OXFORD READINGS IN
Aristophanes

Acharnians   425
Knights   424
Clouds   423·22
Wasps   422
Peace   421
Birds   414
Lys   411
Thesmo
Frogs   405
        S = Warminster
            Summerstein
Eccles   393
Plutus   388

ox comm
                        Acharnians (S)*
                            80
Clouds   S 82 Dover
Frogs   ~~S~~   Dover
Wasps   S 83 MacDowell
Lysistrata S 90 Hend.
Ecclesiazusae   Ussher
            n an Dunbar 95
Birds   S 87
                    *
            Thesmophoriazusae
                (S 94)
        — Knights (Henderson
                or ...
                (S 81)*
        Plutus

        Peace S 85
                    *

OXFORD READINGS IN
Aristophanes

Edited by
ERICH SEGAL

Oxford   New York
OXFORD UNIVERSITY PRESS
1996

Oxford University Press, Walton Street, Oxford OX2 6DP

Oxford   New York
Athens   Auckland   Bangkok   Bombay
Calcutta   Cape Town   Dar es Salaam   Delhi
Florence   Hong Kong   Istanbul   Karachi
Kuala Lumpur   Madras   Madrid   Melbourne
Mexico City   Nairobi   Paris   Singapore
Taipei   Tokyo   Toronto
and associated companies in
Berlin   Ibadan

Oxford is a trade mark of Oxford University Press

Published in the United States
by Oxford University Press Inc., New York

© Oxford University Press 1996

British Library Cataloguing in Publication Data
Data available

Library of Congress Cataloging in Publication Data
Oxford readings in Aristophanes / edited by Erich Segal
1. Aristophanes–Criticism and interpretation.   2. Greek drama
(Comedy)–History and criticism.   3. Greece–In literature.
I. Segal, Erich, 1937–
PA3879.094   1996   882'.01–dc20   95–38110
ISBN 0–19–872156–0
ISBN 0–19–872157–9 (Pbk)
1 3 5 7 9 10 8 6 4 2

Typeset by J&L Composition Ltd, Filey, North Yorkshire
Printed in Great Britain on acid-free paper by
Bookcraft (Bath) Ltd, Midsomer Norton

CONTENTS

ABBREVIATIONS

A & A	*Antike und Abendland*
A.	Aeschylus
A.	A., *Agamemnon*
AARov	*Atti della Accademia Roveretana degli Agiati, Classe di Scienze umane, Lettere ed Arti*
Ach.	Ar., *Acharnians*
AJA	*American Journal of Archaeology*
AJP	*American Journal of Philology*
Alcm.	Alcman
And.	Andocides
Andr.	E., *Andromache*
Annales ESC	*Annales (Économie, Sociétés, Civilisations)*, Paris
Anon. Iamb.	Anonymous Iamblichus
Ant.	S., *Antigone*
Ar.	Aristophanes
Arch.	Archias
Arist.	Aristotle
Ass.	*The Assemblywomen*
Ath.	Arist., *Athenaion politeia*
Ath. Pol.	Ps.-Xen., *Athenaion Politeia*
Av.	Ar., *Aves*
BICS	*Bulletin of the Institute of Classical Studies*
CAF	T. Kock, *Comicorum atticorum fragmenta*, 3 vols. (Leipzig, 1880 8)
CAH	*Cambridge Ancient History*, v. (Cambridge, 1927)
CGF	G. Kaibel, *Comicorum graecorum fragmenta*, vol. i, fasc. i (Berlin, 1899)
CGITA	*Cahiers du groupe interdisciplinaire du théâtre antique*, Université Paul Valéry, Montpellier
Cim.	Plu., *Cimon*
CL	*Corolla Londiniensis*
CP	*Classical Philology*
CQ	*Classical Quarterly*
CR	*Classical Review*
Cyc.	E., *Cyclops*

D.	Demosthenes
D.L.	Diogenes Laertius
Dem.	Hyp., *adv. Demosthenem*
DFA²	A. W. Pickard-Cambridge, *Dramatic Festivals of Athens*₂, rev. J. Gould and D. M. Lewis (Oxford, 1968)
Diod.	Diodorus Siculus
DK	See *FVS*
E.	Euripides
Ec.	Ar., *Ecclesiazusae*
Edm.	J. M. Edmonds, *The Fragments of Attic Comedy*, 3 vols. (Leiden, 1957–61)
EE	Arist., *Ethica eudemia*
Eloc.	Demetrius Phalereus, *De Elocutione [Demetrius on Style]*
Eq.	*Equites*
Eu.	A., *Eumenides*
Eup.	Eupolis
Eux.	Hyp., *pro Euxenippo*
FGrH	F. Jacoby, *Fragmente der griechischen Historiker* (Berlin, 1923–)
fr.	fragment
FVS	H. Diels and W. Kranz (eds), *Die Fragmente der Vorsokratiker* (Berlin, 1951)
G & R	*Greece and Rome*
Grg.	Pl., *Gorgias*
Hdt.	Herodotus
Hel.	E., *Helena*
Her.	Philostr., *Heroicus*
Heracl.	E., *Heraclidae*
Hes.	Hesiod
HG	X., *Historia graeca (Hellenica)*
Hipp.	E., *Hippolytus*
Hippon.	Hipponax
Hp.	Hippocrates
Hsch.	Hesychius
HSCP	*Harvard Studies in Classical Philology*
Hyp.	Hyperides
IG	*Inscriptiones graecae*
Isoc.	Isocrates
JHS	*Journal of Hellenic Studies*
K	See *CAF*
Kassel–Austin	See *PCG*
LCM	*Liverpool Classical Monthly*

LSJ	Liddell and Scott, *Greek–English Lexicon*, rev. H. Stuart Jones (Oxford, 1968)
Lys.	Lysias
Lys.	Ar., *Lysistrata*
Meid.	D., *Against Meidias*
Mem.	X., *Memorabilia*
Metag.	Metagenes
MH	*Museum Helveticum*
N²	A. Nauck, *Tragicorum graecorum fragmenta*² (Leipzig, 1889)
NE	Arist., *Nicomachean Ethics*
Nec.	Lucianus, *Necyomantia*
Nic.	Plu., *Nicias*
Nu.	Ar., *Nubes*
OCD	*Oxford Classical Dictionary*² (Oxford, 1970)
OCT	Oxford Classical Texts
OED	*Oxford English Dictionary*
Or.	E., *Orestes*
OT	S., *Oedipus Tyrranus*
P.	Pindar, *Pythian*
PA	J. Kirchner (ed., *Prosopographia attica* (Berlin, 1901–3); rev. S. Lauffer (1966)
Paneg.	Isoc., *Panegyricus*
Paus.	Pausanias
PCG	R. Kassel and C. Austin (eds), *Poetae comici graeci* (Berlin, 1983–)
PCHPhS	*Proceedings of the Cambridge Philological Society*
Ph.	E., *Phoenissae*
Pherecr.	Pherecrates
Philostr.	Philostratus
Phryn.	Phrynicus
Pl.	Plato
Pl.	Ar., *Plutus*
Pl. Com.	Plato Comicus
Platon.	Platonius
Plu.	Plutarch
Po.	Arist., *Poetics*
Pomp.	Plu., *Pompeius*
POxy.	*Oxyrhynchus papyri*, ed. B. P. Grenfell and A. S. Hunt (London, 1898–)
Ps.-Xen.	Pseudo-Xenophon
QUCC	*Quaderni Urbinati di Cultura Classica*
R.	Pl., *Republic*
Ra.	Ar., *Ranae*
RCCM	*Rivista di Cultura Classica e Medioevale*

RE	Pauly-Wissowa, *Real-Encyclopädie ker classischen Altertumswissenschaft* (Stuttgart, 1893–)
REG	*Revue des Études Grecques*
Rh.	Arist., *Rhetorica*
RhM	*Rheinisches Museum*
RPh	*Revue de Philologie*
S.	Sophocles
SAWW	Sitzungsberichte der Österreichischen Akademie der Wissenschaften in Wien
SHAW	Sitzungsberichte der Heidelberger Akademie der Wissenschaften, Philos.-Hist. Klasse
SIFC	*Studi italiani di filologia classica*
Smp.	Pl., *Symposium*
Sn.-M.	B. Snell and H. Maehler (eds), *Pindarus: Fragmenta* (Leipzig, 1975)
Sol.	Solon
Sol.	Plu., *Solon*
Str.	Strabo
Supp.	E., *Supplices*
Sus.	Susarion
TAPA	*Transactions of the American Philological Association*
Telecl.	Teleclides
Th.	Thucydides
Th.	Ar., *Thesmophoriazusae*
Thes.	Plu., *Theseus*
Tr.	E., *Troades*
Tract. Coisl.	*Tractatus Coislinianus*
TrGF	B. Snell, R. Kannicht, and S. Radt (eds), *Tragicorum graecorum fragmenta* (Göttingen, 1971–)
Tz.	Joannes Tzetzes
WJA	*Würzburger Jahrbücher für di Altertumswissenschaft*
WS	*Wiener Studien*
X.	Xenophon
YCS	*Yale Classical Studies*
ZPE	*Zeitschrift für Papyrologie und Epigraphik*

INTRODUCTION

Aristophanes is the only poet of Greek Old Comedy who has left us more than fragments. And yet his eleven plays—themselves quite various—represent only a quarter of his own output. This places an enormous burden on scholars. Can they examine our playwright and draw *pars pro toto* conclusions about all comedy of the Hellenic age?

The challenge is impossible. To begin with, we lack any evidence of the 'phallic songs' described by Aristotle as the forerunners of literary comedy. Moreover, Aristophanes himself is from the third generation of recognized early comic authors, and we know scarcely anything about his literary predecessors.[1]

In these circumstances, only one critical posture is appropriate. We should conceive of Aristophanes as a single gold piece from a sunken vessel. Rather than idly speculating on the nature of the other coins in the missing treasure, we should welcome what we have in our hands.

In the first third of the twentieth century, two approaches to Aristophanes were especially prominent. First, the scholars of the Cambridge School probed the origins of comedy and its links with ritual; this approach is epitomized in F. M. Cornford's classic work *The Origin of Attic Comedy*.[2] The author's eagerness to infer religious rituals behind the structural forms of comedy was understandable, given the impact of Frazer's *The Golden Bough* (1890) and then of Jane Ellen Harrison's *Themis* (1912)—to which both Cornford and Gilbert Murray contributed essays.

The claim of ritual origins for myth and drama, not to mention the Olympic Games, has undergone at least two *peripeteiai* in the subsequent seventy years: these views have been in and out of fashion as

---

[1] See the excellent discussion of this thorny problem by E. W. Handley in 'Comedy', in *The Cambridge History of Classical Literature*, i: P. E. Easterling and B. M. W. Knox (eds.), *Greek Literature* (Cambridge, 1985), 355 ff.

[2] 2nd edn. 1934; first pub. 1914; reissued Ann Arbor, Mich., 1993, with intro. by Jeffrey Henderson.

they suffered from historicist rejection (as, for instance, by A. W. Pickard-Cambridge), but scepticism has more recently yielded to selective, even enthusiastic, re-evaluation in some quarters.[3]

The second dominant approach several generations ago was preoccupied with pinning down Aristophanes' relationship to the turbulent politics of his time and trying to mine contemporary historical allusions. M. Croiset's *Aristophanes and the Political Parties at Athens* (London, 1909) typifies this method.

On the threshold of the new millennium, we can now discern different, far richer veins in Aristophanic criticism—along with notable advances in the areas of comparative genre studies, metrical analysis, translations, and wide-ranging metaphilological commentaries. The sixteen essays in this volume are intended to exemplify the works of the past twenty-five years, though, understandably, the limitations of space preclude the representation of certain notable scholars, a necessity mitigated by the fact that their works in book form are among the most accessible to the general reader. For example, the landmark survey by Victor Ehrenberg relating the society of the audience to the comic poet's dramatis personae;[4] C. H. Whitman's imaginative study of the protagonists;[5] and K. J. Dover's indispensable overview.[6] There are also the wide-ranging analyses by M. Landfester, K. J. Reckford, and A. M. Bowie.[7] The last-mentioned examined the myths of the Athenian festival calendar as homologies for the myths within the plays themselves.

Although we have made every attempt to give ample coverage to Aristophanes' *œuvre*, there is not a separate essay on each of his comedies. On the other hand, a number of articles discuss more than one work. In general, for *Acharnians*, see de Ste Croix, Foley, and Newiger (Chapters 4, 7, and 8); for *Knights*, see Henderson and Halliwell (Chapters 5 and 6); for *Clouds*, Charles Segal (Chapter 9);

---

[3] See the discussion of Henderson's introduction to Cornford, cited above, with references there, especially to H. S. Versnel, 'What's sauce for the Goose is Sauce for the Gander: Myth and Ritual, Old and New', in Lowell Edmunds (ed.), *Approaches to Greek Myth* (Baltimore, 1990).

[4] *The People of Aristophanes*[2] (Oxford, 1951).

[5] *Aristophanes and the Comic Hero* (Cambridge, Mass., 1964).

[6] *Aristophanic Comedy* (Berkeley, 1972).

[7] M. Landfester, *Handlungsverlauf und Komik in den frühen Komödien von Aristophanes* (Berlin, 1977); K. J. Reckford, *Aristophanes' Old-and-New Comedy, i: Six Essays in Perspective* (Chapel Hill, NC, 1987); A. M. Bowie, *Aristophanes: Myth, Ritual and Comedy* (Cambridge, 1993). Reckford promises a full-scale study of the *Clouds* as a sequel to his 1987 volume.

for *Wasps*, Halliwell and Zimmermann (Chapters 6 and 10); for *Peace*,
Newiger (Chapter 8); for *Birds*, Gelzer and Moulton (Chapters 11 and
12); for *Lysistrata*, Newiger (Chapter 8); for *Thesmophoriazusae*, Silk
(Chapter 13); for *Frogs*, de Ste Croix (Chapter 4); for *Ecclesiazusae*,
Saïd (Chapter 15); for *Plutus*, Sommerstein and Flashar (Chapters
14 and 16). One would have wished for more space to devote to
Frogs. But the reader may profitably consult the volume *Twentieth-
Century Interpretations* on this play edited by D. J. Littlefield (Engle-
wood Cliffs, NJ, 1968), as well as K. J. Dover's introduction to his new
Oxford commentary (1993).

A conspectus of contemporary approaches to Aristophanes may
be roughly divided into ten categories: comedy and the comic;
career and chronology; war, politics, current affairs; language,
imagery, structure; dramatic technique, performance studies,
metatheatre; meter; Aristophanes and art; commentaries; translations; and surveys and bibliographies.

Essays in this volume by Erich Segal, Taplin, and Silk (Chapters 1,
2, and 13) address the development and growth of comedy, its
interrelation with tragedy, and its essentially imagist presentation
of character. Another important group of works—taking its cue from
the early efforts to probe the origins and distinctive structure of Old
Comedy—has dealt with its form and inner dynamic. Here we may
single out Thomas Gelzer, *Der epirrhematische Agōn bei Aristophanes*
(Munich, 1960) and G. M. Sifakis, *Parabasis and Animal Choruses*
(London, 1971). Both authors react against early twentieth-century
scholarship and propose fundamentally new ways of looking at the
two most idiosyncratic structural features of the plays.

The curious territory between comedy and tragedy continues to
be one of the most intriguing areas in ancient dramatic criticism.
Another school of researchers has focused on parodic elements: for
example, the seminal monograph of E. W. Handley and J. Rea on *The
'Telephus' of Euripides* (*BICS*, supp. vol. v; London, 1957), P. Rau's
comprehensive *Paratragodia* (Munich, 1967), and W. Horn's *Gebet
und Gebetsparodie in den Komödien des Aristophanes* (Nuremberg,
1970). In a useful appreciation, Michael Silk observes 'we know of
only one Aristophanic comedy which had a permanent interest in
art or literature, but was not centered on tragedy'.[8] In examining

---

[8] See, 'Aristophanic Paratragedy', a paper that appears with a wealth of other
valuable essays in Stephen Halliwell, Jeffrey Henderson, and Bernhard Zimmermann
(eds.), *Tragedy, Comedy and the Polis* (Bari, 1993). The play Silk alludes to is the lost
Gerytades.

the interpenetration and separateness of comedy and tragedy, we
may especially note works of Taplin, Gruber, Flintoff, Seidensticker,
Levine, and Silk.[9]

A third area is the landscape of comedy's development in the
course of the fifth and fourth centuries BC. Bernard Knox's essay
'Euripidean Comedy'[10] has had a pioneering influence on demonstrating the relationship between late Euripides and the development of later Greek Comedy themes and situations. See also R. G.
Ussher's article 'Old Comedy and "Character": Some Comments'.[11]
His suggestion that some of the 'Characters' in Theophrastus'
famous typological treatise are beholden to Old Comic prototypes
blurs the traditional dividing line between Old and New Comedy.

In a similar vein, see the comments by Carroll Moulton on the
dramatis personae in Old and New Comedy and on the finales of
Dyskolos and *Wasps*.[12] A. H. Sommerstein, 'Act Division in Old
Comedy', goes as far as to discern Menandrian five-act structure
in late Aristophanic comedy.[13] Clearly believing in a kinship among
the four plays, Kenneth McLeish and J. Michael Walton bracket
Ecclesiazusae and *Plutus* with *Dyskolos* and *Samia* in an unusual
volume of translations entitled *Aristophanes and Menander: New
Comedy* (London, 1994).[14]

The papers in this collection by Halliwell, Sommerstein, and
Flashar (Chapters 6, 14 and 16) deal with questions involving the
playwright's development. The first focuses on the poet's youthful
work, while the other two consider the pair of last extant comedies,

[9] Oliver Taplin, 'Tragedy and Trugedy', *CO* 33 (1983), 331–3; W. Gruber, 'System-
atized Delirium: The Craft, Form and Meaning of Aristophanic Comedy', *Helios*, 10
(1983), 97–111; E. Flintoff, 'Aristophanes and the *Prometheus Bound*', *CQ* 33 (1983), 1–5;
B. Seidensticker, *Palintonos Harmonia: Studien zu komischen Elementen in der griechischen Tragödie* (Göttingen, 1982); Daniel Levine, '*Lysistrata* and *Bacchae*: Structure, Genre, and "Women on Top"', *Helios*, 54 (1987), 29–38; Michael Silk, 'Pathos
in Aristophanes', *BICS* 34 (1987), 78–111.
[10] In Alan Cheuse and Richard Koffler (eds.), *The Rarer Action: Studies in Honor of
Francis Fergusson* (New Brunswick, 1970); repr. in *Word and Action* (Baltimore, 1979).
[11] *G & R* 24 (1977), 71–9.
[12] See 'Menander', in T. J. Luce (ed.), *Ancient Writers: Greece and Rome*, i (New York,
1982); and cf. more recently R. L. Hunter, *The New Comedy of Greece and Rome*
(Cambridge, 1985), 41–2.
[13] Sommerstein, 'Act Division in Old Comedy', *BICS* 31 (1984), 139–52; cf. the
comments of Richard Hamilton, 'Comic Acts', *CQ* 41 (1991), 346–55.
[14] Most recently, see Erich Segal, 'The Comic Catastrophe: An Essay on Euripidean
Comedy', in Alan Griffiths (ed.), *Stage Directions: Studies in Honor of Eric Handley*
(London, 1995).

Ecclesiazusae and *Plutus*. The account of the early plays may be compared with three others: G. Mastromarco, 'L'esordio "segreto" di Aristofane',[15] D. M. MacDowell, 'Aristophanes and Kallistratos',[16] and Niall Slater, 'Aristophanes' Apprenticeship Again'.[17]

On the career of the master's most talented and famous contemporary, see Ian C. Storey, 'Dating and Re-dating Eupolis'[18] and 'Notus est omnibus Eupolis?'[19]

Recent studies on dating and production include: A. H. Sommerstein, 'Aristophanes and the Events of 411',[20] S. Bianchetti, 'L'ostracismo di Iperbole e la seconda redazione delle Nuvole di Aristofane',[21] and R. P. Marti, 'Fire on the Mountain: *Lysistrata* and the *Lemnian Women*'.[22]

The examination of war, politics, and current affairs in the comedies reaches well back into the nineteenth century and has not waned. Though A. W. Gomme's landmark essay 'Aristophanes and Politics', in which he reacted sharply to efforts to identify Aristophanes' political beliefs, was written in 1938, its continuing importance justified its inclusion in this collection (Chapter 3). Gomme's argument spawned much fruitful controversy. To a certain extent, the pendulum has swung back again, viewing Aristophanes as at least a modest source for political activity. See as evidence the essays in this volume by de Ste Croix, Henderson, Foley, Newiger, and Saïd (Chapters 4, 5, 7, 8, and 15).

It is striking how many scholarly forays into this area have focused on *Acharnians*. W. G. Forrest's extremely controversial interpretation 'Aristophanes' *Acharnians*',[23] occasioned a vehement attack by de Ste Croix.[24] Among the many other treatments have been L. Edmunds, 'Aristophanes' *Acharnians*',[25] and D. M. MacDowell, 'The Nature of Aristophanes' *Acharnians*',[26] In 1987 alone there appeared two monographs with this critical approach: M. Heath's *Political*

[15] *QS* 5 (1979), 153–96. [16] *CQ* 32 (1982), 21–6.
[17] *GRBS* 30 (1989), 67–82. [18] *Phoenix*, 44 (1990), 1–30.
[19] In Sommerstein *et al.* (eds.), *Tragedy, Comedy and the Polis*.
[20] *JHS* 97 (1977), 112–26. [21] *SIFC* 51 (1979), 221–48.
[22] *Classical Antiquity,* 6 (1987), 77–105. [23] *Phoenix*, 17 (1963), 1–12.
[24] *The Origins of the Peloponnesian War* (Ithaca, NY, 1972).
[25] *YCS* 26 (1980), 1–21. [26] *Greece and Rome*, 30 (1983), 143–62.

Comedy in Aristophanes (Göttingen) and L. Edmunds's *Cleon, Knights, and Aristophanes' Politics* (Lanham, Md.).[27]

Aristophanic language, imagery, and structure have also been a fertile area for recent criticism, represented in this volume by the essays of Newiger, Charles Segal, Moulton, Silk, and Sommerstein (Chapters 8, 9, 12, 13, and 14).

Contemporary scholarship in this domain owes a great deal to the groundwork laid by J. Taillardat in *Les Images d'Aristophane*[2] (Paris, 1965) and by Jeffrey Henderson's bold explication of Aristophanic bawdry in *The Maculate Muse* (first published New Haven, 1975; 2nd edn. Oxford, 1991). Hans-Joachim Newiger's classic study *Metapher und Allegorie* (Munich, 1957) has been followed by a number of investigations of dramaturgy and poetic technique. In addition to important insights in the books by C. H. Whitman and K. J. Reckford cited above, see Horn's, *Gebet und Gebetsparodie in den Komödien des Aristophanes*, H. Hofmann, *Mythos und Komödie: Untersuchungen zu den Vögeln des Aristophanes* (Hildesheim, 1976), C. Moulton, *Aristophanic Poetry* (Göttingen, 1981), and Daphne O'Regan, *Rhetoric, Comedy, and the Violence of Language in Aristophanes' 'Clouds'* (Oxford, 1992).

C. H. Whitman occasioned a series of articles on *Frogs* 1200 ff. when he inferred a phallic reference, unmistakable to the audience, in Aeschylus' quip that some of Euripides' most heroic verses could be concluded by the bathetic phrase 'he lost his little bottle of oil'.[28] The light-hearted debate was joined by Jeffrey Henderson, J. G. Griffith, and David Bain.[29]

K. J. Reckford charts the significance of *katharos* and *katharsis* for

---

[27] With the latter, cf. also L. Edmunds's article, 'The Aristophanic Cleon's "Disturbance" of Athens', *AJP* 108 (1987), 233–63. Other papers dealing with the connections between individual plays and current affairs include: D. Konstan and M. Dillon, 'The Ideology of Aristophanes' *Wealth*', *AJP* 102 (1981), 371–94; L. Miori, 'Attualità politica di Aristofane', *AARov* 20 (1981), 177–95; D. Konstan, 'The Politics of Aristophanes' *Wasps*', *TAPA* 115 (1985), 2746; A. Blanc and J. Taillardat, 'Aristophane, *Thesmophories* v. 366: *tes choras houneka* et l'ambition des oligarques dans l'hiver de 412–411', *RPh* 60 (1986), 183–6; M. Dillon, 'Topicality in Aristophanes' *Ploutos*', *Classical Antiquity* 6 (1987), 155–83; R. F. Morton, 'Aristophanes on Alcibiades', *GRBS* 29 (1988), 345–59; J. E. Atkinson, 'Curbing the Comedians: Cleon versus Aristophanes and Syracosius' Decree', *CQ* 42 (1992), 56–64; and J. Henderson, 'Comic Hero vs. Political Élite', in Sommerstein *et al.* (eds.), *Tragedy, Comedy and the Polis.*

[28] 'Lēkythion apōlesen', *HCSP* 73 (1969), 109–12.

[29] J. G. Griffith, 'Lēkythion apōlesen: A Postscript', *HSCP* 74 (1970), 43–4; Jeffrey Henderson, 'The Lekythos and *Frogs* 1200–1248', *HSCP* 76 (1972), 133–44; David Bain, 'Lēkythion apōlesen: Some Reservations', *CQ* 35 (1985), 31–7.

the *Wasps* in a stimulating article, 'Catharsis and Dream-Interpreta-
tion in Aristophanes' *Wasps*', in *TAPA* 107 (1977), 283–312. S.
Douglas Olson's 'Names and Naming in Aristophanic Comedy', *CQ*
42 (1992), 304–19 perceptively explains why certain characters are
called as they are and why others are left anonymous.

Incisive essays on the playwright's diction include K. J. Dover,
'Language and Character in Aristophanes',[30] as well as H. Diller,
'Zum Umgang des Aristophanes mit der Sprache, erläutert in den
Acharnen'.[31]

There have been increasingly sophisticated appraisals of the
structure of the comedies. A. M. Bowie, 'The Parabasis in Aristo-
phanes: Prolegomena, *Acharnians*',[32] should be considered together
with the recent full-length study of the parabasis by Thomas K.
Hubbard (see below). There are examinations of individual plays by
R. W. Brock, 'The Double Plot in Aristophanes' *Knights*',[33] A. M.
Bowie, 'Ritual Stereotype and Comic Reversal: Aristophanes'
Wasps',[34] D. Konstan, 'A City in the Air: Aristophanes' *Birds*',[35] N.
Slater, 'Lekythoi in Aristophanes' *Ecclesiazusae*,'[36] and Kenneth S.
Rothwell Jr., *Politics and Persuasion in Aristophanes' Ecclesiazusae*
(Leiden, 1990).

'Old Comedy is ubiquitously self-referential: Aristophanes is probably the most metatheatrical playwright before Pirandello.' Taplin's
argument (Chapter 2) has raised a chorus of approval. Indeed, the
concept of metatheatre (a coinage by Lionel Abel in his 1963 book of
that name) has proved fruitful for critics of Old Comedy, especially in
performance studies. The impetus for a recent spate of articles may
well be K. J. Dover's 'The Skene in Aristophanes'.[37] Imaginative
observations may be found as well in books by C. W. Dearden, K.
McLeish, and Laura K. Stone.[38]

Perhaps the simplest and most useful definition of metatheatrical

[30] First pub. in Italian as 'Linguaggio e caratteri Aristofanei', *RCCM* 18 (1976), 357–
71; repr. in K. J. Dover (ed.), *Greek and the Greeks* (Oxford, 1987).
[31] See *Hermes*, 106 (1978), 509–18.   [32] *CQ* 32 (1982), 27–40.
[33] *GRBS* 27 (1986), 15–27.   [34] *BICS* 34 (1987), 112–25.
[35] *Arethusa*, 23 (1990), 183–207.   [36] *Lexis*, 3 (1989), 43–51.
[37] *PCPhS* 192 (1966), 2–17; repr. in Dover (ed.), *Greek and the Greeks*.
[38] See C. W. Dearden, *The Stage of Aristophanes* (London, 1976); K. McLeish, *The Theatre of Aristophanes* (London, 1980); Laura K. Stone, *Costume in Aristophanic Comedy* (Salem, NH, 1984). There is also the important work on later comedy, both Greek and Roman, by Niall Slater, *Plautus in Performance* (Princeton, 1985) and David Wiles, *The Masks of Menander* (Cambridge, 1991).

practice may be inferred from the title of F. Muecke's essay 'Playing with the Play: Theatrical Self-Consciousness in Aristophanes'.[39] Other studies of this nature include G. A. H. Chapman, 'Some Notes on Dramatic Illusion in Aristophanes',[40] the second edition of C. F. Russo's *Aristofane: Autore di teatro* (Florence, 1984; Eng. trans. 1994), and Niall Slater's impressive analysis of a play in performance, 'Space, Character, and *Apatē*: Transformation and Transvaluation in the *Acharnians*'.[41] Lastly there is the important full-length study of Thomas K. Hubbard, *The Mask of Comedy: Aristophanes and the Intertextual Parabasis* (Ithaca, NY, 1991), a book that may finally complete the rescue of the parabasis from the ritual periphery to which it was relegated by Cornford and Murray.

Much recent work on questions of dramatic technique has been inspired by the French school of J.-P. Vernant and P. Vidal-Naquet. D. Auger speculates on the correlation of myth and dramatic representation in 'Le Théâtre d'Aristophane: Le Mythe, l'utopie, et les femmes'.[42] Helene Foley focuses on the oppositions of *oikos* and *polis* in 'The Female Intruder Reconsidered: Women in Aristophanes, *Lysistrata* and *Ecclesiazusae*'.[43]

In 'The Frogs in the *Frogs*',[44] D. A. Campbell discusses the vexed problem of the play's double chorus. Representative of another important aspect are F. Zeitlin, 'Travesties of Gender and Genre in Aristophanes' *Thesmophoriazusae*',[45] Suzanne Saïd, 'Travestis et travestissements dans les comédies d'Aristophane',[46] and Lauren K. Taaffe, *Aristophanes and Women* (London, 1993), which deals with sexual ambiguities in *Lysistrata*, *Thesmophoriazusae*, and *Ecclesiazusae*.

The previously ignored field of metrics has now seen exciting new developments that bid fair to approach the standards set for Plautine comedy in the brilliant work of Cesare Questa.[47] Earlier work on Aristophanic meter such as C. Prato's *I canti di Aristofane* (Rome, 1962) has been superseded by the three volumes of Bernhard Zimmermann, *Untersuchungen zur Form und dramatischen Technik der*

[39] *Antichthon*, 11 (1977), 52–67.   [40] *AJP* 104 (1983), 1–23.
[41] See Sommerstein *et al.* (eds.), *Tragedy, Comedy and the Polis.*
[42] *Cahiers de Fontenay*, 17 (1979), 71–101.   [43] *CP* 78 (1982), 1–21.
[44] *JHS* 104 (1984), 163–5.
[45] In H. P. Foley (ed.), *Reflections of Women in Antiquity* (New York, 1981).
[46] *CGITA* 3 (1987), 217–48.
[47] See e.g. his definitive *Introduzione alla metrica di Plauto* (Bologna, 1967).

Aristophanischen Komödien (Königtstein, 1984–7), vol. i: *Parodos und Amoibaion*, vol. ii: *Die anderen lyrischen Partien*, vol. iii: *Metrische Analysen*. Zimmermann seeks to understand the relationship of meter to character, action, and dramatic structure. His essay in this volume (Chapter 10) analyses in broad strokes the *parodoi* of the comedies, with special attention to the first choral song of the *Wasps*.[48]

Other recent studies in this area are W. T. MacCary, 'Philokleon ithyphallos: Dance, Costume, and Character in the *Wasps*',[49] C. Prato, 'I metri lirici di Aristofane',[50] Zimmermann's 'Parodia metrica nelle Rane di Aristofane',[51] L. P. E. Parker, 'Eupolis the Unruly',[52] and Mario Pintacuda's speculative but intriguing intuitions about the playwright's musical settings in *Interpretazioni musicali sul teatro di Aristofane* (Palermo, 1982).[53]

There has not been a great deal of new work on Aristophanes and the visual arts. Standard compendia include A. W. Trendall and T. B. L. Webster, *Illustrations of Greek Drama* (London, 1971), 117 ff.[54] As usual, K. J. Dover has illuminating observations in his brief paper 'Portrait-Masks in Aristophanes'.[55] The reader can also profit from the overview in B. Sparkes, 'Illustrating Aristophanes'.[56]

Oliver Taplin reconsidered the intriguing question of the relationship of Old Comedy to the phlyax vases (*Comic Angels* (Oxford, 1993)). Taplin's discussion of two recently discovered vases is especially exciting. He argues that the 'Würzburg Telephos' (first published in 1978) reflects a paratragic scene in *Thesmophoriazusae*, and he interprets the scene on the 'Chorēgoi' vase (1991) as an emblematic confrontation between the genres of comedy and tragedy.[57]

In the late nineteenth century philology reached a high standard

---

[48] The reader may wish to compare with this chapter Michael Silk's article 'Aristophanes as a Lyric Poet', *YCS* 26 (1980), 99–151, to which Zimmermann's chapter is something of a riposte.

[49] *TAPA* 109 (1979), 137–47.   [50] *Dioniso*, 57 (1967), 203–44.
[51] *SIFC* 6 (1988), 35–47.   [52] *PCPhS* NS 34 (1988), 115–22.

[53] Pintacuda's especially noteworthy concluding chapter focuses on music composed for modern revivals of Aristophanic plays, as well as on musical compositions directly inspired by the comedies, e.g. Humperdinck's melodies for *Lysistrata*.

[54] See also Webster's *Monuments Illustrating Old and Middle Comedy*, BICS, supp. vol. 23 (1969).

[55] In *Komoidotragemata: Studia Aristophanea Viri Aristophanei W. J. W. Koster in Honorem* (Amsterdam, 1968); repr. in Dover (ed.), *Greek and the Greeks* (Oxford, 1987).

[56] *JHS* 95 (1975), 122–35.

[57] Intimations of Taplin's new approach appeared in his article 'Phallology, Phlyakes, Iconography and Aristophanes' *PCPhS* 33 (1987), 92–104, as well as in the pendant 'Taplin on Cocks', by Don Fowler, *CQ* 39 (1989), 257–9.

in the commentaries on all eleven plays of J. van Leeuwen (Leiden, 1893–1906), which are still immensely valuable.

Dover's *Clouds* (Oxford, 1968) set an exceptional model for the plays' exegesis. In the past quarter century D. M. MacDowell's *Wasps* and R. G. Ussher's *Ecclesiazusae* (1973) have appeared in the same series, together with the especially welcome volumes on *Lysistrata* by Henderson (1987) and *Frogs* by Dover (1993), as well as the long-awaited *Birds* by Nan Dunbar (1995) and Henderson's *Knights* (in progress). The pace is slow, but one hopes that the series will be complete before the end of this century.

A. H. Sommerstein has also published a number of abbreviated commentaries-cum-translations, beginning with *Acharnians* (Warminster, 1980) and followed by *Knights* (1981), *Clouds* (1982), *Wasps* (1983), *Peace* (1085), *Birds* (1987), *Lysistrata* (1990), and *Thesmophoriazusae* (1994).

Until quite recently Aristophanes was poorly served by translators, although there was one exception earlier in the century in the clever renderings by Benjamin Bickley Rogers, published in the Loeb Classical Library in 1924. Blending the lyrical with the satirical, these versions capitalized on the coincidence that the principal meter of the Aristophanic parabasis, the anapaestic tetrameter catalectic, was also the meter of W. S. Gilbert:

> Ye men who are dimly existing below,
>   who perish and fade as the leaf,
> Pale, woebegone, shadowlike, spiritless folk,
>   life feeble and wingless and brief,
> Frail castings in clay, who are gone in a day,
>   like a dream full of sorrow and sighing,
> Come listen with care to the Birds of the air,
>   the ageless, the deathless, who flying
> In the joy and the freshness of Ether, are wont
>   to muse upon wisdom undying.

> (*Birds*, 685–9)

In addition to the renderings noted above, Sommerstein is the co-author with David Barrett of the Penguin translations. These are generally more accurate than the free-wheeling pieces produced in the 1960s by William Arrowsmith and Douglass Parker.[58] Special

[58] The versions of seven plays (*Acharnians, Clouds, Wasps, Birds, Lysistrata, Frogs,* and *Ecclesiazusae*) by Arrowsmith, Parker, and Richmond Lattimore are available in two volumes from the University of Michigan Press (Ann Arbor, 1961–9).

mention should be made of the readable and often inspired translations by Dudley Fitts of *Lysistrata*, *Frogs*, *Birds*, and *Thesmophoriazusae* (under the title *Ladies' Day*).[59] Some Aristophanes has yet
to get its version for our time: one thinks of *Knights*, *Peace*, and
especially *Plutus*.

For surveys and bibliographies, we may list the following studies,
ranging in scope from general to specialist (most include substantial
bibliographies): R. Harriott, *Aristophanes, Poet and Dramatist* (Baltimore, 1986); F. H. Sandbach, *The Comic Theatre of Greece and Rome*
(London, 1977); R. G. Ussher, *Aristophanes* (*Greece and Rome* New
Surveys in the Classics, 13 (Oxford, 1979)); E. W. Handley's survey of
Greek Comedy;[60] A. C. Quicke, *Aristophanes and Athenian Old
Comedy: A Survey and Bibliography of Twentieth-Century Criticism,
with an Essay on the Current State of Bibliography in Classical Studies*
(London, 1982); H.-J. Newiger (ed.), *Aristophanes und die Alte Komödie* (Wege der Forschung, cclxv (Darmstadt, 1975)); T. Gelzer, *Aris-
tophanes der Komiker* (Stuttgart, 1971); and the annual
bibliographical surveys in *L'Année philologique*.

Gilbert Murray's oft-quoted comment that 'Aristophanes died
intestate'[61] is substantiated by the fact that only C. Gum's *The
Aristophanic Comedies of Ben Jonson* (The Hague, 1969) has earned
any notice in this arid field, laboriously worked by Wilhelm Süss in
Aristophanes und die Nachwelt (Leipzig, 1911).[62]

Aristophanes did not become the paradigm for modern comedy,
which descends instead from the Hellenistic tribe of Menander and
his Roman successors. From time to time, however, there have been
attempts to write theatrical presentations in a neo-Aristophanic
vein. In ages past there have been slavish emulations like Racine's
Les Plaideurs, a version of *Wasps*. In our own day, some critics have
singled out popular entertainments like *Saturday Night Live* and its
bold British analogue *Spitting Image*, with its grotesquely caricatured
puppet versions of dignitaries like Prince Charles and Ronald Reagan,
much in the way that Aristophanes is thought to have fashioned the
mask of Socrates. But despite these claims it is indisputable that
there has never been an Aristophanic renaissance. Perhaps that is
because of the abiding vitality of the playwright himself.

[59] *Aristophanes: Four Comedies* (New York, 1959).   [60] See n. 1.
[61] *Aristophanes* (Oxford, 1933), 199.
[62] Hubbard re-explores Ben Jonson's debt to Aristophanes in his recent book *The
Mask of Comedy*, appendix 2.

I

The *Physis* of Comedy

ERICH SEGAL

It all seems perfectly clear. 'Old Comedy' refers to an ancient dramatic genre whose masters were Eupolis and Cratinus and Aristophanes and at least forty other poets. 'New Comedy' is the genre of Philemon, Diphilus, and especially Menander, the prototype and norm for all comedies written since. And if we do not recognize it as a distinct genre, we none the less understand 'Middle Comedy' as a chronological specification referring to plays composed roughly between the fall of Athens and the Battle of Chaeronea. But what valid critical use do we make of these terms?

Alexandrian scholars found 'Old' and 'New' to be convenient labels. 'Middle Comedy' seems to be a much later notion, not antedating Apuleius' description of Philemon as 'mediae comoediae scriptor'.[1] Some would adduce Aristotle's *Nicomachean Ethics* 1128^a, a passage discussing comedies 'of the ancient and modern styles' (*ton palaion kai ton kainon*), as a precedent for distinguishing between comic genres. Still, it is quite obvious from the context that Aristotle himself is making no such distinctions, but simply comparing plays ancient and modern, preferring the innuendo (*hyponoia*) of the present to the indecent language (*aischrologia*) of the past. Moreover, the *Poetics* never makes an explicit distinction between Old and New at all. Nor does Aristotle state—for better or worse—what later

---

[1] *Florida* 3. 16. According to Athenaeus (11. 428c), Antiochus of Alexandria wrote a treatise 'about the poets of middle comedy' (*peri tōn en tēi mesēi kōmōidiai kōmōi-doumenōn poiētōn*). Kock does not recognize this third category and so his edn. of fragments (Leipzig, 1880) is bipartite. Among those who do accept Middle Comedy as a literary genre are Körte *RE*, 1256–5; Philippe Legrand, *The New Greek Comedy*, trans. J. Loeb (London, 1917); Karl Reinhardt, 'Aristophanes und Athen', *Von Werken und Formen* (Godesberg, 1948), 309; T. B. L. Webster, *Studies in Later Greek Comedy*,[2] rev. (Manchester, 1970).

scholars would maintain so often: that Old Comedy 'died intestate'.[2] Poor Old Comedy, no heirs to perpetuate its traditions. What grief its so-called demise has evoked. Neither epic nor dithyramb has had so many scholarly mourners or nostalgic eulogizers.

But it is the present argument that we must not continue to regard Old Comedy as a separate artistic entity and must cease the frustrating attempts to define and describe it as an independent genre.[3] Rather, we must come to grips with a basic fact which literary history has clearly affirmed: Aristophanes *atque alii* represent merely a stage—several stages perhaps—of a work in progress. Quite simply, a step toward the ultimate development of the single genre we all know as Comedy.

The thesis is not presented here for the first time. But for a variety of reasons it has rarely been welcomed. A. W. Schlegel, for example, was outraged at the notion of considering Aristophanes a mere way station to Menander. To him, Aristophanes was beyond dispute 'eine ursprüngliche und reine Gattung'.[4] In our own day, Albin Lesky has categorically opposed any attempt to link Old and New Comedy in an evolutionary scheme.[5] And yet some scholars, including K. J. Dover, have offered arguments in support of a 'comic continuity'.[6] And there is a lengthy advocacy in Wilhelm Süss's *Aristophanes und die Nachwelt*.[7]

Perhaps there would be no dispute if the entire *Poetics* were extant. As it is, we have merely enough to justify our hypothesis.

[2] e.g. Gilbert Murray, *Aristophanes* (Oxford, 1933), 199; Cedric H. Whitman, *Aristophanes and the Comic Hero* (Cambridge, Mass., 1964), 2. Intestate or not, it was unquestionably defunct. With the exception of the *Plutus*, Aristophanes was never revived. The latest to remark upon this is K. J. Dover, *Aristophanic Comedy* (London, 1972), 223.

[3] Despite energetic attempts to prove the contrary by scholars like F. M. Cornford, *The Origin of Attic Comedy* (London, 1914; ed. T. H. Gaster (Garden City, NY, 1961)), and O. Navarre, 'Les Origines et la structure technique de la Comédie Ancienne', *Revue des études anciennes*, 13 (1911), 245–95. Whitman, *Aristophanes and the Comic Hero*, 9 ff. offers a brief defence of Aristophanic structure. But Reinhardt, 'Aristophanes und Athen', 292 reviews the various generic explanations and cautions against attempts to fit Aristophanes into any 'Gattungs-oder Ursprungsformel'.

[4] A. W. Schlegel, *Vorlesungen über dramatische Kunst und Literatur*, lecture 13 (Stuttgart, 1966), 157. Ironically, Schlegel then asserts that New Comedy is not a real genre.

[5] Albin Lesky, *Geschichte der griechischen Literatur*,[2] (Bern, 1963), 425.

[6] K. J. Dover, 'Greek Comedy', in *Fifty Years (and Twelve) of Classical Scholarship* (Oxford, 1968), 147.

[7] Wilhelm Süss, *Aristophanes und die Nachwelt* (Leipzig, 1911), 190 ff.

In chapter 4 (1449^{a}9ff.), Aristotle opens his discussion of comedy and tragedy with tantalizing and ambiguous explanations of their origins. He then considers whether tragedy is a fully developed form and decides affirmatively.

Having begun as improvized episodes, tragedy underwent many changes, *pollas metabolas metabalousa*, and finally stopped growing and came to rest—*epausato*—having reached its fullest natural form, its *physis* (1449^{a}10–15).[8] Aristotle's essential view is that tragedy had been fully developed since the early days of Sophocles' career. This would, of course, admit the *Oresteia* as mature tragedy as well.

Then, in the next chapter, he turns to comedy. He discusses how certain of its elements originated, but he does not consider whether comedy has reached *its physis*. He does note in 5. 3 (1449^{b}1–2) that comedy got a much later start, receiving an official chorus long after the public presentation of tragedies was an old and accepted tradition. But even from the scant remains of fifth-century comedy we can see what drastic changes it underwent in a very short time. There is an infinitely greater difference between the *Acharnians* and the *Plutus* than between the *Prometheus* and the *Bacchae*. And it is of no small significance that Aristotle never once uses the term *komoidia* in reference to Eupolis, Cratinus—or Aristophanes.

Ironically, comedy was reaching its *physis* at precisely the moment Aristotle was composing the *Poetics*. For in Menander we find the 'classic' comedy, what E. R. Curtius calls *Normalklassik*.[9] In Menander the form is canonized; there are no more *metabolai*. Indeed, one of the essential characteristics of classical comedy is its inexhaustible sameness. Menander and Marivaux are cut from the same comic cloth; the *Birds* and the *Ecclesiazusae* are certainly not. Meter, as Aristotle notes at the beginning of the *Poetics* (1447^{b}6ff.), does not a genre make.

Indeed, most Plautine comedies have more lyrics than the *Ecclesiazusae*, three-quarters of which is in iambic trimeter. Moreover, every definition of comedy, from antiquity to our own day, refers

---

[8] Cf. Aristotle, *Politics* 1252^{b}33–6.
[9] E. R. Curtius, *Europäische Literatur und lateinisches Mittelalter* (Bern, 1948), 275 ff. Georg Luck adapts the term as 'normative' (opposed to 'absolute') in 'Scriptor Classicus', in *CL* 10/2 (Spring 1958), 150 ff.

exclusively to the Menandrian form.[10] Like it or not, Menander's comedy has determined the classical tradition for more than 2,000 years.

We may perhaps briefly note some of the aspects of Attic comedy which succumbed to the evolutionary process. The genesis of comedy resembles the Creation as told by Hesiod: in the beginning there was Chaos.[11] The earliest comic writers are criticized for formlessness and chaotic construction. The cry is as old as comedy itself, for even Susarion, its semi-legendary inventor, is accused of managing things sloppily, *ataktōs*.[12] This is a charge hurled often at Aristophanes, and Cratinus was likewise criticized for *ataxia*.[13] One may excuse or explain this as the necessary result of Attic Comedy's attempts to absorb the disparate elements of various popular traditions (Dorian, Megarian, the epirrhematic *agōn*), but the fact needs no apology. For Aristophanes *atque alii* were great artists whose theatrical forte happened to be a kind of episodic vaudeville. One may agree with Pickard-Cambridge that Aristophanes progressively absorbed the various heterogeneous elements into a kind of texture,[14] but Aristophanic comedy is still essentially a string of short episodes.

Yet comedy ultimately rejected loosely jointed vaudeville, growing more and more into tightly structured *mythos*. The chaos in Aristophanic Cloudland became the cosmos of Menandrian Athens. There is a parallel phenomenon in later antiquity: Livy, discussing the beginnings of real theatre in Rome, emphasizes the importance of 240 BC, the date when Livius Andronicus introduced the first play *with a plot*. Thus the appearance of a structured story likewise signals the *physis* of Roman comedy.[15]

---

[10] It is interesting to note that in ch. 3 of his passionate anti-classical manifesto *Racine et Shakespeare* (1823), Stendhal cheerfully announces the end of classical comedy, to be replaced of course by *la comédie romantique*, which firmly rejects each and every New Comedy convention. Stendhal devotes an entire page to listing the titles of fresh new-style comedies destined to sweep the classics into oblivion. Ironically, none of these plays is remembered today, and the list is frequently omitted by editors of *Racine et Shakespeare*.

[11] *Th.* 166 ff. Cf. Aristophanes' parody in the genealogy of *Birds* (693 ff.).

[12] Tz. *Proll. Com.* 3. 16, *CGF* 18.

[13] Platon., *Peri diaphoras*, Kaibel 6; Tz. *Proll. Com.*, *CGF* 18.

[14] A. W. Pickard-Cambridge, *Dithyramb, Tragedy and Comedy*,[2] rev. T. B. L. Webster (Oxford, 1962), 194 ff.

[15] Fredrich Leo astutely noted that the similarities between Livy's account and Aristotle's remarks on the development of comedy were too great to be merely coincidental. 'Varro und die Satire', *Hermes*, 24 (1889), 76 ff. There is further illuminating discussion in G. L. Hendrickson, 'The Dramatic Satura and the Old Comedy at Rome', *AJP*, 15 (1896), 1.

There have been numerous attempts to explain why fifth-century comedy discarded its political and allegorical elements in favour of more personal and domestic matters.[16] But from the very beginning we see in Aristophanes a tendency to domesticate rather than politicize.[17] Aristophanic comedy characteristically reduces statecraft to housekeeping.

In Murray's distinction, Old Comedy deals with *res publica*, New with *res privata*.[18] But which of these distinctions best describes the *Acharnians*? Is Dikaiopolis really concerned with the state at large? Or is he rather a private person who makes a private peace for private *gain* and celebrates a private Dionysia in his private home? His peace treaty is actually a trade agreement which enables him to open his own common market to all cities.[19] In 971 ff. the chorus notes that Dikaiopolis is out to make a fast profit and has amassed a good supply of household items and luscious foodstuffs. His motives are so private and personal that they are downright selfish. At 1018 ff. he flatly refuses to share any of his peace with the visitors who come to request some. The chorus specifically comments for a second time on this selfish attitude at 1037 ff. (especially 1038-9: 'he's not about to share with anybody'). In the finale, Lamachos leaves to fight a national war while Dikaiopolis stays to continue his private party. The *Acharnians* does indeed celebrate the joy of peace and condemn the folly of war, but its tone is as much domestic as polemic.

This domesticating tendency is also manifest in the *Knights*, where the Sausage-Seller is advised that ruling the city is no different

[16] It is not possible to resolve the question of how 'political' Aristophanes really was. One extreme is the view of Reinhardt, 'Aristophanes und Athen', 294: 'politisch ist [die Komödie] ganz und gar, politisch in ihrem Entwurf, politisch in ihrer dramatischen Aktion—und wird unpolitisch durch die Eigentümlichkeit ihrer politischen Symbolik'. On the other hand, simple references to politicians did not disappear from comedy after Aristophanes. There are numerous political names dropped until the time of Demetrius of Phalerum. Cf. Webster, *Studies in Later Greek Comedy*, 37 ff; Dover *Aristophanic Comedy*, 233. Also Viola Guinness Stephens, 'Political Figures in Late Comedy', diss. (Yale University, 1967).

[17] And the very earliest extant fragment of Greek comedy (Sus. 3K) involves the most domestic of *oikeia pragmata*. It is misogynistic in a *nec tecum nec sine te* vein, but concludes that whereas a man may be able to do without a woman, a home cannot do without a wife (lines 4-5): 'Women are an evil thing, without a doubt, | Yet they're a thing no family can do without.'

[18] Murray, *Atristophanes*, 251. Cf. Donat., Kaibel 67: 'Comoedia est fabula diversa instituta continens affectuum civilium ac privatorum . . .'   [19] *Ach.* 623-5; 720-8.

from cooking up meat patties (214ff.). This advice anticipates Lysistrata's lengthy speech (567ff.) in which she predicts how women will run the state as they do their households, and untangle political problems the way they unravel wool. Understandably, the Athenian *proboulos* is outraged by the comparison.

The *Knights* and *Lysistrata* bring government into the kitchen. In an ironic bourgeois reversal of the *Oresteia*, the *Wasps* brings the court into the living-room. Here even the judgement urn is less important than certain domestic crockery. Philocleon can prosecute the household animals while close to the comforts of his chamber-pot.[20]

Finally, there is Praxagora in the *Ecclesiazusae*, who would apply to the state women's rule *en tais oikiais* (210ff.) and domesticate even the municipal buildings to make Athens one big happy household. Even the courts and colonnades will become dining-rooms:

BLEPYROS. But what will you do with the desk for the speakers?
PRAXAGORA. I'll make it a stand for the cups and the beakers . . .

                                    (677–8, trans. Rogers)

There is little need to stress the domesticity of the *Plutus*. The wife is a New Comedy *matrona* and Cario a typical slave who here outfaces Hermes better than Sosia will in Plautus' *Amphitruo*. In the *Plutus* Aristophanes conforms to what became standard New Comedy practice: he offers a unified plot.

And the city street to which Aristophanes here moves is the very one that Menander rarely leaves. In fact it may have been a flourishing comic thoroughfare long before Aristophanes arrived. Simply stated, some of Aristophanes' contemporaries seem to have been moving earlier toward unified domestic *mythos*.

We have enough of Cratinus' *Pytine*, for example, to see that although it contained a few allegorical characters, it was still essentially a domestic comedy in which the hero leaves his wedded wife for a mistress.[21] Later, the protagonist senses a conspiracy against him. One particular fragment (185K) shows him pondering what sort of cabal (*paraskeue*) the members of his household are concocting. This intrigue-making suggests Plautus' *Casina*, not to

---

[20] *Wasps* 763ff., esp. 799–810; 931–5.
[21] Cf. also frs. 181, 182, 188K. The scholiast to *Knights* 400 adds some helpful details.

mention Feydeau.[22]

To Aristotle, only Crates is worthy to be considered as a writer of *komoidia*, perhaps because—as Aristotle emphasizes—he was the first to abandon sheer raillery (*aphemenos tēs iambikēs ideas*) and compose orderly plots (*logous kai mythous*) (*Poetics* 1449^{b}8–9). There is plenty of domestic chatter in the fragments of Crates,[23] but of course we have no real notion what his plots were like. An ancient commentator noted that Pherecrates, some of whose extant citations read like party menus, stopped indulging in raillery (*to loidorein*) and became especially effective at plot-making (*heuretikos mythōn*) producing many 'novelties' (*kaina pragmata*).[24] The poet's *Korianno* presented some sort of romantic rivalry between a *senex amator* and his son.[25] It seems more 'traditional' than the finale of Aristophanes' *Wasps* and anticipates the likes of Menander's *Aspis*, Plautus' *Mercator*, and Molière's *L'Avare*. This comic gamut is traditionally resolved according to 'Figaro's Law', as expounded at the curtain of *Le Barbier de Seville*: 'quand la jeunesse et l'amour sont d'accord pour tromper un vieillard, tout ce qu'il fait pour l'empêcher peut bien s'appeler à bon droit *la précaution inutile*'.

Thus, what is true of Aristophanes' later style may have been characteristic of his contemporaries much earlier. F. M. Cornford observed that 'the fragments of Crates and Pherecrates are hardly distinguishable from the manner of New Comedy'.[26]

New Comedy is essentially bourgeois and emphatically plot-orientated. In late Aristophanes we see another of Figaro's remarks validated: 'l'or c'est le nerf de l'intrigue'. The marked increase in use of financial language in both the *Ecclesiazusae* and the *Plutus* can be explained only in part by the contemporary Athenian financial woes.[27] As comedy develops, Plutus replaces Phales as the central divinity. What is more, especially in Aristophanes' final

---

[22] In an important essay, Bernard Knox proposes Euripides' *Ion* as the first modern comedy, primarily because of the *intrigue*. 'Euripidean Comedy', in *The Rarer Action: Essays in Honor of Francis Fergusson* (New Brunswick, 1971), 68 ff. The limits of this paper precluded an examination of the relationship between Euripides and Aristophanes.

[23] Crates, frs. 14–17K.   [24] Anon., *Peri komoidias*, Kaibel 8.

[25] Cf. *Korianno*, fr. 71K, which clearly articulates the Youth–Age amorous antagonism: 'YOUNG MAN. On the contrary it's perfectly reasonable for *me* to be in love, but *you* are totally out of season.'   [26] Cornford, *The Origin of Attic Comedy*, 189.

[27] Lysias 19. 11 specifically refers to the scarcity of money in the city at about the time the *Plutus* was presented. Cf. Victor Ehrenberg, *The People of Aristophanes*[2] (Oxford, 1951), 253 ff.

play, we see a concern for the rewarding of the just, which will be a key Menandrian theme.

Even Aristophanes seems to have written at least one comedy entirely in the New style. The *Vita* states that the late (now lost) *Kokalos* contained rape, recognition, and 'all those other things Menander loved'.[28] Thus, Aristophanes could be Menandrian, though Menander would never be Aristophanic.

None of this is to overrate Menander's art, although one cannot overstress his influence. Rather, it is to signal the development of the comic genre toward its ultimate *physis*: the structured plot with happy ending.[29] Tragedy underwent a similar development. In both mature genres, Aristotle's constant emphasis on the structure of events, the *systasis tōn pragmatōn*,[30] has proved to be not only the prime critical criterion but the primary popular pleasure. His remark that plot was the *psychē* of drama is substantiated by scientific fact: the happy ending does indeed appeal directly to certain needs of the human psyche.[31]

Aristophanes did not live merely to write Old Comedy. He was a great dramatic poet who well understood that 'the drama's laws the drama's patrons give'. Like any man of the theatre, he wrote for a public, not posterity. The fact that his final plays were vastly different from the episodic vaudeville with which he began his career reflects not a decline in his art or the decay of a genre—for Old Comedy never was one—but a natural evolution. Surely Aristophanes, who himself was young during the infancy of the comic theatre, was delighted to witness as well as present the *physis* of comedy.

---

[28] *Vita Aristophanis*, PCG 3², p. 3: 'phthoran kai anagnōrismon kai talla panta ha ezēlōse Menandros'.

[29] Aristotle (*Poetics* 1453ᵃ36) posits the happy ending as the basic pleasure (*hēdonē*) of comedy. For a fuller discussion, see E. Segal, 'The Meaning of Comedy', *Horizon*, 15/1 (Winter 1973).   [30] Cf. *Po.* 1450ᵃ15 (see also 1447ᵃ2, 1451ᵃ32–3).

[31] In a paper in progress, I discuss the illuminating similarity between the plots of Menandrian Comedy and what psychologists call the 'Family Romance' syndrome, the pleasure in mentally reliving the infantile experiences of separation and reunion. See e.g. Otto Rank, *The Myth of the Birth of the Hero*, trans. F. Robbins and Smith Ely Jelliffe (New York, 1952), 63–4. Also, Geza Roheim, 'The Psychoanalytic Interpretation of Culture', in Warner Meunsterberger (ed.), *Man and his Culture: Psychoanalytic Anthropology after 'Totem and Taboo'* (New York, 1970), 43–5. Martin A. Berezin demonstrates the psychic need for a well-structured 'happy end' not only in comedy but in music as well: 'Some Observations on Art (Music) in its Relationship to Ego Mastery', *Bulletin of the Philadelphia Association for Psychoanalysis*, 7/2 (June 1958), 49 ff.

2

Fifth-Century Tragedy and Comedy

OLIVER TAPLIN

At the very end of Plato's *Symposium* our narrator awakes to find
Socrates still hard at it, and making Agathon and Aristophanes
agree that the composition of tragedy and comedy is really one
and the same thing: 'Socrates compelled them to agree that the
same man could write comedy and tragedy and that a tragedian's
art could also be that of a comedian. And as they were forced to
concede . . .', the two playwrights succumb to sleep, leaving
Socrates triumphant. Socrates had to 'force' his case; and it is a
fact that, though we know of well over 100 fifth-century playwrights, we do not know of a single one who produced both
tragedy and comedy.[1] In a famous fragment the comedian Antiphanes (fr. 191K) complains that the tragedians have an easy time—
familiar stories, the *deus ex machina*, etc.—'But we don't have these
advantages. . . .' It is a matter of 'them' and 'us'. Furthermore, there
was an entire separate genre besides tragedy and comedy. As
Demetrius put it (*De eloc.* 169), 'Tragedy has many graceful features, but laughter is its enemy. No one could conceive of a playful
tragedy, since he would actually be writing a satyr play in that case,
not a tragedy.'[2]

Socrates' proposition does not seem to us at all perverse, because
we live in the post-Shakespearean era. As Dr Johnson observed in
his *Preface to Shakespeare*, 'Shakespeare's plays are not in the rigor-
ous and critical sense either tragedies or comedies, but compositions

---

[1] The nearest thing to a counter-example is the scholium on Ar., *Peace* 835 which
says that Ion of Chios wrote comedies as well (see *TrGF* 19T2b). Athenaeus 9. 407d
says the same of a 4th-cent. Timocles (86T1). It is worth noting that actors also seem
to have been split exclusively between the two genres.

[2] The distinctive middle ground for satyr-play is well discussed in the intro. to R.
Seaford's *Cyclops* (Oxford, 1984), 10 ff. Of special interest for this discussion is his
suggestion (pp. 18, 32) that satyr-play stood outside *to politikon*, the sphere of both
tragedy and comedy, though in very different ways.

of a distinct kind; exhibiting the real state of sublunary nature . . . .'.
Victor Hugo was more rapturous: 'Shakespeare is the [sc. real]
drama, and a drama which blends at one stroke the grotesque
and the sublime, the terrible and the farcical, comedy and tragedy.' Since then, Chekhov and Brecht are two masters who have
further submerged the dichotomy, and so made it hard for us to
assimilate. None the less, the generic separation held good in
accounts of ancient drama until recently. Brilliant articles by R. P.
Winnington-Ingram and Bernard Knox weakened the barrier,[3] and
now it seems to be collapsing in several places at once. For example,
Berndt Seidensticker has argued for the widespread use of comic or
tragicomic elements to intensify Greek tragedy, explicitly invoking
comparison with Shakespeare.[4] Froma Zeitlin regards 'comic and
melodramatic elements' and 'the illusion–reality game' as typical of
Euripides, while claiming that Orestes goes 'beyond any formal
definitions and limitations, beyond parody . . . to a new level of
self-consciousness and authorial extravagance'.[5] Going one stage
further, some critics regard all literature, tragedy not least, as
playful or 'ludic'.[6]

This movement to diminish the distinction between the two
genres might claim solid ancient support. There is the formation
of the very words tragōidia and kōmōidia (let alone trygōidia); both
were put on in exactly the same theatre, as part of the same festival;
both have a chorus, which sings; both have actors who mainly
speak in iambic trimeters; both employ masks, and aulos (double-
reed pipe); and so on. But these very similarities might cut both
ways; they might be the basis for a polarity. It might be argued that,
from their shared setting, the two genres oppose each other, and
even to some extent build up mutually exclusive characteristics.
And this is what I shall maintain: that to a considerable degree

[3] R. Winnington-Ingram, 'Euripides, poiētēs sophos', Arethusa, 2 (1969), 127–43; B.
Knox, 'Euripidean Comedy', Word and Action (1970; Baltimore, 1979), 250–74.
[4] Palintonos Harmonia: Studien zu komischen Elementen in der griechischen Tragödie,
Hypomnemata, 72 (Göttingen, 1982).
[5] F. Zeitlin, 'The Closet of Masks: Role-Playing with Myth-Making in the Orestes of
Euripides', Ramus, 9 (1980), 51–77. This virtuoso piece is evidently becoming a classic.
[6] This position is approached by S. Goldhill, Language, Sexuality, Narrative: The
'Oresteia' (Cambridge, 1984). It may be epitomized by his attempt (p. 119) to improve
on a bon mot of Vernant: 'tragédie . . . ne reflète pas cette réalité; elle la met en
question': Goldhill adds, '"En jeu," he might have said.'

fifth-century tragedy and comedy help to define each other by their opposition and their reluctance to overlap.

There have of course been many sorts of *synkrisis* (comparison by juxtaposition) in both ancient and modern times: much of the material is usefully surveyed by Seidensticker. These are usually put in terms of propriety and plot: noble versus vulgar, sad versus happy, the insoluble versus resolution etc.[7] My *synkrisis* is going to be put in rather different terms: it is based on the *relation of the world of the play to the world of the audience*. The thesis is that this relation is fundamentally different in the two genres. It may be worth observing that any such distinction would be obliterated by those who posit a uniform 'textuality' in all literature. My polarity depends on going beyond the text to the work and the audience in the theatre; and, once in the theatre, it posits two quite different modes of interplay between stage and auditorium.[8]

In pursuing this *synkrisis* I shall look especially, though with excursions, at theatrical self-reference, or 'metatheatre'[9]—at the ways in which plays may, or may not, draw attention to their own 'playness', to the fact that they are artifices being performed under special controlled circumstances. Clearly the nature and degree of self-reference has great bearing on the relation of the world of the play to that of the audience. Old Comedy is ubiquitously self-referential: Aristophanes is probably the most metatheatrical

[7] Seidensticker, *Palintonos Harmonia*, 14–20, 249–71. At 245 n. 33 Seidensticker quotes George Bernard Shaw: 'the popular definition of tragedy is heavy drama in which everyone is killed in the last act, comedy being light drama, in which everyone is married in the last act'.

[8] This way of approaching 'theatrical texts' may be becoming the focus of some contemporary theoretical work. Nothing much is to be found in K. Elam, *The Semiotics of Theatre and Drama* (London, 1980)—see his index, s.v. 'transaction performer–audience'—but rather more in the last few pages of M. Carlson, *Theories of the Theatre* (Ithaca, NY, 1984). He writes (p. 508): 'the relatively minor attention given to the audience's contribution by the first generation of modern theatre semioticians is demonstrated by the fact that Elam's book devotes only 9 of 210 pages to this subject, but more recent work sugests that this may develop into one of the major areas of theoretical investigation of the 1980's.' In its concern with the stage–auditorium relationship my approach looks to the school of 'Rezeptionsästhetik' rather than to that of Derrida and de Man which is trapped within the framework of 'text–reader'.

[9] Although not entered in supp. 2 to the *OED* (1976), this term, presumably formed by analogy with 'metalanguage', goes back to at least 1963, when it was used as the title of a book by Lionel Abel.

playwright before Pirandello.[10] The world of the audience is never
safe from invasion, even appropriation, by the world of the play. The
question is how far tragedy is similar—or different. How true is it
that 'there are many instances of self-reference in Greek tragedy'?[11]
(I should add that any approach which holds that all literature is
necessarily self-referential is, of course, using the terms in a different
sense.)

I am purposely avoiding the traditional language of 'the dramatic
illusion' that can be 'maintained' or 'broken', which has accumulated its own burden of controversy, not least because 'illusion' is a
badly ambiguous term to use of a highly non-naturalistic theatre. At
the same time, it is my own experience as a spectator that on the
whole, when it works well for me, Greek tragedy binds a spell; that
my 'knowledge' that I am watching a play is temporarily charmed
away. I am reassured by the way this tallies with what Gorgias and
others have to say about the *apatē* and *psychagōgia* of tragedy.[12]
Moreover, this spellbinding is quite fragile; it can be dispelled in
all sorts of ways, and it can be difficult to restore. And the enthral-
ment is liable to be broken by a prominent theatrical self-reference—that is my experience at least. It does not, then, seem to
tally altogether with Dr Johnson later in his *Preface to Shakespeare*:
'The truth is, that the spectators are always in their senses, and
know, from the first act to the last, that the stage is only a stage, and
that the players are only players . . .'. I would agree that I do not
mistake the play for reality outside the theatre; my responses as I sit
in my seat are crucially different both internally and externally from
those which would be provoked by similar events in reality. But we
must beware of being forced into a false dichotomy between the
artefact's pretending that it is reality and the artefact's positive
proclamation that it is 'only' artifice. In what sense do I 'know'

[10] For recent studies of self-reference in Greek comedy, see C. F. Russo, *Aristofane, autore di teatro²* (Florence, 1984), D. Bain, *Actors and Audience* (Oxford, 1977), 208 ff., F. Muecke, 'Playing with the Play: Theatrical Self-Consciousness in Aristophanes', *Antichthon*, 11 (1977), 52–67, G. A. H. Chapman, 'Some Notes on Dramatic Illusion in Aristophanes', *AJP* 104 (1983), 1–23. Chapman contrasts comedy with tragedy, but without going into detailed discussion of tragedy. (The wide-ranging study by W. Görler, 'Über die Illusion in den antiken Komödie', *A & A* 18 (1973), 41–57, does not say much about 5th-cent. comedy.)

[11] P. Easterling, 'Anachronism in Greek Tragedy', *JHS* 105 (1985), 6. I am most grateful for an advance view of this valuable article.

[12] See e.g. J. de Romilly, 'Gorgias et le pouvoir de la poésie', *JHS* 93 (1973), 155–62.

all the time that the play is an artifice? How active a part of my experience is that 'knowledge'? Similarly, I would question Coleridge's phrase 'suspension of disbelief '. I suspend disbelief in so far as I respond in a way appropriate to the theatre and inappropriate to 'brute reality'; but how far are either 'belief ' or 'disbelief ' part of my experience during the play? It seems to me that fifth-century tragedy and comedy invite different answers to all these questions by setting up different relationships between the two worlds within the theatre.

The periods for which we can make these comparisons are not entirely synchronous. We can survey tragedy from 472 BC to the end of the century, while our comedy only begins, sufficiently preserved for these purposes, in the 420s. Within this time-span the polarization which I shall be proposing is not constant. It seems to have been at its most marked during the middle careers of Sophocles and Euripides. The ways in which it is diminished before and after this central period (approximately 440 to 415 BC) are different; and it may be best to introduce the earlier and later convergences now since they will crop up throughout this essay.

First, some of the characteristics of later comedy are to be found in Aeschylus, though not in Sophocles or Euripides. For example, the business of knocking at the door is common in comedy, while the only definite instance in tragedy is in *Choephoroi*. Or, more substantially, Aristophanic comedy seems free to shift around in time and place. Thus in *Acharnians* the scene can move from the *ekklēsia* to Dikaiopolis' house, and the time from the Rural Dionysia to the festival of Choes; at one point in *Lysistrata* several days or weeks of sexual privation pass by; the scene in *Frogs* can change from Earth to Styx to the Palace of Hades. It is doubtful whether tragedy ever admits explicit lapses of time without the departure of the chorus. And this kind of shifting of place is to be found in Aeschylus, but not in Sophocles or Euripides—for example, from council chamber to tomb in *Persae*, or from tomb to palace in *Choephoroi*.[13] Phenomena such as these might be explained by the late growth and definition of comedy. Although admitted to the dramatic festivals in the 470s, it seems to have been still a minor element in the lifetime of Aeschylus, leaving little or no textual or

[13] On knocking at the door, see Taplin, *Stagecraft of Aeschylus* (Oxford, 1977), 340–1; on time, pp. 291–4, 377–9; on place, pp. 103–7, 377–9.

pictorial trace. It seems to have been with the rise of Cratinus and Crates in the 430s that comedy really made its mark at Athens, and, I suggest, defined its territory.

Secondly, some of the characteristics of comedy 'infiltrate' tragedy towards the end of the century. It is now orthodox to detect comic touches in later Euripides. Although I would myself not accept all of those alleged by Knox, Seidensticker, and others in *Electra*, *Helen*, etc., I would not wish to deny at least some of those elements in the plays composed after 415 BC, though they are there as often as not in order to accentuate tragic tone elsewhere in the play. A good example is the contrast between the two 'recognition scenes' in *Ion*, the first, between Ion and Xuthus, amusing and mistaken, the second, between Ion and Creusa, true and dangerous.[14] I think, however, that Euripides takes this generic 'interference' to a new degree in the first two-thirds of *Bacchae*, where the unsettling use of Dionysus 'denies us' clear access either to the comic laughter or to the tragic pity by which we control our theatrical experience'.[15] There are, for example, the absurdities of the maenadism of Cadmus and Tiresias, the funny transvestism of Pentheus, and the smiling mask of Dionysus. Such contraventions of the generic boundaries are, no doubt, all part of the crisis in the last years of the fifth century which produced fascinating innovative plays—I think particularly of *Orestes* and *Philoctetes*—but which also marked the end of growth for classical tragedy. In that case, this confirms rather than weakens the distinction between the two genres before this last brilliant breakdown.

I shall roughly group the material under five headings: audience, poet, theatre, disguise, and parody.

1. Consider first audience address and explicit references to the presence of the audience. 'Shall I use one of the old jokes, master—the ones that never fail to get a laugh?' (*Frogs* 1–2). The audience of Old Comedy is never safe from being pointed to, addressed, and implicated in the play. For tragedy, on the other hand, there has been controversy whether the audience is ever addressed or directly

---

[14] See Knox, 'Euripidean Comedy', 260–3; Taplin, *Greek Tragedy in Action* (London, 1978), 137–8.

[15] H. Foley, 'The Masque of Dionysus' *TAPA* 110 (1980), 107–33: 122; see now *Ritual Irony: Poetry and Sacrifice in Euripides* (Ithaca, NY, 1985), 205 ff.

alluded to; and I agree with David Bain that it never was.[16] In many ways the strongest candidate (not discussed by Bain) is Athena at *Eumenides* 681 ff. She begins, 'Hear now my ordinance, people of Athens . . .', but the idea that she turns to the *Attikos leōs* assembled in the theatre is surely contradicted by the next line, where she explicitly glosses her vocative as addressed to the jurors at the trial of Orestes, 'judging this first case for shed blood'. And yet if there was any audience address in tragedy, it would surely have been at such crucial moments (and not in passing second-person plurals like *skepsasthe* at *Ajax* 1028 or *eidete* at *Orestes* 128).

Along the same lines, we might expect the physical line between stage and auditorium to be breached by comedy yet not by tragedy, whether the breach is made by members of the audience being taken into the orchestra or by actors going out into the auditorium. In fact we have no evidence of any such physical 'interference' in either genre (nor in satyr-play). What we do find, however, is nuts and figs thrown by the actors out into the audience. Aristophanes takes a supercilious attitude to such pantomime gimmicks (*Wasps* 58–9, *Wealth* 797–9), though it is more than possible that the 'sacrificial grain' which he has thrown out among the spectators at *Peace* 962 was really edible goodies. In any case comedy breached the stage–auditorium barrier ballistically if not corporeally: tragedy presumably did not.

Comedy also feels free to refer to the Dionysia (though it does not do so often), and to the judges, priests, etc. present at the performance. The nearest tragedy comes to this is the brief address to Nike in the closing words of *Iphigenia among the Taurians*, *Orestes*, and *Phoenissae*. Even supposing these are authentic,[17] they are still the exception which proves the rule, since they come outside the play proper. But, while there are no allusions to tragedy to the Dionysia or its appurtenances, there are plenty to Dionysus. Are these automatically metatheatrical? Any answer to this question should be reached in the light of the whole issue of the relation of the world

[16] D. Bain, 'Audience Address in Greek Tragedy', *CQ* 25 (1975), 13–25; also cf. Taplin, *Stagecraft of Aeschylus*, 130–2, 394–5. I am inclined to agree with Bain (pp. 23–5) that Astydamas 60F4 is wrongly attributed to satyr-play rather than comedy (i.e. the author is wrong also); but D. F. Sutton, *The Greek Satyr Play* (Meisenheim an Glan, 1980), 82–3, prefers the explanation that comedy and satyr-play were losing their generic distinctions in the 4th cent. For illustrations from Old Comedy see e.g. Chapman, 'Some Notes on Dramatic Illusion in Aristophanes', 3, 8–9.

[17] Against authenticity, see W. S. Barrett (ed.), *Euripides: Hippolytos* (Oxford, 1964), 1462–6; he is followed by J. Diggle's Oxford Classical Text (1981), at *IT* 1197–9.

of tragedy to the world of the auditorium. Was the audience
expecting self-reference of this sort—on the look-out for it? At least
it should not be taken for granted without argument that any
reference to 'the god of tragedy' (whtever that means) is thereby
self-reference.[18]

Even those who think that the audience as a whole is sometimes
addressed or that the setting at the Dionysia is sometimes explicitly
brought to mind do not argue, so far as I know, that any individual
member of the audience is ever alluded to by name. In Old Comedy,
of course, however fantastical the plot, individuals who are sitting in
the auditorium are named, and even replicated as dramatis personae. It is, I suggest, a curious and neglected pointer to the different
relation of the world of the audience to that of tragedy that fifth-
century Athenians did not share their names with the characters of
heroic myth (unlike modern Greeks). I have not yet found a single
Athenian name in Aristophanes which is also the name of a
character in tragedy.[19] Surveying Kirchner's *Prosopographia Attica*,
there is not a single example of an Aias, Agamemnon, Hector,
Hippolytos, Odysseus, Oidipous, Orestes, Polyneikes, or Teiresias.
There are a few instances, mainly post fifth-century, of some of
the names which people have in tragedy, for example Aeneas,
Menelaos, Neoptolemos, Kreon, Pelops. The only tragic name I
have yet found which is actually common is Alexandros; Iason
and Lykourgos are not rare.

We do not know whether individuals in the audience were named
in the early dramatizations of recent history by Phrynichus and
others. If they were, that might be because, as I suggested earlier,
the dichotomy with comedy did not yet exist. Note, however, that,
while Aeschylus does not name any Greek in *Persae*, he feels free to
accumulate Persian names: few if any of them were shared with
anyone in the audience. It is, in any case, worth remembering that
Phrynichus was fined by the Athenians 'on the grounds that he
reminded the audience of a disaster close to home' (Hdt. 6. 21. 2)—
that was not the function of tragedy.[20]

It would not be sensible, in this context, to get deeply entangled in

---

[18] As it is in Charles Segal, 'Metatragedy', in *Dionysiac Poetics and Euripides' Bacchae*
(Princeton, 1982), ch. 7.
[19] At first sight Orestes, the highwayman, looks like an exception (*Ach.* 1167, *Birds*
712, 1482 ff.); but that is in fact a nickname.
[20] On this, see C. Macleod, 'Politics and the *Oresteia*', *JHS*, 102 (1982), 131–2; repr. in
Collected Essays (Oxford, 1983).

the never-ending controversy over topical, and especially political, reference in fifth-century tragedy; but a passing brush with it is hardly avoidable. I would strongly maintain that Greek tragedy is through and through political, in the sense that it is much concerned with the life of men and women within society, the *polis*; but that this concern does not necessarily involve any direct reference to the immediate politicking of the Athenian audience at any one particular time. Anyone who wishes to argue that tragedy does make particular topical incursions across the stage–auditorium line has, at least, to concede that they are cryptic; they have to be decoded behind the façade of a distant world of the past. The point should then be made that some of the topical allusion in comedy is cryptic. It is a particular loss that we do not have one single old comedy of mythological burlesque, such as Cratinus' *Nemesis* and *Dionysalexandros*. Our papyrus hypothesis to *Dionysa-ledandros* ends, however, 'Perikles is lampooned in the play very plausibly through *emphasis* as someone who involved Athens in war.'[21] This very probably means that the application to Pericles had to be worked out from clues in the quasi-mythological setting. Even in *Wasps* there are the thin disguises of Labes and the *kyōn Kydathenaieus*, and in *Knights* the slaves are not directly identified as Demosthenes and Nicias, nor even Paphlagon as Cleon. Are we to credit that tragedy used very much the same technique, and thus set up a similar interplay between the play and the world of the audience? I am inclined to go to the other extreme and say that, just because this was comedy's method, no one in the audience would be at all inclined to search for such encoding in tragedy. In other words, I suggest that, for example, the only years which we can exclude with confidence as the date for the first performance of *Oedipus Tyrannus* were the years of the plague.

It is significant that fifth-century satyr-play has been combed in vain for Athenians and for topical allusions to the world of the audience. Nothing has been found more topical than *kottabos* or Corinthian prostitutes.[22] In the next century, however, when

[21] *POxy* 663, col. 2 = *PCG* 4. 140, lines 44–8. For a discussion of *emphasis* see R. Janko, *Aristotle on Comedy* (London, 1984), 202–3, 206.

[22] Seaford, *Cyclops*, 18–19, Sutton, *The Greek Satyr Play*, 162–3. Sutton (p. 10) writes 'Satyr play was rarely if ever a vehicle for the expression of opinion about contemporary events in the arts or in any other sphere, and even veiled personal attacks are not found.' I am not sure what to make of Sophocles 887R, which contains the coined epithets *nikomachon* and *pausanian*. See S. Radt, Fondation Hardt, Entretiens, 29 (1983), 210, 227 (where I suggested it might come from satyr-play).

comedy had banished topicality from its essence to more fringe jokes, satyr-play began to allegorize the affairs of the audience, most notoriously in Python's *Agen*.[23]

2. The *poiētēs* of Old Comedy may refer to himself, and to his own activity of producing comedy. This occurs above all in the parabasis, but not exclusively so, as is shown by *Acharnians* 497ff.: 'Don't bear me a grudge out there in the audience if I, a beggar, dare to speak out in public about the city in a comic play. . .'. This simply does not happen in tragedy. That should also warn us against ever saying (as, for example, Wilamowitz did about *Heracles* 637ff.) that in some particular passage the poet himself is speaking as an individual through his play.[24] In Cratinus' *Pytine* of 423 BC, on the other hand, it seems that Cratinus himself was a dramatis persona.[25]

Closely related to self-reference by the author would be reference to his act of writing or to the text produced. This might be of special significance for those theories which hold 'textuality' as a central concept, and those which hold that all writing is essentially about writing (and/or reading essentially about reading). But, so far as I know, no *explicit* self-reference to the writing or text of tragedy has been claimed. In fact references to any kind of writing or reading, or even literature, are not thick on the ground. It might be claimed that the playwright would not in any case be associated with written texts rather than the oral instruction of actors and chorus; but 'orality' can be over-emphasized.[26] Even so, references in tragedy to writing and poetry tend to be put in rather high-flown and epic terms.[27] The closest that any tragedy comes to

---

[23] B. Snell, *Scenes from Greek Drama* (Berkeley, 1964), 113 ff., Sutton, *The Greek Satyr Play*, 77 ff.

[24] This point is well discussed in Bain, 'Audience Address in Greek Tragedy', 14–17; see also M. Kaimio, *The Chorus of Greek Drama within the Light of the Person and Number Used* (Helsinki, 1970), 92–103. [25] For evidence, see PCG 4. 219.

[26] I now feel that in Taplin, *Stagecraft of Aeschylus*, 12–16, where my prime purpose was to argue that reading plays was only a secondary substitute for seeing them, I underrated the literacy of the dramatists, and indeed of the 5th cent. as a whole. For a better balance, see B. Knox, *The Cambridge History of Classical Literature*, vol. i, pt. 1 (Cambridge, 1985), 6–12. Bear in mind also that in *Acharnians* Euripides' plays are presented as texts which are equated with his ragged costumes (see Macleod, *Collected Essays*, 47–8); and that on the 'Pronomos Vase', where the *aulētēs* is the centre of attention, the playwright is shown sitting with a finished roll of papyrus in his hand. This is unique, but for allied material, see H. R. Immerwahr, in C. Henderson (ed.), *Studies in Honour of B. L. Ullmann* (Rome, 1964), 17 ff.

[27] See Easterling, 'Anachronism in Greek Tragedy', 4–6.

textual self-reference is probably *Troades* 1242–5.[28] Diggle's text reads: 'But if God had not laid us low, we would have perished obscure, unsung, unremembered in poets' songs of later time.'

Both the words *hymnētheimen* and *aoidas* distance the passage from tragedy. Contrast the explicit theatrical language of Shakespeare's *Julius Caesar*:

CASSIUS.　　　　　　How many ages hence
　Shall this our lofty scene be acted over
　In states unborn and accents yet unknown!
BRUTUS. How many times shall Caesar bleed in sport . . .

3. Probably the most obvious kind of self-reference in Old Comedy is reference to its own theatricality and to its own performance in the theatre. One thinks of Dikaiopolis telling Euripides *all' engkuk-lētheti* (*Ach.* 407); or Trygaeus calling out to the *mēchanopoios* (*Peace* 174 ff.); or the chorus's warning later in *Peace* (729 ff.) not to leave property lying around, 'because lots of thieves like to hang around the stage building and ply their trade there'. There are many varied examples of this sort of metatheatre in Old Comedy.[29] Plenty of examples in tragedy have been alleged; but I suggest that we should not be too hasty in joining the hunt for metatheatre here, there, and everywhere.

One problem is that we do not know how highly developed the technical terms of the theatre were in the fifth century. There are many Greek words whose primary association for us is theatrical, while in the fifth century this application may have been minor, or even have not yet existed. It would be a mistake to regard *skēnē*, for example, as metatheatrical in *Ajax* 3—'And now I see, near his tent along the shore . . .'—or its many other occurrences in tragedy. What, then, of *angeloi* at Euripides' *Electra* 759, which is widely regarded as a self-referential joke?[30] The counter-argument is best made by reproducing the full text of Diggle's Oxford Classical Text of lines 757–61:

ELECTRA. You pronounce my doom—why do I delay?
CHORUS. Stay here, till you clearly learn your fate.

[28] Cited by R. Rutherford, 'Tragic Form and Feeling in the *Iliad*', *JHS* 102 (1982), 160 n. 69, as refuting the contention that 'no case of theatrical self-reference can be found in Greek tragedy'.

[29] For a full, if rather rough, collection, see Chapman, 'Some Notes on Dramatic Illusion in Aristophanes', 4–10.

[30] See esp. W. G. Arnott, 'Euripides and the Unexpected', *G & R* 20 (1973), 49–64.

ELECTRA. No, I'm beaten! Where are the messengers?
CHORUS. They'll come. It's no light matter to slay a king.
ANGELOS. Hail, victorious, beautiful Mycenaean maids!

For us *angelos* is primarily theatrical, especially familiar from the
editorial attributions of parts; but we should not necessarily read
that back into Euripides. On the contrary, it might be maintained (as
with the date of *Oedipus* and the plague) that the occurrence of a
word in tragedy—*kommos* or *mēchanē*, for example—is evidence that
at that time the word did not have theatrical associations, or at least
that they were not irrepressibly prominent.

An interesting case is *choros*. In the fifth century this word had, of
course, many other applications as well as to the chorus of drama.
Aristophanes could make it metatheatrical by means of context, as
when Dikaiopolis, instead of telling Euripides that he must address
the Acharnians, says, 'I have to speak a long oration to the chorus'
(*Ach.* 416). But that does not make its use in tragedy automatically
metatheatrical. On *ti dei me choreuein* at *Oedipus Tyrannus* 896, E. R.
Dodds wrote, 'The meaning is surely "Why should I, an Athenian
citizen, continue to serve in a chorus?"'. In speaking of themselves
as a chorus they step out of the play into the contemporary world,
as Aristophanes' choruses do in the *parabasis*.'[31] But he failed to see
the breadth of application of *choreuein*: 'Why should I participate in
religious occasions?'

There is a particularly interesting occurrence of *choros* in the
Cassandra scene in *Agamemnon*. At 1178 ff. Cassandra speaks of
being on the track of ancient evils: 'A chorus never departs from
this house—singing in concert, but with no pleasing sound' (1186–
7). She then goes on to describe this *choros* in terms which fit the
chorus of the *Eumenides* closely: 'It has drunk indeed of human
blood, and grown bolder—a rout of inbred Furies, within the
house, never to be turned away. They sing their song . . .'. Before
this is claimed as a prize example of tragic metatheatricality—
which so far as I know has not happened yet—I suggest that would
be a mistake. Surely the identity of the chorus of the third play of
Oresteia was a closely guarded secret, to be released as an astonishing surprise. The audience of *Agamemnon* did not know that there

---

[31] *The Ancient Concept of Progress* (Oxford, 1973), 75; repr. in E. Segal (ed.), *Oxford
Readings in Greek Tragedy* (Oxford, 1983), 186. (Dodds's article 'On Misunderstanding
the *Oedipus Rex*' was first published in 1966.)

would be a *choros Erinyōn*.[32] So this passage is not a flash of ludic self-consciousness: it is much more effective and Aeschylean than that, planting in the mind of the audience an image, a fantastic metaphor, which later becomes terribly real.

4. Costume is only a further type of possible theatrical self-reference. It is, however, particularly blatant, since the actors have disguised themselves to assume their roles. And, above all, the women are men in costume. So in Old Comedy there is much play with costume, with putting it on and taking it off on-stage; and especially with the *failure* of disguise, since this comically shakes the whole undertaking, and threatens to return the actors to the world of the audience. Tragedy is generally wary of using disguises and avoids putting them on or taking them off on-stage. In her recent article Frances Muecke generally makes more of disguise in tragedy than I would; but even in *Helen*, her chief example before *Bacchae*, she observes an important difference from Aristophanes: 'in Euripides, play with the theatrical illusion is for the sake of the play with ideas in the drama, while in Aristophanes contrast between reality and illusion is used for the sake of reflecting upon theatrical illusion itself'.[33] It is in *Bacchae*, and especially in the transvestism scene, that Euripides finally breaks down this distinction.

On the other hand I am not convinced by Charles Segal[34] that we have a metatheatrical use of *prosōpon*—face, mask—at *Bacchae* 1277, where Cadmus asks his daughter, 'Whose head do you hold in your hands?' Five lines later Agave sees the truth: 'I see the greatest grief . . .'. The time for Dionysus' conjuring-tricks is over; the play has moved on from its metatheatrical juggling with illusion and reality, tragedy and comedy. It has returned, with fresh power, to the grip of tragedy; this is no mere flimsy mask (even if the mask was used as a matter of stage management); it is the heavy head of Agave's own son. This passage shows how resistant tragedy was to ludic infiltration, in that Euripides is able to repair so completely the great breaches made earlier in the play. It is interesting that there is, in fact, no clear case in surviving Aristophanes of a metatheatrical

---

[32] If this is right, it is in itself evidence that the audience did not know the titles of the plays in advance.

[33] F. Muecke, 'I know You—By Your Rags: Costume and Disguise in Fifth-Century Drama', *Antichthon*, 16 (1982), 17–34: 29. For raw material, rather than interpretation, see Chapman, 10–22.

[34] 'Metatragedy', 248 ff. Sec n. 18.

use of *prosōpon*.[35] There are, however, references to masks in
comedy, as we might expect. The most prominent is at *Knights*
230–3, where 'Demosthenes' refers to the appearance of the 'Paphlagonian': 'Don't be afraid of him, because that's not really his
picture. All the mask-makers were too scared to make his like-
ness. But everyone here will recognize him, so clever is our audience.' In view of this, it is all the more implausible that any of the
many other uses of *prosōpon* should be self-referential.[36]

5. The last of my five headings is 'parody'. On the ubiquitous
parody of tragedy in Old Comedy it is worth observing that, as well
as indicators such as metrics and diction, there were almost certainly indications in performance which it is less possible for us to
document. There was surely a tragic timbre in the voice, and a
tragic poise to physical movement and posture, which comedy
would also exploit. I suspect that a single gesture was often sufficient to indicate paratragedy. The many common features of the two
genres make it easy to indicate parody by means of the differences;
and this helps to account for the pervasiveness of paratragedy in Old
Comedy.

There was clearly plenty of paratragedy in satyr-play, though it
was probably less than in comedy, and there is no place in surviving
satyr-play, so far as I know, whose point depends on knowing a
certain passage of tragedy which is being parodied. Here again we
cannot know the extent of performative paratragedy. The new
illustration of Aeschylus' *Sphinx* on the Würzburg hydria indicates
parody of tragedy by means of costume and demeanour: the satyrs
are posing as solemn elders of the city.[37] So satyr-play also exploits
the generic differences.

The parody of tragedy *by tragedy* would, then, be a very different
matter, since all these intergeneric resources would not be available.
(It would, by the way, be easy for tragedy to parody comedy, if that

[35] 'Metatragedy', 248 n. 33 offers *Ach.* 990, *Peace* 524, *Frogs* 912.
[36] I have in mind particularly Aeschylus' *Eumenides* 990, where the Erinyes'
frightening faces are a permanent feature, not a temporary mask; and it would be
even less appropriate at Sophocles' *Electra* 1297, where Electra's expression is not
habitually grim, as she herself explains at 1309 ff. I am not even persuaded by Seaford,
Cyclops, ad loc. that there is a reference to Silenus' mask at E., *Cyc.* 227.
[37] See E. Simon, *Das Satyrspiel Sphinx des Aischylos*, SHAW 1981/5 (Heidelberg,
1981).

were desirable.[38]) In keeping with my overall thesis I am sceptical about allegations of parody in tragedy. Explicit parody would signal an acknowledgement to the audience that they have seen other tragedies, and thus subvert, in the manner of comedy, the independence of the world of drama. Of course, a tragedy may be influenced by earlier works, and may build them into its fabric; but how often does a tragedy draw attention to a predecessor as such? The notorious instance is the parody of *Choephoroi* in Euripides' *Electra*. Assuming these thirty or so lines to be genuine Euripides—and I do not think the case against their authenticity should be lightly dismissed[39]—it must be conceded that they do not have much point without the explicit recognition by the audience of their parodic relationship to *Choephoroi*. Yet it is easy to see how this was signalled without the indicators at the disposal of comedy—diction, gesture, direct quotation, not to mention actual citation.

There is no surviving example even in comedy of a fully fledged play within a play; but the use of *Telephus* in *Acharnians*, or of *Helen* and *Andromeda* in *Thesmophoriazusae*, is half-way there. The nearest that tragedy approaches to this is in certain uses of contrived disguise such as the 'merchant' in *Philoctetes* and the escape scene in *Helen*. Such scenes seem to occur in the 'outer' periods of fifth-century tragedy.

I have argued that tragedy does not pretend to be reality, but that it does not undermine its own fictionality either. We need not be forced into that dichotomy. Analogously I believe that tragedy may make use of other earlier literature, and be greatly enriched by it, without the kind of specific allusion and quotation which are everywhere in comedy (and Japanese Noh, by the way).

It seems to me that recent studies of intertexuality, and especially ludic intertextuality, do not make sufficient distinctions over explicitness and about the relation of the work to the audience. By means of parody comedy openly acknowledges that it is an artefact making play with another artefact. Most tragedy casts its spell in a more exclusive, almost hypnotic way; to be effective it demands the total concentration of its audience, intellectual and emotional. Explicit self-reference breaks that spell. Recent studies of Euripides,

---

[38] Tragedy may 'borrow' from comedy, as is argued, for example, by K. J. Dover, *Aristophanic Comedy* (London, 1972), 148–9 with reference to *Birds* 209 ff. and *Helen* 1187 ff. But this is not parody and does not draw attention to its intertextual relation.

[39] See David Bain, '[Euripides], *Electra* 518–544', *BICS* 24 (1977), 104–16.

like that of Froma Zeitlin on *Orestes* in relation to the *Oresteia*, *Medea*, and other tragedies,[40] raise the questions: how explicit are these allusions; do they call for recognition as such from an audience; if so, how is this signalled; do they sacrifice characteristic tragic spellbinding? These are posed as open questions, not merely rhetorical questions.

We read nervously and self-consciously, observing minute correspondences between those few tragedies we have. We should not forget the quite different state of consciousness experienced in the theatre. Similarly, we are aware of chronology and historical authenticity, and likely to be sensitive to 'anachronisms'. But how much were those a concern in the fifth century? Easterling writes that the technical terms of the theatre were avoided in tragedy because they 'would be too "modern", just the kind of anachronism that is studiously avoided'.[41] But is this chronographic awareness the explanation rather than the mutual exclusivity of the world of the tragedy and the world of the auditorium? I am doubtful whether there are any anachronisms in Greek tragedy to be noticed as such—not even the allusion to Orphics in *Hippolytus* or the demagogic assembly in *Orestes*. The best candidates are probably philosophically avant-garde notions; on the other hand, we are particularly obsessed with the temporal history of ideas. We must ask how far Euripides and his audience thought of the development of philosophy in chronological terms. *Troades* 884 ff. is as strong a candidate as any: Menelaus comments on Hecuba's prayers, 'What's this? What strange new prayers you're praying!' If we leave aside our awareness of the history of philosophy, it might appear that he is commenting on her unconventional phrasing rather than her anachronistic metaphysics.

Aetiologies are rather different from such alleged anachronisms. Certainly, from Athenian justice in *Eumenides* to the offerings at Brauron predicted by Athena in *Iphigenia*, such prophecies allude to the future beyond the play, to the era of the audience.[42] But this is a far cry from the particular topicality of comedy; far from breaking

---

[40] Zeitlin, 'The Closet of Masks'.

[41] Easterling, 'Anachronism in Greek Tragedy'.

[42] This may also be the point of Hecuba's reference at *Troades* 1242–5 to the *aoidas hysterōn brotōn* (the songs of generations to come); this is the nearest that *Troades* has to a prediction *ex machina*.

down the integrity of the distanced setting of tragedy, it reinforces it. The aetiology is part of the 'antiquity' of the world of the play.

This *synkrisis* of tragedy and comedy has looked at only some aspects, leaving others virtually unconsidered. An obvious one, the one which received most attention in antiquity, is decorum: the contrast was put in terms of *semnon* versus *phaulon*, and in many other similar oppositions. Although Euripides is already accused in Aristophanes of degrading the tone of tragedy, the fact remains that there are many areas open to comedy which were still unthinkable even in Euripides. Some lurid examples are gross physical violence and indignity, and the physical manifestations of excretion and of sex. Comedy revels in those very parts which are unmentionable in tragedy; and the more they are the property of comedy, the more inaccessible they become for tragedy. The Nurse in *Choephoroi* may be the early exception who proves the rule for later. Another, less blatant, area of contrast is staging. In my view at least, the stage action of tragedy was austere but weighty; there were not a lot of movements or props, but those there were were clear and full of dramatic significance. The stage of comedy was evidently much more crowded with activity and business. A good example is Old Comedy's delight in bringing on a clutter of stage properties, as in the courtroom scene in *Wasps*, or the bedroom farce of Cinesias and Myrrhine in *Lysistrata*. There may be an analogous contrast in structure. On the whole the formal construction of comedy tends to be uneven, unpredictable, and paratactic. Contrast with tragedy, for instance, the string of characters in *Birds* who turn up trying to gain access to Nephelokokkygia. On the other hand, we should set against this looseness comedy's rigid, and apparently conservative, large-scale epirrhematic *agōnes*.

Endings may be another divergence. Comedy tends towards a united and celebratory ending, such as a victory or wedding procession. The *Oresteia* has that sort of conclusion; but in 'classical' tragedy, once comedy is established, they are avoided. Euripides' later leaning towards such resolutions in his escape-plays of 414 to 412 BC may have been one of the provocations of *Thesmophoriazusai*.

As I approach a conclusion, I shall attempt a couple of ambitious generalizations, both connected with the role of the chorus. First, it was essential for comedy, if it was to succeed, that the audience should interrupt: it was essential for tragedy, if it was to succeed, that the audience should not interrupt. We do not know for sure whether comedy encouraged shouting, whistling, clapping, etc., but obviously it encouraged laughter. It wanted to be stopped by laughter; one of the first things young actors of comedy have to learn is how to accommodate the audience's laughter, leaving enough pause but not too much. The intense concentration of tragedy calls for silence—even your weeping should not disturb your neighbour![43] It is true that we have anecdotes about the noisiness and interruptions of ancient audiences, but these all concern plays that were not liked, and were not succeeding.[44] Theophrastus' character the *bdelyros* is liable 'to clap in the theatre when others stop applauding, and to hiss the actors that the rest of the audience favour'. I doubt whether a really effective tragedy even admitted applause except at the end. And laughter is a great threat to this kind of concentrated emotional sequence; anyone who has been concerned with a modern production will witness that it must be most carefully controlled. Those who enjoy seeking jokes in Greek tragedy seldom have much sense of theatre beyond the text.

The inactivity of the audience is, indeed, a vital prerequisite of the tragic experience, and is an important way in which theatre is quite unlike the 'real world'. The young learn that, however moved, they must not scream or call out, let alone try to intervene physically (like the provincial Chinese spectator who in 1678, so the story goes, stabbed the villain of the piece to death on the stage). Emotions urge us to consequential action—fear to flight, joy to celebration, and so forth. But however moved the tragic audience may be, whether by pity towards giving help, or by anger towards revenge, or whatever, it knows it must sit quiet. The place of the chorus within the play has strong affinities, though it always remains within the world of the play, never stepping outside it. The chorus becomes emotionally very involved, yet is all but helpless to do anything about it. What the chorus does is to divert its frustrated urge to action into lyric expression, into singing of associations—religious, mythical, ethical—and of ideas arising from their helpless emotion. I suggest that

[43] Plato's *Ion* 535e portrays a silent and motionless, though highly moved, audience at performances of epic (and humorously alludes to the danger of laughter).

[44] For the material, see A. W. Pickard-Cambridge, *The Dramatic Festivals of Athens*[2], rev. J. Gould and D. Lewis (Oxford, 1968), 272–6. Chapman, 'Some Notes on Dramatic Illusion in Aristophanes', 1 notes the contrast between the appropriate audience responses to tragedy and comedy.

this supplies the audience of tragedy with its model of a response that is both emotional and intellectual.

The audience of comedy is, on the other hand, allowed, and encouraged, to express its response by laughter, and to interrupt the play when it is moved to do so. It may not be coincidence that the chorus of Old Comedy is, generally speaking, more active and more directly involved in the plot than that of tragedy, at least during the first half of the play.[45] (So the rise of comedy may be one reason why 'protagonist-choruses' like those of Aeschylus' *Suppliants* and *Eumenides* are not found in later tragedy.)

This leads me to my second grand generalization, which was stimulated by Michael Silk's thought-provoking article 'Aristophanes as a Lyric Poet'.[46] He argues that Aristophanes' best and most characteristic lyrics are not his pastiches of high style, but his lively, low, often personal squibs; and he writes, 'traditional Greek lyric, and specifically traditional choral lyric, tends towards the general, the world of myth and timeless truths. Aristophanes' most fundamental instincts go the other way, towards the particular.' I think this notion can be extended to fifth-century comedy and tragedy in general. It is as though they are planets in orbit round two different suns. Comedy may make gestures in the direction of the universal, the more than transient—Aristophanes is already making such moves in the parabasis of *Acharnians* (*kōmōidēsei ta dikaia* . . .). But it is always pulled back by the gravitational influence of the particular, back to individuals and details. Comedy cannot universalize for long without falling over a heap of dung. Tragedy can pay attention to particulars: indeed it is essential for its effectiveness that the particulars of the plot should be sufficiently concrete to be convincing. But the particulars never dominate, they are always overborne by the gravitational pull of the universal. In the long run the particulars serve the general, the 'timeless truths' as Silk put it.

We are left, then, with two genres which are in essence fundamentally different. On the whole they reject overlap rather than invite overlap. They are fascinatingly related yet opposed ways of approaching through art the world and the truth. This may be why

[45] Cf. B. Zimmermann, *Untersuchungen zur Form und dramatischen Technik der Aristophanischen Komödien* (Königstein, 1984), ch. 1.
[46] *YCS* 26 (1980), 99–151, esp. 117–24.

in the *Symposium*, in demonstrating the superior access of philosophy to the truth, Plato did not give the rival—drama—only one representative, but included both Aristophanes with his details about genitals and navel-fashioning and Agathon with his high-flown sweeping generalities.

And, in a sense, Socrates was right in the end. During the fourth century tragedy stagnated, while comedy developed. But it developed from the exuberant topicality of Aristophanes towards the more ethical and restrained Menander. Almost all the distinctions I have been drawing between fifth-century tragedy and comedy do not apply to the New Comedy of Menander.[47] In the terms of Agathon's *tragōidopoios* and Aristophanes' *kōmōidopoios*, Menander is, as Socrates insisted was possible, both. Yet Meander was also inferior to both Old Comedy and Old Tragedy, and closer to one than the other. It would be nearly 2,000 years befoe the dichotomy would be fully bridged and transcended by the master of tragical–comical–historical–pastoral.[48]

[47] For some new discussion of self-reference in New Comedy, see R. L. Hunter, *The New Comedy of Greece and Rome* (Cambridge, 1985), 73–82.

[48] An earlier version of this essay was prepared for the Table Ronde of the Groupe de recherches sur la tragédie grecque held at Paris X-Nanterre in May 1985. I am most grateful to Professors F. Jouan and S. Saïd for the invitation, which prompted me to get my ideas down on paper—and to those present for the discussion. I am also indebted to Michael Silk and to the *Journal of Hellenic Studies'* referee for thought-provoking criticism, not all of which I have been able to meet.

3
Aristophanes and Politics

A. W. GOMME

This is a threadbare subject; and I would not write about it further if it were not that I am convinced that those scholars who have discussed it hitherto, so far as their writings are known to me, have failed to satisfy us because, with hardly an exception,[1] they have started in the wrong direction. They have not by any means all travelled by the same road, and they have reached very different conclusions: inevitably, because some of them have not understood Aristophanes, others are sympathetic and sensitive. But they have begun by asking: What were Aristophanes' opinions? What system or what policy was he attacking or defending? Even, To what party did he belong? That is to say, they have thought of him as primarily a politician: a man with a policy to advocate, opinions to defend, who wants to see certain things done—in this sense, a *practical* man.

Two propositions are generally put forward. First, that Aristophanes was convinced that the theatre had a moral and didactic purpose, in the strictest, narrowest sense, that it was its business to improve its hearers, and especially that it was the business of comedy to give good political advice; and that he himself had always given such advice, consistently (in his 'Old Comedy' period). Secondly, that he was conservative in his attitude both to politics and to cultural movements. It is in the statement of this second proposition that we find most variety of opinion among scholars. For some, as (for example) Starkie, Aristophanes was a 'fanatical conservative', 'the enemy of new ideas'—'the comic spirit of Athens was condemned, by the instinct of self-preservation, to

---

[1] One exception is W. Rennie, *The 'Acharnians' of Aristophanes* (London, 1909); but his few pages in his intro. to *Ach.*, admirable as they are, hint at, rather than explain, his position.

oppose all novel ideas'. So Neil: Aristophanes 'had two objects of attack'—newer intellectual movements and democratic politics. For others, such as Croiset and Murray, he was not opposed to democracy, had no desire to alter the constitution, but was an enemy only of the demagogues who misled the demos, and especially of the militant imperialism which was at the time their particular mark; though Croiset thinks that he 'hated the very name of philosophy and thought it detestable', while Murray says of the *Clouds* 'the whole makes on me the impression not of a satire, like the *Knights* and the *Wasps*, directed against something the poet hated and wanted to destroy, but of a "clash of humours"'. For these scholars Aristophanes, in the main, occupies a middle position—he is a moderate democrat, disliking the extreme oligarch as much as the demagogue: a good, comfortable, essentially British position.

Turn to the plays themselves. Aristophanes, we are told, was the admirer of olden days, of the old way of life, in politics as in culture. Miltiades, Cimon, and Myronides were his military heroes, Marathon and Salamis the great battles (but especially Marathon, for it was a land battle—Salamis belonged rather to the sailor-crowd of Piraeus[2]), Phrynichus and Aeschylus his favourite poets. Whether oligarch or moderate democrat, he was at least a lover of the old ways; that is why Socrates and Euripides, who liked the militant demagogy of the war period as little as he did, are attacked as vigorously as the demagogues—they were dissolvents of the old culture. He was all for the older generation, the men of the country, the small farmer who tilled his own land, of simple thought, of little speech, who had fought hard and loved the old songs of Phrynichus: the *Marathonamachai* (men who fought at Marathon)—'the name which Aristophanes was wont to send thrilling through the theatre, sure of his effect'.[3] That is the general view. It may even be true. But it is a view which, combined with the other theory that Aristophanes had a policy to urge upon his hearers, was a politician, leads at once to contradictions and so to self-deception. It will not hold water for a moment. For a politician there is a right and a wrong side: he urges the right and condemns the wrong; for a dramatist, though he represents a conflict, there is no right or wrong side (whatever his private opinions may be). If

---

[2] Macan, *Herodotus* IV–VI, ii. 186.
[3] Ibid.

Aristophanes was a politician, then a single reading of the plays
makes one thing clear: the older generation, whenever they appear
expressly as such, when they are described as brave old men of
Marathon, are invariably on the wrong side or *are* the wrong side,
the side which Aristophanes is attacking. In the *Acharnians* it is the
old men, the farmers, who are most fiercely patriotic, militant, pro-
war; it is for them treason for anyone to suggest a parley with the
faithless enemy, or to say a good word for him—as wicked as for a
woman at the Thesmophoria to speak in defence of Euripides.[4] In
the *Knights* when Cleon is about to be attacked he calls on the older
generation to support him against the revolutionaries:

Help! Members of the jury! Comrades of the Order of the Three Obols!
Remember how I've fed you all these years with my prosecutions—right
or wrong, I never gave a damn, I just shouted as hard as I could! Come
quickly and help! I'm being assaulted by a gang of conspirators!   (255-7)

The knights, who are the enemies of Cleon, and so the friends of
Aristophanes, are young. Neil[5] in his note here remarks that the
poet's true democracy is always old, and his young men tend to be
oligarchs; but that did not prevent him from asserting that he
consistently attacked new ideas and movements. In the *Clouds*
who is it that cannot stand the conceited, anaemic, cheap lot of
highbrows who study in Socrates' college? Simple-minded old
Strepsiades, who liked the songs of Simonides and Aeschylus, or
his young spendthrift son Pheidippides? The latter, of course. Very
natural, perhaps, since his weakness was horses—very unlikely he
should have any interest in higher mathematics. 'My fellow officers
in the Blues', he says in effect to his father when refusing to enter
the college, 'would find me out, and I should never hear the end of
it.' An excellent reply: but only if Aristophanes was a dramatist, not
if he was a politician whose aim was both to uphold the older
generation and to attack the dangerous new sophistic movement.
In the *Wasps* the chorus enter singing one of the most attractive of all
Aristophanes' songs—the old men helping each other along in the
mud and the dark, regretting the days of their youth—what a time
we had, you and I (do you remember?), on guard duty at Byzantium, when we stole the mortar from that old baker-woman?—but

---

[4] Esp. 562: 'Well, true or false, he had no right to utter treason here.'
[5] *The 'Knights' of Aristophanes*, ed. R. A. Neil (Cambridge, 1901).

still capable of doing their duty today; and then looking for
Philocleon, the most conscientious of them all, the earliest riser,
who would always lead the way, singing some song of Phrynichus:

He's usually first in the line, leading the singing; he's a great one for the old
songs. (269–70)

What more sympathetic picture could you have of the older generation? Aristophanes must surely be going to contrast them with a
younger lot of men, smart, clever, but without grace of manner,
honesty, or character? Not at all: they are the dicasts, the life and
soul of the system which it is the purpose of this play to attack and
overthrow. It is the younger generation which exposes their folly. In
Lysistrata there is no such express contrast between the old and the
young; but the chorus of old men here too refer to a glorious past,
earlier even than Marathon this time: 'the women shall not mock
our ancient city while I live; even Cleomenes, for all his Spartan fire,
had to yield to my spear'. 'It was well', says Rogers[6] in his note here,
'in these dark days of tribulation and despondency that the Athenians should call to their remembrance the successful heroism of
their ancestors.' But what consolation could it bring when these fine
old men are the ardent supporters of the hateful war, who will go on
fighting till Athens and her allies and all Greece are laid waste and
destroyed, the upholders of all that the poet was attacking? Once
more it is not the old men, fire-eaters and dicasts, but the defenders
of a novel idea that are wise and triumph in the end. 'Aristophanes',
says Murray, 'and, as far as we can judge, the other comedians, are
normally defenders of the established custom, and satirize all that is
new or unusual. Hence also the chief character in Aristophanes is
almost always an Old Man, a *gerōn*, who knows and likes the old
ways.'[7] Even though the old fellow is always in the wrong? Is it what
is new and unusual that is satirized in *Acharnians*, *Knights*, *Wasps*,
Peace, *Lysistrata*? Is it not clear that the view is untenable that
Aristophanes was a conservative, an upholder of older things, and
at the same time a propagandist who used the theatre for a practical
end, when his older generation is consistently on the wrong side,

[6] *The 'Lysistrata' of Aristophanes*, ed. B. B. Rogers (London, 1911).
[7] Gilbert Murray, *Aristophanes* (Oxford, 1933), 107.

when it regularly represents the system or the policy to which he was opposed?

Murray, in his recent book, speaking of the *Wasps* and the dicastic system as there portrayed, says:

It is a horrible picture. . . . Yet, the curious thing is that Philocleon and his waspish colleagues are treated with a kind of personal sympathy. It is not war to the knife against them, as it is against Cleon and the Kolakes. The truth is that the juries were largely composed of just the class of men that Aristophanes liked and championed: the old men from the country, prevented by the war from attending to their farms, prevented by their age from going on military expeditions . . . and consequently left in Athens, old, respectable, very poor, embittered and angry, able to serve on juries or sit in the ecclesia, and—according to Aristophanes—offering an easy prey to any smart or unscrupulous speaker who chose to gull them.[8]

But is that the truth or anything like the truth? Are the Wasps disgruntled men, forced into serving on juries for want of anything else to do, embittered at not being on their farms? We must keep in mind what the question is—not 'Is this description true of the actual Athenian jurymen of this time (though we may remember, by the way, that Spartan invasions had ceased since 425, and men were back on their farms)?'—but 'Is it true of Philocleon and the chorus of the *Wasps*, characters in the play?' And the answer is that it is utterly untrue: they are not at all reluctant jurymen—the work is their whole life. They dream about it at night, practise it all day; it is in their bones, it is their very life-blood, so that when Philocleon's vision of his imperial power is shattered, he must still go on *pretending* to serve on juries. But Professor Murray felt that he must reconcile Aristophanes' apparent liking for the men with his practical propaganda against the system, with his general conservatism and liking for country ways.

Consider the question on the supposition that Aristophanes was not a politician but a dramatist, an artist; a man, that is, whose purpose is to give us a picture—in his case a comic picture—not to advocate a policy; and Murray says he 'was after all first and foremost a man of letters': what is there *curious* in his treating his foremost character with a kind of personal sympathy? Nothing. And not only is there nothing curious in it, but Aristophanes could not

[8] Ibid. 82.

have drawn Philocleon without sympathy, if he was to be successful;
no artist could. It is not a question of 'Which side did he favour?',
for as a dramatist he must be sympathetic with all. Impartiality is a
desirable quality for most of us; for an artist is is essential—or rather
a positive sympathy, for impartiality is but a negative quality. Without this sympathy he cannot write. All drama represents a conflict
of some kind; but there will be little success for the writer who can
only take one side. The statement in fact—which is true enough in
answer to the current view—'the older generation in Aristophanes
is always on the wrong side', has really no meaning: there can be no
wrong side in a play. All this is elementary, especially to Murray, and
should not need saying, and would not be said, if it were not so
frequently ignored when Aristophanes is in question. Aeschylus was
a man like the rest of us, and as a man, I suppose, he had little
liking, in real life, for a character such as Clytemnestra's: but we do
not say 'the curious thing is that in the *Oresteia* Clytemnestra is
treated with a certain sympathy'. We are not surprised when
Shakespeare, in the course of making a play out of a cheap melodramatic story of a Jewish money-lender, discovers some understanding for Shylock; we should not think much of his play if he
had not. What we say of all other dramatists is, Are the characters
probable and consistent? Do they convince? Ask the same question
of Aristophanes, and especially concerning Philocleon, his most
successfully drawn character; and the answer is that it is a triumph
of characterization, one of the best comic figures in literature. How
was that possible, if the poet had not understood the character, and
treated it with sympathy? How dull compared with him, how
uneloquent, is the good Bdelycleon, who is supposed to represent
Aristophanes' own views. Contrast the real politician—
Demosthenes: he is not eloquent and sympathetic when presenting
his opponents' policies, and dull when advocating his own.

'Probable and consistent.' By this is meant probable and consistent within the limits of that play. This again is elementary; but the
principle is ignored in the case of Aristophanes, and again by no less
a writer than Murray. In the *Acharnians* the chorus complain of the
ill-treatment of old Thucydides and others of their contemporaries
in the law-courts at the hands of young advocates and the juries.
Murray writes:

Curiously enough it [the sympathy with *old* Thucydides] seems contrary to
the *Wasps*, where the old men are devoted to Cleon and the law-courts

while the other side is represented by young Bdelycleon. In this play too the fierce Acharnians are old men, 'veterans of Marathon, hard as oak'. Perhaps the solution is that while the old men are full of warlike spirit and form severe juries, the dissolute younger generation provide the smooth and tricky orators who badger and entrap the prisoners, especially if they are old and unready, or, of course, if they come from the islands.

But this solution, anyhow difficult, as it is Bdelycleon who represents the younger generation, is not that of his own problem, but of a different one, namely, why, as a matter of historical fact (if it is historical fact), juries consisting largely of older men often condemned men of their own generation attacked by ambitious young demagogues.[9] There cannot be inconsistency, in this sense, between two different *plays*, dramatic productions. The only question we can ask is, Is each play consistent in itself and probable, in the Aristotelian sense? And the answer is obvious: Yes. The only inconsistency between two plays by the same author would be one in general outlook, of the kind that many, for example, have thought to exist between the *Bacchae* and the *Ion* of Euripides; and no one has ever charged Aristophanes with this.

I must be careful not to press this, in the case of Aristophanes; for he is giving portraits not of imaginary, but of real people; and portraits of the same person, by the same artist, we expect not to be inconsistent with each other. If Aristophanes intended to give a full-length portrait of the typical Athenian (in his public activity) in every play, then we should expect consistency between one play and another. But if, as is in fact the case, he shows in any one play only some face of a many-faceted stone, if in some he is only giving us a glimpse, a sketch, not a full portrait, if he is showing us his subject acting at different times and under different conditions, then we must be careful how we find discrepancies. To take an obvious instance: there is no discrepancy between the warlike fervour of the farmers of the *Acharnians* in 425 and the pacific feeling of the farmers in the *Peace* in 421.

It may be asked: Had then Aristophanes no political opinions of his own? And if he had, what were they? To the first the answer is, I imagine, easy: he must have had. In a society like that of Athens, in which public affairs played so large a part, everyone practically, Aeschylus, Sophocles, Socrates, even Timon, will have had political

[9] Cf. *Acharnians* 370–6, which gives a picture just like that in the *Wasps*.

opinions; and not only a general idea—vaguely conservative, vaguely democratic—but positive ones on everyday questions. The *apragmones* of Athens were not isolated from their fellow men. Still more must Aristophanes, who studied public affairs so closely, to whom they formed almost the sole material for his art, have made up his mind about them. But before we come to the second question—What then were his personal opinions?—we must ask ourselves: Assuming that we can find out, of what importance is it to us to know? Is it, for example, essential to the understanding of his plays? To me their interest is almost wholly biographical, with very little relevance to his character as a dramatist. The biographical interest may be a strong one, and it is certainly legitimate. The most austere of Shakespearean scholars, who would pour scorn on attempts to discover the influence of events in Shakespeare's life on his plays, would nevertheless welcome the discovery of more facts about him; but for their own sake, because we cannot help being interested in all that concerned so great a man, hardly at all because they would help us to understand his plays. So do I feel about Aristophanes, as about all Greek writers—with the natural exception of those orators who were also politicians. If we were to find an authentic biography, if we could learn from it how often Aristophanes attended the *ekklēsia* and how he voted there (did he, we wonder, beguiled by Alcibiades, vote for the expedition to Sicily? Did he vote against it?), which of the many ordinary magistracies open to Athenian citizens he held, it would be fascinating. But, except for the light which any addition to our scanty evidence for those times would throw, it would, I am sure, leave his plays and our understanding of them very much as they are. I will, however, discuss the question of his opinions, partly just for the biographical interest, partly because it does throw some light on his method of working—how he brings in his own opinions, and with what success from the point of view of the structure of the play—does the intrusion of the personal view disturb the dramatic picture? To illustrate the point I will take examples from two modern writers. The first has at least a superficial resemblance to Aristophanes, in that he is a writer of comedies and, mainly, of political comedies— plays that deal with public questions: I mean Bernard Shaw. Shaw has himself said that art ought to be didactic—in a vigorous sentence he wrote of connoisseurs who say that 'art should not be didactic, and all the people who have nothing to teach and all who are unable to learn emphatically agree'. Moreover he has been, quite definitely, an active politician—a vigorous member of political societies, a speaker at street corners, a member of a borough council. And he is nothing if not autobiographical: he writes a long preface to every play, in which he tells us his opinions on its main theme. We are in possession in fact of the materials for a very full biography of Shaw in his public capacity—both as politician and as playwright. But take them all away, burn his prefaces and the record of his political activities: would it make much difference to our understanding of his plays? I think not. We should still know the most important thing about him, his general attitude to life; we should know his critical and satiric view of existing institutions— that he was, as artist, neither indifferent to them nor quietly content, that is, that he was neither anarchist nor conservative. We should also be confident that he had been a revolutionary force in his own sphere of art, the theatre.

The other modern whom I will cite in this connection is a writer as different from Aristophanes as could well be—Jane Austen. She is one of the most objective of writers, standing well outside her characters. Yet we feel at times that we can see her own self. In *Emma* the young and dashing Frank Churchill rides to London and back, over thirty miles, just, he says, to get his hair cut. Emma heard of it and 'there was an air of affectation and nonsense about it which she could not approve'. How exact and just a judgement! I feel it is Jane Austen's own; that it comes from some actual experience, which she judged in this way; yet felt there was something priggish in the expression of it. With perfect tact she puts it into the mouth of Emma, who is allowed to be a somewhat priggish and superior person. Take an instance of wider scope. *Persuasion* has in it more warmth of feeling and less wit than her other novels; it has been surmised (I do not know if there is any external evidence) that this is due to the fact that it was written soon after she had had a serious and presumably sad love affair herself; we can perhaps see her in Anne Elliot. Suppose that to be true. It is an interesting biographical detail; it arouses our sentimental interest; it gives us evidence for what after all we know already—that as the foundation for her writing there must be her experience of life as well as her own mother wit. But it does not affect the quality of the novel, nor our appreciation of it.

Turn now to the plays of Aristophanes, consider them in this light, forget for a moment all that we have learnt about the consistent purpose and courage with which he advocated his views. The *Acharnians* was produced early in 425, written therefore in 426—after five and more years of war, marked by the disastrous pestilence, but not by any serious military check for Athens. On the other hand there had been a series of pinpricks in the annual invasions of the country by the Peloponnesians; just in fact what would keep alive an intense and fiery patriotism in the majority, and make for a conviction that an early peace was necessary in a few. That is the atmosphere which Aristophanes depicts. It is a 'probable' picture of Athens at the time. He may or may not have been himself in favour of peace negotiations being then opened by Athens; though we may feel fairly sure that neither the veterans of Marathon nor he simply approved of Dikaiopolis having a jolly time when others were doing their duty. What we can be certain of is that, in this early play, he already shows an original and critical attitude, that he was not therefore to be taken in by the conventional phrases of patriotism (so far was he from always sending a thrill through his audience at the name of Marathon that he mocks its constant use[10]), and that he had immense creative power for comedy— including the ability to observe his countrymen closely. What would it add to his fame to know that he was in favour of peace in 425?

The *Knights*, of the next year, shows in one respect a change worth noting. The young aristocrats appear for the first and only time in Aristophanes in an important if not altogether sympathetic role. (Actually there is less character-drawing altogether in the *Knights* than in any other play, and no character is sympathetically treated.) There is the notable passage in which they declare their loyalty, their readiness to join in battle for their city, and mention a particularly gallant piece of fighting in which they had engaged. 'Only do not grudge us our little affectations and fopperies, when peace comes and troubles end.' They sing an ode both to Poseidon and to Athena—Poseidon, we are told, especially the god of the conservative aristocrats of Athens, the god of horses; but here he is equally the god of the sea, dear to Phormio and the sailors—the democratic sailors—and more necessary to Athens at the moment

[10] *Eq.* 782. One might equally say that he sends a thrill with the democratic and imperialist oracle: *Eq.* 1011–13, *Av.* 978.

than any other god. (The hoplites, the fine yeoman breed, are
curiously out of the picture.) The whole play has a more patriotic
tone; and we should note but not wonder at this—it was written
just after the capture of Pylos and other successes, when Athens
could see victory in sight. No need to ask, has Aristophanes
changed his opinions? Only, is this picture of Athens, or a section
of Athens, in a new light a probable one? The answer is, Yes: and all
we need note is that he could understand such a recovery of
patriotic ardour. Very likely he shared it too; but that is unimportant.[11]

So with the *Peace*, written for 421, after the deaths of Cleon and
Brasidas, when everybody saw the chances of peace and longed for
it, all but a few fire-eaters and armament-manufacturers; and
negotiations were well on the way to success. Aristophanes is not
standing almost alone in a consistent struggle to persuade his
countrymen of the evil of their ways; indeed the scholiast tells us
that many poets about this time were talking of peace.[12] How could
it be otherwise, when the Athens they were depicting was doing the
same? Aristophanes is giving another picture of Athens, somewhat
different from the last because the conditions are changed. The
farmers are especially anxious to be back to their fields for good,
and no longer the bellicose patriots of 426–425. The *Lysistrata*
belongs to 412–411, when Athens was in desperate straits, her
enemies at last confident of complete victory and resolved to crush
her; she determined to fall, if she must fall, fighting. Only the women
can save Greece now, and not the women of Athens only but of all
the big states, especially Sparta. The warlike spirit *everywhere* must
be stopped, and above all, the mutual suspicions, the distrust of each
other's good faith, must be ended. Again a dramatic picture.

[11] I am not saying that there may not be a special, extra-dramatic, point in the
'alliance' between the poet and the Knights. It may be that many of the latter had
actively supported him in his trouble with Cleon after the *Babylonians*. But, if so, it
would be as permissible to argue that their support had been more embarrassing than
helpful, and that Aristophanes intended the *Knights* to be a satire on oligarchic
reformers: these self-styled *kaloi kagathoi, epieikeis, beltistoi* in effect only propose to
get rid of Cleon by putting Athens—including themselves—in the power of a similar
demagogue: demagogy of the right is very like that of the left. (Similarly *Vespae* 1335 ff.
could be taken as a satire on Bdelycleon's improvements.)

But I prefer to believe that though, when he wrote *Acharnians* 300–1, Aristophanes
had in mind a definite *attack* on Cleon, later, when he came to write the *Knights*, his
dramatic genius got the better of him; and that in fact he does not attack, but gives a
picture of contemporary Athenian politics.   [12] *Hypothesis* 1, *ad fin.*

That Aristophanes took many an opportunity to introduce opinions and feelings of his own in jest and earnest is true; as true as it is
of Shaw. He often makes them dramatic, and then we cannot be
sure that they are his; or we may be sure that he shares them with
many others—for example, the satire of the lucky rich who get
comfortable jobs denied to the ordinary man, satire appropriate to
other wars as well as the Peloponnesian; and the brilliant speech on
the meeting of the Boule in the *Knights* is both Aristophanes' own
picture and dramatic. But in some cases we can tell what is his own
view because the particular jest or description is out of place in its
context, or is often repeated. To take two or three instances: his
frequent, often undramatic satire of the dissolute young exquisites of
Athens and the members of the oligarchic clubs, of the seers and
soothsayers trusted by real conservatives like Nicias, and his constant sympathy with the poor soldier and sailor who did all the
fighting for very little pay—especially with the sailors, who
belonged to the democratic city crowd; indeed, except in the
Peace, the hoplite farmers get nothing like so frequent and sympathetic a mention as the sailors.[13] It is clear also from the general
tone of the *Clouds*, and from one or two particular passages in it,[14]
that Aristophanes neither liked nor admired Socrates at that time;
that is, that he lets his own feelings be seen; though I am very far
from thinking that the play was intended as an earnest attack on
the New Learning. I feel it, in fact, to be less a 'clash of humours', to
use Murray's phrase, than any other play except the *Peace* (where
there is hardly any clash): we must confess that in 423 Aristophanes
knew little of Socrates and did not care whether he knew little or
much. After all, he was not perfect. It is the only play, to my mind,
which might give some support to Croiset's view of Attic comedy
providing laughter for country folk at the expense of the wise men of
the town—only we may be sure that the Piraeus crowd laughed
equally; for once Aristophanes seems, at times, simply to be taking
the side of the heavy-handed majority, playing for the easily won
applause. Yet the play did not succeed with that majority: and,

---

[13] As the frequency is relevant, here is a by no means exhaustive list: (1) the
dissolute young oligarchs (the type disliked by the Cleon of the *Knights*, as in
Thucydides): *Ach.* 601 ff.; 716, 843 ff.; *Eq.* 877: *Nu.* 1088 ff.; *V.* 486, 687, 887–90,
1299 ff.; *Ra.* 1513; (2) the sailors: *Ach.* 162–3, 648, 677; *Eq.* 551 ff., 813 ff., 1063–6,
1182–6, 1300 ff., 1366–71; *V.* 909, 1091 ff., 1189; *Lys.* 804: *Ra.* 49–50, 698, 1071 ff., 1465
(cf. 535–7 and 999–1004).   [14] e.g. 362–3.

moreover, Aristophanes thought it especially free from rustic humour, far more intellectual than most, and worthy of success for that reason alone.

It is also clear that he had a real dislike of Cleon, partly perhaps personal, mainly political, and that this appears in all the early plays. But this does not prove that, in general, they are not objective, dramatic, as good plays must be. Compare him in this detail with a man of very different temper, Thucydides. His general objectivity and impartiality is certain; so is his bias against Cleon. But though biased in this, he gives in essentials an accurate picture of Athenian politics of his day. So, in his different way, does Aristophanes; certainly the two fit in very well with each other.

Lastly, there can be no doubt about the seriousness of Aristophanes' desire for internal peace and union expressed in the parabases of the *Lysistrata* and the *Frogs*. The desperate position of Athens by then would have made any one, even Aristophanes, serious; and he is only serious for short passages, especially in the *Frogs*, in which his exhortations are remote from the context of the play and appear therefore perfunctory, in spite of the fine writing, and uninspired.

4

The Political Outlook of Aristophanes

G. E. M. DE STE CROIX

There are three questions I want to ask and answer abut Aristophanes. First, how far can we identify his political outlook, particularly in regard to the war? Secondly, is it worth while trying to do
so? And thirdly, how far (if at all) did he deliberately express political
views in his plays?

I shall begin with the last two questions. The second, whether it is
worth trying to discover Aristophanes' political opinions, is easily
disposed of. It is answered in the negative by many people nowadays: their point of view is well expressed in an influential article by
Gomme, first published in 1938.[1] Having effectively ridiculed various
modern attempts to depict Aristophanes' outlook in entirely unjus-
tifiable terms (Croiset's, for example), Gomme reached a position at
which he could ask himself impatiently, 'Had then Aristophanes no
political opinions of his own? And if he had, what were they? To the
first [question] the answer is, I imagine, easy: he must have had.'
But, 'assuming that we can find out, of what importance is it to us
to know? Is it, for example, essential to the understanding of his
plays?' Gomme concludes not, and he goes on to draw parallels
with Bernard Shaw and Jane Austen. 'Burn Shaw's prefaces and the
record of his political activities: would it make much difference to
our understanding of his plays? I think not.'

It should be obvious that Gomme has not asked all the necessary
questions. What he says may (or may not) be true while we are
thinking of Aristophanes purely as a dramatist, a literary figure in
his own right, on whom alone our attention is concentrated. But
those of us who are Greek historians are obliged to see him *in
addition* in a very different way, *as an important historical source* for
the Athens of the late fifth and early fourth centuries; and when we

[1] See Ch. 3.

approach him in this way we do need to know all we possibly can
about his attitude to the world around him, including his political
opinions, so that we can understand the point of view from which
he saw the world and know how to evaluate his treatment of it, and
what kind of bias and prejudice to allow for. There is no question,
then, but that we must do all we can, *as historians*, to discover
Aristophanes' outlook. I find it astonishing that Gomme and
many others should have failed to appreciate this.

The question whether Aristophanes consciously tried to express
his political opinions in his plays is not so easy to answer to everyone's satisfaction. I myself have not the slightest doubt that he often
did so, and that he used many of his plays, *even while they of course
remained primarily comedies*, as vehicles for the expression of serious
political views—about the Athenian democracy, its institutions, and
its leading figures, and about the Peloponnesian war. Many others
have much the same belief, even if their notion of Aristophanes'
opinions differs markedly from mine. Others again, on the other
hand, believe that Aristophanes wrote his plays as comedies pure
and simple, and that we must beware of attributing to the poet
himself opinions which are either expressed in character by his
dramatis personae, or are simply part of the fooling. I shall return
to this question at the end of this chapter.

At this point I want to make four preliminary observations. First,
it must not be assumed a priori that a comic dramatist of the fifth
century would not use a play or plays as (to put it as crudely as
possible) political propaganda in favour of views which he himself
held. Even a tragic dramatist could do this. Aeschylus went far
beyond what was dramatically necessary, in his *Eumenides*, to stress
the desirability of an eternal military alliance between Athens and
Argos (which could only involve Athens in war with Sparta).[2] And I
do not think anyone would wish to deny that Euripides sometimes
openly expressed in his plays views that may be broadly called
political.[3]

Secondly, I suggest that the best modern parallel for the kind of
mixture of seriousness and foolery that I am suggesting in Aristo-

[2] See G. E. M. de Ste Croix, *The Origins of the Peloponnesian War* (London, 1972),
183–5.
[3] For example, the praise of Athenian democracy, in *Supplices* 352–3 (where it is
instituted by Theseus!), and of Athenian freedom of speech in *Ion* 670–5 (cf. *Heracl.*
181–3); the praise of equality in *Phoenissae* 535–45 (cf. *Supp.* 352–3, 433–8); the

phanes is the political cartoonist. He must always be *funny*: that is
the pre-condition of his genre. But he can be, and very often is,
serious at the same time. The funnier he is, the more likely it will be
that his 'message' will be received and make an impression on the
reader's mind—including the reader who would instantly reject the
message if it were conveyed to him in a purely serious form. It would
be a crude error to insist that a particular passage in a comic
dramatist cannot be conveying a serious idea simply because it is
cast in a humorous form—as a sheer fantasy or absurdity or
impossibility, or a gross exaggeration, or in the guise of a literary
parody: some such comic dress is a necessity of the genre.

Thirdly, given that even intrinsically humorous material may be
making a serious statement (and on the other hand that some
mock-serious passages may in reality be comic),[4] we must keep a
careful watch for passages which express serious opinions and
which *are not funny in themselves*: these are particularly likely to
represent the poet's own views. He may, of course, have found it
desirable to keep them fairly brief and to sandwich them, so to
speak, between lines which are purely comic; but if the bread in
which the meat is delivered is clearly separable from it (as in the
excellent string of examples in *Lysistrata* 1114–77, noticed below),
we may have no difficulty in recognizing the meat for what it is.

And fourthly, even the *kind of joke* Aristophanes makes, the *things
he makes jokes about*, can sometimes give an indication of the out-

insistence on the saving political role of men of moderate possessions, in *Supplices*
238–45; the denial that wealth is a criterion of worth, in *Electra* 367–76, 938–44 (cf. 37–
8, with 67–70 and 247–62; also *Or.* 920); and the hatred of Sparta in *Andromache* 445–
53, 595–601, 724–6; *Supplices* 187, etc. Of the two main Athenian versions of the myth
about Athens' intervention, on the appeal of Adrastus, to recover the corpses of the
Argives who had fallen in the assault of Thebes, Euripides (*Supp.*, esp. 571 ff., 634 ff.)
chose the one in which it was accomplished by force, as against the version in
Aeschylus' *Eleusinians*, in which only persuasion was used (see Plu. *Thes.* 29. 4–5;
cf. Paus. 1. 39. 2; and Isoc. 4. 58 and 14. 53, against 12. 168–71, 172–4). In view of
Herodotus 9. 27. 3, Euripides evidently did not invent his version (see *FGrH* 3b supp.)
1. 445–8, on Philoch. F112–12), but of course it would have had much greater force
after the events at Delium, described by Thucydides 4. 97–9. (I would date the
Supplices 422 or 421. G. Zuntz, *The Political Plays of Euripides* (Manchester, 1955),
88–94, is for 424, but for inadequate reasons: he fails even to mention Th. 4. 97–9,
and he seems unaware of the significance of Th. 5. 14. 4, 22.2, 28.2, 40.3 in relation to
Supp. 1189–95.)

[4] See the acute exegesis of *Knights* 230–3 by K. J. Dover, 'Portrait-Masks in
Aristophanes', in *Komoidotragemata: Studia Aristophanea Viri Aristophanei W. J. W.
Koster in Honorem* (Amsterdam, 1968).

look he must have had, to find these particular things funny. A good example is the jury courts and dicastic pay, dealt with below.

Before taking up individual points in detail, I will give a bare summary of Aristophanes' position, as I see it. There is no indication at all that he was an oligarch, in the literal sense of wanting to restrict the franchise and (like his contemporary Pseudo-Xenophon, *Ath. Pol.* 1. 9) reduce the lower classes to complete political subjection, *douleia*. Indeed, he can sometimes show a real sympathy for the lower orders.[5] But he had an essentially *paternalist* attitude toward them: he clearly resented the political *power* the *dēmos* was beginning to exercise, more particularly in the law-courts, as a result of dicastic pay, his frequent sneers at which betray the irritation felt by the upper-class Athenian at this innovation of the radical democracy. For him, the lower classes were most admirable when they were wearing out their rumps at the oar-bench and crying 'Rhyppapai' (*Frogs* 1072–3; cf. *Wasps* 909); and one should be particularly careful not to cheat them out of their pay for *that*, which was well earned (*Knights* 1366–7; cf. 1065–6; *Ach.* 162–3). But it was intolerable when ignorant and ill-educated men demanded a share in the delicate art of government, and presumed to take the conduct of state affairs into their own hands (cf. Th. 2. 65. 10). Aristophanes also sneers repeatedly at the men not belonging to the old leading families who in the late fifth century began to exercise political leadership, mainly perhaps with the support of the humbler Athenians; and he represents these new leaders (especially in *Knights* 128–43) as jumped-up salesmen: *-pōlai* ('-sellers') of various kinds. Although doubtless a patriotic Athenian, who would fight for his city without question when he had to, he was very much against the war: he thought it should never have been allowed to break out in the first place, and that any chance of bringing it to an end and making peace with Sparta should be eagerly embraced; the admirable situation which had existed before the coming to power of the radical democrats could then be restored, and Athens and Sparta could dominate the Greek world jointly. In this respect, as well as in his general political position, Aristophanes can be described as a 'Cimonian'. There is some evidence to suggest that he may have moved in quite high social circles.[6]

[5] See Gomme, Ch. 3, above, citing a number of passages from the plays, including of course *Ach.* 162–3.

[6] See Sterling Dow, 'Some Athenians in Aristophanes', *AJA* 73 (1969), 234–5, on *IG* II² 2343, a list of Thiasotai of the early 4th cent.

Aristophanes has been the victim of many absurd misconceptions, some of which have been easily demolished by Gomme. But the fact that he has often been misrepresented is not to be taken as evidence that he had no identifiable opinions, or none worth discovering. I hope to have made a fresh start.

A writer's attitude will often emerge clearly from the way he uses political and social terminology, and Aristophanes is no exception here. The most instructive passage is the parabasis of the *Frogs* (674–737), the seriousness of which is not, I think, denied by anyone. The whole passage 686ff. is characterized by a real earnestness, underlined by the opening statement of the chorus, calling itself *hieros* ('sacred' or 'holy') and announcing that it has a duty to give good advice and teaching to the city (686–7). That is not one of the mock-serious statements Aristophanes sometimes makes, which would be immediately recognized as comic, and I know of no one who has tried to maintain that Aristophanes was writing it with his tongue in his cheek. At 706–16 there is a brief burst of invective against Cleigenes, but in 717–37 we move back on to the more exalted plane of 686ff., with one of Aristophanes' most brilliant imaginative pieces: a comparison between the city's politicians and its coins. Here, couched in a vocabulary that would have been perfectly acceptable to Pseudo-Xenophon (whom anglophones usually call 'the Old Oligarch'), we have a plea for political leadership, not by the foreigners and base-born who are now dominant, but by 'the nobly born, the discreet, the civilized'—the *kaloi kagathoi* indeed (728, cf. 719), 'nurtured in the wrestling-schools, in dances, in the arts'. This reinforces the wish expressed earlier, in 686–705 (another passage that shows scarcely any attempt at humour), that those who had suffered some form of disqualification as a result of taking part in the oligarchic revolution of 411 (and who are described euphemistically as having 'sustained a fall in Phrynichus' wrestlings') should be 'forgiven for their one mishap'. Those who had been prominent enough in the revolution to be thought worth disfranchising would have been mainly if not entirely men of leading families, the *dynatōtatoi* (those with the most power of influence) of Thucydides 8. 47. 2 and 48. 1. Later in the play, in the exchange between Aeschylus and Dionysus in lines 1454–7, Athens is again said to hate the *chrēstoi* (the 'good', with the implication, 'of good birth') and use, if perforce, the *ponēroi* (the 'worthless', also with social-political significance: 'the baser sort'). Now these passages are by no means exceptional in Aristophanes: he very often speaks in the same way. I do not intend to multiply examples of the obvious, but it is worth emphasizing that nearly twenty years earlier Aristophanes was using exactly the same language. In *Knights* 181, 185–93, 222–9, 334–7, and 738–40 we find many of the same concepts used in the same way.[7]

It has recently been asserted by a leading authority on Aristophanes, K. J. Dover (whose commentary on the *Clouds* is by far the best we have on any Aristophanic play), that 'the essential spirit of Old Comedy is the ordinary man's protest—using his inalienable weapons, humour and fantasy—against all who are in some way stronger or better than he: gods, politicians, generals, artists, and intellectuals';[8] and that the treatment of Aristophanes himself of politicians (apart from Cleon, who had attacked him for his play the *Babylonians*, and against whom Aristophanes was expressing personal venom) 'does not differ significantly from the way in which "we" satirize "them" nowadays. No class, age-group, or profession is exempted from Aristophanes' satire.'[9] Although there is a certain element of truth in this, as a generalization it does not fit the facts. Certainly Aristophanes pictures the 'demagogues'[10] as rogues who have entirely selfish motives and make handsome profits for them-

[7] The *kalos kagathos* is idealized (*Knights* 185, 227, 738), and the successful politician is presented as *poneros* (181, 186, 336, 337, cf. 415), base-born (218, *gegonas kakōs*), *amathēs* and *bdelyros* (193), unacquainted with *mousikē* (188–9, 191–2) and not *chrēstos tous tropous* (192), for *to sōphronōs traphēnai* is worth nothing in Athenian politics (334). The *chrēstoi–ponēroi* contrast of *Frogs* 1454–7 appears also in *Knights* 1274–5, and the *ponēroi–kaloi kagathoi* contrast of *Frogs* 718–33 in *Knights* 185–6. When Aristophanes speaks of the *kaloi kagathoi* (*Knights* 185, 227, 738; *Clouds* 101, 797; *Wasps* 1256; *Lys.* 1059; *Frogs* 719, 728; and even *Knights* 735, although spoken by the Sausage-Seller), the words almost always have a strongly social complexion.
[8] *OCD*² 270a.   [9] *OCD*² 113b.
[10] I feel impelled to put the word 'demagogue' in inverted commas when I use it of the late 5th- and 4th-cent. Athenian politicians, lest anyone should think that I am attributing to them the unpleasant characteristics usually connoted by that term. Some of these politicians (Hyperbolus, perhaps; cf. Th. 8. 73. 3) may have been demagogues in the bad sense, men who gained their ends by unworthy and flattering appeals to the baser feelings of the people (cf. Th. 2. 65. 10). But the *demagogos* in the basic sense of the word, 'leader of the people', the man who gives leadership above all through *speeches*, is an inevitable feature of any system of democracy which, like the Greek variety, works mainly through direct rather than representative government. Cf. M. I. Finley, 'Athenian Demagogues', in *Past and Present*, 21 (1962), 3–24. And in any form of democracy, the greater the crisis, the greater the need for the 'good demagogue'. One remembers that in recent times it has been during the two world wars above all that Britain has had recourse to 'demagogues', men who were outstanding orators: Lloyd George and Winston Churchill.

selves out of their political activities, at the expense of the ordinary
citizen: the best example is *Wasps* 656–79; cf. *Knights* 128ff., 824–35,
etc. But except for this, what specific features does Aristophanes'
picture of the demagogues and their activities share with attacks on
modern politicians? One may remember some of the gibes at the low
birth and poor education of some working-class politicians of the
Edwardian period and even the 1920s and 1930s (they have hardly
survived the Second World War); but when these sneers were
fashionable, what they represented was the outlook of an upper
class used to governing and irritated at having to admit some of
its 'inferiors' to a position in which they might be able to exercise
some political influence, even power—very much the attitude I am
attributing to Aristophanes. I see little reflection of the true contemporary 'we–them' situation in Aristophanes' plays. The essence
of his presentation of the demagogues in the *Knights* is that the
more crude and uncultured and cunning they are, the more
ardently the *dēmos* will take them to its heart: the 'Sausage-
Seller', who usurps the place of the Paphlagonian slave who is
Cleon has these characteristics in the very highest degree—until
the very end, when he is suddenly and mysteriously transformed
(lines 1316ff.). What modern politician in our generation has been
caricatured in anything like this way?

It is instructive to discover, by way of contrast, who it is that
emerges with credit from the plays of Aristophanes. When Dover, in
the passage quoted above, says that Aristophanes' treatment of
politicians other than Cleon 'does not differ significantly from the
way in which "we" satirize "them" nowadays. No class . . . is
exempted from Aristophanes' satire,' he significantly omits one
category of 'them' which we might reasonably have expected
Aristophanes to include among his targets: the very rich—surely
the most obvious target of all, for a satirist with a real 'we/them'
attitude? In fact, Aristophanes scarcely says a disrespectful word
about the rich as such, although of course he attacks the demagogues (see above) for allegedly making fortunes out of their political
activities.[11] The various terms for 'wealth' and 'wealthy' are not

[11] The accusation seems to have been conspicuously untrue of the man who was
perhaps the most prominent of all the 'demagogues' after Cleon, namely Cleophon
(see *Lys.* 19. 48–9). It is a fact seldom sufficiently realized nowadays that Athenian
politicians in general expected, and were expected, to make money out of politics:

particularly frequent in Aristophanes outside the *Plutus*; but it is very interesting to find that even the words *pachys, hoi pacheis* are used of rich men by Aristophanes only in passages in which he is sympathizing with them: *Knights* 1137–40, *Wasps* 288–9, *Peace* 639–40. In the *Plutus* the nature of the plot is such that occasional unflattering references to the rich are bound to occur, but even here they are few (see 107–9, 502–3, and of course 30–1, and especially 567–70, referring to the orators; cf. *Peace* 644–6 etc.). And in the other plays, as far as I can discover, the rich are never once attacked as such, and on no less than five occasions they are sympathetically treated: *Knights* 223–4, 264–5; *Wasps* 626–7; *Peace* 639–40; *Ecclesiazusae* 197–8. I can find nothing at all in the surviving plays to compare with Euripides' *Supplices* 238–9, or the attacks on the *plousioi* (the rich) in Demosthenes 21.

It is consistent with this attitude that Aristophanes should treat with great respect and sympathy one group forming a distinct social category of the richest Athenians, the Knights (*hippeis*), who receive a grateful compliment in the opening scene of the *Acharnians* (5–8) and another friendly reference later (300–1), and of course form the chorus of Aristophanes' next play. (I am not sure what the best contemporary parallel to these Knights would be—perhaps not so much a chorus of peers or millionaires as of Rolls-Royce owners?) The very favourable treatment the Knights receive from Aristophanes does not at all correspond with Dover's 'we–them' antithesis. And I might remark that although I know of nothing to suggest that the Athenian *hippeis* had an anti-democratic complexion in the 420s, they certainly did at the end of the war.[12]

In the *Knights* we first hear of the *hippeis* as *agathoi chilioi* (a thousand good men, 225), who, according to Demos, will work against Cleon, with the *kaloi kagathoi* and whoever is clever (*dexios*) among the spectators (cf. for *dexios* Ps.-Xen., *Ath. Pol.* 1. 6. 9). From the moment of their entry, at line 347, the Knights are presented in an admirable light: they rebuke Cleon, who is unable to cajole them, and in the parabasis (507–46), after some conven-

---

Hyp. 5 (*Dem.*), cols. 24–5 is particularly illuminating on this point. Taking money for most political activities was perfectly permissible: it was only if his leadership had *bad* results for Athens that the politician might be made to suffer—*then* he could be prosecuted, e.g. for 'speaking not in the best interests of the Athenian people, *chrēmata lambanōn* (making a profit for himself)' (see esp. Hyp. 4 (*Eux.*) 8, 29, etc.).

[12] See X. *HG* 2. 4. 2, 4, 7, 8, 24, 31, 3. 1. 4; Lys. 16. 6; and cf. Th. 8. 92. 6 *fin.* (411).

tional praise of the poet himself (whose outlook they identify with
theirs, 509–10), they speak in a noble and dignified fashion of their
ambition to fight for the city and its gods—without pay, of course:
they will be satisfied if no one begrudges them their long hair and
their luxurious baths (576–80). There are a few comic touches, but
they are all friendly. And in lines 595–610 they are made to speak
with unalloyed pride of a recent military exploit of theirs, described
by Thucydides 4. 42–5. Their other contributions are all creditable to
them. Gomme speaks of the Knights ('the young aristocrats', he
calls them) as appearing in this play in 'an important *if not
altogether sympathetic* role'; and he thinks it would be 'permissible
to argue . . . that Aristophanes intended the *Knights* to be a satire
on oligarchic reformers',[13] because the chorus 'in effect only propose to get rid of Cleon by putting Athens—including themselves—
in the power of a similar demagogue; demagogy of the right is very
like that of the left'. But this ignores the fact that although the
Knights support the Sausage-Seller against Cleon in their competition for the favours of old Demos, there is ultimately a complete
transformation: Demos reveals that he can see through the flattery
of the demagogues after all (1111–50), and at the very end of the
play, taught by the Sausage-Seller (who has now shed his demagogy
and all his unpleasant characteristics, 1316ff.), he appears reformed
and rejuvenated (1216–34), and ready to return to the great days of
Miltiades and Aristeides and perform deeds worthy (as the Chorus
put it, 1334), 'of the trophy at Marathon'. In the concluding lines,
after some interesting talk about the peace which we shall notice
below, Cleon takes over the Sausage-Seller's trade, and all is well.
The Knights had backed the right man indeed!

I have been speaking about Aristophanes' attitude to a particular
social group, the Knights. Most of the individuals referred to in the
plays are of course ridiculed in one way or another, but some of the
exceptions are significant. Cimon is mentioned only once, with
honour (*Lys.* 1144; cf. the single mention of Cimon in the preserved
fragments of Cratinus: fr. 1 *ap.* Plut., *Cim.* 10. 4). Another character
who receives sympathetic treatment (cf. *Ach.* 703–12; cf. *Wasps* 946–
8) is Thucydides, son of Melesias, who must have returned from
ostracism in the spring of 433. I think we may possibly be exaggerating if we speak of Thucydides the son of Melesias as an '*oligarchic*

---

[13] Gomme, Ch. 3 above.

leader'. There was an oligarchic group at Athens in the early 450s (see Th. 1. 107. 4, and the passages in which Aeschylus expresses fear of civil war: *Eu.* 858–66, 976–87); but I feel that Thucydides' followers may have been mainly the more conservative Athenian democrats who had earlier taken Cimon as their leader, rather than actual would-be 'oligarchs'. However this may be, we may find some significance in Aristophanes' respectful tribute to this Thucydides, a conspicuous example of the men he so greatly admired, who were 'nurtured in the wrestling-schools, in dances, in the arts' (*Frogs* 729: for Thucydides as a wrestler, see *Ach.* 703–12).

And if it is true, as to some extent it is, that it is the principal men of the time who are the most natural butts of Comedy and we must accordingly expect the comic poets to attack the most prominent politicians, then it is all the more remarkable how gently Aristophanes treats two men who were certainly among the most conspicuous political figures of their day: Alcibiades and Nicias, each of whom, in his way, might appear a rather obvious target for comic treatment. Aristophanes makes surprisingly few references to the aristocratic Alcibiades, who was certainly prominent by 427 (Ar., fr. 198). Apart from a passing reference in fragment 554 and perhaps another in fragment 907, the only disparaging ones are *Acharnians* 716 (*en passant*, again) and the justified criticism by Euripides in *Frogs* 1427–9, which is followed at once by Aeschylus' plea that Athens should put up with her inconvenient 'lion'—now of course in his second (and final) exile. Nicias escapes Aristophanes' lash altogether, apart from the comic word *mellonikian* in *Birds* 640 and perhaps the mysterious fragment 100 (*ap.* Plu., *Nic.* 8. 4: Plutarch may have misunderstood this). *Knights* 358 is if anything sympathetic. Even if Nicias is the second slave in *Knights* 6ff., he is not blackguarded there; and in fact it seems very doubtful whether Nicias is intended.[14] The other comic poets also dealt very gently with Nicias. Remembered in the fourth century as a *kalos kagathos* (Arist., *Ath.* 28. 5), Nicias had no famous ancestors, and the family may well have been recently enriched by mining activities and slave-owning.[15] But Nicias was an 'establishment figure' of unimpeach-

[14] See Dover, 'Portrait-Masks' in *Aristophanes*, 24–6, and 'Aristophanes, *Knights* 11–20', *CR* 73 = NS 9 (1959), 196–9.

[15] See J. K. Davies, *Athenian Propertied Families 600–300 BC* (Oxford, 1971), 403–4.

able orthodoxy, and he was not very aggressive towards Sparta: that must be why Aristophanes lets him off so very lightly.

Another way in which Aristophanes reveals his political opinions is in his attitude to the jury-courts, in which, during the last generation only, many poor Athenians had become able to serve, owing to the institution of dicastic pay by Pericles. Aristophanes evidently disliked this situation, and he makes a number of references to the *triōbolon* and to dicastic pay generally[16]—which in itself was not in the least funny, except of course to a member of the upper classes, who disapproved of it to the extent of thinking it a fit subject for satire. Aristophanes even makes the very telling point that the dicasts, alone of the Athenian office-holders (*archai*), were *anhypeuthynoi*, not subject to account (*Wasps* 587–8)—a well-known characteristic of the tyrant. He makes Philocleon tell the dicasts that their *archē* is as great as that of Zeus (620–1) and Bdelycleon speak of the paid popular courts, dependent as they were (in his picture) upon the demagogues, as 'an inveterate, old disease engrained in the heart of the State' (651, Rogers's translation; cf. *Ach.* 370–6 and many other passages). Very little of this is at all funny, except to someone who sees the whole system as a form of popular tyranny,[17] and is out to discredit it by ridicule.[18]

Aristophanes hated the war, not simply because it was war and peace was better, but because this particular war made impossible

[16] *Knights* 50–1, 255–7, 797–8 (cf. 1089), 800, 805–8, 1358–60; *Clouds* 863; *Wasps* 300–11, 525, 605–9, 661–3, 682–4, 689–90, 700–5, 785, 813, 1113, 1117–21; *Birds* 1541, 1694–9; *Frogs* 1466. (The three obols of *Ec.* 292, 308, 380, 392, and *Pl.* 329, cf. 125, are Assembly pay, introduced after 404/3.)

[17] It has been customary (see e.g. B. B. Rogers's edn. of the *Wasps*, pp. xvi–xix, and D. M. MacDowell's, 1–4) to pretend that Aristophanes was not criticizing the legal system but only the way in which the courts worked in practice, giving (it is said) too great power to the demagogues. But again (cf. n. 10 above), the demagogues were, so to speak, a built-in feature of Athenian democratic process, and the line of argument I have just described derives from an uncritical acceptance of the Aristophanic caricature, a very clever attack upon the system which enabled many humble men, gulled (as Aristophanes would have us believe) by the demagogues to sit in judgement on their 'betters'.

[18] Among the passages in his 5th-cent. plays in which Aristophanes makes fun of the courts or otherwise denigrates them (in addition to some of those cited in n. 16 above) are *Ach.* 375–6, 676–718; *Knights* 259–65, 307–11, 897–8, 1145–50; *Clouds* 207–8, 620, 1004; *Wasps passim*, e.g. 88 ff., 156–60, 223–7, 240–1, 287–9, 320–2, 400–14, 417–27, 513–726 (esp. 548–51, 577, 587–8, 590–1, 620–1, 626–8, 650–1, 656–72, 682–4), 799–804, 836–1002 (esp. 920–1, 941–3, 976–81, 991–2, 997–1002), 1037–42, 1094–8, 1339–41, 1450–73; *Peace* 505, 639–41; *Birds* 40–1, 109–10, 145–7, 1032, 1046, 1052–3, 1422–69,

the situation he wanted: the joint hegemony of Athens and Sparta over the Greeks, that joint hegemony which Cimon had done his utmost to preserve and a return to which remained the dream of Athenians who felt that Athens and Sparta had no necessary quarrel, right into the fourth century (see especially Isoc. 4, *Paneg.*). Three of Aristophanes' plays (*Acharnians, Peace,* and *Lysistrata*) are mainly concerned with the war against Sparta, and there are other significant references to it. Although there is of course a good deal of sheer fooling in all the three plays just mentioned, each in its very different way shows Aristophanes' disapproval of the war, and the first two (*Acharnians* and *Peace*) make it very clear that in his opinion war should never have been allowed to break out at all.

We begin with the *Acharnians*, and first of all with its principal figure, a 'comic hero' of the special type, who—like many of Aristophanes' characters—has a very interesting name, Dikaiopolis (the full significance of which will emerge presently), and who, alone of Aristophanes' characters of whom we know anything, is *carefully and explicitly identified by the poet with himself*, not merely once but in two separate passages: lines 377–82 and 497–503. 'I myself', says Dikaiopolis, 'know what I suffered from Cleon over last year's comedy' (377–8)—a clear allusion to Cleon's attack on Aristophanes over the *Babylonians* of 426.[19] A little later Dikaiopolis, dressed in beggar's rags, is about to make his principal speech (497ff.), largely a parody of one by Telephus in Euripides' play of that name (produced in 438), which Aristophanes was particularly fond of quoting. 'Don't bear me a grudge, spectators,' he begins, 'if I, as a beggar, am about to speak among Athenians about the City, in a comedy, for truth is no stranger to Comedy. And I am going to say what is both shocking and true' (497–501). It is at this point that the identification of Dikaiopolis with the poet is made all over again, to make quite sure the audience understands it: again Dikaiopolis

1694–1705. In *Knights* 1317 the regenerated Sausage-Seller urges the closing of the courts for the day, which is to be a day of festival. Of course Aristophanes is particularly hostile to those who brought prosecutions ('sycophants') (see e.g. *Ach.* 515–22, 559, 679–718, 725, 818–35, 839–41, 904–58; *Knights* 435–7 ff.; *Wasps* 1094–6; *Peace* 190–1, 653; *Birds* 285, 1410–69; *Ec.* 452–3, 560–2; *Pl.* 30–1, 850–950, esp. 877–9, 905–20). It was naturally the propertied class, to which Aristophanes himself belonged and with which he sympathized, which had most to fear from 'sycophants'.

[19] The nature of this play has so often been misinterpreted that it is a relief to be able to refer to one discussion of it that is sound, sensible, and properly cautious: that of G. Norwood, 'The Babylonians of Aristophanes', *CP* 25 (1930), 1–10.

refers to Cleon's slandering *him* for speaking evil of the city in the presence of strangers (at the Dionysia of 426), and congratulates himself that he is in no danger this time, for it is the Lenaea and the strangers have not yet arrived (502–5).

It is extraordinary how the commentators have failed to grasp the obvious point of these two passages: that Aristophanes is identifying himself with Dikaiopolis, making it quite clear that Dikaiopolis is speaking for him. (Contrast such passages as 659–64, where it is the Chorus which speaks for the poet against Cleon.) Now we know that Aristophanes produced both the *Babylonians* and the *Acharnians* (as well as the *Banqueters* of 427 and the *Birds* of 414) 'through Callistratus', who was the official *didaskalos*, although everyone will have known that the author of the plays was Aristophanes;[20] and some scholars[21] have supposed, on no evidence at all, that the part of Dikaiopolis was *acted* by Callistratus and that lines 377–82 and 497–503 were spoken *in propria persona* by Callistratus, who (and not Aristophanes) had been the subject of Cleon's prosecution after the *Babylonians*. Even Rennie, who rightly rejected this as a 'desperate theory', thought the lines were 'clearly concessions to the timidity of Callistratus'—as producer, presumably: I cannot imagine why. Others, including Starkie and Cyril Bailey,[22] have produced an equally 'desperate' theory: that Aristophanes himself played the part of Dikaiopolis. Certainly the two passages, 377–82 and 497–503, are unique in Attic Comedy,[23] in so far as a character identifies himself with the author of the play. But there is no need to resort to far-fetched theories in order to explain this. There is no hint in any ancient source, even late scholia, that Aristophanes acted the part of Dikaiopolis, nor is there any reliable evidence that he was ever an actor at all. It is true that the *Vita Aristophanis* 3,[24] the Second

[20] See e.g. W. J. M. Starkie, *The 'Acharnians' of Aristophanes* (London, 1909), 247–8; Cyril Bailey, 'Who Played "Dicaeopolis"?', in *Greek Poetry and Life: Essays Presented to Gilbert Murray on his Seventieth Birthday* (Oxford, 1936), 232; K. J. Dover, *Aristophanes' 'Clouds'* (Oxford, 1968), p. xvii and no. 2.

[21] See W. Rennie, *The 'Acharnians' of Aristophanes* (London, 1909), 144; and the edn. by J. van Leeuwen (Leiden, 1901), 67 n.

[22] Starkie, *The 'Acharnians' of Aristophanes*, 84 n.; Bailey, 'Who Played "Dicaeopolis"?' Contrast Wilhelm Schmid, *Geschichte der griechischen Literatur*, part 1, vol. iv (Munich, 1946), 224 n. 3.

[23] Pl. Com., fr. 107, has been cited as a possible parallel, but I find no reason to see a reference to the author of the play. See Bailey, 'Who Played "Dicaeopolis"?', 234–5.

[24] See e.g. the Teubner text of Aristophanes, ed. T. Bergk (Leipzig, 1987), vol. i, pp. xliv ff.; W. Dindorf's edn. of Aristophanes, vol. iv, part 1 (Oxford, 1838), 33 ff.; B. B. Rogers's edn. of *Ach.*, pp. lvii ff.; etc.

Hypothesis to the *Knights*, and the scholium to *Knights* 230 speak of Aristophanes himself as acting the part of Paphlagon in the *Knights*, because neither mask (cf. *Knights* 230–2) nor actor could be procured for the part; but the story has rightly been dismissed as a fiction by most scholars other than Bailey.

Yet another explanation of the two passages we are considering has been offered by Dover: that Dikaiopolis is speaking as 'the comic hero' or 'the comic protagonist', who 'has the right to speak for Comedy. Aristophanes treats Dikaiopolis as if [he] were an annual visitor to Athens who got into trouble on the last occasion on which he attempted to *dikaia legein*.'[25] This seems to me very implausible. I know of nothing to suggest that an Athenian audience was ever likely to recognize 'the comic protagonist' as a kind of personification of Comedy itself, with an existence outside the particular play in question; and in any event, on Dover's own showing, Dikaiopolis is the *first* known hero of the required type—which could not *yet*, therefore, exist as such! And the object of Cleon's attack in the previous year had been not Comedy but *Aristophanes personally* (and conceivably Callistratus also). Dover's note is specifically on 'lines 377–8 and 501–2'; but even if we limit ourselves to these particular lines we find the first passage opening with the very personal *autos t'emauton*, and when we read on we find Dikaiopolis saying in lines 379–82 that Cleon had slandered *him* to the Council and abused *him*. I cannot see how Aristophanes' audience could possibly have taken these words to refer to anything but Cleon's attack on *Aristophanes personally*. An identification of Dikaiopolis with the poet necessarily follows.

To understand the situation in the play in which the main speech of Dikaiopolis (497ff.) is made, we have to go back to the opening scene: this is vital to the understanding of the basic plot, in which Dikaiopolis makes his own private peace with Sparta, and it also sets up the character of Dikaiopolis, whose curious name it explains. Now there are many characters in Aristophanes who have names expressive of their nature or function: not merely Demos, Eirene and Polemos, Penia and Ploutos, but Bdelycleon and Philocleon, Lysistrata, Praxagora, Peisthetaerus, Agoracritus, Trygaeus, Pseudartabas, and others—all have names appropriate to the roles they

[25] K. J. Dover, 'Notes on Aristophanes' *Acharnians*', *Maia*, 15 (1963), 15. The reference (to 'speaking the truth') is to *Ach.* 501.

perform: Lysistrata is a 'dissolver of armies', Praxagora is active in the Agora, Peisthetaerus is highly persuasive, on so on. None of these names is in any way deceptive; all are to be taken at their face value. Similarly, Dikaiopolis must be the 'Just City'. The commentators have been unable to understand this. As a rule the name has wrongly been taken to mean something like 'the Just *Citizen*' (e.g. Gilbert Murray.[26] After noting this, Bailey tried to find a covert allusion to Aegina, which Pindar (*Pythian* 8. 22) once calls *ha dikaiopolis*.[27] Bailey calls this 'the famous Pindaric epithet'; but we have no reason to think it became 'famous', and anyway Athens was the last place where a compliment to Aegina would be remembered and repeated! The nature of the connection between Aristophanes and Aegina, which is the subject of an obscure passage in the *Acharnians* (652–4),[28] is unknown to us. To find the name Dikaiopolis an allusion to 'Aristophanes the Aeginetan', as Bailey does, is to construct another of those 'desperate theories' which have so bedevilled the interpretation of Aristophanes' plays. I cannot myself see the least difficulty in Dikaiopolis' name. In the opening scene Dikaiopolis wants his *City* to negotiate for peace with Sparta and, when no one will listen to him, *does what the City ought to have done*, and successfully negotiates for a peace himself—of course it has now to be a private peace, in which he and his family alone share.

The plot, like those of some other plays of Aristophanes, is an impossible fantasy, something that by its very nature could never actually happen in the manner depicted in the play; but it is worked out, as so often, with a certain logical rigour, within its frame of reference. From the very beginning the personality of Dikaiopolis is sharply delineated: no character in Aristophanes is more carefully built up. There is of course no standard 'comic hero' in Aristophanes.[29] At one extreme, the principal character or characters may be mere buffoons, like most of those in *Knights*, *Clouds*, and *Wasps*; but at the other extreme one character can stand out as a real 'hero' and dominate the action of the play: Lysistrata, Prax-

---

[26] *Aristophanes* (Oxford, 1933).

[27] Bailey, 'Who Played "Dicaeopolis"?', 236–8.

[28] See e.g. Starkie, *The 'Acharnians' of Aristophanes*, 138–9; Dover, *Aristophanes' 'Clouds'* p. xix.

[29] Others may find, though I cannot, some help from C. H. Whitman, *Aristophanes and the Comic Hero*, Martin Classical Lectures, 19 (Cambridge, Mass., 1964).

agora—and Dikaiopolis. One of the main functions of the introductory scene in the *Acharnians* (1–173), which occupies nearly an eighth of the play, is to establish Dikaiopolis as the one really sagacious man in Athens, who is shrewd enough to see through all deceptions, even when all those around him are being taken in: see especially lines 71–2, 79, 86–7, 105–7, 109 ff., 125–7, 135, 161–3. The consistency of the portrait is remarkable. Dikaiopolis can be comic, but he is never at any moment disreputable or dishonest (as comic heroes so often are) or silly—very much the reverse. In case anyone is tempted not to take him seriously, inside the first eight lines he proclaims himself anti-Cleon and pro-Knights; he is able, unlike the ambassadors and the Council, to see through both Pseudartabas (91–125) and Theorus (134–71). In his opening speech (26 ff., especially 26–7, 32, 37–9) he makes it clear both that he himself wants peace, to the extent of being prepared to shout down any orator who talks about anything else, and that the Athenians in general are not at all concerned to obtain peace. At line 46 Amphitheus enters as the negotiator appointed by the gods to arrange peace; but he is refused his journey-money and thrown out (51–5). Dikaiopolis protests, and refuses to be quiet unless peace is discussed (56–60). It is only when Dikaiopolis finds that the Assembly has no intention of discussing peace that he sends Amphitheus to Sparta to arrange a private peace on his own behalf (129–32, 175–9, 186–202). By the time we reach the central scene of the play (204–718) we know we are going to be on the side of this remarkable man. And then, to clinch the matter, comes the identification of Dikaiopolis with Aristophanes, made twice over, as we have seen.

I need not describe at length the speech which Dikaiopolis, as a Pseudo-Telephus, makes to the bellicose Acharnians (509–56). I have analysed it sufficiently in my *Origins of the Peloponnesian War*,[30] after stating[31] some important principles which I believe should be applied when we are using the evidence of comedy (and that of Aristophanes in particular) to draw historical conclusions. The speech of Dikaiopolis has a real logic of its own. The audience has been led to expect something that is *both comic and exceptionally serious*, and that is exactly what we find. As a parody of

[30] pp. 239–44, with 383–6.
[31] pp. 232–7.

the speech of Telephus it is intrinsically funny, and parts of it are also funny in themselves; but *one* serious point is also made: the blame for the war must not be laid *only* at Sparta's door (514, picking up 309–14 and 496–501; cf. 355–6, 369, 482); the war started above all because Pericles 'over-reacted' to a minor provocation with the exaggerated Megarian decree (524–34), and when Athens refused to repeal it, war was inevitable (535–55). This was the one way in which a case, of a sort, could be made against Athens and for Sparta;[32] and I cannot resist pointing out that it nicely represents the consensus of modern scholarly opinion on the outbreak of the war! The Megarian decree must still have been very much a living political issue in 426/5. Six years earlier *many* Athenians (Th. 1. 139. 4) had advocated its repeal as a necessary step to avoiding war with Sparta, and although some had doubtless changed their minds, in view of Athens' unexpected success in resisting Peloponnesian attacks, many will surely not have done so and will have longed for a settlement with Sparta. They may have been only a minority, but I suspect they may have been quite an influential minority.

Let us be very clear about the argument of Dikaiopolis–Aristophanes: it is that Athens too is partly to blame for the war and should now swallow her pride and *open negotiations for peace*. When war was in progress, to take the initiative in asking for peace was to the Greeks an admission of weakness and the fear of imminent defeat. The Athenians in 430 had sent ambassadors to Sparta to propose peace (Th. 22. 59. 2), but were evidently not able to obtain tolerable terms, and Pericles succeeded in dissuading them from making any further such attempts (65. 2). We hear no more of peace proposals until 425, not long after the production of the *Acharnians*, and then it was the Spartans who took the initiative, things having suddenly begun to go badly for them (4. 15–22; cf. 41. 3–4).[33]

In 427/6 something had happened at Sparta which would have appreciably increased the chances of peace: the recall of King

[32] Modern scholars have found no difficulty in taking the argument seriously: thus to Gilbert Murray it is 'a fair and persuasive argument that the war has arisen out of a muddle and is a very bad way of correcting the muddle' (*Aristophanes*, 32).

[33] Purely on the strength of *Acharnians* 652–4, some think the Spartans had negotiated for peace in 426: F. E. Adcock, in *CAH* 226–7; (Karl) Julius Beloch, *Griechische Geschichte*², vol. ii, pt. 1 (Berlin, 1927), 323; and Georg Busolt, *Griechische Geschichte*, vol. iii, pt. 2 (Gotha, 1904), 1079 and n. 5, seem to have no doubts about this. But see A. W. Gomme, *A Historical Commentary on Thucydides*, ii (Oxford, 1956), 391 (with 87), with whom I agree.

Pleistoanax, who had been exiled, or more probably had fled, in
445, as a result of his failure (perhaps the result of deliberate policy)
to press home the invasion of Attica in 446, and who was to be the
leader of those Spartans who wanted peace with Athens in 421. The
significance of this event cannot have escaped those Athenians who
knew anything about the outside world. By 426/5, then, circumstances were more favourable for a peace initiative than they had
ever been since the beginning of the war. The majority of Athenians
were not prepared to put themselves in the position of the weaker
party, by opening negotiations; but the return of Pleistoanax had
created a new situation which it was worth trying to exploit. If the
deadlock had continued and the whole complexion of the war had
not changed dramatically a few months later, with the Pylos affair,
there might well have been some cautious soundings from the
Athenian side during the course of 425/4. Aristophanes was not
backing an entirely hopeless cause in the *Acharnians*.

The next play of Aristophanes, the *Knights*, produced early in 424,
was written and staged at a time when the spirits of the Athenians
had suddenly been sent soaring by their great success at Pylos. This
was actually the peak of Athenian achievement in the whole war,
before Delium and the activities of Brasidas in the Thraceward
region in the autumn of 424 had begun to reverse the tide once
more. We know from Thucydides (4. 15–22, 41. 3–4) how Sparta
sued for peace while the operations at Pylos were in progress, and
repeatedly thereafter (perhaps thrice: see *Peace* 665–7). But her
overtures were all repulsed, the Athenians insisting on terms which
were too humiliating for Sparta to accept. That Athens should take
the initiative in proposing peace was of course entirely out of the
question after Pylos,[34] and what we might have expected to find in
the *Knights* is rather the celebration of victories already won and the
anticipation of final triumph, with some delighted satirizing of the
proud Spartans, who had so far betrayed Spartan principles as to
surrender ignominiously to the Athenians (cf. Th. 4. 40. 2). But if, as
Gomme says,[35] 'Aristophanes shows us in the *Knights* a whole city

[34] According to W. G. Forrest ('Aristophanes' *Acharnians*', *Phoenix*, 17 (1963), 10 n.
22), Aristophanes, if he had really had the outlook generally attributed to him
(miscalled 'pacifist' by Forrest), 'in the *Knights* . . . should have been pressing
furiously for peace'. It would be hard to show a greater misunderstanding of the
atmosphere in Athens in 425/4.
[35] *Historical Commentary on Thucydides*, iii, 527.

on the tide of victory,' we can only feel surprise at what we actually
do find. The great Athenian success at Pylos is glanced at several
times, but as a rule only askance and in such a way as to discredit
Cleon (lines 54–7, 75–6, 355, 702, 742–5, 844–6, 1005, 1052–5, 1058–9,
1167, 1201–5), a target evidently more congenial to Aristophanes
than the Spartans one might have expected him to get his teeth
into. Nowhere is there any glorying over the discomfiture of the
Spartans, now a very easy subject for satire, or any looking forward
to Sparta's ultimate collapse. The only achievement Aristophanes
does allow his chorus of Knights to celebrate is a minor exploit of
their own (595–610), which Thucydides mentions (4. 42–5). Once,
and only once, is there an invocation of Victory in solemn terms
(581–94)—and then it is simply the Chorus asking the city's patron
goddess to make them victorious in the competition! Otherwise, the
Chorus in the parabasis merely hark back to the deeds of their
ancestors (565–74) and proclaim their loyalty in defending their
country and its gods (576–8), with a mild plea that their little
fopperies should not be begrudged them when peace returns and
they cease from their toils (579–80). Lines 794–6 seem to me to
regret a failure to make peace, promoted by Archeptolemus.[36]
However that may be, there is in lines 1388–95, just before the
end of the play, a very clear condemnation of Cleon for procuring
the rejection of the Spartan peace offers of 425; and the reformed
Sausage-Seller arouses the enthusiasm of Demos by procuring a
Thirty-Years Peace—'How lovely!' cries the grateful Demos.

In the *Clouds* (423) and *Wasps* (422) Aristophanes is concerned
with other topics than the war, but it is not without interest that
Labes, the subject of the mock-trial in the latter play (240, 836ff.,
894ff.), stands for Laches, a prominent general and political figure of
the period, who was evidently working for peace at this time: he
proposed the decree accepting the truce for a year in 423 (Th. 4. 118.
11), and he was evidently active with Nicias in promoting the Peace
in 421 (5. 43. 2). And Labes–Laches is sympathetically treated by
Aristophanes (see esp. *Wasps* 952–72) and acquitted (994).

We now come to the *Peace*, produced at the Great Dionysia of 421,

[36] In the context, of course, the name itself is a pun. And see ibid. iii. 482, cf. 732
(where '*Equit.* 704' is twice misprinted for '794': I cannot accept Gomme's last
sentence here). But whether or not this Archeptolemus is identical with the son of
Hippodamas, the Sausage-Seller is certainly being made to rebuke Cleon for prevent-
ing peace from being made.

only about a fortnight before the conclusion of the Peace of Nicias, at a time when everyone in Athens must have known that peace was certainly coming soon, and even approximately what its terms would be. (Hardly any Athenian at this date could have been in favour of continuing the war, provided tolerable terms could be obtained, as by now they obviously could.) In this play Aristophanes would not feel the need to *argue* in favour of peace: he could celebrate it with appropriate jubilation. There are only three passages to which I need draw attention. In lines 605–18 we have Aristophanes' second reference to the Megarian decree.[37] In 664–9 Trygaeus and Hermes agree (cf. 216–20) that the Athenians were wrong to reject the thrice-repeated Spartan peace overtures in 425. But the really illuminating passage is 1080–2, where Trygaeus, in three lines which are not themselves at all funny (although they are sandwiched inside comic material), proclaims what I am sure was Aristophanes' deeply held conviction: we Athenians and Spartans are wrong to fight each other 'when we could make peace, *and rule Hellas jointly*'. This reflects the opinion expressed by the Spartan ambassadors to Athens during the Pylos operations, according to Thucydides 4. 20. 4, that if Sparta and Athens were in accord (literally, if they 'used the same language') 'the rest of Greece would remain in a condition of inferiority and pay us the greatest honour'. Trygaeus is another of Aristophanes' heroes who is anything but a fool or a mere buffoon, and I cannot see why Aristophanes should have put lines 1080–2 into his mouth unless he himself agreed with them. There will certainly have been plenty of Athenians in 422/1 who were looking forward eagerly to precisely this situation. There is no reason to think that Aristophanes was less of an 'imperialist' than the other Athenians of his day. I am happy to be able to agree (for once, as far as Aristophanes is concerned!) with Forrest, when he says that 'Aristophanes never defends the allies against Athens, he never questions the principle of *archē* (ruling) or of tribute, but he does defend both the allies and the Athenians against their own and each other's demagogues, he does believe that the *archē* and the tribute should be used in the interests of "nicer" people.'[38]

The *Lysistrata*, the last of Aristophanes' 'anti-war' plays, was produced at the Lenaea of 411, at a time when Athens's fortunes

[37] See my *Origins of the Peloponnesian War*, 236–7.
[38] Forrest, 'Aristophanes' *Acharnians*', 1 n. 3.

were at a very much lower ebb than they had been at the time of the
Acharnians. Athens had survived the shock of the Sicilian disaster
and the revolts of the allies which had followed, and she had even
begun to recover a little and win back some of the allies she had lost
in 413/12. But Sparta and Persia were now in the act of coming
together at last, an oligarchic revolution was brewing, and at any
moment the situation of Athens might become desperate (see Th. 8).
'Reasonable terms', from Athens's point of view, were almost out of
the question now, for the Spartans naturally felt they had her at
their mercy, and they would certainly not have consented to even
'uti possidetis' terms—which would anyway have left Athens much
worse off than similar terms in 426/5, if only because major allies
had deserted her since then. Yet there can be no doubt at all that
the *Lysistrata* is a plea for peace.

Scattered through the play are passages which demand to be
taken seriously, even if they are mixed in with pure comedy. Most
important are lines 1114–77, which are in effect a speech by
Lysistrata, *completely serious in character and without a single jest*,
interspersed with comic interjections, often obscene, by her Athenian and Spartan hearers. First, Lysistrata gently chides both sides for
fighting each other, Greeks as they are, in the very sight of armed
barbarians (1128–35). After one line of obscene comment by the
Athenians, Lysistrata turns to the Spartans and reminds them of the
time of the earthquake and the Messenian revolt, when Cimon and
his 4,000 Athenian hoplites saved Sparta; and she reproves them for
ravaging the land from which they had once benefited (1137–46).
Again, there is no attempt at humour. The Athenians applaud at
this point, and there is another sexual interjection, this time by the
Spartans. Lysistrata now rounds on the Athenians with yet a third
short speech, again devoid of humour, reminding them how the
Spartans had rescued them from the tyranny of Hippias (1149–56).
After another pair of comments, of the usual sexual character
(1157–8), Lysistrata asks the Athenians and Spartans why they
cannot come to terms (1159–61). This produces a mixture, partly
obscene, of fact and fancy; but one thing emerges clearly enough:
the Spartans demand Pylos, the Athenians are minded to deny it,
but Lysistrata insists they give it up. Of course we must not over-
idealize Aristophanes' attitude, and Gomme has done well to insist
that it is not at all the heroine's arguments that make Lysistrata's

plan succeed, but the men's unwillingness to tolerate their own sexual deprivation.[39]

I return to the question raised, but not answered, at the beginning of this essay: whether the expression of political views in Aristophanes' plays was deliberate and had the conscious purpose of influencing public opinion. I am myself puzzled to find that there are a few people who are reluctant to give an affirmative answer. It seems to me that Aristophanes was a man of very vigorous political views of a conservative, 'Cimonian' variety (not at all untypical among the Athenian upper classes), the general complexion of which is easily identifiable from the plays and remained consistent over the period of some forty years during which he was writing his comedies. Aristophanes' forthright statements on political matters regularly follow particular patterns; and many of them which are not in themselves comic may indeed have seemed rather tiresome to those who did not share his outlook. Why anyone should suppose that they were not meant seriously, or were not intended to influence the audience, I cannot imagine. There are those who feel distaste at the very notion of a 'committed' poet, or who prefer to forget the truth expressed in Dover's remark that Aristophanes' 'portrayal of the effect of Socrates' teaching on the character of Pheidippides is an invitation to violence, or repressive legislation, against such teachers';[40] but even they must at least take account of the role played by the *Clouds* in helping to procure the condemnation of Socrates. And it is an ironical reflection that, irrespective of any effect on Athenian opinion the plays may have had at the time they were produced, the impression they have made on the historical record has been tremendous. The malicious and quite unnecessary side-swipe at Pericles in the *Peace* (605–18), in relation to the Megarian decree, became the foundation for Ephorus' popular version of the origins of the Peloponnesian war;[41] and the speech of Dikaiopolis in the *Acharnians* (514–39) has probably done more than anything else to create the almost universal misconception of

[39] Gomme, 'Aristophanes and Politics', *CR* 52 (1938), 100–1.
[40] Dover, *Aristophanes 'Clouds'*, p. lvi. The whole para. pp. lvi–lvii, is excellent.
[41] Aristophanes can sometimes be kind to a dead man who he had satirized while living: Lamachus, a main butt as a warmonger in *Ach.*, and in *Peace* 473–4, 1290–1, is given respectful tributes in *Th.* 839–41 and *Frogs* 1039; and even Cleon, in *Peace* 647–56 (see esp. 648–9), is dismissed with a mere backhander, venomous but brief. For the dead Pericles there is no mercy. Cf. de Ste Croix, *The Origins of the Peloponnesian War*, 236–7 n. 4. For the Megarian decree, see ibid., ch. 7.

the nature and effects of the Megarian decree in modern times. The caricature of the demagogues as 'salesmen' and *nouveaux riches* has become so firmly rooted that even the information which has become available in modern times about the background of Cleon and Cleophon[42] has not yet completely dispelled the Aristophanic image. And the various travesties of Athenian political and judicial procedures, especially perhaps that of the jury-courts in the *Wasps* (see above), have been taken all too seriously, and few historians have succeeded in escaping their seductive influence, apart from Grote.

[42] See de Ste Croix, *The Origins of the Peloponnesian war*, 235 n. 7.

5

The *Dēmos* and the Comic Competition

JEFFREY HENDERSON

The comic poets of fifth-century Athens aimed, in the words of the Initiate-chorus of *Frogs* (389–93), 'to say much that is humorous and much that is serious, and to win the prize by playfulness and mockery, worthily of the festival'.[1] For students of Old Comedy 'humorous' and 'playfulness' are relatively unproblematic: the words and actions of the performers would make the spectators laugh. But the claim to be 'serious' raises serious issues about the genre of Old Comedy, for the poets consistently said that their advice and admonishments to the spectators were true and just, that their explicit and often mordantly abusive treatment of individuals (through 'mockery') would purify the *polis* and advance the people's interests, and that their portrayal of contemporary reality, however novel or facetious, was essentially believable. According to the poets, their genre was both artistic and political. Indeed, 'worthily of the festival' inseparably links the genre with its civic context: the comic competition was a feature of the Lenaea and the Greater Dionysia, festivals attended by some 17,000 spectators, organized and regulated by the *dēmos* (sovereign people), the winning poet being voted by judges representing them.

In short, the comic poets pictured themselves as competing for the favor of the *dēmos* with a humorous spectacle of a special kind, which the *dēmos' archōn* had granted them permission and funds to put on at the appropriate yearly festival, and as public voices who could, indeed were expected to, comment on, and seek to influence public thinking about matters of major importance—the same

---

[1] They refer (in character) to the Eleusinian festival (addressing Demeter), but their words apply (as comic chorus) also to the comic competition of the Lenaea (addressing the spectators).

matters that were being or might be presented to the voting *dēmos* in other settings and in different ways, by competitors in a tragic competition, for example,[2] or by speakers in an assembly, or by litigants in a lawcourt.

In this essay I will argue that the picture drawn by the Old Comic poets is accurate: they were the constituent intellectuals of the *dēmos* during the period of full popular sovereignty that began with the reforms of Ephialtes in 462/1, and in their institutionalized competitions they influenced the formulation of its ideology and the public standing of individuals. While their role was distinctive, it was also an organic feature of the sovereignty of the *dēmos*.

Ancient critics, beginning with such eyewitnesses as Pseudo-Xenophon in *Constitution of the Athenians* (the Old Oligarch) and Plato, variously applauded or condemned this picture of what poets and spectators were up to at the Old Comic festivals but never questioned its accuracy. For them, as we will see, the Old Comic poets were what they claimed to be, so that ancient historians and biographers included comedy among their valid sources of political information and opinion. But for modern critics, beginning with Müller-Strübing in 1873,[3] the accuracy of the picture is at issue, and so, therefore, is the socio-political significance claimed by the poets. A sceptical attitude has developed which has suspended confident use of comic texts as special evidence for important features of fifth-century social and political life.[4] When Dionysus of Syracuse wanted to study 'the *politeia* of the Athenians', Plato sent him Aristophanes.[5] Nowadays we would probably send Thucydides or the Tribute Lists, or even Plato.

The reason is clear enough: in our world no one picture can contain both seriousness and humour, both festivals and the state, both art and politics. And so the ancient picture has been edited, the editors falling mainly into two groups. The sceptics separate serious-ness and humour: the poets' claim to seriousness must itself be a joke, or, conversely, the jokes are there to make the serious parts

[2] That tragedy was thought to have an edifying, even didactic function is the assumption throughout *Frogs* and part of the point of *Acharnians* 500. See O. Taplin, 'Tragedy and Trugedy', *CQ*33 (1983), 331–3.

[3] For an overview of modern opinion see Walther Kraus, *Aristophanes' politische Komödien*, SAWW, Philosophisch–Historische Klasse, 453 (Vienna, 1985), 25–30.

[4] As opposed to such information as the price of fish.

[5] Ar. *Life* 42–5 K–A. Historical or not, the anecdote expresses the ancient attitude.

more palatable. The carnivalists separate festivals and the state: the poets' seriousness was somehow detached from the 'real' world of the spectators as being 'mere' entertainment (poetry, play, ritual, carnival, satire, fantasy). Both groups separate art and politics: comedy may be topical and political but only in a reactive or alternative way, so that while there can be 'political comedy' there can be no comic politics. But when we examine each new edition of the picture we see that something is missing, that something important should be restored.

The sceptics rely on an a priori assumption that humour, however artful, is not a moral or political determinant: what makes people laugh cannot affect the principles, criteria, and values that determine their choice of action when they are not laughing. In the case of fifth-century Athens, however, this assumption has insufficient explanatory power. The sceptics have not explained away the fact that the comic poets, despite their jokes, argue vehemently and purposefully about the most important and divisive issues of the day. The positions they advocate or denounce represent those of actual groups, and their techniques of persuasion and abuse are practically identical with those used in political and forensic disputes. After all, the comic troupe competed before the same audience—the sovereign *dēmos*—that arbitrated those disputes. What is more, it is not true, as the sceptics say, that anyone was fair game for comic ridicule: the poets show systematic bias in their choice of people and policies to satirize and not to satirize.[6] Indeed, a poet could, as in *Acharnians* and *Knights*, find room in his production to prosecute a personal feud. As for the impact of comedy, it is hard to explain away the crown awarded by the city to Aristophanes for the advice he offered in *Frogs*, or the lawsuits brought by Cleon, or the special decrees defining comic propriety, or the comic portrayal of Socrates which for Plato was a significant factor in his condemnation. Were these mere anomalies or accidents?

Ste Croix, believing that the poets had serious biases and wished to persuade their fellow citizens, confronts the sceptics on their own terms by identifying passages whose primary aim seems not to be humour, or which can be aligned with other contemporary voices.[7]

[6] G. E. M. de Ste Croix, *The Origins of the Peloponnesian War* (London, 1972), 359–62.
[7] App. xxix, with the reaction of G. A. H. Chapman, 'Aristophanes and History', *Acta Classica*, 21 (1978), 59–70.

But this is again to edit the picture: in the former case humour is removed, in the latter the distinctive outlook of comedy. The comic poets may as well have delivered their criticisms and advice in Assembly or court. The rules of evidence on which the sceptics insist are, it would seem, necessarily distorting. They rule out in advance the possibility that comic humour might have been a persuasive mode parallel to those we call serious. One of the special powers of humour is 'fool's privilege': to mediate between the poles of polite silence and impolite expression, to express ideas that want a public outlet but that would be too disruptive if expressed otherwise. What the fool brings out into the open the king and his court can pretend, if they like, not to have taken seriously. I will suggest that fifth-century comic poets played a similar mediating role: what might be too disruptive in Assembly or court could find an outlet at the comic competition. Thus the problem is not to distinguish humour and seriousness but rather to analyse the dynamics of comic persuasion.

The carnivalists, who examine the institutional status of comedy, seek to side-step this problem by claiming that the comic festival was a holiday world, a world unto itself which could not have had any impact on the world where political decisions were made. This claim is an induction from the many features fifth-century comic plays undeniably share with carnival and that in fact belong to a vast tradition of popular grotesque which ignores the boundaries of time and place. In its typical carnivalesque form, this tradition appears as a counter-world embedded in an autonomous festival. When this counter-world mirrors the official world it can even be called political (as in 'political comedy'), but it cannot itself be a form of politics. The counter-world of fifth-century comedy, however, differs from that of carnival in important ways, and the festival in which it was embedded was not at all autonomous.

As Bakhtin has shown, the counter-world of carnival in its political aspect typically has only the negative role of ridiculing and criticizing a dominant class and ideology. Thus it cannot generate positive positions and does not take sides in political debate. Fifth-century comedy, however, is a local variant which does not fit this model. Its counter-world contained not only ridicule and criticism but also positive alignments and appeals by the poet and sympathetic characters. Although they typically championed minority positions, they did so from a stance of ideological solidarity with the official culture, with those who had sole power to act on such positions: the sovereign *dēmos*. Moreover, their stance was essentially the same for everyone else who appeared before the *dēmos*. The counter-world of fifth-century comedy, unlike that of typical carnival, paralleled rather than opposed the official world, so that it cannot be used to support the claim of autonomous detachment for the festival. But we need not rely on the plays alone to reject that claim.

Unlike autonomous carnival, the comic festival shared with all other public assemblies an institutional structure whose common denominator was the *dēmos*, in this particular instance convened as a theatrical audience. The comic festival took place in a *polis* that devoted at least one-third of its year, and its largest special expenditure of wealth, to public festivals and that considered them to be a distinctive glory of their democracy; was itself a competition where decisions were made; was part of a larger festive complex that included unarguably political elements; was governed by the same official mechanisms as all other public assemblies; and was not, contrary to the 'anything goes' view of the carnivalists, exempt from the laws regulating other forms of public discourse. Moreover, Old Comedy as a genre shows rapid evolution in ways not explainable in terms of aesthetic criteria alone. To point out that such features of comedy as obscenity, parody, transvestism, and role-reversal were restricted to special poetic and festive contexts (and not only comic ones) merely begs the question, for we have not thereby determined the status and function of those contexts in the culture at large.

In this essay I will examine these problems by forsaking the modern consensus that we are too shrewd to be taken in by the comic poets' claims to seriousness and know better than those spectators whose opinions survive. If we contemplate the picture painted by the comic poets unedited, we will find that it makes sense after all. A good place to begin is with the Athenian *dēmos*, which ran the comic competition as it ran everything else, and with our earliest extant opinion about the connection between *dēmos* and comedy: the Old Oligarch, who wrote his treatise in the mid-420s, when Aristophanes was beginning his career.

1. DISPLAYS FOR THE *DĒMOS*

For the Old Oligarch, democracy was rule by the lower classes in their own interests, a poor form of government but not an irrational one: democratic institutions do preserve the role of the *dēmos* and are not to be underestimated (cf. 1. 1–9). One of those institutions is comedy. His description of comedy as an institution (2. 18) appears not in a section on the arts or festivals but in a description of democratic decision-making, which he envisages as displays by individuals for the voting *dēmos*. Before we consider the particular comic display we must examine those which took place in deliberative contexts.

The *dēmos*, says the Old Oligarch, is pragmatic but unprincipled and unaccountable. It makes policy in its own self-interest but cannot be made to take any responsibility. Instead, it can blame the individual who had advocated or called for the vote on a policy or an agreement. 'And if anything bad results from a policy the *dēmos* has decided, its excuse is that a few persons have ruined it by acting against the interests of the *dēmos*, but if the result is good they take all the credit' (17). Comedy exemplifies the same phenomenon (18, quoted in Section 2, below): the *dēmos* may not be ridiculed or criticized, but rich, well-born, and influential citizens may. Such individuals are the same ones who propose policies. Thus he concludes (19) that the *dēmos* can recognize which of the citizens are good (*chrēstoi*) and which bad (*ponēroi*) but does not let this interfere with pursuits of its interests. 'It prefers bad ones who are devoted to its interests to good ones, whom it rather hates, for it does not think that their inborn excellence (*aretēn*) is to its good but to its harm. On the other hand there are some who are undemocratic by nature who nevertheless take the side of the *dēmos*.'

The *dēmos* is here sponsor, spectator, and judge of agonistic performances in which ambitious competitors make their appeals, and only the competitors are at risk. It is a valid description of fifth-century decision-making and jibes with the picture drawn by Thucydides: 'When they recognized the facts, they turned against the public speakers who had favoured the [Sicilian] expedition, as though they themselves had not voted for it' (8. 1). Both Pericles (1. 140. 1) and Nicias (7. 14. 4) complain that the *dēmos* accepts sole credit for good fortune but assigns to its advisers sole blame for bad. If a speaker loses a debate, the *dēmos* has 'slighted' him, and his reputation and influence decline (3. 42. 3–5). Even if he wins, the *dēmos* can vote to punish him, on charges brought by a citizen who wants to volunteer as prosecutor, for having proposed an illegal or inexpedient decree or law or policy should the result be not as predicted: Pericles himself was such a scapegoat (Th. 2. 65. 3).[8] In cases where the *dēmos* could not decide between the contestants, one of them could be expelled from the city by ostracism: each year the *dēmos* decided whether to hold one (*Ath.* 43. 5). All office-holders were subject to official reviews of their fitness to hold an office and then of their conduct when leaving it. The Old Oligarch does not mention litigants in a law court here, but their situation was similar.[9]

Thucydides' Cleon, who thought that the members of the *dēmos* should assume control of their own deliberations, rebukes them for having 'mistakenly' made decision-making a series of 'competitive displays (*kakōs agōnothetountes*)' and as a consequence having become 'victims of your own pleasure in listening and more like spectators sitting at the feet of professional speakers than men deliberating the affairs of the city' (3. 38. 4, 7).[10] Compare the picture in *Knights* of 'slave' politicians competing in the 'city of Open-mouthenians' (*Kechēnaiōn* 1263)[11] for the favour of Old Master Demos, who bestows privileges or floggings, and Plutarch's application to Nicias of Agamemnon's lines in Euripides, *Iphigeneia in Aulis*

---

[8] Jennifer T. Roberts, *Accountability in Athenian Government* (Madison, 1982), describes the legal mechanisms, and Martin Ostwald, *From Popular Sovereignty to the Sovereignty of Law* (Berkeley and Los Angeles, 1986) traces their use in the 5th cent. For voluntary prosecution, see further R. Osborne, 'Law in Action in Classical Athens', *JHS* 105 (1985), 40–58.

[9] Cf. Pl., *Ap.* 31e (Socrates to the jury): 'No one who conscientiously opposes you . . . can possibly escape with his life.' From the dicast's point of view, cf. *Wasps* 546–630.

[10] The whole of the debate on Mytilene between Cleon and the office-holder Diodotus (3. 37–48) examines the decision-making scenario and shows that the Old Oligarch's analysis was hardly idiosyncratic; see Martin Ostwald, 'Diodotus, Son of Eucrates', *GRBS* 20 (1979), 5–13. Note also the attitude of Isocrates (in a pamphlet purporting to address the Assembly): 'It is hazardous to oppose your views, and even though this is a democracy there is no freedom of speech except here in the Assembly for the most thoughtless and self-interested and in the theatre for producers of comedy' (*On the Peace* 14). For the similarity of actors and orators (many of whose speeches were written for them by professionals), see Arist., *Rh.* 1430^{b}32–5.

[11] Alan H. Sommerstein's translation in *Aristophanes' 'Knights'* (Warminster, 1981); see also 261, 755. L. B. Carter, *The Quiet Athenian* (Oxford, 1986), 118, remarks that 'the Athenians did look for something like selfless devotion to duty in their public servants'.

449–50: 'As master of our lives we nobles have magnificence, but we serve the crowd as slaves' (*Life of Nicias* 5. 7).

Thucydides (2. 65), the comic poets,[12] and Aristotle (*Ath.* 28. 1) tell us that Pericles was the last fifth-century leader who was both rich and well-born: Cleon was the first who was 'not of good repute among the better sort' (*tois epieikesin*, Aristotle). These sources also tell us that the new politicians introduced a change of political style (identifying themselves directly with the *dēmos*) and that this style went together with a new source of wealth (not inherited in a distinguished family but earned by 'selling'). How accurate is this picture?

The disappearance of men from the 'better sort' of families seems real enough: before 429 all political leaders had been from the great archaic families or capable of marrying into them, except for Themistocles, who was of the lesser aristocracy.[13] After 429 only Alcibiades and Critias belonged to the old families. 'We need not be surprised at the time-lag between the creation of democratic institutions and the rise of men of the *dēmos* to positions of political importance, but the disappearance of the old aristocracy from such positions is strikingly abrupt.'[14]

That the advent of Cleon as the speaker 'having the greatest power of appeal to the *dēmos*' (Th. 3. 36. 6) marked a change in the traditional (well-bred) style of political persuasion also seems real. Cleon paraded his devotion to the *dēmos* rather than to a circle of friends (whom he is said to have formally dismissed),[15] opposed anyone who thought himself superior to the *dēmos*,[16] eschewed such aristocratic practices as the performance of liturgies, and claimed lower-class affiliations himself.[17] 'More than anyone else he corrupted the *dēmos* by his violent impulses and was the first man who, when on the platform, shouted, slandered and made speeches

[12] *Knights* 180–222, *Frogs* 732–3; Eup., fr. 219, 384.
[13] In *Knights* (810–19; cf. 84, 884) Cleon compares himself to Themistocles.
[14] P. J. Rhodes, *A Commentary on the Aristotelian 'Athenaion Politeia'* (Oxford, 1981), 345.
[15] Ar., *Knights* (*passim*), Plu., *Moralia* 806f–807a; cf. W. Robert Connor, *New Politicians of Fifth-Century Athens* (Princeton, 1971), 91–94, 121–2, 127–8.
[16] Th. 3.374d with Connor, *New Politicians of Fifth-Century Athens*, 94–6.
[17] e.g. *Knights* 335–9, Platon, fr. 219 = Arist. *Rh.* 1376^a. 9–12. Compare litigants, e.g. *Wasps* 548–630, D. 42. 20, where one of Demosthenes' clients boasts, 'In early life I made a lot of money from the silver-mines, working and toiling myself with my own hands.' Sommerstein, in *Aristophanes' 'Knights'*, 314, thinks that 'metaphors from handicrafts may have been typical of Cleon's oratory (cf. 461–3)'.

with his clothes hitched up, while everyone else spoke in an orderly way' (*Ath.* 28. 3).

Clearly the *dēmos* was now ready to listen to men who gave undivided attention to its own interests. Cleon's scornful remarks about 'competitive displays' (Thucydides 3. 38, quoted above) were thus a slap at the upper-class speakers the *dēmos* was used to hearing and an exhortation to the *dēmos* to assume control for itself (with Cleon, of course, as leader). The reply made on this occasion by Diodotus, who as an office-holder could not speak so recklessly as Cleon, aligns Cleon with the unaccountable *dēmos*: 'Faced with issues of utmost importance and in such a position as ours is, we must be expected, as we make our speeches, to be thinking ahead rather further than you who give the issues but a moment's attention, especially as the advice we give is subject to an accounting, whereas the hearing you give is unaccountable' (3. 43. 4). Cleon's demagogic manner may safely be aligned with that fomentation of class antagonism (*dēmos* and its new champions versus the traditional leaders) that would erupt into class warfare before the end of the century.

That the new politicians were actually 'men of the *dēmos*' (sellers without land or family) is, however, harder to document. What little we know of the families of men like Cleon, Hyperbolus, and Cleophon suggest that they were entirely respectable.[18] If Cleon dismissed his friends he must have had friends to dismiss, and there would be no point in dismissing them were they mere sellers, not to say slaves, aliens, thieves, the sons and husbands of shady women. In our world, where seriousness and humour have been separately institutionalized, cartoonists and comedians can indulge in such name-calling, but officials or leaders cannot: contrast Nicias and Cleon (Th. 4. 27) or the speeches of Demosthenes and Aeschines, whose mutual vilification resembles that of the comic poets in all essentials. In evaluating the literary response to the new politicians we must attune ourselves to varieties of wild exaggeration and outright satire that today are largely absent from official and political discourse but that in classical Athens were rhetorical modes common to oratory and comedy. The violent abusiveness

[18] See J. K. Davies' review of Connor, *New Politicians of Fifth-Century Athens*, in *Gomon*, 47 (1975), 374–8.

that characterizes the contest for Old Master Demos' favour in
Knights is not entirely Aristophanes' own invention.

It looks as if the backgrounds that our literary sources supply for
the new politicians were an exaggerated way of saying that an
opponent had 'no family' and of attributing to them that solidarity
with the lower classes that they rhetorically claimed for themselves.
Cleon was no more a tanner than he was a Paphlagonian. This
humour was complex and in its own way as demagogic as Cleon's
portrayal of the men of the old families as 'tyrants': part snobbery
(the victims were not of the 'better sort' of families) and part
exposure of demotic pretensions (nor were they common folk).
Thus both superior and inferior social classes could say 'not one
of us' and so share in the sneering.

For our purposes it is most significant that the new politicians
derived their ascendancy not, like Pericles and his predecessors, by
holding official positions but by success in competitive displays
before the *dēmos* in council, Assembly and court, where rhetorical
ability and force of personality were everything.[19] A new class of
'speakers' (*rhētores*) developed who could be distinguished from
'politicians' (*politikoi*).[20] The latter were statesmen (as in the title
of Plato's dialogue) or men who regularly served the *polis* in
constitutionally specified (and therefore accountable) roles: magistrates allotted from a list of men nominated by their demes; elected
generals and treasurers; liturgists. Such offices meant time-consum-
ing service and, as often as not, more expense than profit:[21] they
were for men of wealth and standing. By contrast, anyone could be
a speaker, and speaking was, compared to office-holding, a relatively
safe way to seek personal advancement: by advising the *dēmos*, or by
taking sides in a lawsuit or review of conduct against the office-
holders. Most speakers were either well-born young men who had
decided not to 'mind their own business' but to become politically
active (*polupragmones*) and who sought out sophists for rhetorical

---

[19] After 429 only Cleon and Thrasybulus among the new politicians are known to
have held a generalship.
[20] Cf. Pl., *Ap.* 23e–24a (Socrates accused by Meletus on behalf of the poets, by
Anytus on behalf of the craftsmen and politicians, by Lycon on behalf of the speakers).
The 'speakers' were constant butts of comic ridicule.
[21] See the Old Oligarch 1. 3, Carter, *The Quiet Athenian*, 35.

training,[22] or they were 'outsiders' like Cleon.[23] The informal
(paraconstitutional) 'office' of speaker enabled such men to get
into the competition, at the expense of the aristocrats, who had
hitherto enjoyed a monopoly. Their new and peculiar styles of
rhetorical appeal were a principal means of establishing their
status, and their caricature in our literary sources was part of the
response.

For Thucydides, people like Cleon harmed the Athenians in
several ways (2. 65). Because they identified themselves with the
dēmos, a whimsical mob, they could not lead it; because their
families had no political importance they espoused policies that
looked to their own advancement and profit rather than to the
public good; and because they were selfishly competitive their
policies were inconsistent and led to that factionalism on which
Thucydides blamed Athens's defeat more than any other factor. The
Old Oligarch had these changes in mind when he said (above) that
the *dēmos* was willing to choose 'bad' men as leaders. The almost
whimsical election of Cleon, on Nicias' ironic proposal, to a command (hitherto reserved for generals: aristocrats and their protégés)
was a sensational instance of the new mood of the *dēmos* (Th. 4. 27–
8). If comedy as a competitive display was analogous to deliberative
ones, Thucydides' account here indicates that the analogy works
both ways: politics could come to resemble comedy.

But there were other 'new politicians' who offered a different
choice. Nicias, who like Cleon was the son of the man who founded
the family fortune,[24] kept to the style represented by Pericles:
accountable leadership by the 'best' in the interests of all classes.
Like Pericles, he frequently performed liturgies, avoided symposiums
and other social distractions, and based his political career on social

[22] See Ostwald, *From Popular Sovereignty to the Sovereignty of the Law*, 229–50,
Carter, *The Quiet Athenian*, 119–25.

[23] The comic poets abused both the aristocratic young speakers and the outsiders,
but also recognized their mutual hostility. Likewise Thucydides, who has Cleon say
(appealing to class antagonism) that his younger counterparts are unpatriotic: 'As for
the speakers who delight you with their way of speaking, they should hold their
competitions about less important subjects and not about a matter where the *polis*
may for its light pleasure pay a heavy price, while the speakers themselves will be well
rewarded for speaking well'. (3. 40. 3). Cleon's 'sophistic' way of saying this aligns him
with those he criticizes: an example of Thucydidean humour.

[24] Silver-mining (X., *Poroi* 4. 14, *Mem.* 2.5.2; Plu., *Nic.* 4. 2), which, however, was far
more lucrative than (say) tanning and therefore could not be ridiculed as a low or
banausic occupation: at *Knights* 362, 'buy mining leases' equals 'be rich'.

alliances and generalships.²⁵ Also like Pericles, he saw the war not as an opportunity to expand the empire but only as a chance to make Sparta and her allies acquiesce in its existence. Things would then be as they had been before the war. For Cleon and the other new men, however, the war was a chance for personal ascendancy and an opportunity to expand the empire.

The war policy created internal division principally by requiring that the countryside be evacuated and left to the predations of the enemy;²⁶ by redistributing the accumulated wealth of the empire; and by creating political openings for men like Cleon, who appealed to the *dēmos'* confidence and aggressiveness. If everyone benefited from the empire, it was the masses who benefited most from the war and the 'best' who were presented with the bill. Pericles' confidence in Athens's ability to finance the war from existing resources had been based on the expectation that the war would not last long (Th. 2. 13). In the event, these resources quickly evaporated, so that by 428 the war began to require ever more borrowing, ever more tribute from the allies, ever more levies on the wealthy.²⁷ All this made the urban populace—rowers and provisioners especially—the beneficiaries of the war, and the landed aristocracy, together with the peasants, the losers. It also changed the make-up of the voting *dēmos* and therefore the character of the appeals made to it.

Since the *dēmos* stood to gain much by going along with men like Cleon and little by going along with men like Nicias, it is easy to see why the 'best' began to take a hostile view of the *dēmos* and its champions. Nevertheless, there seems to have been general agreement about following the war policy in spite of such unanticipated hardships as the plague and the tenacity of the Peloponnesians: the empire was unsafe until its enemies abandoned their resolve to 'liberate' it. The task of the 'best' was to keep the *dēmos'* eye on

---

²⁵ Plu., *Nic.* 3, 5. Nicias was general every year from 427/6 (the aristocrats' counter to Cleon?) to 421/0 (the peace that bears his name) and again from 417/7 until his death in 413: Charles Fornara, *The Athenian Board of Generals from 501 to 404*, Historia Einzelschrift, 16 (Wiesbaden, 1971), 56–65. D.L. 1. 110, providing him with an ancestor who was important in Solonian times, reflects 5th-cent. propaganda the opposite of that directed at Cleon.   ²⁶ For the effect see Th. 2. 16.

²⁷ See Russell Meiggs and David Lewis, *Greek Historical Inscriptions* (Oxford, 1969), 184–201 on *IGi³* 68, 71 (tribute), 205–17 on *IGi³* 369 (borrowing); Th. 3. 19. 1 (capital levies on the wealthy begin in 428, perhaps on Cleon's initiative: *Knights* 773–5). In *Knights* 912–26, Cleon threatens to make the Sausage-Seller a trierarch and to enrol him among the rich so that he can be squeezed for levies.

this goal and to curb the ambitious adventurism of the demagogues, who chafed under Pericles' warning about not 'hoping for more' until the Peloponnesians gave up.[28] The victory at Pylos in 425 might have achieved this goal. Unhappily for the 'best', the Pylos victory meant triumph for Cleon and disgrace for Nicias, and it encouraged the *dēmos* to 'hope for more'.

Those who claim that the comic poets were mere humorists must explain why they consistently and one-sidedly championed the position of the 'best': like Thucydides, they refrain from criticizing Nicias (who could just as fairly be called a slave and a seller as Cleon); they explain away, play down, or even omit to mention the victories both military and financial that were achieved by the new politicians; and they hold profoundly ambivalent views about the ability of the *dēmos* at large to choose responsible leaders (like themselves!).

Those competitors for the favour of the *dēmos* who made their appeals as office-holders, as speakers in council and Assembly, or as litigants in court were thus engaged in a political and ideological contest that the ascendancy of Pericles had postponed and that the war with the Peloponnesians exacerbated. There was no settled Athenian policy, no unanimity. Men competed for the votes that would determine policy and crossed their fingers. The comic poets were part of the contest, just as Socrates says in Plato's *Apology*: in 423 a comic poet was one of his 'most dangerous accusers' (18c2–d2), and in 399 Meletus represented the poets in seeking his death (23e–24a). As the 'Open-mouthenian' *dēmos* looked from one side to the other, trying to decide which way its interests lay. Aristophanes arrived on the scene and joined the contest, attacking the new politics in his very first play (427) and Cleon in his second. But by what mechanisms, social, political, or institutional, did comic poets have access to such a contest?

2. THE COMIC DISPLAY

Let us return to the Old Oligarch's description of comedy as an institution of the *dēmos* that illustrates its practice of holding

---

[28] In *Knights*, Cleon hopes to extend the *dēmos'* sway over all of Greece (236–8, 797–800) and Hyperbolus has his eye on Carthage (1303–4). In 425/4 three generals were cashiered by the *dēmos* for having failed to subdue Sicily (Th. 4. 65. 3). Such ambitions culminated in 415 in the expedition against Sicily.

prominent men responsible for whatever goes wrong while taking credit for everything that turns out well.

And again, they do not tolerate comic ridicule and criticism of the *dēmos*, lest their reputation suffer, but they encourage this in the case of individuals if there is anyone somebody wants this to happen to. For they well know that the victim is generally not one of the *dēmos* or the crowd but a rich, well-born or powerful individual. A few of the poor and the demotic are ridiculed in comedy but only if they are politically active or seek to have more than the *dēmos*. Therefore they are not offended if such people are ridiculed. (2. 18)

Leaving aside for the moment the function here ascribed to comedy (ridicule and criticism), let us see in what ways it was a competitive display comparable to the displays with deliberative functions that were discussed above.

The comic festivals are often thought of as holiday[29] or static ritual[30] or carnival,[31] and thus as opportunities for 'unbridled freedom of speech', and 'release from the normal obligation to heed the restraints and subordinations of social hierarchy', since they were occasions whose 'conventions . . . separated the festivals from the normal life of the city'.[32] But comic festivals, as occasions for competitive display by poets, producers, and *chorēgoi*, show not only as much institutional structure as the deliberative occasions with which the Old Oligarch aligns them, but also much the same structure.[33] And, like all festivals organized by the *dēmos*, they had social and political as well as religious significance: no decisions

[29] C. L. Barber, *Shakespeare's Festive Comedy* (Princeton, 1959) has most influenced classicists.
[30] Francis M. Cornford, *The Origin of Attic Comedy* (Cambridge, 1914; 2nd edn. 1934) first systematically made the case, but his understanding of ritual (*à la* the Cambridge School of Fraser and Harrison) as a static behaviour embedded in a society is no longer the understanding of cultural anthropologists, who see it as an integral and therefore flexible mode of all social organization, even if self-conscious rituals (notably religious ones) often refer to themselves as unchanging.
[31] Mikhail Bakhtin, *Rabelais and his World*, trans. H. Iswolsky (Cambridge, Mass., 1968), whose model is discussed above, made no special study of classical comedy but has had the greatest influence on classicists: see most recently J.-C. Carrière, *Le Carnaval et la politique* (Paris, 1979), whose summary of comedy as carnival appears on p. 32; cf. also pp. 41–50, 167–75, and W. Rösler, 'Bakhtin und die Karnevalskultur im antiken Griechenland', *QUCC* 23 (1986), 25–44.
[32] S. Halliwell, 'Aristophanic Satire', *Yearbook of English Studies*, 14 (1984), 6–20: 8.
[33] The role played by real carnival in political struggles (rebellions against dominant classes) depends on its autonomy and its separateness from official structures

were made about the city or its individual citizens, but the city and its citizens were the festival's theme and focus. Comic festivals were not 'carnival' but civic business—and big business.

Consider the Great Dionysia, into which the *dēmos* inserted the old *kōmōidia* (song of the *kōmos*) as a competition in 486 and where comedy had its unique home until 440, when it was admitted also to the Lenaea.[34] Like the Panathenaea, the Dionysia was a comparatively recent institution created and developed largely for civic and political ends. There were marches, parades, processions, sacrifices, ceremonies honouring benefactors both foreign and Athenian, diplomatic demonstrations like the renewal of the oath to abide by the Peace of Nicias (Th. 5. 23), recognition of the new (ephebic) warriors, including those war orphans who had been wards of the *dēmos*, the presentation of tribute in talents to the presiding (allotted) *archōn* by representatives of each 'ally'. All this was a display of the authority, the power, and the character of the *dēmos*, which was arrayed in the theatre exactly as it was on the Pnyx.

Then came the choral contests, paid for through liturgy (the Old Oligarch would say extortion) by rich competitors: dithyramb (involving 1,000 dancers, 50 men, and 50 boys from each tribe), comedy (120 dancers) and tragedy (36, later 45 dancers). Like the Panathenaea, the Greater Dionysia was exceptionally grand and costly, but we must view it against the background of a city that boasted of having more festivals than any other city (to say nothing of those at the deme-level)[35]–a phenomenon closely connected with

(though officials sometimes connive in it for their own purposes): a thorough case-study is supplied by B. Scribner, 'Reformation, Carnival, and the World Turned Upside-Down', *Social History* 3 (1978), 303–29.

[34] Athenian festivals, except perhaps for the central holy acts performed by priests or other hieratic personnel, were as dynamic and ever-changing as the society of which they were a part, not 'ritual' in the older sense of the word (n. 30 above), so that historians must read them not as fixed texts but as palimpsests-in-process. M. Ozuf, *Festivals and the French Revolution* (Cambridge, Mass., 1988), examines the processes by which festivals can be changed or created in response to political–ideological upheavals.

[35] 'The costs of cult—upkeep of temples and shrines, offering of regular sacrifices, celebration of recurrent festivals—surely represented, for any deme, the major object of regular expenditure'; David Whitehead, *The Demes of Attica* (Princeton, 1986), 163–4. For theatrical activity at the deme level, see P. Ghiron-Bistagne, *Recherches sur les acteurs dans la Grèce antique* (Paris, 1976), 86–97.

democracy by the Old Oligarch (1. 13, 3. 2, 8)—so that to exclude
them from the 'normal life of the city' is misleading. Festivals were
one of the chief ways in which the city organized itself, established
who was who, and demonstrated what was important. With this in
mind, let us examine the organization of the comic festival within
the larger framework of the Dionysia and its institutional relationship to the city (the *dēmos*).

The appropriate (allotted) *archōn* granted the poet a chorus and
authorized payment for actors, honoraria, and prizes.[36] One of the
citizens (about 1 per cent of the total number) rich enough to be,[37]
and therefore required[38] by the *dēmos* to be, *chorēgos* recruited and
paid for the lodging, training, and outfitting of the twenty-four
singer-dancers who would be his comic chorus as well as for all
other expenses required for the production and for the banquet
afterwards. The competition itself was governed by rules carefully
established by the *dēmos*. Following the festival, an assembly was
held to determine whether these rules had been scrupulously
followed and to hear complaints from anyone who thought they
had not been.[39] We know nothing specific about how these rules
controlled what was said and done on the comic stage. But there is
solid evidence that they did.

The Old Oligarch, at 2. 18, says that ridicule and criticism of the
dēmos was 'not tolerated' and in fact is not found in extant comedies: in *Knights* and *Wasps*, for example, Aristophanes blames the
dēmos only to exhort it to recapture the ideals and the glory which it
has lost by listening to false leaders like Cleon. What is more, the
personal experience of Aristophanes shows that comic poets were

[36] Plato says that each poet read specimens of his songs (*ōidai*) to the *archōn* (*Laws*
817d), but it is likely that patronage in the form of help from influential or experienced
friends also played a role: see S. Halliwell, 'Aristophanes' Apprenticeship', *CQ* 30
(1980), 33–45.
[37] Only some 400 of the 30,000 citizens could meet the three-talent qualification
(about 50 years' wages for a skilled craftsman): see J. K. Davies, *Athenian Propertied
Families 600–300 BC* (Oxford, 1975), pp. xxi–xxiv.
[38] That *chorēgiai* were required like any other liturgy is clear from the Old Oligarch,
who mentions *diadikasiai* over them, cf. Arist., *Ath.* 56. 3 (with Rhodes, *A Commentary
on the Aristotelian 'Athenaion Politeia'*), J. H. Lipsius, *Das attische Recht und Rechtsver-
fahren* (Leipzig, 1905–15), 590–9. No one was required to perform the same liturgy
twice in a lifetime, but one could volunteer: old-style politicians like Nicias made
voluntary liturgies a primary element of their political ascendancy (Plu., *Nic.* 3); the
speaker of Lysias 21 boasts of performing 8 *chorēgiai* in 9 years (1–5).
[39] See *DFA*² 64, 68–70.

not considered immune from *all* complaint by fellow citizens, as some critics in ancient and modern times have thought. He was sued by Cleon after his victory with *Babylonians* in 426 on the grounds that he had slandered the magistrates, councillors, and people in the presence of foreigners (scholiast on *Ach.* 378),[40] and again after his victory with *Knights*, on grounds unclear (*Wasps* 1284–91): recall the possible consequences to victors in political debate described by the Old Oligarch in 2. 17. It would seem that comic poets, like other office-holders, were accountable.

The victims of comic abuse (as opposed to the *dēmos*) were prominent competitors and were evidently expected to take it in good spirit (the spirit of the traditional *kōmos*-song), and in any event an appeal to the *dēmos* that one had been unfairly abused (as in the case of Socrates, which will be considered later) would amount to a claim of superiority and so would most likely earn only more ridicule. But there is no reason to think that comic poets were exempt from the laws about slander, and they may even have been controlled by special ones: Plutarch mentions a law of Thurioi (an Athenian colony and ally) restricting comic ridicule of citizens to 'adulterers and troublemakers (*polupragmones*)' (*Moralia* 519b).[41] There may well have been rules of this sort in fifth-century Athens. Their particulars can only be inferred as by the dog that didn't bark in the night: the absence of certain explicit charges or the avoidance of certain targets. They will turn out to be the same as for the orators. I notice, for example, that the wives and mothers of prominent men were, as in oratory, insulted and even portrayed

---

[40] Probably by *eisangelia*; see Alan H. Sommerstein, *Aristophanes' 'Acharnians'* (Warminster, 1980), 32–3 and, for Cleon's use of *eisangelia* in general, Ostwald, *From Popular Sovereignty to the Sovereignty of the Law*, 207–13. For the 'presence of foreigners', see *Ach.* 502–8. *Knights* 512–13 is evidence that in the period before 424 Aristophanes was known as the author of those plays produced by Callistratus: see Halliwell, 'Aristophanes' Apprenticeship', 35–6. With this episode compare the 1,000 drachma fine levied against the tragic poet Phrynichus in 493 for having in his (topical) *Capture of Miletos* 'reminded the Athenians of misfortunes close to home' (Hdt. 6. 21).

[41] If there was Thurian comedy in the 5th cent., was it one of those institutional exports by which Athens sought to encourage and safeguard democracy in allied cities? For some others, see J. P. Barron, 'Religious Propaganda of the Delian League', *JHS* 84 (1964), 35–48, Russell Meiggs, *The Athenian Empire* (Oxford, 1972), 295–8, J. Alty, 'Dorians and Ionians', *JHS* 102 (1982), 1–14, Edmunds, 'Aristophanic Cleon', 254–6.

on-stage, but their unmarried daughters were not.[42] In fact a
marriageable citizen-girl appears only once in extant fifth-century
comedy, in *Acharnians* (241–79), where *Dikaiopolis'* daughter is the
basket-carrier in his procession. To be chosen basket-carrier was in
real life a great distinction, and to be denied was a great humiliation
to the men of the family: this was the insult that got Hipparchus
assassinated in 514 (Th. 6. 56. 1).[43]

The rules could also be reformulated. The year 440/39, when the
Athenians went to war against their own ally Samos (Th. 1. 115–
17), saw the passage of a decree in some way limiting comic freedom
of criticism and lasting until 437/6 (scholiast on *Ach.* 67). And in
415/4, Syracosius[44] secured the passage of a decree prohibiting
reference by name in comedy to persons condemned for mutilating
the herms or celebrating mock Mysteries (*Birds* 1297 with scholiast;
cf. Phryn., fr. 26). The reality of this decree has been doubted, but
nothing else explains why not one of the some sixty-five persons
known to have been condemned is mentioned by name in the some
4,550 surviving lines of comedy from the period 415–411 (when
Alcibiades' condemnation was repealed: Th. 8. 97. 3), although
many others are.[45] Evidently the decree was part of a general
damnatio memoriae against Alcibiades and the others, comedy being
a civic occasion when they might be mentioned in memorable
fashion.[46] It was possible also to change state-authorized allowances
to the poets, even if the reason might not have been the one given
by the chorus of *Frogs*, who would ban from the festival such

[42] The protocol of not naming respectable women in comedy was the same as in
oratory: D. Schaps, 'The Woman Least Mentioned: Etiquette and Women's Names'.
CQ 27 (1977), 323–30, Alan H. Sommerstein, 'The Naming of Women in Greek and
Roman Comedy', *Quaderni di storia* 11 (1980), 393–418. Curiously, no comic poet seems
to have subjected Cleon's wife or mother to the abuse freely heaped on those of other
'demagogues' (lechery, foreign birth, selling in the markets, membership in strange
cults, etc.).

[43] Note that in *Lysistrata* the maidens are the only class and age-group of citizen-
females who do not appear on stage.

[44] Evidently a politician in the mould of Cleon: Eup., fr. 220, compares him to
'watchdogs running on the walls' because when speaking on the platform he 'runs
around and barks'.

[45] See Alan H. Sommerstein, 'The Decree of Syrakosios', *CQ* 36 (1986), 101–8. The
short life and apparent infrequency of such decrees indicate the people's liking for
comic attack.

[46] Perhaps even in a not unsympathetic fashion: two of the men condemned,
Archippus and Aristomenes (And. 1. 12–13), may have been the comic poets: see
Douglas M. MacDowell, *On the Mysteries* (Oxford, 1961), app. N.

'uninitiated and unhealthy' people[47] as 'the person who as speaker proceeds to nibble away the rewards of poets because he was ridiculed (*kōmōidōtheis*) in the ancestral festivals of Dionysos' (367–8).

Victory for poets was primarily for artistic achievement, whose importance is amply elucidated in Aristophanes' plays (particularly in the parabases), as is the bitterness of a defeat like the one in 423 when he 'retired, defeated undeservedly by crass men' (*Clouds* 518–62). There was also the kind of social celebrity that 'stars' enjoy in all ages: see *Wasps* 1023–8.[48] And there might be political consequences as well: not only lawsuits like the ones brought by Cleon but also special honours like the 'crown of sacred olive, reckoned equal in honour to a golden crown' which the *dēmos* bestowed on Aristophanes for the splendid advice he had offered in *Frogs*,[49] which was given an unprecedented second performance.[50] These honours recognized the advice given in the parabasis, in particular lines 686–705, which recommended the restoration of the rights of disfranchised citizens. The decree and second performance were voted either in connection with the decision of the *dēmos* to follow that advice, in late 405 by the decree of Patroclides,[51] or (less likely) after the democratic restoration and general amnesty of 403, when sacred olive-crowns were also decreed for the defenders of Phyle against the Thirty (Aischines, 3. 187).[52]

The Old Oligarch seems to be so far justified in speaking of the comic festival as an institution of the *dēmos*, as part of that mosaic of occasions when competitive appeals were made and whose common denominator was the sovereignty of the *dēmos* over all individuals, however distinguished. From what social class did the comic poets come? Were they, like the politicians and *chorēgoi*, wealthy and (until Cleon) well-bred? The evidence is very scanty but inclines me to say yes. One had, I think, to be well-bred to have a career as a

---

[47] The 'demagogues' Agyrrhius and Archinus: see Rhodes, *Commentary*, on Arist., *Ath.* 34. 3, 41. 3.

[48] I see no reason to read this passage as empty conceit: a young poet with at least three victories behind him will surely have attracted the admiring glances of at least some boys at the palaestra. Plato remarks (*Laws* 658d2) that 'the older boys' especially enjoyed comedy.   [49] Ar., *Life* 35–6, PCG 3², pp. 2–3.

[50] Dichaearchus, quoted in Hypothesis 1 of *Frogs*.

[51] And. 1. 73–80; X. *HG* 2. 2. 11.

[52] See J. T. Allen, *California Publications in Classical Philology*, 11 (1930–3), 143–51: but advice to entrust the polis to *chrēstoi* and *kaloi kagathoi* would have been more appealing before the regime of the Thirty than after the democratic restoration.

dramatic poet: this was no job for 'the demotic'. Nor for the poor: when we do have information, as for Aeschylus, Sophocles, and Euripides,[53] we find that the poets were also from well-to-do families. The social personality of Old Comedy (surely not mere affectation) suggests that what was true of tragedians was true of their comic counterparts.

Aristophanes, like Cleon from the urban deme Kydathenaion, apparently came from a cultivated family. Plato in the *Symposium* portrays him as a lover of good living, if not the sturdiest of drinkers (176b–c, 185c), on friendly terms with the other guests, the élite of social and intellectual Athens, and as a man of old-fashioned ethical values (190b–d, 193a–d). In *Acharnians* (6–8, 299–302) and *Knights*, he aligns himself with the upper-class cavalry corps, one of whom was Simon (*Knights* 242, 351), the fellow demesman who wrote a treatise on horsemanship and dedicated a bronze statue of a horse at the Eleusinion (X., *De re equestri* 1. 1), and another of whom (243) was probably the Panaitios later condemned in the scandal of the Mysteries (And. 1. 13, 52, 67).[54] Simon was also the priest of a *thiasos* of Heracles, among whose sixteen members (all of Kydathenaion) were Philonides, the producer of *Wasps*, *Proagōn*, *Amphiaraos*, and *Frogs*, and one Amphitheus, whose name occurs nowhere else in Attica except as the friend of Dikaiopolis, who fetches the Treaties in *Acharnians* (45–203).[55] Early in the fourth century Aristophanes served as Councillor[56] and two of his sons also became comic poets.[57] I see no reason to doubt that Aristophanes' rivals, whose

[53] Aristophanes, who thought that Euripides' plays appealed to the lowest common denominator, invented a suitably squalid background for the poet himself, insisting that his mother was a vegetable-seller, but she was in reality of high birth (Philochorus, *FGrH* 328F218); cf. Carter, *The Quiet Athenian*, 150.

[54] See Sommerstein, 'The Decree of Syrakosios', 104 n. 26.

[55] For the *thiasos* (*IGII*² 2343) see S. Dow, 'Some Athenians in Aristophanes', *AJA* 73 (1969), 234–5; Thomas Gelzer, 'Aristophanes der Komiker', *RE*, supp. 12 (1971), 1398. 14 ff.; D. Welsh, '*IG* II² 2343, Philonides, and Aristophanes' *Banqueters*', *CQ* 33 (1983), 51–5; and H. Lind, 'Neues aus Kydathen', *MH* 42 (1985), 249–61. For its possible location see P. Stauropoullos, '*Chronika Athenai, Attike*', *Arkhaiologikon Deltion*, 20 (1965), 52–5 with pl. 41b. Such cults were fraternal organizations that would appeal to the upper classes: S. Woodford, 'Cults of Heracles in Attica', in *Studies Presented to G. M. A. Hanfmann* (Mainz, 1971), 211–25; D. 57. 46, where the speaker lists among his credentials that he 'was selected by my fellow-demesmen among the highest-born to cast lots for the priesthood of Herakles'. Why Aristophanes was not a member is unclear.

[56] *IG* II² 1740. 21–4.   [57] Ar., testimonia 7–8, *PCG*.

tendencies appear to be the same, also came from the same kind of background.

It would seem that the advent of the new style of appeal introduced by Cleon to political contests was not paralleled at the comic festivals. Although Aristophanes thought that there were 'new' (demagogic) tragic poets (principally Euripides and Agathon) who were ruining the tragic festivals as surely as Cleon and Socrates were ruining the city, there seem to have been no 'new' comic poets. The comic poets who did compose in the period after 429 poured scorn on the new style and, in their way, sided with those who held to the old. To understand comedy's contribution to this struggle we must take up the Old Oligarch's description of its function: that ridicule and criticism of individuals which pleased the *dēmos* and confirmed its sovereignty.

3. RIDICULE

Comedy had no uniform style in the fifth century. Not all comedies took direct notice of contemporary public affairs. There were mythological burlesques like the *Odyssēs* of Cratinus,[58] and there were domestic comedies that foreshadowed the Hellenistic style, the speciality first of Crates,[59] later of Pherecrates.[60] These to some degree overlapped with tragedy and satyr-drama. There were two specialities of fifth-century comedy, however, that were distinctive and closely related: the offering of useful advice and criticism about

[58] See Platon. *Diff. Com.*, PCG 4 (192), who notes that there were very many plays of this type; the statement that they had no *chorika* or parabases means that they had no abusive songs or partisan–topical tendencies. Eight of the titles of Aristophanes' plays suggest mythological burlesque, all apparently produced after 415. Note, however, that figures from mythology might 'stand for' contemporaries, as is alleged of Cratinus' *Dionysalexandros* in an ancient hypothesis (*POxy*, PCG 4 (140), lines 44–8): 'Perikles is very clearly ridiculed by innuendo (*emphasis*) for having brought the war on the Athenians.' In the same year (430), Hermippos' *Moirai* seems to have assimilated the 'king of the satyrs' to Pericles. We must keep open the possibility that political innuendo was often (perhaps always) a feature of mythological burlesque. Those who see topical allusion in tragic myths claim a similar kind of *emphasis*.

[59] Arist., *Po.* 1449^{b}7–9, Ar., *Knights* 537–40. It may be significant that he won three times at the Greater Dionysia (*IG* ii² 2325. 52) but never at the Lenaea.

[60] Platon. *Diff. Com.* Arist., *Po.* 1449^b, says that this style was first developed in Sicilian comedy.

important issues of the day, and the ridicule of individuals.[61] How common comedies in this style were will probably never be known. But these were the specialities that most impressed contemporaries and posterity and that account for the canonical status and favoured transmission of Cratinus, said to have pioneered the 'political' type of comedy,[62] and his successors Eupolis and Aristophanes. Let us look first at ridicule, since an understanding of its functions is the key to the useful advice.

There are several varieties of ridicule in the comedies,[63] occurring both in choral songs, which carry on the traditions of the *kōmos*, and in the speeches and conversations of characters, which carry on the traditions of *iambos*.[64] The ridicule in comedy, however, differs from that of *kōmos* and *iambos* in significant ways.

Public ridicule of individuals, in the form of shouted jests and more or less formal lampoons, was a venerable tradition of many festive occasions (particularly those honouring Dionysus and Demeter), and continues as a feature of carnivalesque practices everywhere.[65] Old Comedy includes this tradition both in the agonistic epirrhematic choral complex and also in the type of choral song that often articulates episodes after the parabasis and consists of free-form mockery of particular spectators.[66] In its agonistic role the comic chorus, like a group of *komasts*, entertains the community by abusing its own enemies (e.g. 'Knights' versus Cleon). We might compare the masked men who mocked prominent initiates in

[61] The latter never occurs in tragedy or satyr-drama, the former only obliquely, through the veil of plots drawn from heroic legend, set in the distant past and usually in remote places, and peopled by characters whose names were not by and large borne by the Athenians (in contrast with modern Greeks). For the polarity of dramatic genres as an aspect of their development in the 5th cent., see O. Taplin, 'Fifth-Century Tragedy and Comedy: A Synkrisis', *JHS* 106 (1986), 163–74.

[62] See Cratinus, testimonia 17–19, Kassel–Austin. Cratinus anticipates Aristophanes in assimilating comic victory to political victory, fr. 52 (*Dionysoi*): 'let the victory go to him who gives the best advice to this city'; cf. *Frogs* 686, 1420.

[63] For overviews, see Wilhelm Schmid, *Geschichte der griechischen Literatur*, part 1, vol. iv (Munich, 1946), 13–26; Ralph Rosen, *Old Comedy and the Iambographic Tradition* (Atlanta, 1988).

[64] Both *kōmos* as a festive form and *iambos* as a poetic form flourished in the classical period alongside comedy.

[65] See the excellent overview in P. Burke, *Popular Culture in Early Modern Europe* (New York, 1978), 178–204.

[66] That the mockery was expected at this point in a comedy is indicated by *Lysistrata* 1043–9, where the newly united chorus announces its intention to eschew it. The context of one example, *Frogs* 416–30, clearly reveals the traditional derivation.

the procession to Eleusis and the groups who abused one another at women's festivals.[67] A special feature of the agonistic chorus is the prominence of its leader who, in a parabasis-speech, often represents the poet, abusing his own enemies and admonishing the spectators. Later in the play, however, the chorus drops the special identity it had during its involvement in the plot and becomes mere onlookers, like the spectators. Here the comic chorus differs from a *kōmos* in representing the celebrating community as a whole.

Insulting allusion to spectators in the conversation of characters reproduces as a public entertainment 'the wit and abuse of ordinary conversation; and its range of tone is therefore ribald, spiteful and irreverent'.[68] In comic reproduction of personal enmities we see a continuation of the ancient *iambos* in dramatic form.[69] But comedy differs from *iambos* in that the characters often reproduce the arguments and invective of political dispute as well, and in highly partisan fashion. In such cases the enemies of sympathetic characters are portrayed also as enemies of the city.

In traditional, face-to-face communities such ridicule reflects, circulates, comments about, enshrines, puts a kind of imprimatur on, what is widely thought, discussed, or enjoyed privately but has no other public outlet. Often the victim's notoriety is based on an incident simply too amusing to forget and so becomes part of community myth, like Hegelochus' error of pronunciation which spoiled a performance of Euripides' *Orestes*.[70] And often the victim is cast in the role of scapegoat, like Cleonymus, who (uniquely) was repeatedly mocked for having thrown away his shield, apparently in the Athenian retreat at Delion, where 'the army was put to flight, and he ran with the rest: it was his bad luck that his fatness made him conspicuous'.[71] But, we may add, it was also the good luck of the others to find a publicly acceptable scapegoat. The comic poets in this case did what modern political leaders call 'containing the damage': Cleonymus lost his respect as a warrior so that the

[67] See Walter Burkert, *Greek Religion*, trans. J. Raffan (Cambridge, Mass., 1985) 244, 287. Good Aristophanic examples are, respectively, the Initiate Chorus of *Frogs* and the hostile semichoruses of *Lysistrata*.   [68] Halliwell, 'Aristophanic Satire', 14.

[69] See Arist., *Po.* 1448^{b}25, 1449^{b}8; *EN* 1128^{a}22.

[70] Cf. *Frogs* 302–4, Sannyrion, fr. 8. The scholiast on E., *Or.* 279 tells us that many comic poets mocked Hegelochus for this.

[71] Sommerstein, 'The Decree of Syrakosios', 104, who compares Demosthenes' flight from Chaeronea, for which he was never prosecuted, even though Aeschines, in his speech *Against Ktesiphon* (3), repeatedly brings it up against him.

Athenians could keep theirs. And he was lucky too: knowing what his defence would be, no one cared to prosecute him.

But more often the ridicule uses complaints about disruptive but otherwise unpunishable behaviour (that is, gossip and malice) as a form of social control: the community emphasizes its norms and discourages their violation, and by doing so as a festive entertainment allows for the release of pent-up tensions before they can become dangerous.[72] Festive ridicule, in punishing misbehaviour not, or not yet, in the community's power to punish by force (as in court), thus lies somewhere between doing something about misbehaviour and doing nothing about it. Ridicule as a mode and festival as a venue exemplify the characteristic mediating power of humour. In the *Frogs* song (416–30), for example, Callias Hipponikou becomes Callias Hippobinou ('Super Fucker'), who fights his battles in bed (428–30). Callias was a very rich man who avoided political commitments and spent his money on his own pleasures instead.[73] Here Aristophanes voices the spectators' resentment of this kind of selfishness at a time when the city is fighting for its survival. The spectators feel that something has been done about Callias, even if nothing has been changed, and hope that people like Callias, present and future, will take a lesson, even if they can choose not to. Part of a successful comic poet's business was to keep his eyes and ears open during the year for just this sort of misbehaviour: the audience expected him to make comedy of it.[74]

Comic ridicule differs from that of *kōmos* and *iambos* by being part of a national festival whose celebrants were the entire city, of which the *dēmos* was in charge: the comic troupe ridicules its enemies in the interests of the *dēmos*. In this respect *kōmos* and *iambos* are to comedy as neighbourhood graffiti are to nationally syndicated political cartoons. But the social mechanism is the same: ridicule is a kind of kangaroo court. In a democracy, the rule of law, not

[72] See Scribner, 'Reformation, Carnival, and the World Turned Upside-Down', 319–22,

[73] Eupolis' *Flatterers*, victorious at the Great Dionysia in 421, ridiculed Callias and his circle; the fragments (156–90) are instructive.

[74] At *Knights* 525, Aristophanes says that Magnes was 'driven from' the competitions because his power of mockery (*skōptein*) failed him. 'A man who was not himself a comic dramatist might use comedy to injure or blackmail another by asking for the help of, or retailing scandal to, a dramatist friend, much as he might today enlist the help of a gossip columnist or a satirical magazine'; Alan H. Sommerstein, *Aristophanes' 'Wasps'* (Warminster, 1983) on lines 1025–6.

men, prevails. If *A* benefits at *B*'s expense, his behaviour, however shameless, is permissible unless legally actionable, and *B*'s only recourse is by appeal to 'those unwritten laws which it is an acknowledged shame to break'.[75] The contest of Logoi in *Clouds* is instructive here: Worse Logos appeals to a legalistic concept of *nomos* (do it if you can get away with it), Better Logos to the imperatives of custom (self-restraint enforced by shame). Thus comedy generally chose as a victim a person who was, or who could be, popularly suspected of getting away with something at the expense of the *dēmos* or its benefactors, and who is made an example of widespread misbehaviour, like Callias (the selfish rich) or Cleon (dishonest leaders) or sycophants (predatory troublemakers).

Comedy is therefore good evidence about the attitudes of the *dēmos* (what they collectively disapproved of, what they thought laughable and mockable) and the communal problems they thought, or might be made to think, were widespread and important. It is also good evidence for the strength of democratic principles in fifth-century Athens: lawcourts and assemblies were not the only officially established restraint on misbehaviour. In any society, the more repressive the government, the narrower the scope of satirical humour.[76]

Much, perhaps most, comic ridicule (*kōmōidein*) has no other apparent motivation than jesting: it is not formulated in terms of a charge (as the orators would say, it is *exō tou pragmatos*), or it is an offhand remark (*parapsogos*), or it refers to personal failings or misbehaviour that most people are already talking about, or it simply mimics the abuse that some spectators had actually invented themselves (as in the case of the comic Cleon). Thus even the portrayal of Cleonymus as a shield-thrower, an actionable slander, is a jest, not (serious) abuse. In *Laws*, Plato notes this characteristic of comic ridicule but also observes that it was a common trick of disputants to pretend that their slanders were jests (935c–d). Thus the speaker of Lysias, fragment 5. 3, Thalheim:

---

[75] Pericles in his Funeral Oration (Th. 2. 37), that occasion when one lists civic virtues that need constant emphasis.

[76] Even outside the former Soviet Union and Communist China political satire can be dangerous. In April 1988 one of the best-known and most outspoken satirists in Mexico, Hector Felix Miranda ('The Cat'), was assassinated in Tijuana: the latest of some two dozen assassinations of journalists critical of the government since 1972. None of the assassins has been charged by the police.

'Isn't this Kinesias the offender against the gods in ways you hear
about every year from the producers of comedy but which it is
shameful for other people even to mention?' The orators often
accused their opponents of using ridicule when their material
claims were weak: thus Plato's Socrates when he stressed comic
diabolē (unfounded accusation),[77] and the speaker of Lysias 24. 18:
'My accuser is not being serious but playful, his purpose not
persuasion but ridicule (*kōmōidein*), as if making some fine joke.'

Among the honour-sensitive Athenians, however, the distinction
between abuse and jesting often called for nice judgement, and it
became a topic of concern for ethicists. When Aristotle says that
'the law forbids serious abuse (*loidorein*) of some things and perhaps
should have forbidden jocular abuse (*skōptein*) as well' (EN 1128^{a}19),
he is talking about the trouble that can arise when a jester goes too
far or his butt is over-sensitive. One man's joke is another man's
slander, depending on the skill of the jester and the butt's reaction.
Comic poets, like orators, had to be able to sail very close to the
wind. Ridicule by definition covers areas beyond the reach of
actionable claims, where votes can be taken, but the victim was
the one who decided to cry foul. Thus Cleon's suit against Aristophanes for slander (whether to defend himself or the city) may
indicate either that Aristophanes' abuse was seriously intended or
that Cleon was over-sensitive to jesting.[78]

The laws about slander (defined very loosely by a variety of
terms)[79] provided redress for abuse whose untruthfulness could be
proved to a jury (the *dēmos*). Solon's laws forbade slander of the
dead, or slander of the living in temples, in lawcourts, in places of
official business, or at festive competitions.[80] Individuals could sue
not only as private citizens but also as allotted (D., 21. 32) or elected
(Lys., 9. 5–6) office-holders. Although the speaker of Lysias 10. 6ff.

[77] *Ap.* 18b–d, 19b–c, 23c–d, at the same time distracting attention from the more
serious charge that many of his close associates had in fact harmed the democracy
(Aeschines 1. 173).

[78] In a recent case, televangelist Jerry Falwell was caricatured in the pornographic
magazine *Hustler* as having lost his virginity with his mother in an outhouse. *Hustler*
publisher Larry Flynt publicly acknowledged malicious intent: 'He's just a big wind-
bag. He's right in there with . . . all the rest of them, and the sooner they're exposed,
the better off it will be for everybody.' For the Supreme Court decision in Falwell's libel
suit, see n. 86 below.

[79] To those used by Plato, *Laws*, add *kakōs legein, kakōs agoreuein, hybrizein*. For the
laws about slander, see Lipsius, *Das attische Recht*, 646–54.

[80] Plu., *Sol.* 21. 1–2; c. Pl., *Laws* 935b.

mentions such specifically forbidden charges (*aporrhēta*) as murder, father- or mother-beating, and shield-throwing, it is clear that any accusation of wrongdoing (*rhēta kai arrhēta*, D., 21. 79) could be called slander if the accused wanted to press the issue, just as any accusation could be passed off as empty ridicule if the victim did not want to press it. A determination of slander was left to individuals and their potential juries (what in Athens amounted to public opinion).

We observed above that comic poets seem to avoid the same 'forbidden' targets as the orators, so that they had the avoidance of actionable slander in mind when they resorted to abuse. To the example of maiden daughters we may add the avoidance of actually naming a target (*onomasti kōmōidein*), however obvious the identity. Thus Cleon is 'the Paphlagonian' and Nicias and Demosthenes are home-bred slaves throughout *Knights*, and an obvious allusion to Alcibiades' arrest in *Birds* (145–7) does not name him, in accordance with the Decree of Syrakosios. Similarly, Aristophanes apologizes for not using a portrait-mask for Cleon: surely not (as he says) because it was the mask-makers who were afraid (*Knights* 230–2). Further investigation of the areas of inhibition common to comic poets and other public speakers would yield interesting information about social and political restraints in classical Athens.

According to etiquette, it was base to abuse gratuitously, by starting a fight[81] (like Thersites), but honourable when wronged (like Achilles), illegal to abuse falsely but legal when exposing true misbehaviour.[82] Thus the speaker of Lysias 10. 3, 'I consider it mean and very litigious to go to law for slander (*kakēgoria*). But in the present case I feel it would be shameful—since it concerns my father, who has deserved so much both of you and of the city—not to take vengeance on the man who said this.' The comic poets told the *dēmos* that speakers, demagogues, and sycophants were ones who use abuse to pick fights for selfish reasons and who abuse falsely (*diabolē/diabellein* is thematic for Cleon in *Knights*); speakers,

---

[81] *loidorias archein*, Pl., *Laws* 935c3.

[82] It has often been observed that Thersites and Achilles blame Agamemnon on the same grounds. For the ethical norm, cf. Hes., *Op.* 708–11, 'Do not wrong a friend first, nor lie about him to please the tongue, but if he wrongs you first, either by making a malicious statement or by deed, remember to repay him double'; cf. Democritus, *FVS* 68B192, 'It is easy to praise and blame (*psegein*) inappropriately, either one being the mark of a bad character (*ponērou ēthous*)'; Hippias, *FVS* 86B17, 'unfounded accusation (*diabolē*) is a dangerous technique'.

demagogues, and sycophants portrayed themselves as 'watchdogs of the *dēmos*' who exposed anti-democratic misbehaviour in no uncertain terms. For the new politicians and the comic poets, abuse was a persuasive strategy in appeals to the *dēmos*.

The comic claim to be both humorous and serious, and the Old Oligarch's statement that comic poets attacked both by ridicule (*kōmōidein*) and by abuse (*kakōs legein*), now seems to make better sense. Not all comic attacks were made in ridicule, as defined above: in the passage from *Laws* cited there, Plato also mentions seriously motivated comic abuse.[83]

Aristophanes' abuse of Cleon, for example, is explicitly identified and formally motivated as serious: Cleon started it by abusing Aristophanes unjustly (*Ach.* 377–82), so that the poet is justified in defending himself (630–64) and in launching a counter-attack in next year's comedy on behalf of his friends the Knights, who have also been victimized (299–302). To this personal motivation Aristophanes adds good citizenship: he 'dares to say what is just, and nobly steps forth to confront the typhoon and the whirlwind [Cleon]' (*Knights* 510–11), for 'there is nothing invidious about abusing bad men, but it is an honour to good men for those who reckon well' (1274–75). In attacking Cleon, Aristophanes appeals both to personal enmity (like iambic poets) and to the interests of the city (like speakers in assembly and court), and he uses abuse to characterize his opponent as a bad citizen, so enhancing the credibility of his claims. When viewed in this light, Cleon's subsequent lawsuit—no doubt another *graphē*—looks like a serious response to serious abuse rather than merely an over-sensitive reaction to harmless ridicule.

The comic attack on Socrates in *Clouds* is another example of extensive and explicitly motivated abuse, though here the element of personal enmity was not (explicitly at least) a factor. Aristophanes sought an individual who could exemplify the kind of misbehaviour popularly associated with the 'new learning'—so popular with the young 'speakers'—and picked Socrates. The fact that a real person was thus turned into an exaggerated stereotype for the purposes of ridicule does not mean that the ridicule was mere jesting and

---

[83] 'No comic or iambic or melodic poet will be allowed to ridicule (*kōmōidein*) any citizen in any way either by word or gesture (*eikoni*), either with or without anger', 935e.

without effect. The stereotype embodied real social hostility and Socrates seemed to fit it. Nor were the charges ridiculous: other intellectuals of the day had been tried on the catch-all charge of 'impiety' (*asebeia*).[84] Indeed, the charges were not forgotten twenty-four years later: Plato tells us the *Clouds* helped to circulate and fix in the popular mind a prejudice against Socrates that contributed to his condemnation.[85] This prejudice, created by skilful ridicule, could not be argued away, because one cannot disprove ridicule. If people—in this case the jury—believed it, it was true, and one only compounded his difficulties by accusing people of wrong beliefs. Unfair, maybe. But it is the fate of prominent people to life, or die, by their public images.[86]

The precise effects of comic ridicule and comic abuse are impossible to gauge. But surely no prominent Athenian imagined that the laughter of the *dēmos* at his expense could possibly do him any good, and the better the joke the less comfortable he would be thereafter. For this very reason the *dēmos* institutionalized the comic competitions. In return for accepting the guidance of the 'rich, the well-born, and the powerful' it provided that they be subjected to a yearly unofficial review of their conduct in general at the hands of the *dēmos'* organic intellectuals and critics, the comic poets. Like Socrates' pupil Plato, or like Cleon the aspiring demagogue, the victims did not like this institution. For the former it epitomized the low prejudices and invidious character of the *dēmos*; for the latter it was an unwelcome reminder that what the *dēmos* gave the *dēmos* could take away. For all public competitors it meant potential

---

[84] For these trials see Ostwald, *From Popular Sovereignty to the Sovereignty of Law*, 528–36.

[85] Cf. n. 77 above. Osborne, 'Law in Action in Classical Athens', 51 shows that in *graphai* where there was no injured party, like those brought by Meletus, Anytus, and Lycon against Socrates and threatened by Andocides against Archippus, the action usually was more political than legal in its motivation.

[86] In the libel case *Hustler* v. *Falwell* (n. 78 above), the Supreme Court ruled that even outrageous satire of public figures is protected by the free-speech provisions of the First Amendment: 'The appeal of political cartoon or caricature is often based on exploration of unfortunate physical traits or politically embarrassing events—an exploration often calculated to injure the feelings of the subject . . . [but] our political discourse would have been poorer without them. . . . Outrageousness in the area of political and social discourse has an inherent subjectiveness about it which would allow a jury to impose liability on the basis of jurors' tastes or views, or perhaps on their dislike of a particular expression. . . . We doubt that there is any standard that would separate sharp satire from defamatory attack' (US Supreme Court, 86–1278).

deflation. But compared with the other institutions the *dēmos* could bring to bear against them, comedy must have seemed no worse than fair warning.

4. THE COMIC APPEAL

For the Old Oligarch, who was showing how the *dēmos* kept 'the best' on a short leash, ridicule was the distinctive feature of comedy. So also for the anti-demotic critic-philosophers of the fourth century. It is true that comedy mentions or portrays living individuals only for ridicule, never for praise,[87] and that the prominent and would-be prominent, not, as we will presently see, the *dēmos*, were its victims. But these critics fail to mention the positive tendencies of comedy, its heroes and its advice to the *dēmos*, for an obvious reason. The comic poets claim that their ridicule exposes people to whom the *dēmos* has granted success but who are in fact wrongdoers, and through the chorus-leader or a sympathetic character they offer alternative choices. But the denunciation of those responsible for the *dēmos*' unsatisfactory status quo and a demonstration of how to make it satisfactory was the appeal of all who competed for victory in the fifth century, including comic poets. What was distinctive about the comic appeal?

The world depicted in political comedy was the world of the spectators in their civic roles. We see the *dēmos* in its various capacities; we see the competitors for its favour; we listen to formal debate on current issues, including its characteristic invective; we get a decision, complete with a winner and a loser; we see the outcome of that decision. But there is something strange about the depiction, like seeing yourself in a fun-house mirror. Everything is grotesquely exaggerated and caricatured, the image is all backwards and seems to reflect things that aren't there and omit things that are. But you must admit that your presence in front of the

[87] Praise is actively avoided: Nicias is ridiculed for losing out to Cleon in *Knights* but is not mentioned at all in *Peace*, a play celebrating the treaty which he engineered and which Aristophanes had repeatedly urged. Sometimes individuals are mentioned as victims of 'bad men' or (what amounts to the same thing) unwise decisions by the *dēmos*: Nicias is pitied for being the constant target of malicious prosecutors (Teleci., fr. 41, Eup., fr. 193), and in *Knights* Archeptolemus (*PA* 2384), who had unsuccessfully opposed Cleon over policy toward the allies (327) and Spartan peace proposals (794–6), is mentioned sympathetically.

mirror is the cause of the image in it. How does the reflection we see on the comic stage differ from what it reflects?

The villains and their dupes are recognizable enough, despite the distortion: they are identifiable among the spectators and most often have their actual names. The *dēmos* is recognizable too: the chorus usually represents some subset thereof,[88] its members sometimes having real names, and at a certain point its identity becomes continuous with that of the spectators collectively.[89] But the villains and their dupes are not the people whom the *dēmos* has in fact recently voted against but the ones they voted *for*, not the social failures but the successful. And the *dēmos* is not the all-sovereign *dēmos* that chooses as leaders those best able to serve its interests, but a poor mob whose role models and heroes are bad people and which is eager to carry out the policies of self-serving con men to its own disadvantage. The more we enjoy this debunking of our leaders—which draws on their acknowledged shortcomings, evokes our own worst suspicions, and plays on the anti-authoritarian invidiousness that festivals only intensify—the more persuasive our own negative caricature becomes. The reaction of the spectators was as the Old Oligarch describes: 'When the *dēmos* makes policy it can blame the individual who made the proposal or took the vote and everyone else can protest, I was not there and don't like it either!—even when one knows the Assembly had been fully attended' (2. 17). The comic poets encouraged this feeling. The first message was, You are unhappy because you (and your neighbours) have made a big mistake!

But there, on-stage, is a rather likeable person. Not an actual person, and in fact not the sort of person who would be prominent at all: a farmer, a seller from the markets, the debt-ridden victim of a socialite wife and a social-climbing son, a juror, the target of too many lawsuits who has decided to try his luck elsewhere, a

[88] Choruses can change their identity, most spectacularly in *Peace*, where they are all Greeks, then Greek farmers, then Athenian farmers, then the generic comic chorus.

[89] As it is theatrically throughout: 'The world of Old Comedy was fundamentally a choral space, in which the twenty-four amateurs of the chorus, trained in song and dance by the poet, functioned as both center and bridge, the heart of the performance and a mediation between the whole city, present as audience, and the by now professionalized actors on the stage'; N. W. Slater, 'Transformations of Space in New Comedy', in *Themes in Drama*, ix: *The Theatrical Space* (Cambridge, 1987), 2.

housewife.[90] This person is in the same fix as most of us and it is
pleasant to see someone like that in the spotlight for once. It is even
more pleasant to see that this person gets what all of us would like
to have: a chance to eliminate, painlessly and with impunity, those
forces, human, natural, or divine, which are arguably responsible
for our unhappiness and discomfort. Or even to have all the food,
wine, luxury, power, sexual partners, and admiration we want, and
at the expense only of bad people! This person says that it is in our
power, as members of the *dēmos*, to have these things, if only we did
not keep forgetting them, if only we did not submit to people who
keep the good things for themselves while we do all the work. In the
play everything turns out happily: the people who are like us win
out, the bad ones who were so arrogant are gone. Life resembles the
festival. The second message was: Now that you see your mistake,
give me the prize and remember what you have learned!

This was the city of political comedy, where the *dēmos'* ideal goals
could be achieved as they could not be, or not yet be, in the
Assembly; where the distance between ideal norms of civic behaviour and the actual performance of civic authorities was exposed
and punished as it could not be, or not yet be, in court; where the
difference between collective sovereignty and individual subordination was eliminated. At the comedies the members of the *dēmos*
enjoyed a picture of their imperial democracy in which the intract-
able problems of communal life and the frustrating requirements of
political compromise were magically, but at the same time plausibly,
resolved.

It is this idealistic transformation of the *dēmos* from unhappy and
misguided to happy and united that vindicates its initial caricature
and justifies the Old Oligarch's statement that comic poets did not
ridicule and abuse the *dēmos*. *Knights*, which contains the most
thoroughgoing criticisms of the *dēmos*, also contains the most
glorious picture of it in the transformation of Old Master Demos

[90] The women who appear in plays after 411 either obstruct the *dēmos* (*Ly.*, *Th.*) or
usurp its corporate structures (*Ec.*) from positions outside the world of the *dēmos*.
Among other uses, they were a way to criticize the behaviour of citizens without
attributing the critical voices to a male character. The chief difference between a
Lysistrata and a Dikaiopolis is that the latter's real-life counterparts could, like him,
address the assembly (*Ach.*, prologue), whereas the former's could not. But in all three
'women's' plays the motive complaints ring true to life.

with which the play ends.[91] And even the criticisms Aristophanes does level at the *dēmos* concern only the personal shortcomings and political style of its leaders, or the folly of individual decisions, both of which are shown being amended in the course of a play: *Knights* 1356–7 (to Old Master Demos), 'Don't worry, you're not to blame: it was those who deceived you.' Similarly *Frogs* 1454–7: the *dēmos* hates bad men and uses them only because it has no choice. He never attacks the constitutional structure of the democracy or questions the inherent rightness of the *dēmos'* rule.[92] This was after all an inheritance from the sacrosanct dead and therefore immune from comic or any other public criticism. When he insults and upbraids the *dēmos* for choosing bad leaders or making bad decisions he does what all poets and public speakers had a traditional right to do,[93] just as all public competitors had a right to ridicule political opponents and abuse personal enemies. Aristophanes' criticisms of the *dēmos* are in fact, like those of the orators, praise by exhortation (cf. Pericles at Th. 2. 65): the *dēmos* may be deceived but it is not, like its leaders, base in character. Comedy uses the language of democracy to attack the leaders whom the *dēmos* chose. Contrast the Old Oligarch, who is hostile to the *dēmos* and considers it just as base as its leaders.[94]

[91] See H. Kleinknecht, 'Die Epiphanie des Demos in Aristophanes' Rittern'. *Hermes*, 77 (1939), 58–65; repr. in H.-J. Newiger (ed.), *Aristophanes und die alte Komödie* (Darmstadt, 1975); Edmunds, 'Aristophanic Cleon', 256–62.

[92] See Kenneth J. Dover, *Aristophanic Comedy* (Berkeley and Los Angeles, 1972), 33–4.

[93] On this 'didactic tradition', see K. J. Dover, *Greek Popular Morality in the Time of Plato and Aristotle* (Berkeley and Los Angeles, 1974), 29–30.

[94] 'In every land the best sort is against the democracy. In the best people there is the least licentiousness and injustice, but the most care for what is good (*ta chrēsta*), while in the *dēmos* is the most ignorance, disorder and wickedness (*ponēria*). For poverty rather leads them to what is shameful, as do lack of education and in some cases that ignorance which is due to lack of money' (1. 5; cf. also 1. 1). No public speaker could afford to take this line: in Aristophanes such characteristics are attributed to leaders, not to the *dēmos*. For anti-democratic views of the *dēmos* in Aristophanes' day generally, see Ostwald, *From Popular Sovereignty to the Sovereignty of Law*, 224–9.

For helpful advice and criticism I am grateful to Sir Kenneth Dover, Lowell Edmunds, Anthony Edwards, Bruce Heiden, Gregory Nagy, Martin Ostwald, Ralph Rosen, Oliver Taplin, Alan H. Sommerstein, John J. Winkler, Froma Zeitlin, and Bernhard Zimmermann. Plays of Aristophanes are cited from the Oxford texts of Maurice Platnauer, *Peace* (1964), Kenneth J. Dover, *Clouds* (1968), Douglas M. Mac-Dowell, *Wasps* (1971), Robert G. Ussher, *Ecclesiazusae* (1973), Jeffrey J. Henderson, *Lysistrata* (1987); otherwise from Victor Coulon (Paris, 1923–30). Fragments of comedy and the *Life of Aristophanes* are cited from PCG (Aristophanes–Magnes); otherwise from *CAF*.

6

Aristophanes' Apprenticeship

STEPHEN HALLIWELL

The basis of this article is a reconsideration of some old and familiar problems about Aristophanes' early career. In the course of trying to supply firm solutions to these problems I hope also to present evidence for an early and inconspicuous stage in Aristophanes' development as a comic dramatist, and as a reflection on the resulting picture I shall make some general observations on our understanding of the relationship between the various activities involved in the creation of a comic production in the fifth-century theatre. Practically all the material I shall deal with comes from the plays themselves, and I should state at the start that I both work with and hope to justify the principle that Aristophanic disingenuousness does not normally operate where hard facts of chronology, law and theatrical conditions are concerned.

In an attempt to explain why Aristophanes did not himself apply for a chorus for any of his own plays before *Knights* in 424, the scholiast on *Clouds* 510 refers us to what he claims was an Athenian law forbidding anyone under 30 from performing a drama in the theatre or addressing the Assembly. Partly because we know from independent evidence that a statutory minimum age did exist at Athens for some kinds of political service,[1] though apparently not for addressing the Assembly,[2] and partly because at *Clouds* 530 Aristophanes, talking of the circumstances in which *Banqueters* was produced in 427, says that 'it wasn't right for me to give birth

---

[1] Arist., *Ath.* 4. 15 gives 30 as the minimum age for *bouleutai* and for those who hold *tas allas archas*—which includes dicasts (cf. 63. 3). Cf. X. *Mem.* 1. 2. 35.

[2] *Pace* K. J. Dover on *Clouds* (Oxford, 1968), 530–2. X., *Mem.* 3. 6. 1 does not suggest a statutory age for speaking in the Assembly, just a general assumption that an essential qualification was age and experience; cf. Aeschines 1. 23, and see W. Wyse on Isaeus 7. 41. 4.

[sc. to a play]',[3] this theory of a legal explanation for the fact that Aristophanes did not produce his early plays himself has strongly attracted a number of modern scholars too.[4] Others have remained agnostic, but open to the possibility.[5] Those few scholars who have rejected the idea have found in the practice of other poets, and indeed of Aristophanes himself, some good reasons for scepticism, but their arguments are not conclusive enough to have settled the issue.[6] Yet the question will permit of a clear answer, and the crucial piece of evidence is to be found in one of the passages very often cited in connection with this issue. It is *Knights* 512–16:

He says that many of you have come up to him in amazement
And asked why he didn't long ago request a chorus in his own name:
He's told us to give you the explanation. He lets it be known
It wasn't stupidity which made him keep behaving this way.
No, he thought that producing comedies was the hardest thing in the world.

These lines, which will prove relevant to some other parts of this enquiry as well, introduce a passage which certainly contains some Aristophanic irony; it is not a wholly ingenuous account of the reasons for the poet's *sōphrosynē* (cf. *Knights* 545). However, these lines themselves are only intelligible on the assumption that in 427 and subsequent years Aristophanes had a real choice, legally at any rate, whether to apply for his own chorus.[7] The implication is reinforced by the particular choice of words, especially *thaumazein*, *pollous*, *ouchi palai*; *palai* carries us back to 427, when an Aristophanic

[3] *'ouk exēn* is not "it was impossible" but "it was contrary to the rules"' (Dover, *ad loc.*). I should prefer 'circumstances did not allow it', a vague insinuation of propriety. For my interpretation of this whole passage see n. 22 below.

[4] e.g. U. von Wilamowitz-Moellendorff, 'Über die Wespen des Aristophanes', *Sitzungsberichte der königlich Preussischen Akademie der Wissenschaften* (1911), 461; rep. in *Kleine Schriften* (Berlin, 1935), i. 284 ff., where the pagination of the original article is given in the margin; V. Steffen, 'De Aristophane a Cleone in ius vocato', *Eos* 47 (1954), 9 f.; V. Coulon, Budé edn. of Aristophanes (Paris, 1964), vol. i, p. ii.

[5] e.g. G. Kaibel, *RE* ii. 972–3; G. Murray, *Aristophanes* (Oxford, 1933), 14; R. A. Neil, edn. of *Knights*, p. v n. 2; K. J. Dover on *Clouds* 530–2; T. Gelzer, 'Aristophanes der Komiker', *RE*, supp. vol. 12 (1971), 1396.

[6] See W. Schmid and O. Stählin, *Geschichte der griechischen Literatur*, part 1, vol. iv (Munich, 1946), 177 and n. 7 there; A. Lesky, *A History of Greek Literature* (Eng. trans., New York, 1965), 427; *DFA*² 84–5.

[7] In the course of composing this article I have noticed three references, themselves obviously disregarded in recent times, to this implication of *Knights* 512 ff.: J. van Leeuwen, *Prolegomena ad Aristophanem* (Leiden, 1908), 39 n. 4; B. B. Rogers, edn. of *Acharnians*, p. vii: R.G. Kent, 'The Date of Aristophanes' Birth', *CR* 19 (1905), 153–4.

play was produced for the first time; and the idea that Aristophanes
could have done differently *from the start*, if he had wanted to, is also
strongly suggested by *diatribein* (515). Aristophanes is bragging to
his audience, and there is no doubt some hyperbole here (see below
on *pollous*), but the passage would make a pointless piece of nonsense
if in fact he had been prevented by law from producing his own
plays before 424. There is no strength in the objection that most of
the audience would not know the poet's age, and so would not
know how he stood in relation to any law there might have been
regarding *kōmōidodidaskalia*. If the audience were aware of a law of
the kind in question, they would naturally assume when they heard
Knights 512 ff. that Aristophanes had been above the minimum age
since at least 427. The lines, in other words, dictate this supposition
to the audience.

I do not believe we can be at all confident about Aristophanes'
date of birth.[8] I therefore do not infer from *Knights* 512 ff. that a law
prescribing a minimum age for *kōmōidodidaskalia* was not in force
during the latter part of the fifth century—though I think it very
unlikely. What I do take to be shown is that the issue of such a law
should cease to matter to our understanding of Aristophanes' early
career.

The fact that Aristophanes did not apply for a chorus in his own
name before 424 has long posed a problem about the business
referred to at *Acharnians* 377–82 and 502 ff. At those two places
Dikaiopolis speaks in the first person on behalf of someone whom
Cleon had 'dragged before the boule' in the preceding year. The
audience must have known who was meant. Was it the author or
the producer of *Babylonians* who got into trouble? There is now
probably a consensus that it was Aristophanes himself, but the
issue has not been properly settled and it is still possible for a
leading Aristophanic scholar to consider the matter insoluble and
to opt for the cautious opinion that both author and producer are
likely to have had a share in the trouble.[9] This last view cannot be

---

[8] For the possibilities, or some of them, see Kent, 'The Date of Aristophanes' Birth',
153–5, Gelzer, 'Aristophanes der Komiker', 1396, and the apt caution of Dover, edn. of
Clouds, p. xix n. 1.
[9] Dover, 'Notes on Aristophanes' *Acharnians*', *Maia*, 15 (1963), 15; but cf. his
Aristophanic Comedy, (Berkeley, 1972), 13. For details of the controversy in earlier
days see Excursus 5 (pp. 274–5) in W. J. M. Starkie's edn. of *Acharnians* (London,
1909). See also n. 29 below.

refuted, and indeed may well be right. However, I wish to argue that all the evidence that we do have is evidence for the prosecution (I imply nothing specific by that term)[10] of the author of *Babylonians*, and that it is decisive evidence.

We must start with two passages from the parabasis and the so-called second parabasis of *Wasps*, lines 1015–59 and 1284–91, and with the observation, restricted by MacDowell to 1017–22 but applicable to the larger passages indicated, that the utterances made in these places are unintelligible 'unless the audience knows that the author is Aristophanes'.[11] MacDowell goes on from this observation to argue that *Wasps* must have been produced in Aristophanes' own name, and not by Philonides, as the first Hypothesis to the play states.[12] I shall tackle MacDowell's case radically below, and in particular his positive reasons for believing that where author and producer were different the author's name would not be made public, but I want first to give some reasons for retaining the testimony of the Hypothesis and consequently for believing that the first audience of *Wasps* must have been informed before the performance of the separate identities of author and producer. In the first place MacDowell's supposition runs counter to the likelihood, established on the evidence of inscriptions, that the poet who applied for a chorus in someone else's name nevertheless received the prize himself and had his name recorded in the document drawn

---

[10] The nature of the clash between Aristophanes and Cleon remains a subject for speculation: cf. Gelzer, 'Aristophanes der Komiker', 1398–9. That Cleon brought a *graphē xenias* against Aristophanes at any point, as schol. *Ach.* 378 asserts and as many have believed, seems to me highly improbable. I believe that the idea arose from an amalgamation of two things: the attack on Aristophanes after *Babylonians*, and the notion, inferred from *Ach.* 654, that Aristophanes was an Aeginetan. But the poet's citizenship seems proved by the information about his father in the lives and else-where, and by *IG* ii² 1740, line 40: cf. *The Athenian Agora*, vol. xv, p. 33. Nor do I believe that *Wasps* 1284 ff. refer to a clash with Cleon later than *Knights*. MacDowell's reason for taking it this way is the word *nun* in 1291: D. M. MacDowell, edn. of *Wasps*, 299. But we must consider the whole phrase *eita nun*, and also the fact that *exēpatēsen* (1291) is aorist, not perfect as we should expect if MacDowell were right. On *eknise* in 1286 MacDowell comments: 'The aorist perhaps implies that there was one occasion . . .'. There is an equivalent implication in *exēpatēsen*, and its past reference rules out the possibility that *Wasps* itself is meant. Consequently, I take *nun* in 1291 in its atemporal sense ('after all': cf. *LSJ* s.v. 1. 4) and translate the whole line: 'But then, after all, the pole (Ar.) deceived the vine (Cleon).' The reference is to *Knights*. I think that the caution of *Ach.* 502 ff. squares with the allusion at *Wasps* 1284 to some sort of concession by Aristophanes after the trouble over *Babylonians*.

[11] Edn. of *Wasps*, 124.   [12] Hypothesis 1, line 32.

on for the compilation of *IG* ii². 2325.[13] But the strongest reason for
believing that a poet's identity was known even where he did not
produce his own play lies in two lines from the passage of *Knights*
that I considered above. For it is an obvious but unnoticed implication of *Knights* 512–13 that in the period before 424 Aristophanes
was known as the author of those plays which were produced in the
name of Callistratus. MacDowell is aware of the threat to his own
position from *Knights* 512–13 and tries to effect a reconciliation by
asserting, quite fairly, that in *Knights* 512 '*pollous* may mean merely
"a number of his friends" '.[14] MacDowell is making full allowance, as
I did above, for hyperbole, but he fails to notice that this is immater-
ial to the implications of the passage. Aristophanes may indeed be
claiming something quite fictional, but we must distinguish here,
and not for the first or last time, between on the one hand whatever
reality did or did not lie behind the claim, and, on the other, the
intelligibility of the remark to the original audience. Now the
audience of *Knights* could only have made sense of what Aristophanes (or rather the chorus) was talking about if they knew that
he had written the plays produced by Callistratus during the past
three years; and Aristophanes could only have written the lines in
this way if he was sure that his audience knew this. The minimum
requirement by this argument is that the authorship of Aristophanes' early plays should have been disclosed at some stage prior
to the first performance of *Knights*. But we can surely go further
than this, for how could this disclosure have been made if not at the
first performances of the plays concerned?[15]

If the above reasoning is valid, then there is no reason to reject
the statement of the Hypothesis to *Wasps* that the play was produced *dia Philōnidou*. Instead we should conclude that the separate
identity of author and producer was known, and that the relevant
references in the two parabases were naturally understood as
applying to the poet, Aristophanes, as on any argument they
must have been. The consequences for *Acharnians* 377–82 and

---

[13] See E. Capps, 'Epigraphical Problems in the History of Attic Comedy', *AJP* 28
(1907), 179–99, and *Hesperia*, 12 (1943), 3 n. 5. There is, as Capps shows, a strong
possibility that the formula *ho deina edidaxe dia tou deinos* is an ancient one: cf. *IG* xiv
1098, line 9.   [14] Edn. of *Wasps* (Oxford, 1971), 124.
[15] Most likely at the Proagon, for it appears from Pl., *Smp.* 194a that each poet
made an appearance with his unmasked actors on that occasion. Cf. *DFA*² 67–8.

502–3 are apparent: the audience will have taken these passages as references to the author, not the producer. The two parts of my thesis are inseparable: if Aristophanes was known as the author of *Acharnians*, assertions about the *poiētēs* (633, 644, 649, 654) or first-person references in connection with *Babylonians* would have to be understood as applying to him; and for such references to be taken satisfactorily in this way, the poet's identity would have to have been known in the first place. As far as *Acharnians* itself is concerned, this leaves one difficulty. Why do the chorus talk about *ho didaskalos hēmōn* in line 628, and what does the whole of that line refer to? Dover has suggested: 'It may well have been a convention that the chorus in the parabasis should speak of the *didaskalos* of the play as if he were also the *poiētēs*, whether or not he was.'[16] This seems highly implausible to me; surely the very reverse was the case. More often than not the roles of *didaskalos* and poet were combined, and so we should not be surprised to find that it was possible to refer to the poet who produced his own play by either term. This is in fact what we find in the parabases of *Knights* and *Peace*. Both passages are reminiscent of *Acharnians* 628 ff. In *Knights* Aristophanes is first called *kōmōidodidaskalos* (507), then *poiētēs* is used from 509 onwards (509, 519, 548). *Peace* shows an even freer variation of terms: *kōmōidopoiētēs* (734), *kōmōidodidaskalos* (737), *didaskalos* (738), *poiētēs* (772). Given the practices of the fifth-century theatre this freedom is perfectly intelligible. The facts do not at all lend credibility to the idea that the producer of someone else's play could be called *poiētēs*; but they do tend, I think, to support the possibility that at *Acharnians* 628 Aristophanes could be intelligibly called *didaskalos* by the chorus, even though he was not officially the producer of this play. As to the significance of the line as a whole, I shall return to this problem below in my general remarks on the various components in the preparation of a comedy for production in the fifth century. For the real solution to this problem lies, I believe, in a refinement of our understanding of the general theatrical background and of the development of Aristophanes' career.

I want now to return to the positive side of MacDowell's case for the proposition that an author's identity was not made public when

---

[16] Edn. of *Clouds*, p. xix. See also his *Aristophanic Comedy*, 14 n. 5.

he did not produce his plays himself. The basis of MacDowell's case is an interpretation, which it is fair to call orthodox,[17] of *Wasps* 1018–22. In this passage, so the orthodox interpretation runs, Aristophanes is drawing a contrast between his practice during the period 427 to 425, when he did not produce his own plays officially, and the period from 424 onwards when he started to take full responsibility for at least some of his own comedies. One immediate objection to this interpretation—that Aristophanes uses a plural, *heteroisi poiētais*, in line 1018, even though he seems to have used only *one* producer before 424—has often been acknowledged, and a variety of solutions have been proposed.[18] It is significant that MacDowell finds it difficult to endorse any of them. But even if a satisfactory solution to this problem were to be agreed on, there remain several other major obstacles in the way of the orthodox interpretation of the passage. These have not, so far as I can see, been given any airing; I set out below what seem to me to be the most important:

1.   The description puts a very heavy emphasis on secrecy— something much more severe than the absence of official or public recognition of Aristophanic authorship. After *ou phanerōs all'* . . . *krybdēn* comes the ventriloquism simile, and the point is remade by *kai phanerōs* in 1021. If this is a description of the production of Aristophanes' early plays, we have no choice but to suppose that the poet's identity was quite unknown not only at the first performance of the plays but at least until after the Lenaea of 425. MacDowell seems well aware of this when he talks about 'spectators who thought that *Banqueters*, *Babylonians* and *Akharnians* were all written by Kallistratos'.[19] No convincing explanation of the reasons for this putative secrecy has ever been given, but it is in any case hard to give credence to in simple practical terms. There is, for example, the difficulty of reconciling such secrecy with the reasonable supposition that, in Dover's words, 'the written and circulated version of the play . . . would bear the name of the poet'.[20] There is also the Proagon, and the poet's customary appearance at it, to be kept in mind.[21] But there is the further and more important problem that if

---

[17] It starts with schol. *Wasps* 1018 and was subscribed to by, among others, Kock, Wilamowitz, Merry, Starkie, Rogers, and van Leeuwen.
[18] See MacDowell, edn. of *Wasps*.   [19] Ibid. 124.
[20] Edn. of *Clouds*, p. xvii n. 2.   [21] See n. 15 above.

it was not known until after *Acharnians* that Aristophanes was the
author of *Banqueters* and *Babylonians*, then how are we to suppose
this revelation to have been made? For by the time of *Knights*
Aristophanes, as we have seen, could certainly count on his audience's familiarity with the facts.

2.   The passage contains a strong suggestion of artistic subordination to other poets: *epikourōn* is a strikingly self-effacing term, and
Aristophanes is not noted for modesty. What point could there be in
equating his role as author of those earlier plays with one of
'assisting other poets'? MacDowell fairly glosses 1022: 'exercising
full control over his own artistic activities, instead of merely assisting other people's'. How could Aristophanes have offered this as a
way of talking about plays he had written himself? Surely since 427
the *Mousai* (1022) had been his all along; it was the *hēniochos*
(charioteer) that had changed. But our passage talks of the reverse
of this. Where Aristophanes is certainly talking about those earlier
plays, as at *Clouds* 528–33, the emphasis is different. He explains that
he was not officially responsible for the production (*tekein*, 530) of
Banqueters: he does not pretend that the play was not really his, or
that he was merely giving Callistratus a bit of help.[22]

3.   On *Wasps* 1023 ff., MacDowell comments: 'Ar. refers primarily
to the success of *Knights*.' Indeed he must, for the interpretation to
be consistent; for how could the poet refer to the success of earlier
plays by *artheis de megas* etc., when he has just told his audience
that his identity was not known to them until after *Acharnians*? But
the orthodox interpretation suggests an odd purpose, for it makes
Aristophanes switch from disowning responsibility for at least one
first prize to describing as 'great and honoured like no one else'

---

[22] *Clouds* 530–2 is patently the basis of the scholiast's assertion on *Frogs* 501 that
Aristophanes was still a *meirakiskos* in 427, and of schol. *Clouds* 510 (discussed in the
text above) regarding a law on *kōmōidodidaskalia*, though the scholiast on *Clouds* 530–
2 itself more sensibly talks in terms of *aidōs* and *eulabeia*. My own view is that by
parthenos, which it is vital to realize refers only to 427 and the circumstances in which
Banqueters was produced, Aristophanes means to signify his newness as a dramatist
and his consequent lack of status in the eyes of the *archōn*, but that he is not
necessarily saying anything about his practical involvement in the production. I
would not accept that *hetera tis labous' aneileto* implies that *Banqueters* was passed
off as Callistratus's own play. We have to decide how strictly to understand Aristophanic metaphors on the basis of all the available evidence. If we took *Clouds* 531
really strictly, we should be bound to believe not just that *Banqueters* was presented as
Callistratus's own, but that the production of the play was accidental—for the play
was a 'foundling'—and that in no sense was it on behalf of or for Aristophanes.

(*megas kai timētheis hōs oudeis*) his record during a two-year
period in which he had suffered what we know he felt as the
ignominy of a third place.[23] We should expect Aristophanes, I
submit, to be bragging about his success before *Wasps*.

4. Wilamowitz, who subscribed to the orthodox reading of
the passage, remarked on what seemed to him the crucial
significance for his interpretation of the qualification 'when he
first began to produce' (*hote prōton g'ērxe didaskein*) at line 1029.[24]
Without it, Wilamowitz correctly observed, Aristophanes would
seem to be implying that his vendetta with Cleon was later than
Knights. That qualification does look important; it ought to
matter in the sequence. According to Wilamowitz's suggestion,
though, Aristophanes has organized the narrative somewhat
ineptly, and has had to introduce a saving qualification to avoid
a misleading impression. I believe that the clause should and can
be given a more natural function in the sequence of thought.

5. At *Clouds* 528–9 Aristophanes implies that his identity as
author of *Banqueters* was known to at least part of the audience
at the time of the first performance of the play, or not long after.
The second half of line 528, *hous hēdu kai legein*, makes it clear
that Aristophanes has not the general class of *sophoi* spectators
in mind but a specific group of real individuals. This is brought
out well by Dover's paraphrase: 'It is agreeable <to me now>
even to mention them <let alone know them personally and hear
their praise>.'[25] If these people received well Aristophanes' first
play in a way which meant something to the dramatist, it is hard
to imagine how the identity of the author can have been all that
much of a secret or why he should later have wanted to talk of
his early success and good reception as though it did not belong
to him.

---

[23] Cf. *Clouds* 524–5.

[24] Wilamowitz, 'Über die Wespen des Aristophanes', 465 ff.

[25] Dover, edn. of *Clouds* (Oxford, 1968), 166, working with Blaydes's very necessary
emendation.

6. There is no evidence outside *Wasps* which suggests that Callistratus was himself a comic dramatist.[26] To call him a poet, in singular or plural, would therefore be strange.

The above objections to the orthodox reading of *Wasps* 1018 ff. constitute, it seems to me, good grounds for seeking a fresh interpretation of the passage. In doing so we ought, I believe, to take note of the other description which Aristophanes offers us of the development of his artistic career, that at *Knights* 541–4:

It was out of these fears that he followed that course. And he says, moreover,
That he needed to train as a rower first, before handling the tiller,
And then become bow-officer and watch the winds' directions,
And only then become his own ship's captain.

The striking feature of this passage is the complexity of the nautical metaphor for what ought by the orthodox understanding to be the poet's purpose. If Aristophanes' early career fell into two neat stages—writing but not producing, then taking on both jobs—why does he here employ an analogy with three, or maybe even four, stages of a nautical career?[27] This is perhaps to expect too strict a correlation, but there surely is about this passage a definite impression of *gradual* development to full *kōmōidodidaskalia*, and of what we might call a complex apprenticeship. We have here a clue, if we need one, to the true sense of *Wasps* 1018 ff. I suggest that these lines should be understood much more literally than is usual. Aristophanes is revealing to his audience the fact that even before he was known to them as a comic poet and was having his own plays produced, he was actually providing them with entertainment in the form of comic material contributed to the plays of other dramatists.[28]

---

[26] Contrary to what is sometimes asserted: see e.g. P. Ghiron-Bistagne, *Recherches sur les acteurs dans la Grèce antique* (Paris, 1976), 129, with a reference to *PA* 8127, where it is admitted that no evidence exists for this belief. Poor old Callistratus was divined to be a 'wretched poetaster' by Starkie, edn. of *Ach.*, 248. See *AJP* 28 (1907), 89 together with *IG* ii² 2318, col. 5 and *DFA*² 118 for the better restoration of Cantharus' name in *IG* ii² 2325.   [27] See Neil's note, edn. of *Knights*, ad loc.
[28] About the details we can only guess, but it seems an attractive possibility that Philonides was involved. We know him to have been a comic poet in his own right: see *PA* 14904 and *IG* ii² 2325 (*DFA*² 112). He seems also to have belonged to a circle which contained a number of well-to-do friends of Aristophanes: see Sterling Dow, 'Some Athenians in Aristophanes', *AJA* 73 (1969), 234–5.

The advantages of this theory for our understanding of the whole
passage, *Wasps* 1018–29, are considerable. The emphasis on secrecy,
the modest suggestion of subordination to others (1022), now make
natural sense. Lines 1023 ff. can now easily be taken as referring to
all Aristophanes' dramatic successes before *Wasps*, from *Banqueters*
onwards, and the temporal qualification in 1029 fits perfectly into
the sequence of argument by marking a further stage in the career,
the assumption of full *kōmōidodidaskalia*. I would add that on my
interpretation *kōmōidika polla* (1020), which suggests comic material
rather than whole plays, perhaps makes easier sense. One detail
alone seems to pose a difficulty for my reading, the phrase *kath'
heauton* in 1021. Aristophanes uses the same phrase at *Knights* 513,
where he is describing application for a chorus through someone else
rather than 'in his own name'. However, the precise contrast made
by *kath' heauton* in each case can only be determined by reference to
the context. At *Knights* 513 the point is quite clear. In *Wasps* 1021,
though, *kath' heauton* must represent the opposite of what is
described in 1018 and 1022, and if the reasons given above for taking
the reference to be to collaboration with other poets and not to the
production of Aristophanes' early plays are good ones, then *kindu-
neuōn kath' heauton* must mean 'taking a risk with one of his own
plays'—that is, bringing out *Banqueters* in 427.

I believe, then, that in *Wasps* 1018 ff. we have some little noticed
evidence for an early stage in Aristophanes' apprenticeship as a
comic dramatist.[29] It is important here, however, to reinvoke a
principle used earlier in this article—that there is a logical distinction to be drawn between the reality behind the authorial assertion
and the intelligibility of the assertion to the original audience. It is
the area of overlap between them that concerns us. At *Wasps*
1018 ff. Aristophanes is expecting his audience to understand him

[29] I have discovered a number of scholars who have noticed the implications of
Knights 541–4 and dissented from the orthodoxy on *Wasps* 1018 ff., but none of them
puts the full case against the orthodoxy or gives more than a hint at an alternative
reading. Most confuse the matter, in my view, by introducing reference to Eup. fr. 89
PCG (see the following note): cf. Kaibel, *RE* ii. 973; Kent, 'The Date of Aristophanes'
Birth', 154; Schmid and Stählin, *Geschichte der griechischen Literatur*, 179. I am very
grateful to *CQ*'s referee for alerting me to the review article by E. Hiller in *Phil. Anzeig.*
17 (1887), 361 ff. Hiller suggests a reading of *Wasps* 1018 ff. very similar to my own: see
pp. 366–7. He also discusses many of the other points raised in my article and reaches
some similar conclusions, though he differs from me notably on *kath' heauton* at
Knights 513 and on *Wasps* 1029. I have made no changes in my text since reading
Hiller.

to be claiming to have contributed to the work of other poets. He uses the plural 'other poets' even though he may in fact, for all we know, have helped only one man. But though that detail may be an exaggeration, the manner of the claim seems to me to guarantee that there was *something* behind it. If we were dealing with an attempt to invent an achievement or to glorify the poet's image, we should expect a racier presentation with a colourful and perhaps detailed dressing. Comparison with the exchange of allegations of plagiarism between Aristophanes and Eupolis is instructive.[30] There detailed claims are thrust at the audience, and the satirical purpose behind them does not require us to believe what they assert. *Wasps* 1018 ff. is very different. Despite an admixture of humour and exaggeration, Aristophanes has a real aim, to remind the audience of his past achievements, justify *Clouds* and the standards of comedy it represented, and generally impress on his audience the quality of his plays. The framework of references to events in his career hitherto therefore needs to be substantially accurate, as we know it to be as far as *Knights* and *Clouds* are concerned. At 1018–20 Aristophanes is describing a stage in his career, and relating it to something the audience have first-hand knowledge of, his subsequent development as an independent poet (1021 ff.). If we resist the assumptions of the orthodox reading, the sequence yields the sense I have outlined above, and the context demands that we take Aristophanes' words seriously.

If I am right in finding at *Knights* 541–4 and *Wasps* 1018 ff. references to a more complex development to full *kōmōidodidaskalia* in Aristophanes' early career than has commonly been imagined, then some important questions are raised regarding the preparation of plays for production in the fifth-century theatre. I wish now to

---

[30] See *Clouds* 554 with Dover's note, and Eup. fr. 89 *PCG*, which is a reply to the Aristophanic gibe. I can see no evidence regarding a collaboration between these two poets which cannot be traced back to these jokes, and no reason at all for taking the Eupolis fr. as itself evidence of collaboration. As for the jokes made by Aristophanes' rivals involving the proverb *tetradi gegonas*, which are sometimes treated as confirming the view that the authorship of Aristophanes' early plays was not known, and that the prize for a play did not go to its author when he was not full *kōmōidodidaskalos*, I must protest that the frs. in question, in their unspecific and contentless form, tell us next to nothing about anything. See Gelzer, 'Aristophanes der Komiker', 1396–7 for the references and a statement of the customary interpretation. It may be significant that Sannyr. fr. 5 is to be dated to 410 or later; P. Geissler, *Chronologie der altattischen Komödie* (Munich, 1925), 67. I discuss Pl. Com. frs. 106–7 *PCG* in 'Authorial Collaboration in the Athenian Comic Theatre', *GRBS* 30 (1989), 515–28: 521, 524–6.

make some remarks about the theatrical background as involved in
and affecting the apprenticeship and early career of a new dramatist, though some of my points are, I believe, of wider importance.
Fortunately an increase in scholarly interest in the practical aspects
of ancient theatre production prevents most of us from visualizing
the origins of Aristophanes' dramatic career simply in terms of the
force of genius, patriotism, and personality, important though these
may have been.[31] However, these origins have generally been dealt
with in recent times on the basis of a rather inflexible model of the
distinction between the roles of poet and producer. If we wish to
understand the evidence which Aristophanes provides us with for
the beginnings of his career in the theatre, we need to refine this
poet-producer model. The terms translate, of course, *poiētēs* and
didaskalos. These translations are convenient and perhaps unavoid-
able, but by evoking the conditions of our own theatre they carry
with them the danger of a simplified understanding of the reality
they represent. It is convenient to assert that Aristophanes did not
produce his early plays himself, that he was not his own producer in
the years 427 to 425. But what are we committing ourselves to when
we say such things? It is often supposed that the key to Aristophanes' early career lies in the fact that though he could write plays
capable of being produced in the theatre he did not yet have the
practical experience to produce them. (A caution is normally added
to take care of the fact that he did not always take full responsibility
for his own plays later in his career.)[32] This way of looking at the
matter seems to me to be only a partial truth. If we are to get nearer
to an appreciation of the conditions in which Aristophanes developed into a practising comic poet, a full *kōmōidodidaskalos*, I believe
we should attend to the following factors:

  1. We should not underestimate the complexity of activities
involved in the preparation of a comedy for production. We need
to separate conceptually the request for a chorus, the practical
running of rehearsals, and the more general business of finance
and overall supervision, including dealings with the *chorēgos*, who
might not always be as accommodating as the defendant of Antiphon VI.[33] It seems never to have been sufficiently emphasized that

---

[31] Cf. the romanticizing speculations of van Leeuwen, *Prolegomena* etc., 19 ff.
[32] See e.g. *DFA*² 84–5, Gelzer 'Aristophanes der Komiker', 1517.
[33] Antiphon 6. 11–14.

at *Knights* 513 the chorus refer to the fact that for the past three years Aristophanes has not been *asking for a chorus in his own name*. We should not glibly assume that this must necessarily have entailed taking no other part in the preparation of the play for production, or that *choron aitein* is a straight synonym for what we mean by 'to be the producer', though certainly *Knights* 515–16 and *Wasps* 1029 show that it was not simply the request for a chorus that Aristophanes had performed vicariously from 427 to 425.

2. In the theatrical milieu of the fifth century, where the focus of dramatic activities was the single public performance of a play, it is misguided to imagine the text and the production as two quite separate things. We know that alterations were sometimes made in the script relatively late on in the preparations for performance.[34] When the poet himself supervised rehearsals, he would clearly have had full control over the interaction between script and production. But if, to take an important example, the text of *Frogs* was altered in places at a late stage in the preparations for performance in response to the death of Sophocles,[35] it was done despite the fact that Philonides was the official *didaskalos*. We should therefore not lightly assume that when the responsibilities of production were shared with someone else the author's role would necessarily be confined to producing a script, handing it over to a producer, and then taking no further part himself in the production. We cannot be sure that this did not ever happen, but we must beware of simply accepting without question that this was the procedure when a poet applied for a chorus through someone else.

3. To produce a dramatic text capable of production within the strict limits of the available resources and prevailing conventions implies in itself some degree of practical theatrical knowledge. Those who wish to maintain that Aristophanes could write *Acharnians* unassisted but could not produce it without help should be explicit about what it was that production entailed which the author could not manage, and should explain how the poet grew sufficiently in practical experience to produce *Knights* if he was not involved at all in the production of his earlier plays.

[34] On the relation between the stage of *choron aitein* and the time of performance see the remarks of Gelzer, 'Aristophanes der Komiker', 1517–18.
[35] The case is put best by Wilamowitz, *Einleitung in die griechische Tragödie* (Berlin, 1910), 2–3, and Dover, *Aristophanic Comedy*, 180–1. For arguments against see L. Radermacher's edn. of *Frogs*, 254–5.

4. We do not know on what basis the *archōn* allotted choruses, and in particular what personal factors may have been involved.[36] Where a new poet was concerned, the help of influential or experienced friends might well have been invaluable. The fact that it is *choron aitein* which Aristophanes refers to at *Knights* 513 may carry a good deal of significance.

5. (4) raises wider questions of patronage or backing in the fifth-century theatre.[37] This is a subject about which, of course, we know singularly little, but I think it is worth considering the possibility that what we have at *Clouds* 528–9 is a reference to some form of patronage. Whatever form the support of the *sophoi* took, it seems to have been the act of a group of individuals to whom Aristophanes thought it worthwhile to show his gratitude by a special mention. The likelihood that we have here a form of patronage would be increased if the good reception which the *sophoi* gave to *Banqueters* was prior to the public performance of the play. There are, I believe, indications in the text that this might have been so:

Since the time when some men here, whom it's agreeable to mention,
Gave an excellent reception to my two characters—the virtuous and
    debauched—
And I, as it wasn't right for an unmarried girl to give birth,
Exposed the child, and another girl picked it up,
While *you* gave it such a splendid rearing and education . . .

(Clouds 528–32)

Aristophanes here seems to describe a temporal sequence of events: first the backing of the *sophoi*, then the decision to apply for a chorus through someone else, then (notice the switch from the particular *andres* of 528 to *humeis*, the general audience, at 532–3) the public performance of the play.

There is obviously a great deal that we do not know about Aristophanes' early career, but if we keep the above factors in mind I believe we can construct an outline derived from the evidence to be found in the poet's own plays. The progression to full *kōmōidodidaskalia* involved a number of stages, and this is the reason why at *Knights* 541–4 Aristophanes chooses to use a

---

[36] See *DFA*[2] 84.
[37] I should perhaps note that by 'patronage' I mean mainly to suggest forms of support other than financial.

metaphor that suggests a complex development. Part of the apprenticeship entailed contributing to the plays of others—a collaboration which may have been an established way of encouraging new dramatists, and which is not to be thought of as purely literary but rather as experience in the creation of a dramatic script for production. By 427 Aristophanes was in a position to provide a whole play for performance, and it was one which may have gained him some patrons even before it was publicly produced. The task of applying for a chorus was given to Callistratus, who probably also had a large hand in the preparations for the production; but no attempt to conceal the identity of the author was made, and Aristophanes will have received the appropriate official recognition. The poet was not to attain to full *kōmōidodidaskalia* until 424, but the impression given by *Knights* 541–4 is of a gradually increasing involvement by the author in his own productions. It therefore seems very likely to me that Aristophanes took part in the rehearsals of his own plays from the start, and that he did not simply leave to Callistratus all the work of preparation which the poet-*didaskalos* would normally perform. It is this kind of background, I think, which we must visualize to make sense of *Acharnians* 628:

Since the time when our trainer first took charge of comic choruses . . .

In a theatrical context *didaskalos* is a term for the poet. We have in fact no evidence relevant to the fifth century which suggests that when a poet applied for a chorus through someone else or shared the responsibilities for production he relinquished the title of *didaskalos*.[38] However, even if that were normal practice, a reference to Aristophanes as *didaskalos* in *Acharnians* would still be possible. If the poet's involvement in his productions was by this stage almost complete, as my argument suggests, the fact that it was Callistratus who had applied for the chorus would surely not automatically entitle him to be called *didaskalos*. An Athenian audience would

---

[38] Even 4th-cent. practice may not tell us anything about the 5th cent; D., *Meid.* 58 proves little, for by that date a greater separation of the roles of poet and producer seems probable. There is a reference in *POxy* 2737, fr. 1, col. 2, lines 21–2 (= Ar., fr. 590. 55–6 PCG) to *toutous tous neous didaskalous*. It follows closely on a reference to poets' having their plays produced by others, but I can see no compelling reason not to take *didaskalos* in the standard sense of 'poet' here.

not expect to hear the 'voice' of anyone other than the poet in a
parabasis; they had already heard the author speaking at 377–82
and 502–3. *Didaskalos* would at once suggest the poet, and if anyone
did happen to be momentarily puzzled the ensuing series of references to the *poiētēs* (633, 644, 649, 654) would make the meaning
clear. *Acharnians* 628 perhaps represents Aristophanes' first attempt
to claim for himself the full status of *kōmōidodidaskalos*.

In the above discussion I have been using the phrase 'the early
plays of Aristophanes' to refer to the phase of the dramatist's career
from *Banqueters* to *Acharnians*. In addition to the three plays securely
dated in this period, it has sometimes been thought that there was
a fourth play, produced at the Lenaea of 426.[39] This belief is an
inference from *Acharnians* 1154–5, where the chorus abuse one
Antimachus, a *chorēgos*, and give as justification that he sent
them away without any dinner at the Lenaean feast. The validity
of this inference has been questioned by Dover,[40] but I wish here to
try to re-establish it by some detailed considerations.

Dover has argued that in the given line *eme* refers to 'the comic
choreutēs' and implies nothing about either Aristophanes himself or
the members of the chorus in the first performance of *Acharnians*.
That nothing is implied about the individual members of the chorus
cannot be disputed. Rather more challenging, though, is the belief
that the chorus of *Acharnians* could speak for 'comic *choreutai* in
general', or rather, as Antimachus presumably *was* a *chorēgos* in
426, for the chorus of some other comedian than Aristophanes
(some, of course, might have said 'than Callistratus'). Dover draws
an analogy with Athenian juries: it was possible to address a
particular jury as though its membership were coterminous with
that of the whole citizen body in its judicial aspect. Consequently,
individual jurors could find themselves being addressed as though
they had taken decisions in cases in which they had not actually
been involved. But the case of Athenian juries is explicable in terms
which are simply irrelevant to comic choruses. All juries were taken
functionally from the body of male citizens of the polis; the repre-
sentativeness of the individual jury is a principle of the whole
democratic system. It is pertinent to recall Aristotle's definition of

---

[39] e.g. C. F. Russo, *Aristofane Autore di Teatro* (Florence, 1962), 26; Gelzer, 'Aristophanes der Komiker', 1408.   [40] 'Notes on Aristophanes' *Acharnians*', 23.

a citizen: 'one who has the right to sit on the council or on a jury'.[41]
In the case of individual choruses and 'comic *choreutai* in general'
this relationship is not established, and the line from *Acharnians*
with which we are dealing is not sufficient to establish it. On the
evidence of the extant plays of Aristophanes we can assert that
when the chorus refers to itself in the first person it must be
characterizing itself in one of the following three ways:

1. as a dramatically defined group of Acharnians, knights or
   whatever;
2. as a body of representative members of the *polis* of Athens;
3. as the Aristophanic chorus, which is assumed to be a constant
   entity because of the influence and identity of the author and
   despite the varying dramatic character of the chorus and the
   presumable change from year to year in the actors or dancers
   who make it up.

The first of these types of reference is too common and obvious to
need illustration. Examples of the other types can be found in the
parabasis of *Acharnians*. In line 628 *hēmōn* means 'we the chorus of
the poet Aristophanes', and not 'we the comic chorus', as *ho
didaskalos* shows. In line 631, where *hēmōn* occurs again, the chorus
undoubtedly speak simply as members of the *polis*, representative
Athenian citizens. Perhaps the closest an Aristophanic chorus
comes to speaking in the way that Dover attributes to them at
Acharnians 1154 is in the quasi-parabatic passage in the *parodos* of
Frogs (354ff.). The term *choros* is used ambivalently in this passage of
both the comic chorus and the band of initiates. Leaving aside this,
though, what prevents us from finding support here for Dover's
thesis is the way in which the context makes evident the special
nature of the chorus's status at this moment. Firstly there are the
plurals: *choroisin* (354), *chorois* (370). Secondly, the references to
Cratinus (357) and to general service in a comic chorus (356). These
details define the peculiar role of the chorus here as a mouthpiece
for the genre. This is not at all equivalent to a chorus representing
all comic choruses when simply making a first-person reference.
Indeed, even the chorus of *Frogs* no more acquires *that* identity in
the *parodos* than it does when in line 686 it makes a general
comment on the political function of *ton hieron choron*. A chorus

<hr>

[41] *Pol.* 3. 1275[b] 18–19.

can speak in a manner which acknowledges the existence of other comic choruses; but there are no grounds for supposing that without warning or explanation an Aristophanic chorus could speak for a particular chorus belonging to a different poet, or speak as if its identity were the same as that of all other comic choruses. I therefore conclude that the inference from *Acharnians* 1154–5 that Aristophanes had a play produced at the Lenaea of 426 is a valid one.

I am very grateful for the suggestive criticisms of a draft of this article that I received from Sir Kenneth Dover and Mrs Barbara Mitchell.

7

Tragedy and Politics in Aristophanes' *Acharnians*

HELENE P. FOLEY

Aristophanes' second play, *Babylonians*, included an attack on state offices and politicians and, probably, the city's treatment of its allies.[1] According to the scholia of *Acharnians*, the play provoked Cleon to indict Aristophanes (or the play's producer Callistratus) for *adikia* and *hybris* towards the *dēmos* and the *boulē* on the grounds that he treasonably embarrassed the city before strangers at the City Dionysia.[2] Cleon may also have questioned Aristophanes' citizenship, suggesting that the poet (or Callistratus) was really a native Aeginetan, not a true Athenian.[3] Aristophanes returned fire at the Lenaea of 425 with *Acharnians*, a play that renews *Babylonians'*

---

[1] See schol. *Ach.* 378 for *Babylonians'* attack on many unnamed persons, on state offices, whether filled by lot or by vote, and on Cleon. For the attack on the allies, see the ambiguous *Ach.* 642, which makes it unclear whether the play addressed Athens' treatment of its allies or the implications of democratic rule within these states. The fragments of *Babylonians* suggest that the allies may have been represented as slaves of Athens.

[2] Schol. *Ach.* 378. Aristophanes may, of course, have invented these charges, and the scholiast may have derived his evidence from the plays; on the other hand, the poet repeatedly attacks both Cleon and his purported charges against him (see esp. *Ach.* 376–82, *Knights*, *Wasps* 1284–91, and *Clouds* 581–94). One can hardly suppose that the topic would continue to amuse the audience if the threat of censorship were absolutely meaningless. Debate continues on whether Aristophanes or Callistratus (or both) was the object of Cleon's charges; since I am concerned only with the nature and content of the attack, the issue is largely irrelevant. For discussion of these and other aspects of Aristophanes' early career, see esp. W. J. M. Starkie, *The 'Acharnians' of Aristophanes* (London, 1909; repr. Amsterdam, 1968), excursus 5, D. M. MacDowell, 'Aristophanes and Callistratus', *CQ*, NS 32 (1982), 21–6, S. Halliwell, 'Aristophanes' Apprenticeship', *CQ* NS 30 (1980), 33–45, and G. Mastromarco, 'L'esordio "segreto" di Aristofane', *Quaderni di Storia*, 10 (1979), 153–96.

[3] See schol. *Ach.* 378 for Cleon's purported charge (it may also have occurred after *Knights*) and W. J. W. Koster, *Scholia in Aristophanem* I.1a: *Prolegomena de comoedia* (Groningen, 1975), xxviii–xxxiib for (probably comic) allegations, typical in the

attack on Athens' misguided politics and politicians. Even more important, by making a separate peace with Sparta and by offering in his speech of self-defence before the chorus to defend the enemy, the comic hero Dikaiopolis commits 'crimes' equivalent to those for which Aristophanes was indicted.

In *Acharnians* Aristophanes takes the unusual step of linking his own difficulties with Cleon and his case for the justice of comedy explicitly with Dikaiopolis' speech in self-defence. A comic poet normally speaks in his own voice only in the parabasis, and nowhere else in extant comedy does Aristophanes identify himself with his hero as extensively as in *Acharnians*.[4] At 377–82, when Dikaiopolis announces that he will make a speech in defence of the Lacedaemonians and at the opening of the speech itself (502–3), the comic hero refers in the first person to Cleon's attacks on himself of the previous year. Taking a cue from the scholiast, some scholars have even insisted that Aristophanes played the part of Dikaiopolis himself, perhaps wearing a portrait-mask.[5] How, then, did Aristophanes persuade his audience that a play whose hero glories in being a traitor to his city in wartime was in fact patriotic and beneficial to the *polis*? The question is not a trivial one. An Athenian decree of 440/39 formally restricted the freedom of the political comedian for several years before it was repealed.[6] Other legislation followed and by the fourth century Old Comedy had largely abandoned the biting political satire so popular in its formative years. This chapter will examine the means that Aristophanes uses in *Acharnians* to defend his comedy against the Cleons of his audience. In particular it will investigate why the poet has his hero borrow Euripides' *Telephus* in order to do so,

biographical tradition, of Aristophanes' foreign or slave extraction. Whether or not Cleon made such an attack (now or later), some explanation must be found for *Ach.* 652–4, which deliberately links the poet (or Callistratus) with Aegina; the scholiast on 654 asserts that Callistratus (not as in schol. R on 653, Aristophanes) may recently have acquired property on Aegina. See Starkie, *The 'Acharnians' of Aristophanes*, 139 for further possible associations between Aristophanes and Aegina.

[4] Cratinus, for example, was a character in his *Pytine*, and Aristophanes speaks for himself in fr. 471K.

[5] For a discussion of these issues, provoked by schol. *Ach.* 377, see C. Bailey, 'Who played Dicaeopolis?', in *Greek Poetry and Life: Essays Presented to Gilbert Murray on his Seventieth Birthday* (Oxford, 1936) and K. J. Dover, 'Portrait-masks in Aristophanes', in *Komoidotragemata: Studia Aristophanea viri Aristophanei W. J. W. Koster in Honorem* (Amsterdam, 1967). Bailey's thesis has not generally been accepted.

[6] See the possibly untrustworthy assertion of schol. *Ach.* 67. The decree was passed after the Samian revolt in the archonship of Morychides and repealed in 437/6. Schol.

and how he manipulates tragedy to serve the licence, argument, and prestige of comedy. In a broader sense, I hope to illuminate further the political stance that Aristophanes takes in his peace-plays and how tragic imitation in comedy serves a range of purposes beyond its witty exposure of Euripidean dramaturgy.

I

Even if the popular Telephus myth and, as is less likely, Euripides' play of 438 were thoroughly familiar to the audience, Aristophanes needed in *Acharnians* to establish for the first time in his career his own special relation to Euripides and to tragedy.[7] In this play Aristophanes goes out of his way to give the audience clues for recognizing his major tragic source and for interpreting his use of it,[8] and second to call attention to the way his text defines and

---

Ach. 1150 offers a possible identification of the *syngrapheus* Antimachus mentioned there with the author of a *psēphisma* which forbade *kōmōidein ex onomatos*; in *Acharnians* the chorus accuses Antimachus of being a *chorēgos* who denied the expected feast to the chorus of a comedy presented at the Lenaea (1154–5). We also know of a law of Syracosius in 415 BC. On comic censorship, see also Ps.-Xen., *Ath. Pol.* 2. 18, which notes that attacks on the *dēmos* were not tolerated, whereas attacks on powerful individuals were acceptable (see *Ach.* 515–16). The question of comic censorship in the 5th cent. is too complex to address fully here; the laws probably restricted satire of the state constitution, state policies, or named individuals, not all political comedy (see Starkie, *The 'Acharnians' of Aristophanes*, excursus 2).

[7] *Banqueters* and *Babylonians* apparently gave little if any attention to tragedy. K. J. Dover, *Aristophanic Comedy* (Berkeley and Los Angeles, 1972), 215, suggests that earlier comedy, at least as represented by the fragments of Cratinus, may have parodied Homer and other archaic poets, but that Aristophanes' generation was the first to exploit tragedy for comic purposes. When the Peloponnesian War led the city to reduce the number of comedies at the City Dionysia from five to three (as in the case of *Acharnians*; cf. the argument to the play) and, we think (see Ar., *Birds* 786–9), to produce them at the conclusion of each of three days following the production of a tragic poet, the changed structure of the festival may have sparked a new kind of confrontation and even rivalry between the genres. For the complex problem of the number and place of comedies at the City Dionysia, see A. W. Pickard-Cambridge, *The Dramatic Festivals of Athens*, rev. J. Gould and D. M. Lewis (Oxford, 1968), 82–3.

[8] For the Telephus myth, and its popularity in tragedy and art, see esp. W. H. Roscher, *Ausfürliches Lexikon der Griechischen und römischen Mythologie* (Leipzig, 1884–1937), v. 274–307, G. Brizi, 'Il mito di Telefo nei tragici greci', *A & R* NS 9 (1928), 95–145, and L. Séchan, *Études sur la tragédie grecque* (Paris, 1926), 121–7, 503–18. For recent reconstructions of Euripides' *Telephus*, see E. Handley and J. Rea, *The 'Telephus' of Euripides*, BICS Supp. 5 (London, 1957), and T. B. L. Webster, *The Tragedies of Euripides* (London, 1967), 43–8. In my view, Aristophanes' audience would have needed to know little more than the major episodes of the plot of Euripides' *Telephus* and, preferably, the major points made in Telephus' speech before the Greeks in order

creates what he calls *trygōidia*, a wine-song, or *kōmōidia* with a tragic accent.⁹

Telephus, son of Heracles and Auge, daughter of King Aleus of Arcadia, became by a series of accidents king of barbarian Mysia. He was wounded by Achilles while resisting an attack by Achaeans who were on their way to Troy. In some versions, his disaster was brought on by Dionysus, who caught Telephus' foot in a vine because he had neglected his worship. When the wound would not heal, Telephus sought oracular advice. According to Euripides' version of the myth, he then went to the Greek mainland to seek a cure from Achilles. In disguise as a beggar, he defended himself and the Mysians by assuring the Achaeans that they too would have answered an unprovoked attack on their country. He may also have impugned the Greeks' motives for undertaking the Trojan War, perhaps by denigrating Helen and by representing events from a Trojan perspective. After his disguise was penetrated, Telephus took refuge at an altar with the baby Orestes as hostage. By the conclusion of the play he was recognized as Greek rather than barbarian and promised a cure for his wound by Achilles; in accordance with another oracle he became guide for the expedition to Troy.

Borrowing from *Telephus* is pervasive in *Acharnians*. Although the hostage scene and the speech in self-defence proved most apt for Aristophanes' purposes, verbal allusions to the play range from a half line in the prologue (8; fr. 720N²) to a possible paraphrase in a messenger's description of Lamachus' disaster in the concluding scene (1188; fr. 705a *TrGF*). Neither of these last two Euripidean references need have been recognized by the audience for it to grasp that an important allusion is being made to a tragic context. In the prologue a sprinkling of high-style diction and meter and explicit references to the pleasures and pains evoked by tragic performances (9–16, immediately following the Telephean allusion in 8) link

to appreciate Aristophanes' parody–paratragedy. R. M. Harriott's study 'Aristophanes' Audience and the Plays of Euripides', *BICS* 9 (1962), 1–8, indicates that Aristophanes generally parodied tragic speeches, especially speeches of self-defence; it is likely, then, that Athenians were familiar with such speeches outside of their original context.

⁹ On *trygōidia*, see P. Ghiron-Bistagne, 'Un calembour méconnu d'Aristophane, *Acharniens* 400, *Oiseaux* 787', *REG* 86 (1973), 285–91 and O. Taplin, 'Tragedy and Trugedy', *CQ*, NS 33 (1983), 331–3.

initially the comic hero's situation with the opposite genre.[10] The language of the final scene pointedly contrasts the mock tragic fall of the wounded general with the comic triumph of Dikaiopolis.

Although Aristophanes does not openly name *Telephus* as the source for Dikaiopolis' hostage scene in *Acharnians*, he repeatedly stresses a shared theme—the making of a self-defence by defending the enemy—and draws the audience into a sort of guessing-game about his hero's strategem with the coal basket–'child'. The chorus says, inviting the audience to recall Telephus' seizure of the baby Orestes as hostage, 'Does he have one of our *children* confined inside?' (329–30; Dikaiopolis also swears—perhaps significantly— by Heracles, Telephus' father, at the beginning of the scene, 284). In any case, if the audience had thus far failed to notice Aristophanes' clever adaptation of this popular Euripidean scene,[11] the hero acquires the role, the costume, and the *rhēsis* of Telephus in the scene at the tragic poet's house. Dikaiopolis abandons the role of Telephus by the conclusion of his first encounter with the general Lamachus,[12] but in the final scene of the play Lamachus acquires the lameness of a Euripidean hero. Just as Telephus was wounded because he caught his foot in a vine shoot, Lamachus wounds himself with a vine prop while leaping over a ditch.

In short, Aristophanes frames and unifies the argument of his comedy through repeated references to Euripides' tragedy and makes gradually more explicit for the audience a relation, which cannot be viewed as strictly ironic or absurd, between Dikaiopolis, Telephus, and himself. For however much Aristophanes makes fun of

[10] On the language of the prologue and its complex mixture of poetic and colloquial diction, see esp. P. Rau, *Paratragodia: Untersuchungen einer komischen Form des Aristophanes*, Zetemata 45 (Munich, 1967), 185, and K. J. Dover, 'Lo stile di Aristofane', *QUCC* 9 (1970), 7–23. Rau, 37–8, notes the rarity of monologues in Old Comedy and the frequency of paratragic diction in such passages. Hence, while this passage is by no means a parody of Euripidean prologues (as argued by Starkie, *The 'Acharnians' of Aristophanes*, 6 and 249), and its eclectic style evokes the comic far more than the tragic, the monologue form itself may have prepared the audience for allusions to tragedy. The last scene of *Acharnians* includes lines adapted from other Euripidean plays as well.

[11] The scene appeared frequently on vase paintings. See Webster, *The Tragedies of Euripides*, 302 and E. Simon, *The Ancient Theatre*, trans. C. E. Vafopoulou-Richardson (New York, 1982), pl. 15, for an Apulian Bell Crater by the Schiller painter, *c*.370BC, that parodies the scene.

[12] C. Russo, *Aristofane, autore di teatro* (Florence, 1962; 2nd edn. 1984 unavailable to me), 87 suggests that Dikaiopolis throws off his rags at 595. See further C. Segal's review of Russo (*AJP* 86 (1965), 308) and R. M. Harriott, 'The Function of the Euripides Scene in Aristophanes' *Acharnians*', *G & R* 29 (1982), 39–40.

Euripides in the scene at the poet's house, Dikaiopolis makes his tragicomic[13] Telephean *rhēsis* the basis for a set of claims for both himself and Aristophanes that are repeated by the chorus, when they speak again for the poet and the justice of comedy in the parabasis. In contrast to *Thesmophoriazusae* and *Frogs* in *Acharnians* we find no references to Euripidean immoral heroines or new gods; here Aristophanes has no wish to jeopardize Dikaiopolis' case by emphasizing from the start the moral ambiguities of his tragic model.

II

Ostensibly, Dikaiopolis and Aristophanes lay claim to tragedy in order to acquire the courage to make a convincing and moving self-defence. But what particularly attracts Aristophanes to the choice of Telephus, out of all Euripides' ragged heroes? By having Dikaiopolis at Euripides' house run through a long list of alternative roles from his tragic rag-bag (412–34), Aristophanes not only mocks the tragic poet's propensity for these pathetic figures, but wants his audience to consider the range of tragic models available to him and to pay special attention to the apt choice of Telephus. Dikaiopolis rejects the pathetic rags of Oeneus, Phoenix, Philoctetes, and Bellerophon before accepting from Euripides the Telephean rags that perceptive members of the audience, who recognized allusions to *Telephus* in the previous scene, have already anticipated. Notice how the passage builds up to and stresses the choice of Telephus (414–34):

DIKAIOPOLIS. But I beg you by your knees, Euripides,
give me a little rag from some old drama.
I need to make a long speech to the chorus.
It will bring death, if I speak badly.
EURIPIDES. What sort of garments? The ones in which
this unfortunate old Oeneus played his role?[14]
DIKAIOPOLIS. No, not those of Oeneus, but of someone still more wretched.

[13] Following P. Pucci, *Aristofane ed Euripide: ricerche metriche e stilistiche* (Rome, 1961), 277–8, it is important to distinguish between parody, which deliberately mocks, deforms, or criticizes tragic style, and tragicomedy or paratragedy, which aims not to mock tragedy but to use high style to express comic ideas; *trygōidia*, to use Aristophanes' own term for his hero's comic adaptations of tragedy, has a mixed style which refers to the formal structure of tragedy (monody, stichomythia, and so on).
[14] Here Euripides points to a mask, costume, or manuscript. On the use of demonstratives for the costumes of Oeneus and Bellerophon at 418 and 427, see

EURIPIDES. Those of the blind Phoenix?
DIKAIOPOLIS. No, not Phoenix.
But those of another more miserable than Phoenix.
EURIPIDES. Whatever rent robes can the man be asking for?
Do you mean those of the beggar Philoctetes?
DIKAIOPOLIS. No, but of one far more beggarly.
EURIPIDES. Do you mean you want the filthy clothing
that this lame Bellerophon wore?
DIKAIOPOLIS. Not Bellerophon. But of one who
was lame, importunate, and a clever speaker.
EURIPIDES. [*quoting from his own text*] I know the man, 'Mysian Telephus'.[15]
DIKAIOPOLIS. Yes, Telephus. I beg you to give me his outfit.[16]
EURIPIDES. Slave, give the tatters of Telephus to him.
They lie above those of Thyestes, between them and those of Ino.

Old Oeneus and blind Phoenix were unjustly exiled and justly restored to society at the conclusion of these Euripidean dramas, Ino and Thyestes experienced the pain of exile, and Philoctetes and Bellerophon suffered both lameness and social isolation. Telephus is a supposed alien among Greeks, lame, and eloquent. Yet unlike the other ragged heroes, Telephus is not a helpless victim of exile, but deliberately adopts the disguise of a beggar to defend the justice of his past actions. The hero's manipulation of a humble disguise makes his role particularly attractive to a poet who aims to defend the justice of comedy through the mouth of his comic hero.

The role of Telephus has more extensive advantages for Aristophanes' self-defence than is generally realized, however. For Aristophanes, due to his recent difficulties with Cleon, has in fact even more in common with Telephus than does his comic hero. Both

---

C. Macleod, 'Euripides' Rags', *ZPE* 15 (1974, 221–2 and 'Euripides' Rags Again', *ZPE* 39 (1980), 6; repr. in *Collected Essays* (Oxford, 1983). Macleod suggests that the rags are a source of words for Dikaiopolis (*Ach.* 447) because they may in fact be texts as well as costumes (see *Ach.* 415).

[15] See *Telephus*, fr. 74N². The original line also apparently referred to the recognition of Telephus.

[16] H. Erbse, 'Zu Aristophanes', *Eranos*, 52 (1954), 8 emphasizes that *spargana* mean swaddling-clothes or tokens of recognition as well as rags. Macleod ('Euripides' Rags', 222) thinks that the term makes *Telephus* the exposed 'brain-child' of the tragedian (perhaps Euripides has the original of his text here as well). Pucci (*Aristofane ed Euripide* 413–14) sees here a parody of Euripides' plays of romantic intrigue, which often featured exposed children (such as the baby Telephus himself) who are finally recognized as royal. Euripides thus legitimizes Dikaiopolis as the father of Telephus–*Telephus*. Significantly, Dikaiopolis later uses the rags in his 'recognition scene' with Lamachus.

Telephus and Aristophanes, have suffered and incurred hostility and slander (*Ach.* 630) because of a successful and, we learn, fully justified previous 'attack' on their countrymen. Telephus was wounded by Achilles, and Aristophanes nearly 'perished' from Cleon's suit (381–2). Telephus defends his choice to drive off the invading Greeks from Mysia, and Aristophanes deserves his prize for the offending *Babylonians*, which really did not do violence to (*kathybrizei*, 631; see Cleon's charge of *hybris*) or mock (*kōmōidei*, 631) the city, but offered it justice (*ta dikaia*, 645, 655; see Cleon's charge of *adikia*).

Both claim to be true countrymen, despite appearances to the contrary. Telephus, although ruler of barbarian Mysia and a relation by marriage to Priam, is Greek by birth and said to be the son of Heracles most like his father (and hence a source of courage for Dikaiopolis; see *Ach.* 480–9 and *Telephus* fr. 702N²). His true identity as Greek is recognized in the concluding scenes of Euripides' play. The reference to Aristophanes' connection with Aegina in the parabasis (652–4) makes it likely that Cleon had indeed raised the issue of Aristophanes' Athenian citizenship in 426, even if he had not, as ancient testimony suggests, formally prosecuted the poet at this time for *xenia* as well as *adikia*.[17] Through both Dikaiopolis–Telephus and the parabasis, Aristophanes asserts his value as a true citizen of Athens.

Finally, both Telephus and Aristophanes end by achieving or claiming to have achieved recognition by their countrymen. Telephus, on the strength of an oracle and in gratitude for the cure of his wound, agrees to become the guide for the Greek expedition to Troy. Aristophanes argues in the parabasis that the Persian king has confirmed to the Spartans the strategic value of the famous poet who risks telling his city awkward truths and thus leads it through his advice to *victory in war* (646–55): 'and having this man [Aristophanes] as adviser [the city] will conquer decisively in war' (651). Here Aristophanes exploits the implicit analogy between himself and Telephus—both will lead their countrymen to victory in war—and ignores the plot of his play, which aims at peace (see 626–7). In 652–4, however, the chorus claims that the Spartans are offering to make peace in order to acquire Aegina and above all the poet himself. Thus, although it is difficult to reconcile Aristophanes' insistence on his military value to the city (596, 651) with the

[17] See n. 2 and 3.

powerful case made for peace in the play, I think that we must assume that the victory in war Aristophanes promises as Athens' adviser is an advantageous peace treaty.

The issue of recognition receives special emphasis in the Lamachus scene, which exposes the true identity of the beggar Dikaiopolis (and, by implication, of Aristophanes) as a good citizen (*politēs chrēstos*, 595) and soldier (*stratōnidēs*, 596) who thoroughly warrants the public acclaim he (and the poet) receive from Athens in the concluding scenes. If the audience at first fails to catch all these implicit parallels between Telephus' and Aristophanes' situations— an unlikely possibility given Cleon's recent prosecution and Aristophanes' identification with both heroes in the defence speech—the parabasis immediately following reinforces the similarities in the two cases by reiterating issues raised in Dikaiopolis' speech and by emphasizing the justice of comedy and the value of the slandered and clever poet to his society.[18] The allies come to Athens expressly to see the great poet who dared to speak justice to the city (643–5). Comic poets are just precisely because they satirize and do not flatter (like foreigners, 634–8) or deceive (656–8). How absurd, the parabasis implies, that only Athens's enemies and allies can see the poet's virtues; has the fickle audience forgotten the reception it gave *Babylonians* (see 630–2)?[19]

III

In *Acharnians*, then, Aristophanes borrows the role of a tragic hero whose dilemma corresponds in a number of crucial respects with his own. Yet whereas Aristophanes appropriates *Telephus* to reinforce

---

[18] On the parallels between Dikaiopolis' stance in the early scenes and Aristophanes' claims in the parabasis, see A. M. Bowie, 'The Parabasis in Aristophanes: Prolegomena, *Acharnians*', *CQ*, NS 32 (1982), 27–40. In both the assembly scene and the scene with Lamachus, Dikaiopolis, like Aristophanes in the parabasis, aims to expose those who wish to exploit the war for monetary gain. *Acharnians* 659–64, the *pnigos* of the parabasis, may be adapting *Telephus* 918N² to bolster comedy's claim to justice. Bowie (p. 40) sees a possible parallel between Dikaiopolis' separate peace and Aristophanes' own avenue of escape from the war in Aigina, an island described as *dikaiopolis* by Pindar (P. 8. 22).

[19] The *Babylonians* may have won first prize (see the pride in the play indicated in the parabasis of *Acharnians*, Cleon's reaction, and *IG* ii² 2325, which indicates that Aristophanes may have won a first prize at the Dionysia as early as 426). Others have contested this view, however (see Russo, *Aristofane*, ch. 2).

the case for the justice of his comedy, Dikaiopolis uses Telephus'
speech above all to make the chorus accept his central act of
injustice, the separate peace. Like Telephus and Aristophanes,
Dikaiopolis needs to defend himself on a charge of *adikia* before a
hostile audience. Initially provoked to act by his failure to gain a
hearing in the Assembly and the stealing of his garlic, he too
encounters after making his peace an attack on his person (from
which, however, he escapes unscathed).[20] Yet unlike Telephus,
Dikaiopolis deliberately engages in treason, and does so for purely
selfish gain. Telephus' speech apparently defended himself, the
Mysians, and, less certainly, the Trojans. Dikaiopolis' speech contains the promised defence of the Spartans (369, 482, 514, 541–55; in
509, he asserts that he hates the Spartans) and an exposure of
Athens's dubious motives for war and its tendency to act too
precipitously.[21] Dikaiopolis shares with Aristophanes the legitimate
claim that his speech will protect the city from flattery and deception from both native and foreign speakers corrupted by monetary
gain, and tell it unpalatable truths. Yet he does not defend his
separate peace. It is only by riding on the coat-tails of the truly
wronged Telephus and Aristophanes that he can distract his audience into recognizing his secession from society as the act of a soldier
and patriot(!). We will return later to the implications of this
important ambiguity in Dikaiopolis' (and to a lesser extent Aristophanes') defence. Up to this point we have seen that the relation
established in *Acharnians* among Telephus, Aristophanes, and
Dikaiopolis is quite complex; the closing scene of the play, however,
creates an additional link between Telephus and Lamachus.

---

[20] The third argument to *Peace* suggestively links *Peace*, *Babylonians* and *Acharnians*. If *Babylonians* were a 'peace play', then the connections between Dikaiopolis
and Aristophanes would be even stronger here.

[21] For the discrepancy between what Dikaiopolis claims he will say and what he
actually delivers, see esp. C. Whitman, *Aristophanes and the Comic Hero* (Cambridge,
Mass., 1964), 67, Dover, *Aristophanic Comedy* 82 (on the distracting effect of the speech)
and 86–7, Bowie, 'The Parabasis in Aristophanes', 33, and Harriott, 'The Function of
the Euripides Scene in Aristophanes' *Acharnians*', 38. Dikaiopolis at first conducts his
dialogue with the chorus on a flattering note, calling them sons of Acharneus (322)
and thus attributing to them an invented heroic ancestor. He urges them to hear and
judge why he made peace (294 and 306), leaving aside the Laconians (305). When this
meets with no response, he offers to show in what respects the Spartans have been
wronged (313–14), then to speak on their behalf (369). Hence his outrageous speech
appears forced on him by the hostile chorus.

IV

Dikaiopolis finishes exploiting *Telephus* in the first Lamachus scene, where the hero resists the general.[22] Having secured a Telephean recognition as citizen and patriot, he finally abandons his tragic disguise. After the parabasis Dikaiopolis, with the exception of a mock-tragic recognition of the Boeotian's eel (to be served by implication to Aristophanes' victorious chorus, 886), operates in a forthright comic mode, mocking and expelling his opposition, and revelling in the pleasures of peace, food, sex, festival, and social applause. Now, having created through tragedy the necessary audience for his comedy, Dikaiopolis seems no longer to need to borrow tragic devices to make his point. His summons to dine with the priest of Dionysus (1087) and his victorious exit to encounter the judges (1224) hint that his comic and Dionysiac victory will soon be shared by the poet.[23] The pompous Lamachus, however, whose self-presentation evokes the ethos of epic and tragedy, now suffers the consequences of his chosen style. In an absurd military encounter, Lamachus is lamed like so many Euripidean heroes. The similarity to the fate of Telephus, whom Dionysus punished by shackling him with a vine shoot as he fled from Achilles, is pointed, although the messenger speech describing Lamachus' fall borrows additional tragic pathos by echoing

---

[22] Rau, *Paratragodia*, 40–2 denies that Lamachus plays the role of Euripides' Achilles here. Nevertheless, the scene continues to borrow from *Telephus* (fr. 712N², *Ach.* 577 and the repeated references to the beggar disguise) and prepares for Lamachus' adoption of Telephus' lameness and his pleas for help in the final scene (see Pucci, *Aristophane ed Euripide*, 342).

[23] On the hints that Dikaiopolis' victory in the Dionysiac drinking-contest presages a comic victory for the poet in the Dionysiac theatrical festival as well, see on 886 and 1224, W. Rennie, *The 'Acharnians' of Aristophanes* (London, 1909). The celebration of a comic success would have included wine, and the original prize for a comic victory was said to be figs and wine (the Marmor Parium, *IG* xii 5. 444). Starkie, *The 'Acharnians' of Aristophanes*, 63, and A. W. Pickard-Cambridge, *Dithyramb, Tragedy and Comedy*, rev. T. B. L. Webster (Oxford, 1962), 145 ff. see in Dikaiopolis' celebration of the Rural Dionysia a reference to the origins of drama in Dionysiac phallic processions (see Arist., *Po.* 1449ᵃ12). L. Edmunds, 'Aristophanes' *Acharnians*', *YCS* 26 (1980), 6, while denying this view, nevertheless sees Dikaiopolis in this procession as a proto-poet. 'Paradoxically, the political function of comedy rests on its association with wine,' Edmunds argues, for Dikaiopolis' peace is wine, and 'wine is the occasion of festivals in honour of Dionysus' (p. 11). Dikaiopolis also drinks down Euripides (484) to give himself the courage to make his speech.

Euripides' dying Hippolytus.[24] Like Telephus, Lamachus is headed not for a tragic demise but a (here unheroic) cure.[25] Telephus was wounded in the thigh by Achilles; Lamachus, pretending that he was pierced by an enemy spear (1192), receives a less dignified ankle wound. As the visible transfer of lameness from Euripides and Telephus to Dikaiopolis to Lamachus makes clear, Aristophanes' comedy here insouciantly plays the double game of borrowing *Telephus* to defend itself and then allowing tragedy, in the person of Lamachus–Telephus, to take the rap that Dikaiopolis deserves for his treacherous peace.

V

Let us now consider more generally how Aristophanes' comedy exploits tragedy in its own defence. The role of hero disguised as beggar allows Aristophanes and Dikaiopolis, despite the absurd masks and lowly diction of comedy, to assimilate Telephus' heroic stature and authority. Even more important, however, Aristophanes' comedy imitates in the Telephean *rhēsis makra* tragedy's mode of making social criticism safely distanced and disguised through myth. Dikaiopolis is forced to turn to tragedy because, up to the hostage scene, the hero's purely comic mode of persuasion proves ineffective. The absurdity of Athenian war politics in the Assembly scene is presented as visible to the hero alone—despite his exposure of the impostors—and the chorus is impervious to such comic satire and advice. By contrast, Greek audiences had for generations tolerated from serious literature extensive questioning of the origins of the Trojan war and the notorious Helen. Lyric

[24] *Ach.* 1190–7 and *Hipp.* 1347–52 and *Ach.* 1183 and *Hipp.* 1239. See J. van Leeuwen, *Aristophanis 'Acharnenses'* (Leiden, 1901; repr. 1968), 1178 ff. (contested by Rau, *Paratragodia* 139 n. 5). Schol. R on *Ach.* 1190 sees here a comic adaptation of tragic *thrēnoi*. In the final scene of *Hippolytus*, Theseus gloats (in ignorance of the truth) over the body of the dying Hippolytus just as Dikaiopolis gloats over the wounded Lamachus. On the messenger speech generally, see Rau, *Paratragodia* 137–44.
[25] See Rau, *Paratragodia* 144. See also his comments (142) on Lamachus' unheroic rise from the ditch to pursue soldiers already in flight. Lamachus and Telephus are also linked in the messenger speech by *Ach.* 1188 (*Telephus*, fr. 705aSn.) Both are further linked by 'crimes' against Dionysus and their ultimate commitment to war rather than peace. For Telephus ends Euripides' play by departing for Troy and a betrayal of his father-in-law, Priam.

poetry and Aeschylus offered doubts similar to those presented in the texts that Aristophanes alludes to here, *Telephus* and, perhaps, the opening of Herodotus' *Histories*.[26] Through its imitation of serious literature, comedy makes its political satire seem comparable to what audiences traditionally accepted from tragic poets like Euripides simply because they cloaked their iconoclastic message with myth and an elevated style.[27] 'For *trygōidia* also [or even *trygōidia*] knows justice,'[28] says Dikaiopolis (500), implying that tragedy would automatically be granted such authority.

But above all, by providing Aristophanes with opportunities to create multiple roles, audiences, and disguises, as well as to play off one style of dramaturgy against another, the borrowing from tragedy makes Cleon's prosecution of Aristophanes look like the result of a bumbling and literal-minded misinterpretation of comedy, and especially of political satire in comedy. Aristophanes, adapting a quotation from *Telephus* (fr. 698N², *Ach.* 440–1), stresses to his *audience* that it will *not* be fooled by Dikaiopolis' adoption of a tragic role. By contrast, the rigidly anti-Spartan chorus, who accuse Dikaiopolis (as Cleon accused Aristophanes) of being a traitor, are to

---

[26] Recently D. M. MacDowell, 'The Nature of Aristophanes' *Akharnians*', *G & R* 30 (1983), 151, has renewed the argument that Pericles' wrath over the theft of Aspasia's courtesans—the event that began the war—is not a parody of Herodotus. He cites the problem of the date of publication of the *Histories* and of the audience's familiarity with its text, as well as the lack of any Herodotean turns of phrase in the passage. Others have speculated that *Telephus* was Aristophanes' source here (see C. W. Fornara, 'Evidence for the date of Herodotus' publication', *JHS* 91 (1971, 25–34). Cratinus' recent *Dionysalexandros* may also have offered a similar parody. If the audience knew any of Herodotus' text, however, they would be likely to be familiar with the opening, and the *rhēsis* does not mark all of its borrowings from *Telephus* with tragic language.

[27] See *Telephus*, fr. 706N² and 918N² for the tragic hero's own claims to speak justice to the Greeks. Edmunds, 'Aristophanes' *Acharnians*', arguing that comedy can only claim justice in disguise (p. 12), asserts that the 'paratragic play-within-the-play insulates the justification of peace with Sparta, which might otherwise be offensive, no matter how laughably presented. . . . The question of peace is transposed into a new sphere. . . . Once again Dicaeopolis, or Aristophanes, has left the hostile political milieu behind in order to make a political statement' (10–11). I would qualify these remarks by arguing that the play-within-the-play works differently for its internal and external audiences, and that tragedy as well as comedy may adopt disguise to make political statements (as in the case of Telephus himself). Mythologizing politics (associating Pericles with Zeus and Aspasia's courtesans with Helen) can remind the spectators that politics operate as well in terms of myths of another sort.

[28] On the translation, see Taplin, 'Tragedy and Trugedy', 333.

be rudely humiliated (*skimalisō*, that is, given the finger)[29] by
Dikaiopolis' Telephean rhetoric (440–4):

> It is necessary for me to appear as a beggar today,
> to be as I am but not appear to be so.
> The spectators must know who I am
> but the chorus will be fools enough not to,
> so that I may humiliate them with my clever phrases.

The staging reinforces the verbal point. For although Dikaiopolis
immediately before this passage dons the attire of Telephus, his own
comic costume remains visible through the multiple holes in the
rags (435)—visible to the audience if not to the chorus or to
Lamachus, who both swallow the dramatic illusion produced by
the tragic beggar costume (558, 578). The arbitrariness of the
disguise—Dikaiopolis does not need to conceal himself as Telephus
did, but simply wants to create a tragic tone—reinforces this effect.
Similarly, the audience knows from the start the irony of borrowing
from Euripides the role of 'Mysian Telephus' (430), since the whole
point of Euripides' play is that Telephus is actually Greek. Dikaiopolis' acquisition of Telephus' revealing Mysian cap (439, immediately prior to the passage quoted above) expresses visually the same
ambiguity. Aristophanes' chorus stupidly fails to grasp the implications of this clue to Dikaiopolis'–Telephus' identity, while the audience is further reminded that Dikaiopolis is simultaneously playing
many incompatible roles: beggar, nobleman, and comic hero, Greek
and foreigner. (The scholiast on *Ach.* 439 implies that tragic actors
wore such a cap when playing Telephus. Is Aristophanes mocking
Euripides for providing an absurdly imperfect Greek disguise for his
hero?[30]) In addition, whereas Euripides' tragic beggar is recognized
first merely as Telephus, and finally as both Greek and indispensable

---

[29] Holding up the middle finger implies that the objects of the insulting gesture are
pathics (schol. *Peace* 549). The word can also describe feeling inside a chicken to detect
the presence of an egg (schol. *Ach.* 444), a gesture that might have similar sexual
connotations.

[30] The scholiast knows of contemporary actors who did not wear the *pilidion*.
While some vase paintings of the hostage scene show Telephus bare-headed (as
would fit the dramatic context, since his disguise has already been penetrated), the
two vases with pilos (a Campanian bell krater in Naples, 350–325 BC, and an Attic
pelike, 350–325 BC, *ARV²* 1473; see Webster, *The Tragedies of Euripides*, 302) confirm the
strong association of the cap with the role. The cap serves to keep the issue of
Telephus' identity (and thus also the citizenship of Aristophanes or Callistratus)
visually before the audience. On the irony of 'Mysian Telephus', see Olympiodorus
on Pl. *Grg.* 521b. I wish to thank Eric Handley for drawing my attention to this issue.

to the Greek cause, Aristophanes can ask his audience through Dikaiopolis to recognize his citizenship, as well as to interpret his triple disguise (see *Knights* 512–16) as Callistratus, under whose name he has produced his comedies, as Telephus, and as Dikaiopolis.

The poet's use of tragic rhetoric further serves to separate the play's internal audience from Aristophanes' Athenian audience, who are prepared to read through the tragic smoke-screen to the comic truth beneath. Dikaiopolis, with the ironic self-mockery of a 'mere' comic hero, limits his ambition to borrowing for his speech Euripidean words and phrases, his diminutive *rhēmatia* (444, 447). (Indeed, Aristophanes suggests, the task is made easier because the tragic poet composes by gathering and combining such delightful little phraselets, *epyllia*, 398.) Those in the audience who recollect the actual text of *Telephus* are thus prepared to hear exactly what will happen in the *rhēsis makra*. Here, as scholarly analysis has confirmed, Aristophanes interpolates into the largely comic diction of the speech occasional tragic phrases, many but not all from *Telephus*.[31] Nearly all of these phrases, which help the audience to recall at the beginning and end of the speech central points that Aristophanes has borrowed from *Telephus*, are tranformed or adapted to a new context which distorts in a complex and often double-edged fashion the meaning of the original line(s).[32] For example, whereas Telephus' speech addressed the leaders of the Greeks, the play's internal audience (fr. 703N²), and apologized for speaking as a beggar among noblemen, Dikaiopolis borrows his lines to address—in a pointedly metatheatrical fashion—the *spectators* of *Acharnians* and defends comedy's right to speak among Athenians (by implication, a noble audience) about the city in a *trygōidia*. Dikaiopolis–Aristophanes says, self-consciously playing on the

---

[31] See Rau, *Paratragodia*, 19–42, Webster, *The Tragedies of Euripides*, 43–8, Handley and Rea, *The 'Telephus' of Euripides*, esp. 25, and H. W. Miller, 'Euripides' *Telephus* and the *Thesmophorizusae* of Aristophanes', *CP* 43 (1948), 174–83. On *epyllia* as small erotic poems as well as light verses, see C. del Grande, 'Epyllia in Aristofane', in *Komoido-tragemata: Studia Aristophanes viri Aristophanei W. J. W. Koster in Honorem* (Amsterdam, 1967). The text also paraphrases lines on important ideas from the speech. No one seems to have noticed, however, that Aristophanes gives his audience precise information about how the paratragic speech will work (its borrowing of little phrases) in the scene with Euripides.

[32] Many of the Telephean fragments are too short (or too distorted by Aristophanes' adaptation of them) to allow for an interpretation of how Aristophanes is reworking them. My two examples come from sections where we have enough of the original to be able to speculate (at least two lines, if the scholia give fully correct versions of frs. 698 and 703, as they very probably do not).

supposed inferiority of comedy and the name of Dikaiopolis himself
(496–500): [33]

> Do not be angry with me, spectators,
> if in making my trugedy I am about to speak about the city
> among Athenians, disguised as a beggar.
> For even, trugedy (or trugedy also) knows justice.

A similar example occurs before the *rhēsis*. The Telephean passage about adopting a beggar disguise quoted earlier (440–4) must
have dealt in the original with Telephus' spiritual integrity or with
the simultaneous truth and falsity of his disguise—Telephus *is*
Greek, though not a beggar; appearing a beggar, he must be as he
is (noble) but not appear to be so.[34] Dikaiopolis borrows Telephus'
words to stress instead the issue of theatrical illusion; the chorus
will accept the tragic disguise that the audience is primed to
penetrate. At the same time, Aristophanes in a Telephean manner
does adopt a tragic disguise while being true to himself as comic
poet; for the language, argument and open political satire of the
rhēsis remain comic—to the audience, if not to the chorus, who
again view it as tragic. Dikaiopolis' *rhēsis* does not in fact transpose
political questions into another realm in the tragic manner, but
gains authority by borrowing phraselets from Euripides and the
larger literary tradition to continue to make the kind of pointed
comic criticisms of the causes of the war and of Athens' political
leaders for which Cleon attacked him.[35] Finally, the role of hero
disguised as beggar, although Dikaiopolis uses it to exploit and
deceive the chorus, aptly describes Aristophanes in the role of
Dikaiopolis and thus allows the poet to defend both himself and
the noble nature of comedy;[36] Aristophanes' extravagant claims of
his value to the city in the parabasis here become equivalent to the
(typical) assimilation of heroic language and authority by his comic

[33] Aristophanes goes on to stress (502–7) that he is no longer, as in *Babylonians*,
addressing strangers as well, since the play is being presented at the Lenaia (a festival
that occurred too early in the year for outsiders to attend).
[34] As the scholiast on line 441 says, he changes not his nature (*physis*), but his
shape (*morphē*). Rau, *Paratragodia*, 33, argues that Aristophanes turns this typically
Euripidean philosophizing on being and seeming into a play on theatrical illusion.
[35] MacDowell, 'The Nature of Aristophanes' *Akharnians*', 151–5, makes a strong
case that Aristophanes' remarks concerning the role of Pericles and the Megarian
decree in causing the war have a good deal of substance beneath the absurd comic
detail.   [36] See Edmunds, 'Aristophanes' *Acharnians*', 10–11, on this point.

protagonist and the actual heroism of a tragic protagonist. In short, Aristophanes' treatment of Euripides' costumes sets the tone for his more subtle but comparable misuse and fragmenting of the tragedian's rhetoric. The audience laughs knowingly while the duped chorus maintains its conversion to the tragic mood by responding to Dikaiopolis' speech—as they have throughout this scene (358–571)—in dochmiacs.

In borrowing Euripides' plot Aristophanes again diffuses the Telephean tragic pathos for his audience by fragmenting and reshaping the original as he did costume and rhetoric. Current reconstructions of *Telephus* suggests that Euripides' hero opens the play in disguise, and perhaps uses the beggar role to enter the palace and gain Clytemnestra as ally; his famous speech then provokes a quarrel between Menelaus and Agamemnon.[37] After his disguise is penetrated, Telephus resorts to using the baby Orestes as hostage. Finally, he is recognized as Greek, promised a cure by Achilles, and sets off to serve a predestined role as guide of the troops to Troy. Aristophanes makes random selections from this plot and puts the search and exposure and the recourse to the hostage device *before* not after the *rhēsis* and thus plagiarizes from Euripides prior to the visit to the poet's house. Indeed, Dikaiopolis' deme name *Chollēidēs* (406) punningly establishes his natural right to Euripides' lame (*chōlas*) heroes, and he is wordy, importunate, and a clever speaker (429) long before he pretends to acquire these attributes from Telephus. As Dikaiopolis later tells Euripides, he has no need for a *plekos* (wickerwork) for which he asked (454, very possibly punning on *tekos* and recalling the coal basket that was substituted for the child),[38] because, as the audience knows, he has already used one in the hostage scene. He simply needs the tragic label in order to fool the chorus, who are to be impressed by arguments made in tragic guise that they stupidly reject in comic form. In *Thesmophoriazusae*, where he is letting Euripides run into

[37] Here I follow Handley and Rea, *The 'Telephus' of Euripides*. In his reconstruction of *Telephus*, Rau, *Paratragodia*, 22 puts the speech after a quarrel between Agamemnon and Menelaus about whether to attack Mysia; Telephus responds to the threat to Mysia with a speech that is exclusively one of self-defence. If Rau is correct, Aristophanes has further distorted the plot of the original. Yet Aristophanes expects his audience to recognize a speech 'on behalf of the enemy' as Telephean. If the enemy is Mysia rather than Troy, the richness of the allusion for the war against Sparta is considerably diminished.

[38] See the parody of this same motif at *Peace* 528 with its pun on *tekos–plekos* and *Telephus* fr. 727N[2].

difficulty on his own, Aristophanes apparently sticks in his parody of
Telephus much more closely to the original order of the plot of the
play.[39] But here, by putting the hostage scene before the speech, he
deliberately destroys the logic of Euripides' plot (while enhancing
the impact of his own) and gets away with it; for the hostage device
only makes 'dramatic sense' in a tragic context after all verbal
means have failed.

Having dispensed in advance with Telephus' climactic stratagem,
Dikaiopolis goes on after the *rhēsis* to reveal his 'true' identity as
good citizen and soldier voluntarily (595–6), thus depriving Lamachus of his chance to expose him as impostor (as Cleisthenes,
apparently following Euripides' original, does in *Thesmophoriazusae*[40]) and reducing the general to feeble expostulations about
Dikaiopolis' outrageous abuse of his beggar disguise (an anticlimac-
tic conclusion to the Telephean line expectantly fed him at the
opening of the scene by the chorus, 577, fr. 712N[2]). Having made
Lamachus' 'tragic' role redundant, Aristophanes in this scene
allows Euripides' plot to dissolve in a barrage of comic insults.
Dikaiopolis not only mockingly side-steps the tragic consequences
(involuntary exposure) that should logically have come with his
Telephean disguise but even turns the tables on his opponent, as
the comic hero reveals both Lamachus' pretentiousness (his costume) and his mercenary motives. Again, as with costume and
rhetoric, the unnecessary and improbable Aristophanic plot divides
Aristophanes' spectators, who because of their knowledge of *Telephus* can observe its absurdity and are thus immune to its supposed
pathetic power, from his dupes, Lamachus and the chorus. At the
same time, by turning at once to Euripides' device of last resort,
comedy implies that, unlike tragedy, its central problem is to acquire
a proper hearing. Just as Pindar must make the discerning members
of his audience understand why he must offer advice and criticism
in a praise poem to those who hire him to celebrate their successes,
Aristophanes must persuade an audience to see, for example, how
his peace play does not in fact undermine the war effort.

[39] See Miller, 'Euripides' *Telephus* and the *Thesmophoniazusae* of Aristophanes', and
my n. 37. Erbse, 'Zu Aristophanes', 95–8, surprisingly thinks that Aristophanes has
improved on Euripides' plot.
[40] Rau, *Peratragodia*, 24–5 doubts that the original contained a comparable scene.
Yet Telephus' disguise must have been penetrated in some fashion.

VI

To summarize the argument thus far, then, Aristophanes uses Euripides' tragedy first to defend comedy's social and political criticism (even during a war). By linking his comedy and Euripidean tragedy (a link characterized in this play by the term *trygōidia*), he claims for it the moral authority, literary prestige, and latitude that audiences have always given to more pretentious genres. Why, then, should the audience not allow to Aristophanes the kind of argument about war that it permitted to Euripides and his outrageous Telephus (see *Ach.* 555–6, *Telephus* fr. 710N²)? Second, the poet aims to create a discerning audience for his comedies. Like Pindar, he compliments, though less directly, the perceptive members of the audience. Those who have already picked up the allusion to *Telephus* in the hostage scene do not need something as explicit as the Euripides scene to understand what is going on. He flatters—and educates—his other viewers by having his chorus and characters misread comic satire and be deceived by tragic rhetoric and dramaturgy even as he reveals so explicitly the mechanics of his paratragedy.

Above all, Aristophanes uses the contrast between genres to define his own comedy; indeed, comedy's deliberate violation of tragic limits becomes the basis of its self-defence, of its claim to free speech, truth, and justice. Aristophanes' borrowing of *Telephus* consistently flouts the dramatic illusion and pathos upon which tragedy depends.[41] For example, whereas Euripides' Telephus did not disguise himself on stage, but enters disguised, Aristophanes' audience sees Dikaiopolis begin to adopt the importunate behaviour of a beggar as he acquires each aspect of his excessively 'realistic' and hence ultimately untragic Telephean guise.[42] As in

[41] Recent critics have rejected the claim of G. M. Sifakis, *Parabasis and Animal Choruses* (London, 1971) that dramatic illusion does not exist in comedy. Especially useful are the discussions of D. Bain, *Actors and Audience* (Oxford, 1977), esp. 4–7 and 87–99, and F. Muecke, 'Playing with the Play: Theatrical Self-consciousness in Aristophanes', *Antichthon*, 11 (1977), 52–67, and '"I Know You—By your Rags": Costume and Disguise in Fifth-Century Drama', *Antichthon*, 16 (1982), 17–34. Both help to distinguish precisely where in comedy the author can maintain or violate dramatic illusion. Muecke ('Playing with the Play', 59) suggests that the humour of breaking illusion in comedy nevertheless depends on tragedy. Bain prefers the term 'pretence' to 'dramatic illusion', since no audience fails to know that it is watching a play; comedy thus disrupts the actor's pretence to be the person he plays (pp. 6–7). See also Dover, *Aristophanic Comedy*, 56.

[42] Harriott, 'The Function of the Euripides Scene in Aristophanes' *Acharnians*', 36. The same effect occurs with props. Dikaiopolis staggers off from Euripides' house

Aristophanes, Telephus' reference to his disguise gives his audience
(not the other characters) privileged knowledge of his identity. Yet
whereas Telephus' gesture enhances and makes visible his unjust
suffering, Aristophanes' dramaturgy undercuts tragic pathos to
stress the different ways that costume and dramatic identity can
be read self-consciously by his audience.[43] In addition, Dikaiopolis
finally uses the beggar role less to evoke pity than to establish his
heroism and good citizenship.[44]

By having Dikaiopolis call for Euripides to be rolled out from
within his house on the *ekkyklēma* (408),[45] Aristophanes not only
stresses in an untragic fashion the mechanics of tragic theatre, but
suggests that comedy reveals the unglamorous but important truths
that tragedy (drama that depends on dramatic illusion) hides behind
the stage. Whereas the politicians of the first scene or the tragedians
may use costume or rhetoric to deceive their audience, as the
disguised Dikaiopolis does to the chorus, Aristophanes uses it to
reveal the truth to his audience. In the first scene of the play,
Dikaiopolis exposes the disguises of impostors in the Assembly.
Later he lets his audience, if not the chorus, see through his
Telephean costume with double vision. He makes the mesmerizing
persuasiveness of tragic dramaturgy and rhetoric, like the rhetoric
of politicians, bamboozle the chorus into swallowing not only

---

loaded with more props than the tragic poet could have imagined or Aristophanes'
comedy can use. He even tries to borrow the herbs belonging to Euripides' mother
that are in fact the product of the comic tradition itself. For comedy's illusion-
breaking literalization of tragic metaphors (the axe metaphorically poised at Telephus' throat, fr. 706N[2], an image he invents to insist that nothing will silence him,
becomes a prop on stage, the chopping-block on which Dikaiopolis promises to place
his head while speaking), see esp. H.-J. Newiger, *Metaphor und Allegorie*, Zetemata, 16
(Munich, 1957), Rau, *Paratragodia* 3, and Edmunds, 'Aristophanes' *Acharnians*'.

[43] For a perceptive treatment of the conventions governing comic and tragic
costume, see F. Muecke, 'I Know You—By your Rags'. See Rau, *Paratragodia*, 36, on
the contrast between comic and tragic costume in this passage. Distinguishing the
conventions governing tragic and comic use of disguise is complex—such disguise has
its origins in the *Odyssey* and divine disguise in epic. Aristophanes' texts do tend to
associate tragedy, as here in the case of *Telephus*, with disguise with deliberate intent
to deceive. In *Acharnians* Dikaiopolis first *tells* the chorus that he will get a pitiable
costume in which to make his defence (383–4), and then announces that his tragic
costume will deceive the chorus (443–4; see Rau, *Paratragodia*, 33 n. 38). For another
interpretation of this inconsistency, see Muecke, 'Playing with the Play', 63 n. 59.

[44] On this last point, see Harriott, 'The Function of the Euripides Scene in
Aristophanes' *Acharnians*', 36–41.

[45] A. M. Dale, *Collected Papers* (Cambridge, 1969), 288, comments that the *ekkyklēma* allows Euripides to come out while remaining technically within. This is where
as a tragic poet he belongs, since poets cannot speak for themselves in tragedy.

Aristophanes' defensible Telephean criticisms of his country but even Dikaiopolis' treasonable secession from Athens. By contrast comedy, by exposing all its tricks and strategems, by fragmenting tragic rhetoric and logic, by undercutting the borrowed tragic pathos, by creating absurd plots, and by making its dramaturgy depend on the unnecessary, the excessive, the inconsistent, and the absurd, implicitly argues that it plays fair with its audience and hence better defends comedy's proclaimed agenda—to offer justice to its audience and to make the city examine the errors and absurdities committed by certain of its politicians.

Aristophanes' treatment of tragic dramaturgy here seems to be motivated by concerns similar to those Brecht showed in the twentieth century in choosing to present 'epic theatre'[46] For Brecht the author of epic theatre tries to distance the audience from both characters and action in order to appeal to reason over emotion. Rather than implicating the spectator emotionally (through pity and fear) in a stage situation like tragedy or opera, epic theatre turns the spectator into a critical observer, politicizes him, and arouses his capacity for action outside the theatre. Its characters are alterable and able to alter, not caught in a net of destiny; each scene is taken for itself, rather than forming part of a linear and inevitable sequence. Brecht makes the mechanics of theatre an organic part of his anti-illusionary and non-Aristotelian dramaturgy precisely to prevent the spectator's 'passive empathy', to 'alienate' him from the action, to make him question it and wish to change it. Although his characters do at times maintain the dramatic illusion (or produce the pathos) native to serious drama, the audience is never allowed to maintain this illusion for long, an illusion often created precisely to prepare for a later dispelling of such theatrical magic. At the same time, Brecht argues, theatre must never sacrifice to didactic ends its capacity to move and amuse its audience. Although Aristophanes' aims in defending his political theatre were considerably less activist and revolutionary than Brecht's—and, of course, unlike Brecht he is a comic poet—each adopts or proposes a similar theatrical strategy in urging his audience to examine itself and its politics and to make changes for the better. Each takes seriously the educational role of theatre, and exploits a contrast between his own dramaturgy and that of

---

[46] This paragraph summarizes arguments made in Brecht's *Schriften zum Theater* (Frankfurt, 1957). See also Bain, *Actors and Audience*, 3–7.

tragic-style dramaturgy in order to do so (see *Ach.* 500, 645, 650, 661–2, 655–6).

VII

In *Acharnians*, after half the old men of the chorus fall victim to Dikaiopolis' paratragic arguments in the *rhēsis makra*, they are distracted from their hostility to Dikaiopolis into turning against each other, as Agamemnon and Menelaus apparently did in Euripides' *Telephus*.[47] Finally the whole chorus collapses into blatant admiration of the hero's newly claimed good citizenship and his outrageous and utterly selfish success. The city later follows suit; the treacherous Dikaiopolis is now invited to dinner by the priest of Dionysus (1087) and wins a public drinking-contest at the Anthesteria. In short, the borrowed tragedy helps to make the gulled chorus (444) forget that Dikaiopolis failed to offer an adequate defence of his separate peace (despite his good criticism to the city of its previous errors) or to fit fully the role of Telephus (a comic hero, after all, never faces either a tragic destiny or the lawsuits of the real world), and permits him to claim the justice due to Telephus and Aristophanes. By contrast, the audience to Aristophanes' *trygōidia*, which is in on Dikaiopolis' strategy, is first primed to see through Dikaiopolis' disguise and defence and then warned again against flattery, meaningless high-style rhetoric, gullibility, and misinterpretation of Aristophanes' comedy in the parabasis (633–40). Urging the city to make peace and making a separate peace are not the same thing—although presenting the delightful effects of the latter should indirectly promote the former. The poet celebrates his own value as a speaker of (often unpalatable) truths to society through his hero, but the justice of comedy and the justice of Dikaiopolis' individual peace cannot after the *rhēsis* be simplistically equated in the audience's mind.

Dikaiopolis' behaviour in the scenes following the parabasis puts to the test the audience's ability to distinguish between the comic hero's outrageous behaviour and the true justice of comedy. His private market ultimately displays the vices that were said to lead to or support the war in the earlier scenes: traffic in sexuality

---

[47] See n. 37 above. Whitman, *Aristophanes and the Comic Hero*, 67, emphasizes this point.

(Aspasia's whores and the Megarian's daughters), exclusion from markets (Megara; Lamachus and finally all Athenians),[48] and the exploitation of war to make individual profits (the ambassadors in the first scene and Lamachus; Dikaiopolis). His trading-partners are tricked into accepting the worst of Athenian vices (sycophants, who are nevertheless not unjustified in informing against Dikaiopolis). He shows no generosity to those who are victims of the war as he was once himself (Dercetes),[49] or for his converts, the chorus. True, Dikaiopolis, who in his opening speech expresses a rural distaste for buying and selling (35), was forced by the chorus to abandon his initial plans to celebrate an innocent rural Dionysia in favour of the market;[50] true, Dikaiopolis no doubt pleased his audience by making the enemy as much the victim in his economic exchanges as they would have been while still at war. True, Dikaiopolis' name (if it means 'he of the just city' or 'just city') hardly seems to fit a hero who has no real claim to just behaviour.[51] But in contrast to

[48] I cannot agree with MacDowell, 'The Nature of Aristophanes' *Akharnians*', 158 that all gradually join in Dikaiopolis' peace, despite the choral passage at 971–99; the chorus can be converted to peace without sharing it, the scene with the bridegroom emphasizes the exclusion of all men from the peace, and the Anthesteria could ·be celebrated within the walls of a city at war. In addition, the audience knows that the chorus have been duped by Dikaiopolis (the chorus of *Birds* is similarly duped). Nevertheless, choral exclusion and misperception is certainly not emphasized in the festive final scene, and, given the inconsistencies of comic dramaturgy, I would not want to put too much weight on this point. See Whitman, *Aristophanes and the Comic Hero*, 79, for a subtle treatment of this problem.

[49] Several critics have recently argued that Dercetes fully deserves his rejection; Edmunds, 'Aristophanes' *Acharnians*', 21, argues that Dikaiopolis in 1019 aims to remove the misfortune brought by the unlucky Dercetes, and McDowell, 'The Nature of Aristophanes' *Akharnians*', 159–60, thinks the joke has not been understood because Aristophanes is here satirizing a real person for some unknown offence.

[50] He still gets all things *automata*, as in the traditional Golden Age (976), and enjoys all the delicacies provided by peace and festival, and one could argue that the market involves barter rather than buying and selling. Yet he does not in fact, as Edmunds suggests ('Aristophanes' *Acharnians*', esp. 27 ff.), return to the simple pleasures of the country. In the Golden Age men collectively enjoyed a peaceful life; here Dikaiopolis' *oikos* alone gets the benefits. The Golden Age won by Dikaiopolis is a corrupt and perverted version of the original.

[51] On the name, see Russo, *Aristofane*, 59–60, de Ste Croix, *The Origins of the Peloponnesian War* (London, 1972), 365, Edmunds, 'Aristophanes', *Acharnians*, 1 n. 2, and MacDowell, 'The Nature of Aristophanes' *Akharnians*', 160. The play also shows Athens to be a city that has been persuaded to act unjustly. Critics are divided on how to interpret Dikaiopolis' peace. For Dover, *Aristophanic Comedy*, 88, *Acharnians* is a 'fantasy of total selfishness'. Whitman, *Aristophanes and the Comic Hero*, esp. 76–8, and Bowie 'The Parabasis in Aristophanes', 39–40, see the peace as an expression of the Aristophanic hero's typical *ponēria* or *alazoneia*. Edmunds ('Aristophanes' *Acharnians*';

Aristophanes' later peace plays *Peace* and *Lysistrata*, the hero's countrymen are not only excluded from the benefits of peace but are foolish enough to admire and reward him for his secession as if he were still their own citizen.

Nevertheless, Dikaiopolis' practice of injustice ultimately makes Aristophanes' defence of his *Babylonians* on charges of *adikia* more, rather than less, effective. *Babylonians* it seems, used comic satire to expose the misguided policies of the city's politicians and, the poet claims in the parabasis, won rather than alienated the loyalty of the allies for its justice (641–5). *Acharnians* continues in the tradition of *Babylonians* to expose the city's politicians and to promote the positive cause of peace for the city. Yet it manipulates tragedy to make the stronger claim that a comedy can offer justice to its discerning audience while allowing its outrageous hero openly to advocate and pursue treason (*adikia*). Hence Dikaiopolis' (and comedy's) language is *deina men dikaia de* (501). Literal-minded interpreters of comedy—the chorus or a Cleon—who demand from comedy pleasing deception, unthinking patriotism, literalism, and flattery come off as the easy dupes of arguments perpetrated in tragic style. The discerning audience sees how Dikaiopolis uses tragic rhetoric to distract the chorus from his treachery and then goes on in later scenes to win their positive admiration for it. The outrageous extremes to which Dikaiopolis exploits his peace repeat more shockingly—in part because his success is so seductive—the abuses perpetrated in the Athenian Assembly, where politicians in wartime 'buy and sell' (374) their audience with deceptive rhetoric, material success, and disguise. For the discerning audience, the comic injustice of the hero thus reinforces the justice of comedy—above all, Aristophanes' exposure throughout the play of the dangerous effects of high-style (political and tragic) rhetoric on a gullible and volatile populace.

---

see also MacDowell, 'The Nature of Aristophanes' *Akharnians*', 158–60) has recently made the strongest case for viewing the peace as 'just'. But his argument depends on assuming that Dikaiopolis wins with his peace an ideal rural self-sufficiency; I cannot interpret as such a peace that brings festival through markets, rather than agricultural labour and close contact with the land, as in *Peace*. As in Plato's *Republic*, a 'city of pigs' has in *Acharnians* become a 'fevered city'.

VIII

What can we conclude from *Acharnians* about Aristophanes' politics and Aristophanic parody of tragedy?[52] The analysis offered in this chapter above all reconciles Aristophanes' patriotic claims in the parabasis with the rest of the play. By separating the comic argument from the comic plot, by writing a peace-play that can lead to victory, Aristophanes seems to be arguing that his comedy is far more patriotic than it might appear and that its outrageousness is more apparent than real. Of course, Aristophanes' comedy is not uncritical and it would never be so foolish as to prefer war to peace; but its attack is not aimed at the city (515–16), only at individuals, rhetoric, or policies which deflect the city from its best interests. Hence, for example, Dikaiopolis' *rhēsis* is less the promised defence of the enemy than a defence of the poet and an education of his audience concerning its motives for war.

Aristophanes' fellow comic poet Cratinus (fr. 307K, 342 Kassel–Austin) mocked him for his tendency to 'euripidaristophanize'—that is, apparently, for his artistic dependence on or imitation of (*mimeisthai*) the tragic poet he so frequently mocked (*skōptein*). The clever spectator, says Cratinus, could hardly miss noticing that Aristophanes himself employed the refined, epigrammatical, and overly intellectual style of Euripides. Elsewhere, Aristophanes seems to have admitted borrowing Euripides' stylistic elegance without his vulgarity.[53] While Cratinus shows his awareness that Aristophanes' parody aimed at something more than criticism of contemporary tragedy, scholars have generally given more attention to what Aristophanes says about Euripides than to how Aristophanes uses tragedy to communicate comic meaning to his audience.[54] Yet an

---

[52] For the pros and cons of interpreting *Acharnians* as a serious plea for peace, see, among recent views, W. G. Forrest, 'Aristophanes' *Acharnians*', *Phoenix*, 17 (1963), 1–12, H.-J. Newiger, 'War and Peace in the Comedy of Aristophanes', *YCS* 26 (1980), 219–37, Dover, *Aristophanic Comedy*, esp. 84–8, and the (in my view) largely convincing argument of MacDowell, 'The Nature of Aristophanes' *Akharnians*'. The dimensions of the problem were earlier well stated by A. W. Gomme, 'Aristophanes and Politics', *More Essays in Greek History and Literature* (Oxford, 1962), ch. 5.

[53] Fr. 471K. schol. Areth. (B) Pl. *Ap.* 190.

[54] Most recent critics of Aristophanic parody, such as Pucci, *Aristofane ed Euripide*, or Rau, *Paratragodia*, esp. 182–4, are well aware that Aristophanes borrows tragedy for many purposes; yet their primary focus is either on comic mockery of Euripides or on the philological details of the paratragedy. See Muecke, 'Playing with the Play', 67, for a helpful emphasis on the metatheatrical aspects of Aristophanes' use of Euripides.

artistic relation so symbiotic cannot be understood as merely satirical, and mockery of Euripides may in fact at times be incidental to Aristophanes' main goals. The study of tragic parody–paratragedy has remained largely isolated from an examination of the comedies as a whole; too often critics assume that the poet's imitation and travesty of Euripides is monolithic throughout his corpus. My aim in this chapter has been to broaden our sense of the range of purposes for which Aristophanes drew on tragedy. Aristophanes' audience, after all, was engaged in judging comedies in relation to each other and for themselves, often in the wake of a tragic performance. Certainly the comic poet would not adopt a strategy which would make comedy appear the derivative or inferior genre. In *Acharnians* tragedy indeed serves in multiple ways to make the case for comedy at the cost of exposing tragedy's dependence on pathos and theatrical illusion. Indeed, comedy uses the authority of tragedy to bolster its claims to free speech, and goes on to use this licence to accomplish what tragedy itself did not undertake—for there were only a few tragedies based on recent historical events. Indeed, it is interesting to note that Aristophanes proceeds to draw on Euripidean models to a greater or lesser degree in defending his hero's or heroine's pursuit of peace in the later *Peace* (*Bellerophon*) and *Lysistrata* (*Melanippe Desmotis*), and seems to lose interest in using paratragedy for such purposes as his plays become less internationally and politically oriented in the fourth century. Furthermore, by opening up the question of how drama represents truth, Aristophanes can raise the critical consciousness of his audience and educate it to expect from comedy a new intellectual and artistic complexity. Parody of tragedy affords to the comedian advantages not offered by parody of epic—and it may not be accidental that Aristophanes begins to parody Euripides shortly after Cratinus offered a major parody of Trojan war epic, *Dionysalexandros*—because the manipulation of dramatic technique makes possible a visual as well as verbal means of commenting on the relations among language, art, truth, and reality that characterize a sophistic age.[55]

[55] A version of this paper was first presented in 1984 at the FIEC Conference in Dublin. I would like to thank the anonymous referees and the editor of *JHS* and discerning audiences in Dublin, at Columbia University, at Swarthmore College, and at the University of Cincinnati for their comments and questions.

8

War and Peace in the Comedy of Aristophanes

HANS-JOACHIM NEWIGER

The successful production in recent years of the so-called peace-plays of Aristophanes in a number of German theatres provides a challenge for classical scholars to renew analysis of these comedies. Peter Hacks' adaptation of *Peace*, which opened in Berlin, has been a popular success in many theatres. *Acharnians*, in the adapted translation of Wolfgang Schadewaldt, was accepted much less readily, but *Lysistrata*, for many years the most frequently performed comedy of Aristophanes, has since 1972 had outstanding success in a new translation by Schadewaldt.[1] In this essay I shall attempt to answer the challenge posed by these theatrical successes primarily by examining the differences between the three comedies in their treatment of war and peace. In addition, I hope to demonstrate an aspect of *Lysistrata* that has until now received scant notice.

Accordingly, let us turn directly to the question of exactly how Aristophanes represents war and peace in his peace-plays and how he brings the concept of peace to dramatic life on the stage; for while he manages to accomplish peace in all three comedies, the nature and presentation of peace differ greatly from play to play.

The action of *Acharnians*, produced in 425, the sixth year of the Peloponnesian War, is highly political from the very opening scene. The farmer Dikaiopolis is shocked that all attempts to deliberate about peace in the Assembly have failed. During the Assembly

---

[1] Aristophanes is frequently performed in Greece. In 1974 the festival programme featured performances of *Lysistrata* at Epidaurus, *Thesmophoriazusae* at Philippi and Dodona, *Birds* at Philippi, Dion, and Athens, *Frogs* at Athens—in the ancient theatres themselves. I do not know how many presentations fell victim to the crisis in Cyprus, but in Athens on 20 Sept. I had the pleasure of witnessing *Frogs* performed before a vivaciously sympathetic audience.

(represented as exceedingly grotesque) he sends a certain Amphitheos (whose name means 'divine on both sides [of the family]') to Sparta to negotiate a private peace solely for himself and his family. At the end of the Assembly Amphitheos has already returned and offers Dikaiopolis three kinds of peace, or, more precisely, three kinds of peace treaty embodied by three types of wine. 'Treaty' in Greek is *hai spondai*, an offering, consisting of libations solemnly poured at the conclusion of a treaty. The designation 'five-', 'ten-', or 'thirty-year' can thus be as accurately attributed to the wine itself as it can to the treaty. Dikaiopolis naturally chooses the thirty-year wine and with it the thirty-year treaty, as it had existed before the outbreak of the war between Athens and Sparta.[2]

If we have already seen in the Assembly scene that peace is in no way desired by the majority of Athenians, we are again made aware of its unpopularity when the chorus of Acharnians appears in the following scene. They are looking for the wretch who brings peace with Sparta (Amphitheos) in order to stone him, but instead come upon Dikaiopolis. This situation requires some historical background. The Acharnians, who form the chorus of the play and give it its title, are the inhabitants of the most thickly populated deme of Attica, which alone provided 3,000 hoplites.[3] They had especially suffered from the invasions and pillaging which the Spartans carried out in Attica almost every summer. The country population, having retreated according to Pericles' war plan into the city during these enemy incursions, had to surrender their land to destruction. Athens had formed behind her famous 'long-walls' a single fortified area including the harbours of Piraeus and Phalerum. Here the country population had been dwelling on and off for a few months, miserably and to some extent without proper housing. Many remained in the city, since their farms had been irreparably destroyed and their farm work either constantly interrupted or rendered useless altogether. In addition, there was frequent military service and guard duty. These people, forced by cruel circumstances to endure a city life quite alien to them, were of

---

[2] Here as elsewhere in this chapter my explanations, as the expert will recognize, are based upon the interpretations given in my book *Metapher und Allegorie* (Munich, 1957), 52–3, 104–27, and appear without reference to specific passages.

[3] Thucydides (2. 20) gives this number, but it may need to be corrected to 1200. See A. W. Gomme, *A Historical Commentary on Thucydides II* (Oxford, 1956), 73–4, *ad loc.*

divided minds. They wanted to return to the country to rebuild their farms in peace, but they were also filled with rage at the enemy who had injured them so grievously. They were now frequent participants in the Assembly, whereas in peacetime, because of their work and their distance from Athens, they had exercised their political rights only sporadically. They were less experienced in politics and therefore perhaps easier to influence.

The farmer Dikaiopolis personifies the desire for peace and the impulse to return to the countryside and its ancestral way of life. The Acharnians, rough charcoal-burners sorely distressed by the war, confront him; hatred for the enemy prevails among them and with it the will for war. Now Dikaiopolis alone has his peace and is celebrating his Dionysus Festival in the country with a phallic procession when the Acharnians assail him. He succeeds in obtaining a hearing only by saying that he holds hostages, that is, pieces of charcoal, which by comic metaphor become valued countrymen of the charcoal-burners from Acharnae. He stakes his head, which he promises to lay on the chopping-block, on the assertion that he has convincing arguments for peace. This metaphor is presently made literal. The chopping-block comes on to the stage; he lays his head on it; but for a while he does not present his arguments. On the contrary, he first wants to dress up as a tragic beggar-hero, since otherwise he would not appear pitiable enough. We are thus diverted from the arguments against the war for over 100 verses by an exquisite scene in which our hero borrows a tragic costume from none other than the tragic poet, Euripides. Tragic parody displaces politics, and we are made aware that in this comedy the poet is parodying a series of episodes and dialogues from Euripides' *Telephus*.[4]

Now Dikaiopolis, his head on the chopping-block, makes his great political speech. But, leaving to one side the affirmation that 'even Comedy stands up for truth and right', he brings forth no serious discussion but instead represents the causes of, and responsibility for, the war in a manner at once highly flippant and highly literary: the cause of the war was the kidnapping of women, and the audience is meant to recall not only fair Helen and the Trojan

---

[4] See P. Rau, *Paratragodia* (Munich, 1967), 19–50, who cites the earlier literature.

War, but most of all the reciprocal rapes at the beginning of
Herodotus' history! This is the argument (524–39):[5]

> But some young tipsy cottabus-players went
> And stole from Megara-town the fair Simaetha.
> Then the Megarians, garlicked with the smart,
> Stole, in return, two of Aspasia's hussies.
> From these three Wantons o'er the Hellenic race
> Burst forth the first beginnings of the War.
> For then, in wrath, the Olympian Pericles
> Thundered and lightened, and confounded Hellas,
> Enacting laws which ran like drinking-songs,
> *That the Megarians presently depart*
> *From earth and sea, the mainland, and the mart.*
> Then the Megarians, slowly famishing,
> Besought their Spartan friends to get the Law
> Of the three Wantons cancelled and withdrawn.
> And oft they asked us, but we yielded not.
> Then followed instantly the clash of shields.

Although Dikaiopolis' speech brings half of the chorus over to his
side, the other half calls in the war-hero Lamachus as their suppor-
ter. This Lamachus, who comes forward in a martial manner, is
lustily ridiculed by Dikaiopolis, and here another metaphor is made
literal: the farmer manages to get hold of the officer's helmet and a
feather from its plume, tickles himself in the throat with the feather
and vomits into the helmet, because to him helmets are, if the
expression may be excused, only for puking into.

Finally, by emphasizing the great gulf that separates officers and
office-holders on the one side from the mass of have-nots (to which
the Acharnians belong) on the other, Dikaiopolis brings the rest of
the chorus over to his side. In the parabasis that follows the chorus
praises the courage and merit of the young poet and laments the ill-
treatment of old people in the city, particularly in the courts. This
we may pass over.

The remainder of the play represents the contrast between war
and peace in scenes simultaneously comical and symbolic. We see
chiefly how Dikaiopolis, with his private peace, can obtain a succession of bodily pleasures from hostile foreigners, since he now has a

---

[5] The English translations are those of B. B. Rogers, 3 vols., Loeb Classical Library
(Cambridge, Mass., 1924).

kind of open market. His behaviour, however, is shown to be purely egotistical, and neither in a bourgeois-political nor in a personal sense does he behave in an altruistic or social manner. He refuses to give a share of the profits he has gained to anyone else.[6] The opposition between war and peace reaches its climax (and the comedy its conclusion) in a sequence of scenes which contrast the separate destinies of Colonel Lamachus and the carousing farmer Dikaiopolis. Peace is manifested exclusively in bodily pleasures of an erotic as well as a culinary nature. Lamachus receives an order, now, in the middle of winter, to garrison the passes to Boeotia, where an enemy invasion threatens, but Dikaiopolis is invited to a banquet and drinking-contest at a great festival. In a section of stichomythic dialogue both men make their separate preparations. The chorus concludes the scene with the following suggestive strophe (1143-9):

> Off to your duties, my heroes bold.
> Different truly the paths ye tread;
> One to drink with wreaths on his head;
> One to watch, and shiver with cold,
> Lonely, the while his antagonist passes
> The sweetest of hours with the sweetest of lasses.

This fundamental opposition of war and peace is maintained in the closing scene.[7] Once more our heroes, their concerns as different as their destinies, return: Lamachus from battle, wounded in the leg and supported by two soldiers; Dikaiopolis from feasting, thoroughly drunk and supported by two girls. Both heroes express their condition in parallel verses (1190-1202):

> LAMACHUS. O lack-a-day! O lack-a-day!
> I'm hacked, I'm killed, by hostile lances!
> But worse than wound or lance 'twill grieve me
> If Dikaiopolis perceive me
> and mock, and mock at my mischances.
> DIKAIOPOLIS. O lucky day! O lucky day!
> What mortal ever can be richer,

---

[6] See K. J. Dover, *Aristophanic Comedy* (London, 1972), 86 ff.

[7] I have intentionally overlooked the messenger's speech (1174-89) with its notorious textual and interpretative difficulties. For the various interpretations, see A. M. Dale, 'A Heroic End', *BICS* 8 (1961), 47-8; repr. in *Collected Papers* (Cambridge, 1969); also pp. 292-3); Rau, *Paratragodia*, 139 ff.; M. L. West, 'Aristophanes' *Acharnians* 1178-86', *CR* 21 (1971), 157-8.

> Than he who feels, my golden misses,
> Your softest, closest, loveliest kisses.
> 'Twas I, 'twas I, first drained the pitcher.

The sexuality becomes still more apparent in the following section, but I believe that even here the contrast between war and peace is evident. The comedy ends with the departure of an exceedingly dissipated Dikaiopolis, with his retinue of female companions and the chorus, to accept a wine-skin, his victory prize. The exuberance of a country Dionysus festival thus provides the conclusion.

Through supernatural and magical means a single dissatisfied person obtains an utterly unreal private peace whose joys, portrayed from the standpoint of the farmer, are of a primarily culinary and sexual nature; these joys are then contrasted with the unpleasantness ('horrors' would be too strong an expression) of war. There is no talk of the preservation of the fatherland or even of the extension of this private peace to other sufferers.[8]

War and Peace do not appear as characters on the stage in this comedy as they do in the next peace-play, *Peace* of 421; rather, the peace treaty is symbolized concretely in the wine of the drink-offering accompanying the treaty. But in the poet's words and in the songs of the chorus, war and peace (or more precisely, war and reconciliation) are in fact already represented as characters in *Acharnians*; we can thus find a bridge to *Peace* as well as to *Lysistrata* purely in the play's imagery and the poet's conceptions. Of Polemos, War, it is said in *Acharnians* (978–87):

> War I'll never welcome in to share my hospitality,
> Never shall the fellow sing Harmodius in my company,
> Always in his cups he acts so rudely and offensively.
> Tipsily he burst upon our happy quiet family,
> Breaking this, upsetting that, and brawling most pugnaciously.
> Yea when we entreated him with hospitable courtesy,
> *Sit you down, and drink a cup, a Cup of Love and Harmony,*
> All the more he burnt the poles we wanted for our husbandry,
> Aye and split perforce the liquor treasured up within our vines.

War is an evil table companion, a drunkard who in spite of every attempt at appeasement dashes to pieces all that is dear to the

---

[8] See Dover, *Aristophanic Comedy*, 87–8.

peasant. This is less than a depiction of the actual horrors of war, but more than a description of the inconveniences involved in military service, wretched lodgings in the city and the renunciation of many bodily pleasures. It must be stressed, however, that in the representation of war in *Acharnians* a high propriety holds sway: no mention is made of the dead, and Lamachus' injury is represented as a ridiculous mishap.

Of Diallage, Reconciliation, the chorus sings (989–99):

> O of Cypris foster-sister, and of every heavenly Grace,
> Never knew I till this moment all the glory of thy face,
> RECONCILIATION!
> O that Love would you and me unite in endless harmony,
> Love as he is pictured with the wreath of roses smilingly.
> Maybe you regard me as a fragment of antiquity:
> Ah, but if I get you, dear, I'll show my triple husbandry.
> First a row of vinelets will I plant prolonged and orderly,
> Next the little fig-tree shoots beside them, growing lustily,
> Thirdly the domestic vine; although I am so elderly.
> Round them all shall olives grow, to form a pleasant boundary.
> Thence will you and I anoint us, darling, when the New Moon shines.

Reconciliation, like 'treaty' another word for peace, is portrayed as a longed-for bride. Agricultural metaphors paraphrase love-making and procreation—a connection obvious to an Athenian audience, for the official Attic wedding ceremony contains the phrase 'for the ploughing of legitimate children' (*epi paidōn gnēsiōn arotōi*).

The bride of the wine-grower Trygaeus, who brings about the peace in *Peace*, is not the goddess of peace herself (that would be, according to Greek thought, hubris and sacrilege)[9] but her attendant Opora, the Harvest, a happy invention of Aristophanes and a personification typical of those which occur abundantly in this comedy. In a manner immediately clear to those of an anthropo-morphic cast of mind, the poet creates in these personifications partners for the plot, or even characters participating in the action whose symbolic names emphasize the main issues of the plot. If the Harvest is intended for the farmer Trygaeus, so another attendant of the goddess of peace, Theoria, which I might translate Festival, is

---

[9] See Alcm., fr. 1. 16–17P: 'No man should seek to fly to heaven, nor to marry Aphrodite . . .'.

designated for the Council of Athens. We are to understand that as
a result of peace it will become possible to hold festivals outside of
Athens, and that the Council must concern itself with them as part
of its authority. And the manner in which the Council could
'concern itself' with the young female character Theoria, embodiment of the festival, is reflected once more in sexual imagery made
possible by Theoria's sex. Thus in Theoria and Opora, Festival and
Harvest, the spiritual union (the Council is concerned with the
festival, the farmer with the harvest) is represented as carnal union
and sensual activity. I might add at this point that as early as
Knights, performed the year after *Acharnians*, the peace treaty,
symbolized in the previous year concretely as wine, is now procured for the rejuvenated Sir Demos, the embodiment of the Attic
people as politically sovereign, in the guise of two maidens (Spondai,
in accordance with the plural *feminini generis*), and thus as actual
characters. The nameless girls with whom Dikaiopolis appeared at
the end of the play as a sign of his joyousness and as objects for his
delight have now, in *Knights* and *Peace*, become maidens with
symbolic names that impart immediate significance to the action
of the play. A metaphorical manner of speaking is thus taken
literally and represented symbolically on stage.

This transformation of the metaphorical into the literal also
underlies the scenes of the first half of *Peace*, which I consider to
be among Aristophanes' most brilliant conceptions. Trygaeus wants
to fetch from heaven the peace which has disappeared, and rides
there on a dung-beetle. A metaphor—'to fetch from heaven', which
ought to express an impossibility—is actually staged, and for the
fantastic and ingenious art of comedy the impossible turns out to be
thoroughly possible. Moreover, because the ride on the dung-beetle
also parodies the ride of a tragic hero on the winged horse Pegasus,
the scene gains another stratum of meaning and a further dimension.[10] The task of bringing back peace (which in Greek is feminine,
Eirene) in the form of a statue of the goddess of peace naturally
proves to be difficult. The difficulties of peace negotiations are
symbolized by the stones heaped up before the cave in which the
goddess of peace has been confined by War, and by the labours of
Greeks from all tribes and cities as they try to haul the goddess back
into the light. The farmers, having an especially strong interest in

[10] See Rau, *Paratragodia*, 89 ff.

peace, finally succeed in recovering the goddess together with her companions, with whom we have already become acquainted. Here again is a marked complexity of dimension: the recovery of an object by means of a chorus pulling on a rope has its prototype in a satyr-play of Aeschylus in which the satyrs drag a chest, in which the heroine Danae has been abandoned with her little son Perseus, from the sea by means of a rope.[11] I believe that we can here recognize remarkably well the workings of the poet's fantasy and the comic technique by which he transposes imprtant and meaningful models and ideas into a grotesque-comic plot.

To return, however, to War. He (Polemos) and his companion Tumult (Kydoimos) appear, before the rescue of the entombed Peace from her cave becomes at all possible, *in persona* on the stage, not, as in the lyrics of *Acharnians*, as evil house-guests, but as a cook and his handyman. This cook is much more dangerous than the drunken guest in *Acharnians*; he wants to pulverize in a mortar the belligerent cities, which are symbolized through their agricultural products: cheese for Sicily, onions for Megara, honey for Attica, and so forth. But his handyman Tumult can no longer procure for him a pestle or pounder to carry out the destruction. The Spartans as well as the Athenians have lost their pestle, and thus the war-cook is deprived of his craft—he can make nothing without a pestle. Trygaeus seizes this opportunity to drag Peace out into the light. The pestles are of course the generals of both sides, Cleon and Brasidas, who until now (to continue the metaphor) had served as tools for war; but now they have fallen in the same battle. With the pestle Aristophanes resumes a comparison he has used before: in *Knights* the detested Cleon was compared to a pestle by which everything is tossed into confusion and mixed up. What was previously expressed in metaphorical language is here enacted in a scene on stage.

In conclusion we can say of this play that the peace brought about here is both real and truly panhellenic. Trygaeus does not obtain a private but rather a universal peace, and, totally unlike Dikaiopolis, deserves well of his city and of all Greece. The chorus, appearing on behalf of all the Greeks, represents the common struggle for peace. Peace might be seen here again predominantly from the perspective of the farmer; the spirit of a panhellenic conception, however, of a peace for all cities and classes, imbues the first part of this comedy. On the other hand, in contrast with *Acharnians*, the play is less a protest against the war than a celebration of the official conclusion of the peace treaty[12] which followed at most ten days after the performance. A British colleague formulates, 'Thus Trygaios is not the mouthpiece of a far-sighted minority lamenting the continuation of an apparently unending war, but a man who performs on a level of comic fantasy a task to which the Athenian people had already addressed itself on the mundane level of negotiation.'[13]

Ten years later, in 411, four years after the second outbreak of the war and in a time of great tribulation, Aristophanes produced *Lysistrata*.[14] In the autumn of 413 Athens had not only lost vast numbers of troops in Sicily, almost her entire fleet and her most capable generals, but since the spring of 413 the Spartans, on the advice of the turncoat Alcibiades, had established themselves under King Agis in Decelea,[15] only fifteen miles from Athens, and from there maintained continuous control over the Attic countryside. The conditions of the Archidamian War, so monstrous for the country folk, but during which it had only been necessary to withdraw behind the city walls for a few months at a time, now became permanent. Provisioning the city-dwellers also became more difficult because command of the sea was no longer certain, and it was believed throughout Greece that Athens would soon be forced to capitulate. Slaves deserted to the enemy in droves, the silver mines at Laurium had to be shut down, and most of the allies were becoming disaffected.

But Athens continued the war with unbelievable obstinacy. Through the introduction of new tariffs and the expenditure of her last financial reserves she built a new fleet, and in the autumn

[12] Even C. M. J. Sicking, 'Aristophanes Laetus?' *Komoidotragenata* (Amsterdam, 1967), 115 ff., will not deny that it has happened thus *de facto*; that, however, a better peace than that of Nicias was desired is certainly correct. When Sicking finds it 'more correct to interpret the majority of Aristophanic comedies as imaginary solutions to a menacing state of affairs perceived by the poet as problematic', and stresses the *adynaton* in his comedies, he must be certain of universal agreement.

[13] Dover, *Aristophanic Comedy*, 137.

[14] At the Lenaea, as I assume in spite of T. Gelzer, 'Aristophanes der Komiker', *RE* supp. vol. 12 (1971), 1467–9, 1473–5; cf. also Dover, *Aristophanic Comedy*, 150, 169–72.

[15] On the hill, in fact, on which the cemetery chapel of the former Greek royal house stands today.

of 412, at approximately the time when Aristophanes was putting the final touches on *Lysistrata*, over 100 ships, based on Samos, stood off the Ionian coast of Asia Minor. In Athens the saying resounded just as it had fourteen years earlier, 'Let the war continue!' The women at the beginning of *Lysistrata* also use this saying (*ho polemos herpetō*, 129–30) as they hear what they must do to end the war.

Athens's perilous external situation went hand-in-hand with an extremely threatening domestic situation. The military failures of the democratic administration gave the oligarchs their opportunity to restrict and perhaps even eliminate the democracy which since Pericles' death had become more and more radical and whose leaders were the driving force behind the continuation of the war. The oligarchs were also intent on a settlement with Sparta for reasons of internal politics. The establishment of a new governing body of ten *probouloi* (to which the so-called 'Councillor' appearing in the first part of *Lysistrata* belongs) represented the first restriction of the democracy, for these *probouloi* curtailed the rights of the *prytaneis* and the Council; Sophocles, incidentally, was one of them. These tensions existed even in the fleet on Samos, and from there the oligarchic rebellion, which followed a few months after the performance of *Lysistrata*, gained significant momentum. Thus the conception and performance of this comedy took place in a constantly worsening situation which threatened Athens (and this must be stressed) in both the internal and external political spheres.

The greater universality with which Aristophanes now treats the old theme of war and peace stems to some extent from the tendency of all the extant plays after *Birds* to be less limited to a particular time and situation. The explanation is, however, also to be sought in the political situation, which would scarcely have tolerated any partisanship on the part of the poet. Such partisanship might not only have proved dangerous, but would certainly have deprived him of any possibility of influence as a poet and would have diminished the validity of his declarations. This the chorus of *Lysistrata* announces explicitly (1043–9):

> Not to objugate and scold you,
> Not unpleasant truths to say,
> But with words and deeds of bounty
> Come we here to-day.

> Ah, enough of idle quarrels,
> Now attend, I pray.

A plot summary will show how the old theme of war and peace is handled here. Under the leadership of Lysistrata, married women from Athens as well as Sparta, Boeotia, and Corinth meet and form a conspiracy, after Lysistrata has persuaded them that the only plausible method of obtaining peace must be a refusal to perform their conjugal duties. That this ticklish theme is treated coarsely and explicitly is quite understandable, given the nature of Old Comedy. In particular, the women doubt their own ability to hold out, but finally take a pledge not to surrender themselves to their husbands willingly, but in fact to excite them through provocative behaviour. Employed in all the warring states simultaneously, this method has an immediate success. Hand in hand with this plan, however, comes a sort of *coup d'état* in Athens.[16] While the younger women plot the marriage strike, the old women occupy the Acropolis (which shelters the treasury of Athens in its temples) in order to shut off the main source for the continuation of the war, that is to say, the money.

The next scene shows the attempt of the chorus of old men to gain forcible entry on to the Acropolis by assailing the barricaded gates of the Propylaea with fire. The chorus of old women confronts them and extinguishes the fire, which again is not without symbolic force. Then one of the new *probouloi* approaches to take funds from the Acropolis; his attempt to break in forcibly also fails, and he must instead engage in a long discussion with Lysistrata, after his attempt to have her arrested is frustrated by the women. She takes this opportunity to say several things: first, she identifies the money as the source of the war; the women want to manage it exactly as they manage money in their homes. Second, she stigmatizes the political failures of the high-handed men: they should have obeyed the reasonable counsel of their wives, who were so hard-pressed by the war. Third, the heroine explains in a simile that the women plan to handle politics and the state like wool: they will clean it, unravel the threads, and weave everything beautifully again into a

---

[16] Since this was written J. Vaio has carefully illuminated the two 'planes' or 'themes' (marriage strike–uprising) and their interaction in the whole play: 'The Manipulation of Theme and Action in Aristophanes' *Lysistrata*', *GRBS* 14 (1973), 369–80. Vaio frequently supports the position I have developed here concerning comic technique, without expounding the distinction, essential to our study, between external and internal politics.

cloak for all the people. The central idea of her statement is obviously more concerned with internal politics, with civic harmony and the reconciliation of opposing factions in Athens than with external politics and war, and (like the famous parabasis of *Frogs*) recommends inner strength through disentanglement of the complicated domestic situation.[17]

A later scene shows how Lysistrata, who feels no temptations herself, manages to prevent the weakening women from rushing to their husbands, and finally, the scene between Cinesias and his wife, Myrrhine (notorious on account of its explicit sexuality), demonstrates how a woman, seemingly ready to surrender, excites her husband to the utmost in order to deny him fulfilment—all according to plan.

After it has been made clear through the appearance of a herald from Sparta that the Spartans are also in a state of high sexual excitement and for that reason ready for peace negotiations, the choruses of the old men and women of Athens are the first to be reconciled. As the deputies from Athens and Sparta, manifestly *in statu erectionis*, proceed to peace negotiations, Lysistrata summons Reconciliation to the stage in the form of an attractive girl, and with this symbol of the attainment of their fervid desires before their eyes, both sides quickly consent to easy terms. Lysistrata invokes the days of the Persian War and other earlier times when Athens and Sparta stood together, and refers to that national unity of all Greeks manifested in the panhellenic religious festivals at Delphi and Olympia. The rest of the play portrays a peace festival at which the Spartans in particular have their say, thus showing how beautiful peace among the Greeks could be.

The means by which peace is brought about here seems to us, as compared with *Acharnians* and *Peace*, less fantastic and impossible. The marriage strike requires neither the magic of enchanted wine nor a ride to heaven, but only good intentions. But it is doubtful whether at that time this was a less fantastic means than the wine or the ride to heaven.[18]

---

[17] See Dover, *Aristophanic Comedy*, 161: 'her recipe . . . insensibly passes into what is a recipe not so much for peace as for strength (574–86, in many respects comparable with *Frogs* 686–705), implying that from a position of strength one can get a peace which is to one's own advantage'.

[18] For further discussion, see Gelzer, 'Aristophanes der Komiker', col. 1479, and Dover, *Aristophanic Comedy*, 159–60.

The poetic means of bringing peace and reconciling the hostile
sides turns into a main theme what was in the earlier plays a
subsidiary theme. In the earlier period there also appeared, as
part of that full enjoyment of life made possible by peace, the sexual
aspects of life, in *Peace* (and *Knights*) symbolically emphasized
through the significant names of the female characters. Here the
sexual (or as I would prefer to say, erotic) desire is made the means
by which readiness for peace becomes possible. If, in a poetic simile
in *Acharnians*, the chorus imagined Reconciliation (Diallage) as a
longed-for bride, now Reconciliation actually appears on stage,
embodied as a desirable woman and naked[19] like the companions
of Dikaiopolis, the Spondai (Treaties) in *Knights*, and Festival and
Harvest in *Peace*. The great Wilamowitz, in his 1927 commentary,
took the strongest offence at this scene with Reconciliation which
depicts the peace negotiations. He wrote, 'The terms of the peace
could not of course have been treated seriously. The poet had to
wriggle through dangerous reefs. The way he did it is more unbear-
able than the ithyphalloi. He has introduced Diallage as a naked girl
and transformed the yearning for peace into lascivious desire for
this wench's charms. The vulgar obscenities accompanying Lysistrata's admonitory speech are truly shocking' (58–9). Now, shocking
or not, Wilamowitz overlooked the fact that the women's scheme,
and with it the essential poetic idea of the whole play (if we may
formulate it less aggressively), is the transformation of the yearning
for peace into the yearning of men for women. The scene with the
personified Reconciliation again makes this most emphatically clear,
and thereby the peace negotiations are actually trivialized. Peace
negotiations with moderate terms for Athens were at that time
certainly impossible, and the people preferred to continue the war
to the bitter end of capitulation.[20]

[19] Cf. J. Vaio, 'The Manipulation of Theme and Action in Aristophanes' *Lysistrata*',
379 n. 48: 'such roles were played by extras wearing female masks (cf. Hp. *Lex* 1) and
exaggerated female *sōmatia* with painted genitalia but without chitons. Holzinger
argues cogently from the weather at the time of performance and the physical
requirements of the theater: the spectators in the last rows should be able to see
something of the described particulars. One might add the tendency of Old Comedy
not to reflect reality but grotesquely to distort it.' I agree. (But see now my 'Drama und
Theater', in G. A. Seeck (ed.), *Das griechische Drama* (Darmstadt, 1979).)
[20] That they had unfortunately rejected a possible peace in the summer of 410, and
after the Battle of Arginusae in the late summer of 406, does not fall within the scope
of this discussion.

The men's yearning after women—and thus also after peace—is certainly more deeply founded than is commonly recognized, because it centres round their own wives, and the yearning is mutual, so that this droll and audacious play is actually a celebration of conjugal love and companionship.[21] In the scene in which the hostile choruses are reconciled, the women are clearly represented as more understanding, sympathetic, and mature than the men, who are possessed by fixed ideas (1014–15). That the representation of the war is also more deeply founded is expressed clearly when it is said that the mothers must give up their sons, and when the losses suffered by the women, whom the war has cheated of their most beautiful years and the meaning of their lives, are expounded (587 ff., 648 ff.).

This comedy, as opposed to the earlier peace-plays, thus acquires a deeper human dimension. It seems to me that, to the extent to which its utopian conception distances it from the political reality of a conceivable peace, the play acquires a more human reality. That must be the reason why of all Aristophanes' plays this one moves us the most today, even (and especially) if we free ourselves from the false notion that the play is pacifistic. In particular the scenes in which the choruses of old men and old women dominate bring a new note of understanding humour; and they are reconciled even without the erotic means which reconciliation requires in the external political sphere.

I venture to speak at this point of a domestic reconciliation within this play, and to work out an element which has been almost completely overlooked: the domestic reconciliation, the mediation between opposing factions within Athens, and I offer for consideration the possibility that the play has a much weightier and less theoretical significance than the propagation of what was at that time a practically impossible peace.

The peace striven for in *Acharnians* and *Peace* (and in *Knights* as well) can be fixed historically as the Thirty-Year Peace by which Athens and Sparta were bound before the outbreak of the war. It is the representation of the possibilities of attaining peace that is fanciful and unreal in these plays; the possibilities themselves are thoroughly real. This much is clear from the settlement of the so-called Peace of Nicias immediately after the production of the

[21] Cf. Dover, *Aristophanic Comedy,* 160–1.

comedy entitled *Peace*. If the peace striven for and represented there
is the state of affairs before the outbreak of war, the status quo ante,
so in *Lysistrata* it is a distant happy past in which Athens and Sparta
stood side by side, the time of the Persian Wars; indeed, there are
allusions to events of 100 years earlier, because they show the
present enemies as allies (271 ff., 664 ff., 1149 ff.). It is a Golden
Age, and thus this peace is a utopian conception. But a reconciliation of domestic factions struggling among themselves seems to me
to be not a utopian conception but a plausible aspiration, bringing
internal strength to Athens. This alone could perhaps still avert the
threatening doom. That such a reconciliation between oligarchs
and democrats was possible became evident a few years later
when after the reign of the Thirty Tyrants and after much
bloodshed and open civil war, such a domestic reconciliation actually occurred, and the idea of amnesty, of forgetting wrongs suffered, became so significant. Such pardoning and domestic
reconciliation for the strengthening of Athens is recommended in
the famous parabasis of *Frogs*;[22] we know that on account of this
parabasis the rare honour of a second performance was accorded to
this play. If we see this as the true goal of *Lysistrata* as well, then we
shall better understand a few especially significant passages in the
play.

I have already pointed out that the choruses of old men and
women are reconciled without recourse to the marriage strike or
to Lady Reconciliation. These choruses, however, had fallen out
over the *coup d'état* of the old women who were occupying the
Acropolis, while the younger women plotted for the denial of
intercourse. Thus, to put it simply, external and internal politics
go hand in hand. Lysistrata's great discussion with the *proboulos*
concerns war and peace, the role of money and the political failure
of the men, but the main point of her exposition is represented by
the simile of the handling of the wool, which is clearly intended to
refer to domestic politics. If the cleansed and unravelled threads are
to be woven into a cloak for the entire populace, this must be an
exhortation for civic harmony, for the reconciliation of domestic
differences (565–86) and the strengthening of Athens, just as is
recommended in the parabasis of *Frogs*.

In the parabasis of our play, the role of women in cult is stressed,

[22] *Ra.* 686–705, but also 718–37, where the idea is continued.

specifically the cults of Athena and Artemis on the Acropolis, before
which the action takes place (638–45):

> Right it is that I my slender
> Tribute to the state should render,
> I, who to her thoughtful tender care my happiest memories owe;
> Bore, at seven, the mystic casket;
> Was, at ten, our Lady's miller; then the yellow Brauron bear;
> Next (a maiden tall and stately with a string of figs to wear)
> Bore in pomp the holy Basket.
> Well may such a gracious City all my filial duty claim.

When Lysistrata, perhaps armed with shield and spear, appears
on the citadel (706ff.), she, who feels no temptation herself, reminds
us of the virginal goddess who protects the city, Athena Polias. We
now know that the priestess of Athena Nike (Victory) in these years
was named Myrrhine, like the woman who excites her husband to
the utmost while she herself remains steadfast and thereby provides
an example of how the women could be victorious. The priestess of
Athena Polias, on the other hand, was at that time a certain
Lysimache.[23] Her name is similar not only in sound to that of
Lysistrata, but in meaning as well: the priestess's name means
'Disbander of Battles', our heroine's 'Disbander of Armies'. The
women will some day be called Disbanders of battles, *Lysimachas*,
says Lysistrata to the *proboulos* (554), in an obvious pun on her
name. I believe that this double coincidence of the names of
characters in the play with those of actual priestesses of Athena
on the Acropolis should not be explained away as even Dover has
done.[24] I would prefer to see this not only as evidence of how
seriously the poet takes the fate of his native city, about which
Athena Polias herself (as it were) is concerned, but also as evidence
for the new stature which the play, in spite of all its madly audacious
activity, gives to women, although they are politically without
rights. The significance of the names must be taken together with
the emphasis on the women's interest in the state (648ff.) and their
role in cult (638ff.)—the cult on the Acropolis; it must be taken

---

[23] See D. M. Lewis, 'Notes on Attic Inscriptions (II)', *ABSA* 50 (1955), 1ff., and
further literature in Gelzer, 'Aristophanes der Komiker', cols. 1480–1, with whose
judgement I largely agree. It is significant in this connection with Lampito, the
name of the Spartan woman in the play, is also the name of the mother of the
Spartan king Agis, who was at that time in command at Decelea.

[24] *Aristophanic Comedy* 152 n. 3.

together with the proposal, given in the form of a simile, to clean and untangle the matted and soiled wool of the domestic situation and weave it into a cloak for the *dēmos*, the people (567ff.). Thus the meaning of this play is internal unity and the strengthening of Athens as a pre-condition for peace with external enemies.

I would like to add a word about pacifism, which is nowadays frequently attributed to Aristophanes, and not only in theatre programmes and newspaper reviews. In my opinion, pacifism was unknown to the Greek of that time, least of all the free, self-confident citizen of democratic Athens. It went without saying for him that he should fight and, if necesary, die not only for his fatherland and his gods, but also for his political ideals, rights, and achievements, for the freedom and equality of his democratic state. For even these were being threatened in this war; measured against Athens, Sparta seems almost a totalitarian state, whose aim in war was not only the destruction of Attic power, but also the elimination of democracy. A peace from which the government and the constitution would not emerge even half-way intact was not acceptable to the citizens of Athens. Thus one can hardly speak of pacifism, which views life as the highest good.[25]

Of course it also goes without saying that the Greeks, and Athenians in particular, preferred peace to war, but not peace at any price, and least of all peace at the price of democratic freedom. The peace for which *Lysistrata* strives is a peace among the Greeks, such as had existed at the time when they waged war together against the Persians. The peace which the Sophists and their pupils preached in their speeches is also a peace among the Greeks, often precisely in order to be able to wage war against the barbarians even more effectively.

I am certainly far from trivializing Aristophanes' frequent advocacy of peace,[26] but one should not forget that he could only appeal to one of the warring sides, Athens. Pacifism can be spoken of least of all with reference to *Lysistrata* if the poet was here encouraging domestic strength, as he did in *Frogs*. His democratic and patriotic sense of duty, his concern as man and citizen, are nevertheless remarkable, when on the eve of the oligarchic *coup d'état* he stood

[25] See *Aristophanic Comedy*, 84–5.
[26] He seems to surpass the other comic writers in this, and to have taken it especially seriously; see Gelzer, 'Aristophanes der Komiker', cols. 1458–9, 1481–2.

before both political factions and advocated a civic harmony and a true democratic settlement within the state that can no more be ignored than the famous parabasis of *Frogs*. Only a year after the performance of *Frogs* came the capitulation of Athens and the loss not only of 'the splendor and glory of the Attic empire' (Wilamowitz) but also (much worse) of democratic freedom itself. The Thirty Tyrants, behind the screen of a quasi-totalitarian occupation, seized the helm of state. I am sorry that I must close with the tragic feelings which Aristophanic comedy evokes in us because we know the outcome of this war. But we have known since Plato's *Symposium* that it should be possible for one and the same man to create both comedy and tragedy; indeed, comedy by itself is often very serious, and that was quite true even before Plato.[27]

[27] This essay represents the abridged draft of a lecture which I gave apropos of the new production of W. Schadewaldt's adaptation of *Lysistrata* in the winter of 1972 at the Deutsches Theater in Göttingen, and afterwards before different associations in Berlin, Bremen, Hamburg, and Konstanz, as well as at the Universities of Bern and Kiel—this last on 20 Nov. 1973 in the presence of Hans Diller, to whom I therefore dedicate this essay. In keeping with the original design, the scholarly references are very selective.

9
Aristophanes' Cloud-Chorus

CHARLES SEGAL

One of history's amusing ironies has charged professors with being the interpreters, even the defenders, of Aristophanes' *Clouds*, a work which cheerfully fumigates all of our critical and philological subtleties with the smoke of the burning Think-factory. But just for that reason we need the play all the more and may be the more drawn to its problems, if only to retain dialogue with alter egos on the other side of Academe.

It is a healthy sign, then, that recent interpreters have expressed lively interest in this comedy. Healthy too that their disappointment has been not with the chaos to which the play seems to invite, but, with the insufficiency of such chaos for the liberation which it seeks to perform.[1]

Any interpretation of the *Clouds* must reckon with three problems: the role of the Cloud-chorus, the function of the debate between the Just and the Unjust Argument, and the abrupt change of direction at the end. This last issue will be our principal focus, but it will soon become clear that the three questions are interdependent.

I

The Clouds begin as sophistic air-goddesses, protector of the windy, up-in-the-air nebulosities of Socrates and his crew. But suddenly, at the very end, they become Aeschylean moralizers who, like Darius in the *Persians* (742), explain that they take a hand in punishing a man bent on evil ways in order to teach him fear of the gods (1454–

---

[1] See esp. Cedric H. Whitman, *Aristophanes and the Comic Hero*, Martin Classical Lectures, 19 (Cambridge, Mass., 1964), ch. 4, and the valiant protest that we 'not be disappointed' by Kenneth J. Reckford, 'Aristophanes' Ever-Flowing Clouds', *Emory University Quarterly*, 22 (1967), 234–5. Despite differences of interpretation I am indebted to both of these stimulating discussions.

62, especially 1458–61). Whitman finds this change of character insufficiently motivated and considers the ending 'an anomaly in Aristophanes'.[2] Newiger tries to find parallels with shifts of character in other comedies, but finally admits that the Clouds reverse themselves only 'because the good must win out' and that the 'Cloud chorus in conception and role stands in the way of a moralizing ending.' And he regards this sudden theodicy of the new divinities as 'a weakness of the play'.[3]

More recently K. J. Dover, in his masterly edition of the play, has noted the Chorus's 'strange and equivocal role'. He too observes the departure from the practice of other plays: 'After the parabasis, at the stage at which in other comedies the Chorus tends to degenerate into the hero's claque, the Clouds' alienation from Strepsiades becomes apparent.' Dover does not explore the possible implications of the change; but, in comparing the first *Clouds* to the comedies written just before and just after (*Knights* and *Wasps*), he notes that 'during the period when the first version of *Clouds* was written the type of comedy which ends with unalloyed triumph and leaves no uncomfortable questions in the audience's mind was not the only type in which Ar[istophanes] was interested.'[4] We suggest that the ambivalent characterization of the Clouds is a feature of this more complex kind of Aristophanic comedy. It follows, though we do not lay heavy stress upon it nor is it essential to our main argument, that this ambiguity in the Cloud-chorus belongs to Aristophanes' original conception of his subject.

Even with the likelihood (and, with Dover's demonstration, virtual certainty) that the present *Clouds* is an incompletely revised version of the first play, there is no clear evidence that the characters and function of the Clouds themselves were involved in the revisions (fr. 379K is no exception).[5] And even a revised (or partially

---

[2] Whitman, *Aristophanes and the Comic Hero*, 129. See also Theodor Kock, *Ausgewählte Komödien des Aristophanes*, 4: *Die Wolken* (Berlin, 1894), 24; W. J. M. Starkie, *Aristophanes, 'The Clouds'* (London, 1911), *ad* 1458 ff.; Piero Pucci, 'Saggio sulle Nuvole'. *Maia*, NS 12 (1960) 40–2, who also stresses (p. 31) the 'irregularity' of the chorus' change of sentiments; Peter Rau, *Paratragodia*, Zetemata, 45 (Munich, 1967), 173–5.

[3] Hans-Joachim Newiger, *Metapher und Allegorie: Studien zu Aristophanes*, Zetemata, 16 (Munich, 1957), 60 and 68 n. 4, respectively.

[4] K. J. Dover, *Aristophanes, 'Clouds'* (Oxford, 1968), intro., pp. xxiv, lxix, and xxv, respectively.

[5] For full discussion of the revisions and a useful setting out of the evidence see Dover, *Aristophanes, 'Clouds'*, pp. lxxx ff. For fr. 379K, see p. lxxxix with n. 1.

revised) play of a poet as skilful as Aristophanes will have a
substantial aesthetic coherence, especially in the main features of
the plot if not in every last detail.

Nor will the notion, implicit in the criticisms of Whitman and
Newiger, that the present ending is a flight into moralism, an
attempt to escape the imputation of a too intellectual or too
atheistic position, satisfactorily account for the Clouds' reversal. It
is possible, of course, as Whitman suggests, that the point of the
revisions was to soften the impact of the immoralist ideas presented
by the Unjust Argument. Yet in the present version the Unjust
Argument still triumphs; Strepsiades is still beaten by his son; and
the son, despite the burning of the *phrontistērion*, still goes unchas-
tized. Neither the audience nor poor Strepsiades is given the consolation of seeing him de-Socratized.

Even if one accepts Whitman's hypothesis of the moralizing
revisions, Aristophanes did not have to make the Clouds sound
like Aeschylus in order to avoid the charge of radicalism. Even
without the present ending, none but the most obtuse spectator
could leave the theatre of Dionysus thinking Aristophanes an
enthusiastic admirer of the new intellectual movements. Over
twenty years later Socrates still felt that 'Aristophanes' comedy'
was one of the strongest sources of the prejudice against him (Pl.,
Ap. 19c).

If the reversal of the Cloud-chorus was part of the poet's original
aesthetic conception, does it have a meaning beyond moralistic self-
insurance? We suggest that it has, and therefore that we need to
look again at the play to see if we have not conceived the meaning of
the Clouds, and therefore of the play as a whole, too narrowly.
Aristophanes himself, let us recall, accounted the *Clouds* 'the wit-
tiest of [his] comedies' (522); and a later commentator placed it
'among those very powerfully made'.[6]

II

As befits its sophistic material, the play is organized in terms of
interlocking antitheses: youth and age, the new education and the
old, airy theorizing and the practical necessities of paying bills,

[6] Hypoth. 3. V. Coulon, Budé edn. of Aristophanes (Paris, 1964), i, *ad fin.*

traditional morality and unscrupulous *adikia*. The various antitheses ultimately all centre upon different forms of the same
thing, though, as Whitman and Dover have very well pointed out,
the divisions are not always so sharp and simple as they at first
look.[7]

We are interested in one set of antitheses, and one that recurs
with many variations in other Aristophanic comedies. We may align
these as follows:

Old (Good)	*New* (Bad)
Country	City
Agriculture	Skills in the lawcourts and politics
Good health and physical vigour	Pale complexion and a sickly, moribund constitution
Hard work	Idleness and impractical theorizing
Outdoor exercise	Mental gymnastics performed indoors
Old-fashioned honesty	Sophistic trickery and sharp practice

These antitheses take on clear dialectical shape in the contest
between the Just and Unjust Arguments. But they inform the
action of the entire play as well.

They could be reduced more simply to outdoors versus indoors,
with vitality versus lifelessness as a subheading. When one recalls
how much the Greeks lived (and live) out of doors and when one
remembers that the Athenians witnessed the play in the open air
with the long line of Hymettus and the broad view over the Ilissus
toward Phaleron and the sea before them, one realizes that these
antitheses were more than abstract ideas for Aristophanes and his
audience.

Generally speaking, Strepsiades with his rural background and
the pre-*phrontistērion* Pheidippides with his passion for horses
belong to the positive category, Socrates and his pupils, including

---

[7] On the antitheses of the comedy and their complexity, see the excellent discussions of Whitman, *Aristophanes and the Comic Hero*, 126 ff. and Dover, *Aristophanes, 'Clouds'*, pp. lix ff.

the 'half-dead' (*hēmithnēs*, 503) Chaerephon to the negative.[8] This
division is over-simplified, however, for Strepsiades' rusticity can
verge on stupidity, and Pheidippides' love of racing, the source of
all the woe, is a city-bred vice. Yet the division is essentially
reaffirmed at the end. Here Strepsiades once more assumes his
agroikia (1457) and old-fashioned honesty (1463–4) and prefers the
old, horse-racing Pheidippides to the new, sophistically primed
amoralist (1406–7).

The opening scene of the play firmly states the antithesis between
the simple goods of the country and the cloying luxuries of the city.
Before his marriage with the niece of the aristocratic Megacles,
Strepsiades smelled of 'new wine, wicker crates, wool, abundance'
(50), and his life was 'brim full of bees and sheep and pressed olives'
(45). While his wife envisions their son driving in state to the
Acropolis, Strepsiades imagines him pasturing his goats in the
hills, as he used to do himself (69–72). Both passages sound a
pastoral note (taking the word in a broad sense) which will become
important later in our consideration of the Cloud-chorus.

Over against this hard, but invigorating, rustic life stands the
phrontistērion. The terms in which it is introduced are significant:

That is a Reflectory for clever spirits.[9]   (94)

The opening *psychai*, with its suggestion of the disembodied Homeric
dead, carry us far from the fresh air of the Attic uplands.[10] Pheidippides, at least half-way his father's son, feels an instinctive loathing
for the paleness of the inhabitants, *tous ōchriōntas* (103; also 120), a
sentiment which he continues to feel later in the play (799, 1112),
until he is properly re-educated, or, in more current terminology,
reorientated. At that point Socrates proudly leads him forth from the
phrontistērion, and Strepsiades gives a cry of glee as he observes the
appropriate complexion which the lad has now acquired:

---

[8] By 'Socrates' here and elsewhere I refer only to the Socrates who functions as a
dramatic character within the structure of Aristophanes' play. On the question of the
relation of the historical Socrates to that of the play, I am in agreement with Hartmut
Erbse, 'Sokrates im Schatten der aristophanischen Wolken', *Hermes*, 82 (1954), 420,
who stresses 'die gediegene Schönheit aristophanischer Kunst, in der alle Einzelbes-
tandteile, welcher Herkunft sie auch seien, zu einer höheren Totalität und Selbstän-
digkeit gesammelt erscheinen . . . Denn so viel ist gewiss: Die Wahrheit der Dichtung
lässt sich nicht in ihren literarischen Quellen finden, und wer das Kunstwerk dort
sucht, sucht es da, wo es recht eigentlich nicht ist.' On the whole issue, see now
Dover, *Aristophanes*, '*Clouds*', pp. xliiff.   [9] Trans. A. H. Sommerstein.
[10] *Psychai* here in 94 has other points of reference too, of course: see Starkie,
Aristophanes, '*The Clouds*', ad loc.

How delighted I am right away to see the colour of your skin![11]   (1174)

Strepsiades' first encounter with sophistry is structured in terms of the contrast between the cramped confines of the *phrontistērion* and the open country where he feels (or used to feel) at home. Having accidentally aborted a disciple's thought, Strepsiades alleges his rusticity as an excuse (138). The formidably locked doors of the Thinkery image the enclosed, indoor quality of its life. It takes the rustic protagonist fifty lines (133–83) to get them opened. 'You must think these things mysteries (*mysteria*)', he is told (143). The comparison with mystery rites is not only a spoof of alleged Socratic secrecy and humbug (see 824); it is also a hint of the shut-away quality of *phrontistērion*-life and its darkness.[12]

Strepsiades' first sight of the pupils connects the themes of enclosedness and lifelessness. Seeing their faces fixed on the earth, he offers a comparison with the dejected Spartans who surrendered at Pylos (186). He finds others all hunched over (191), searching out the dark depths of Tartarus (193). One is again reminded of the ghostly *psychai*, fit inhabitants of such realms, at line 94. But Strepsiades interprets the posture of the first group as that of searchers for onions or truffles (whichever *bolboi* means).[13] In any case, Aristophanes, with wonderfully ironic naïvety, has him volunteer the information that he knows where to find 'big and fine ones' (190). Strepsiades thus not only punctures quackery with sound common sense, but he also sets nature's healthy exuberance (*megaloi kai kaloi*, 190), if only as manifested in the lowly *bolbos*, against the unnatural realm of pale and sickly thought. As a rustic he naturally knows (and cares) about finding onions (or truffles).

[11] Trans. Sommerstein.

[12] On the *mysteria* and the connection between 143 and 824 see Wolfgang Schmid, 'Das Sokratesbild der Wolken', *Philologus*, 97 (1948), 212. For the initiatory image and its reversal in the play, see Reckford, 'Aristophanes' Ever-Flowing Clouds', 229: 'Strepsiades' initiation should ideally have led to a kind of rebirth, a passing from the "cave of Trophonius" into the sunlight of true wisdom.' Note also Socrates' reference to his *teloumenoi* at 258. See also Pucci, 'Saggio sulle Nuvole', 32: Dover, *Aristophanes, 'Clouds'*, p. xli.

[13] The scholiast on 188 takes *bolbos* to be the truffle, (if that is what *ta hydna* actually are); and he is followed by Starkie, *Aristophanes', 'The Clouds'*, ad loc., and by B. B. Rogers (ed.), *The 'Clouds' of Aristophanes* (London, 1916), ad loc. But according to LSJ the word can also mean other bulbous plants. H. Van Daele (above, n. 6) translates 'oignon'. Dover, *Aristophanes, 'Clouds'*, ad loc. cites Pl. R. 372c, which supports this translation. If the truffle was as expensive in Aristophanes' day as it is in ours, the humble onion is more to the point.

For him the earth is a practical source of edibles, not a cavern of mysteries.

The contractedness of the *phrontistērion* receives amusing confirmation in another way. The famous anecdote about Socrates and the lizard (171–3) reveals that the master too, for all his walking on air, does not have happy experiences when he ventures to explore the open tracts of the heavens (171–2).

Hints of death and darkness throughout this passage abound. After his encounter with the Tartarus-searchers (192) Strepsiades fears that he may become, like Chaerephon, *hēmithnēs* (503), 'half-dead' (or possibly 'half-mortal', with a reference back to Socrates' *ōphēmere* in 223). His entrance into the *phrontistērion* is a descent into the grotto of Trophonius (508), a place which came to be known as one of the entrances to Hades.[14] This downward journey (cf. Tartarus in 192) is a return to the atmosphere of that endless dark night of troubles from which he is at the beginning of the play trying to escape:

What a length of night-time! It's unending![15]   (2–3)

III

These rather obvious negative associations of the *phrontistērion* create the perspective in which the Cloud-chorus can be understood. The Clouds are first mentioned in lines 251–2, when Socrates offers to his new pupil the opportunity 'to associate and converse with the Clouds, our divinities' (252–3). The response of the two main characters at this point is typical. Each comprehends the Clouds after his own fashion.

Socrates blithely assumes that the Clouds are 'his' to bring into 'converse' with whomever he wishes. For him their chief attraction is their 'up-in-the-air' ethereality.[16] He also makes a point of specify-

---

[14] See Lucian, *Nec.* 22.   [15] Trans. Sommerstein.
[16] For the 'up-in-the-air' qualities of the Clouds and their connections with Socratic and other doctrines (chiefly those of Diogenes of Apollonia), see Whitman, *Aristophanes and the Comic Hero*, 138–40; Newiger, *Metapher und Allegorie*, 59 and p. 50 n. 2; Erbse, 'Sokrates im Schatten der aristophanischen Wolken', 403–4, 406 ff.; Wolfgang Schmid, 'Das Sokratesbild der Wolken', 215 ff.: Pucci, 'Saggio sulle Nuvole', 34–6; Dover, *Aristophanes, 'Clouds'*, pp. xlvii–xlviii; U. von Wilamowitz, *S. B. Berlin* (1921), 739.

ing their 'converse' as *logoi* (250). The old rustic, however, knows them not as givers of words or airy thoughts, but as bringers of rain. More cautious than his mentor, he recognizes their physical power and thinks of the practical problem of keeping dry (267–8). The response is in the spirit of his earlier remark about *bolboi* (188–90). In this saving earthiness of his initial response to the Clouds we have perhaps a clue to their concern with setting him right at the end.

The lovely dactylic chorus in which the Clouds appear (275 ff.) reveals them to us as figures who far transcend the understanding which either of the two human characters has of them. Their flowing and stately rhythms establish the opposite pole to that enclosed mental existence which Socrates would have them sponsor. True, their airy nature makes them the natural companions of the windy speculations of these *meteōrosophistai*. But is it not possible that, in the poet's conception, Socrates and his disciples have mistaken their gods? The poetry of their entrance song entitles us to think so.

This chorus (275–90, 299–313) is one of the most beautiful lyrical passages of Attic literature. It depicts not the friends of abstraction and intellect, but joyful nature-goddesses. The Clouds are happy, lucent beings whose vision encompasses the tree-covered peaks of lofty mountains, the far-shining headlands, the holy earth and its fruits, rivers, and the deep-thundering sea (275–84). Associated with light and life-giving water, they partake of the Dionysiac joy of the burgeoning spring (311). They delight in festal processions, banquets, music, the dance (299–313).[17] When Socrates, a few lines later, invokes these 'great goddesses' for dialectical tricks and rhetorical technicalities (316–18), we feel at once the sharp constriction of spirit, and we wonder how fully they are 'his goddesses' (253).

To Strepsiades, now under Socrates' spell, the Clouds bring fluttering hopes of verbal intricacies and eristic subtleties, all light and smoky (319–22 and cf. 330). Yet the Clouds themselves bring relief from this world of flimsy and sterile cerebration as Socrates describes them slipping quietly over the hollows and thickets of Parnes:

[17] For the Dionysiac associations of the Clouds, see Reckford, 'Aristophanes' Ever-Flowing Clouds', 225.

Then look this way, towards Mount Parnes; for now I see them coming
gently down . . . There they come, a great many of them, through the
woods and the hollows . . . [18]   (323–5)

The peacefulness of their movements (*hēsychēi*, 324) suggests the
blessing of serenity, so far removed from the noise of sophistic fast-
talk or the anxious twistings of Strepsiades. Strepsides says that he
thought them mist and dew and smoke (330); but Socrates at once
assures his doubtful scholar-to-be that they nourish the idle quacks,
cheats, and pedants of meteorosophistry (331–4).

We touch here upon that multiplicity of meaning which is
essential to the Cloud-goddesses. As divinities of life and nature,
they have a certain kinship with the rustic background of Strepsiades shown to us at the beginning (43–72); and they are diametrically opposed to their would-be worshipper, Socrates. They are the
very essence of the out-of-doors, the free sky, and the open air. Yet
they promise to Socrates' eager protégé a life of idleness and
dubiously gained success in the city's lawcourts (416ff.). Bursting
with Dionysiac exuberance, they are yet the patron-divinities of
sophists who must keep away 'from wine, gymnasia, and other
foolish things' (417).[19]

Goddesses who are, to quote Newiger, the 'shifting outlines of
clouds'[20] are not easily pinned down. As Socrates explains, 'They
become whatever they wish' (348). Thus they are what each man
wants them to be.[21] Socrates turns their life-fostering powers almost
literally to smoke and mist. To Strepsiades they hold out the promise
of change and evasion, of avoiding the realities, the firm 'necessities'
of life. Under their guidance he would turn his back on (or, to keep
the metaphor of the play, twist away from) not only his debts, but
also his rustic background, with its twin commandments of hard
work and simple honesty.

The enormous horizons which the Clouds encompass only mirror
back to Strepsiades his own pettiness. When he is finally brought
into 'converse' with them, they address him as a man who 'desires

[18] Trans. Sommerstein.
[19] These abstentions, however, do not have an entirely negative significance: see p.
173 with n. 25.
[20] Newiger, *Metapher und Allegorie*, 59–60. See also Reckford, 'Aristophanes' Ever-
Flowing Clouds', 223.
[21] 'Spirits that mock the madnesses of men', suggests Reckford, 'Aristophanes'
Ever-Flowing Clouds', 223, and see also 225–6.

great wisdom from us' (412). But he replies, 'Don't tell me great thoughts, for I don't want them' (432). And they answer him with a confirmation of that very smallness which he seeks from them: 'You will get your desire; for your desires are not great' (435).

Not only are the Clouds not to be fully identified with Socrates, but later in the play they in fact reveal a number of discrepancies between their beliefs and his. While Socrates maintains that Whirl has expelled Zeus, the Clouds still sing of 'lofty-thoughted Zeus, ruler of the gods' (563 ff.). Soon after they sing another ode in praise of traditional Olympians: Apollo, Athena, Dionysus (595–606).

They can also take sides against humbug and dishonesty. During Cleon's candidacy for the generalship they tried to do *ta chrēsta tēi polei* (cf. 577). With lightning, thunder, and contracted brows they sent forth dire warnings and now give advice for the future (581–94). Here, as at the end too (1458–61), they claim special knowledge of the ways of the gods; and, also as at the end, they present the gods as the traditional upholders of the social and political order: 'Ill-counsel (*dysboulia*)', they say, 'plagues this city; but whatever errors you commit the gods turn to the better course' (587–9). This passage, incidentally, which is a clear survival of the First *Clouds* as Cleon died in 422 BC, helps confirm, though it cannot prove, our view that the ambiguous characterization of the Cloud-chorus was part of Aristophanes' initial conception.

IV

The Clouds' association with light, life, and the good things of the country is by no means confined to their entering lyrics. It is equally strong in the latter two-thirds of the play. In the same ode which celebrates Zeus' power they invoke Aether as 'the nurturer of life for all' (570) and the sun, 'who enfolds the earth with rays of surpassing brilliance' (571–3). In the second parabasis they proudly affirm their connection with farming (1115–25), enumerating the blessings which they will (literally) shower upon the fields and vineyards of the judges who vote for the play. Here, too, despite the obviously light tone, they take their place on the positive side of the antitheses sketched earlier: they stand with the rustic elements against the urban.

Of special importance is their behaviour in the *agōn* and their

sympathy for the Just Argument.[22] In the debate between the two
Logoi they remain fair and dignified. They break up the petty
bickering (934–8) and introduce the contest without favouritism
to either side (949–60). When the Just Argument rests his case,
they praise him in no uncertain terms:

> O you who cultivate the noblest, lovely-towered wisdom,
> How sweet a bloom of chaste restraint (*sōphron anthos*)
>   there lies upon your words.
> Happy indeed were those who lived in times before.
>
> (1024–6)

Their praise of the Just Argument here takes the form of siding with
the old (1026) against the new, with traditional *sōphrosynē* (1025)
against the amoralist appeal to *physis* and the 'necessities of nature'
(1075). They go on to make clear what a hard task they think the
Unjust Argument will have: 'You're likely to need your clever wiles
against him if you intend to surpass him and not turn out a
laughing stock' (1034–5). When the Unjust Argument emerges
victorious, they make no comment at all, and say only that Strepsiades will regret his son's exposure to the 'new education'.

There is a further affinity between the Clouds and the Just
Argument, and one which forms part of the antithetical scheme
set forth above. Like the Just Argument, the Clouds believe in hard,
steady work. When the Clouds, in Socrates' behalf, represent to
Strepsiades the legal skills he will gain (412–19), they also urge
hard work, physical endurance, seriousness, and a life of frugality.
Happy will you be, they say,

if you have a good memory and the capacity for thought, if there is
endurance in your soul, if neither standing nor walking tires you, if you

---

[22] I retain the terms 'Just' and 'Unjust Argument', which are convenient and
familiar and have some justification in the text (e.g. 900), despite Dover's excellent
suggestion Aristophanes, *'Clouds'*, pp. lviiff. that we call them simply 'Right' and
'Wrong'. Dover's terminology, in fact, is still a little confusing, for it conceals (as
does the old terminology too) the deliberate ambiguity of language upon which
Aristophanes is playing and for which English has no equivalent. The terms *kreittōn*
and *hēttōn* can be used in both a moral and a physical sense. The 'defeat' (cf. 1102) of
the 'stronger' (*kreittōn*) Argument by the 'weaker' (*hēttōn*) when it is the *kreittōn* that
ought to be superior (*kratein*) has an essential dramatic function. It is an enacted
example of the inversion of traditional values by Socratic–sophistic intellectualism
and another instance of that transformation, or *Umwertung*, of moral terminology
which is so crucial a factor in the ethical crisis of the late 5th cent. Th. 3. 82–3 is, of
course, the *locus classicus* (see also 2. 52–3).

are not too put out by being cold or yearn for your breakfast, if you abstain from wine and physical exercise and all other follies, and if your notion of the ultimate good is what one might expect a clever man to hold, that it is success in action and deliberation, and in the warfare of the tongue.[23] (414–19)

Aside from the obvious deference to Socrates in *phrontistēs* (414) and the concluding *tēi glōttēi polemizōn* (419), there is not much here that the conservative moralist could take amiss.[24] The abstention from *gymnasia* (417) is not at variance with the Just Argument's advocacy of healthful exercise, for, as Rogers rightly observes, *gymnasia* 'is here used not (as *infra* 1002) in reference to athletic exercises, for which Strepsiades would be far too old, but in the sense of haunting the gymnastic schools for idle or immoral purposes'.[25] Hence the term is properly co-ordinate with 'other silly things' (417). The final line (419), despite the sophistic ring at the end, is an echo of an ethical and didactic programme sanctioned by no less a hero than Achilles, whom Phoenix was to teach 'to be a speaker of words and a doer of deeds' (*Iliad* 9. 443).

The strongest link between the Clouds and the Just Argument lies in the fact that both of them share a vital affinity with the outdoors and the beauty of nature. In beautiful anapaests the Just Argument points out the superiority of games under the olive trees over logic-chopping in the Agora (1002–5). He dwells upon the joy of 'wearing a chaplet of slender reeds with a sound companion, smelling of honeysuckle and freedom from cares and the white poplar, and rejoicing in the season of spring, when the plane tree whispers to the elm' (1006–8). The Clouds too, we recall, also delight in the coming of spring (311; cf. 1008).

Nature here forms a background which unites related elements and clarifies the antitheses which govern the movement of the play. Simultaneously, related forms of utterance and vocabulary contribute to this symbolic alignment of the different forces. The Clouds can speak the windy language of the sophist and sharpster if called

[23] Trans. Sommerstein.
[24] See Erbse, 'Sokrates im Schatten der aristophanischen Wolken', 402: 'In den berühmten Versen 412–19 wird nichts anderes als Beharrlichkeit, Konzentration und saubere Gesinnung gefordert . . .'. Pucci, 'Saggio sulle Nuvole', 38 cites the discussion of Socrates' simple life in X. *Mem.* 1. 6. 1 ff.
[25] Rogers, *The 'Clouds' of Aristophanes, ad loc.*; also Dover, *Aristophanes, 'Clouds', ad loc.*

upon to do so. But their native tongue is the pastoral mode (275 ff.), and this they share with the Just Argument's clean and sweet promises of whispering platans, clear complexion, broad shoulders, and so on (1005–14). Strepsiades can, or could, speak that language too, albeit in the rougher accents of the Attic goatherd (43 ff., 71–2).

The Clouds' sudden alliance with the Just Argument at the end will now, I hope, seem neither sudden nor unholy. From their first appearance they stand in opposition to the pale shut-ins who invoke them. That opposition ripens throughout the play and drops upon us full-grown at the crucial moment, Socrates has been taken in as well as Strepsiades. The development is perhaps the play's finest 'twist' of irony, an irony of which these mobile, volatile goddesses should be fully capable.

V

The nature-imagery, however, only alerts us to what is hinted at, subtly but fairly clearly, in the dialogue itself. From the beginning the Clouds intend a reversal for Strepsiades. The 'change' in 1454 ff., therefore, is only the fulfilment of a well-developed plan and the natural consequence of the Clouds' implicit partnership with the Just Argument.

We have already noted line 435: 'You will get what you desire,' they tell Strepsiades, 'for your desires are not great.' The line may contain more than a recognition of the relation between Strepsiades' character and the smallness of his goals. It points ahead to the irony of the ending when Strepsiades does in fact get what he wants, with a vengeance. His 'not great desires' prove after all to have a disturbing magnitude. One cannot overthrow the social fabric, even in individual cases, with impunity.

Ironic foreshadowing may be present also in the briefly stated advice of the Clouds in 794–6. In reply to Strepsiades' request (793), 'Come, O Clouds, give us good counsel (symbouleusate),' they answer. 'Old man, we counsel you, if you have a son raised up, send him to learn in your own place.'

The formal o presbyta, symbouleuomen, answering symbouleusate (793), and the pompous language of line 795 suggest that tone of paratragic solemnity which prepared for the doom of a hero.

Even more explicit is the final line (812) of this scene in which the Clouds say, 'Such things are accustomed to turn somehow the other way.'[26] The verb *trepesthai* refers ironically to the recurrent image of twisting and turning; and, as we learn, Strepsiades' 'twists' work against him. At 1114, just as he entrusts his son to Socrates, the Clouds pronounce, 'I think that you will regret this.'[27] There is probably an ironic reference back to this passage a little later: Strepsiades, confident in his son's new abilities, dismisses his impending lawsuits with the bravado of *oligon gar moi melei* (1142). Even without the warning echo of the Clouds' *metamelēsein* thirty lines before, Strepsiades' statement fits into the archaic pattern of rash confidence before disaster. Thus it prepares for the Aeschylean formula of 1457–61.

Just before the last cataclysmic scene in which Strepsiades' 'twistings' 'turn' on himself, the Clouds make the clearest use of foreshadowing. As Strepsiades drives off his most bothersome creditors, the chorus sings,

So it is to love evil practices (*pragmatōn eran phlaurōn*). For this old man, in love with them (*erastheis*), wants to deprive (his creditors) of the money he's borrowed. For he certainly shall receive something (*ti pragma*) which will perhaps make this sophist get some unexpected trouble for the evil tricks he's begun to practise.   (1303–11)

The reference to Strepsiades' 'love for evil ways' points ahead to the Clouds' final statement that they lead to evil 'the lover of bad ways' *pragmatōn phlaurōn* (1459). The phrase may also point back to the earlier irony of Strepsiades' 'not great desires' (432, 435), for *phlauros* means 'petty', 'mean', as well as 'base'.

All this stress on the *pragmata* which Strepsiades will receive continues the contrasts between the main antagonists in the play. The Just Argument promises *apragmosynē* (1007) as part of the pastoral simplicity and health he upholds. A term closely related to *apragmosynē* is *hēsychia*, and we may recall the peacefulness (324) of the Clouds' descent over Parnes.[28] Both of these super-characters

---

[26] See Wilhelm Schmid, in W. Schmid and O. Stählin, *Geschichte der griechischen Literatur* part 1, vol. iv (Munich, 1946), 259 n. 5.

[27] For these foreshadowings see ibid. 260; C. H. Whitman, *Aristophanes and the Comic Hero*, 198 with n. 28; K. J. Dover, *Aristophanes, 'Clouds'*, p. lxix and his note on line 1114.

[28] For the associations of *hēsychia* and *apragmosynē* as opposed to Athenian *polypragmosynē*, see Th. 1. 70. 8–9, 1 71. 1 and 3, II. 63. 2–3, II. 64. 3–4. In 1. 70. 8 he

stand together against the *pragmata*, whether *phlaura* or *ponēra*, of Strepsiades' sophistic pettifogging.

The reversal of the Clouds in 1454 ff. is only one item in a whole series of carefully calculated reversals which make the ending seem like the *peripeteia* of a tragedy. Tragedy, and perhaps Aeschylean tragedy, lies behind Strepsiades' exultant hyperboles of 1154–68.[29] He is jubilant as Socrates here leads forth the new Pheidippides (1165–8); but, as in a tragedy, his momentary elation at appearances will soon suffer a cruel reversal (cf. Sophocles, *OT* 1076–85). The Clouds' warning that Strepsiades may not be so happy with a son able to defeat any one 'with whom he associates' (1316–17) ironically takes up Socrates' promise to lead Strepsiades into 'association' with the goddesses who will aid him (252). Pheidippides, impervious to his father's insults, echoes the words of Strepsiades' once would-be champion, the Unjust Argument, when the father tries to ward off the blows (with 1330, compare 910 and 912). The son now accuses the father of old-fashioned ways (1357–60), as Strepsiades had accused him earlier (820–1). Finally, the lines in which the Clouds moralize to Strepsiades and attribute the cause of his troubles to his 'twisting' himself to 'bad deeds' (1455) point us back with poetic justice to the opening of the play, for here Strepsiades urged his son to 'twist' his ways about and learn sophistic rhetoric (88).

This use of the moral structure of tragedy recalls the *Knights*, performed the year before the First *Clouds*. Since it would be natural for Aristophanes to adopt in a new comedy a technique which had won him a prize the preceding year, this use of tragedy suggests that the reversal of the Chorus was part of the First *Clouds*, i.e. that it was part of the original conception of the plot.

In any case, the Clouds, embodiments of change and fluidity, make a 'twist' of their own which mocks Strepsiades' attempt to be what he is not. Yet the Clouds possess, after all, a more sub-

---

opposes *hēsychian apragmona* to *ascholian epiponon*. For *apragmosynē* as a wishful ideal see *Birds* 40–5. *Hēsychia* is an important issue in the period: see E., *Ion* 585 ff., esp. 600–1; D. B3, B243 (DK⁶). Note also the contrast between *pragmata* and *erga* in the Anon. Iamb. 7. 3 (DK) and also in Prodic. (84A18 DK).

[29] Aeschylean echoes in 1154–65 are suggested by H. N. Couch, 'On Aristoph., *Nub.* 1161–1162', *AJP* 54 (1933), 59–62, who calls attention to A., *A.* 896–901, 607–8, 966–72. Rau, however, *Paratragodia*, 148–50, notes the frequency of such a 'Jubellied' in Sophoclean tragedy. See also Dover's general note, *Aristophanes, 'Clouds'*, 1154–70 and his specific notes on 1154, 1159, 1160, 1162, 1165.

stantial character than just mutability. This lies in their association with the joy, life, light of nature, and with that fecundating moisture, their *drosera physis*, of which they speak in the second line of their *parodos* (276).[30]

VI

As divinities allied with the procession of nature, the Clouds are relevant to the antithesis between *nomos* and *physis*, the antinomy between the 'conventions' of human society and the amoral world of 'nature'.[31] On this division rest the cases of the Unjust Logos (1075 ff.) and of Pheidippides, who derives his new learning from this spirit (1421 ff.). It is in part their connection with the supposedly amoral processes of the natural world which encourages Socrates to espouse the Clouds as his divinities now that he has expelled Zeus and the Olympians.

Yet 'nature' is an ambiguous term, and its processes may be understood in different ways. Aristophanes doubtless knew of earlier modes of thought in which these processes themselves followed moral laws (Anaximander B1 TDK, Heraclitus B94 TDK).[32] The Clouds' Aeschylean moral stance at the end is perhaps a glance back at this earlier feeling for a natural world governed by a coherent moral order, a refusal to allow the reign of Dinos, for Whirl's ascendancy signifies (at least in part) the amoral, impersonal materialism and determinism of the Atomists and their disciples. But protest in the name of order is not confined to the end alone. It pervades the play, yet does not limit its scope to a narrow moralism or anti-intellectualism.

For even at the end the Clouds retain their multivalent significance and their mysterious vitality. It is doubtless disturbing to be left a bit confused about whose side they have been on. But the

---

[30] Reckford, 'Aristophanes' Ever-Flowing Clouds', 224 calls attention to the creative associations of their wetness.

[31] For the *physis–nomos* dichotomy in the play, see Whitman, *Aristophanes and the Comic Hero*, 129 ff.

[32] Even among some of the *physiologoi* of the period whom Aristophanes has in mind in the play the processes of nature are not entirely without moral laws. See W. Theiler, *Zur Geschichte der teleologischen Naturbetrachtung bis auf Aristoteles* (Zurich, 1925); also Karl Reinhardt, *Hermes*, 47 (1912) 499 apropos of Anaxagoras A102 (DK), and now F. Hüffmeier, 'Teleologische Weltbetrachtung bei Diogenes von Apollonia?', *Philologus*, 107 (1963), 131–8.

confusion is not the sign of a hopeless muddle or of 'the blurring of apparently clear values'.[33] It is instead a momentary effect, a *coup de théâtre*, which shocks us into a realization of how independently intelligent and purposive these airy beings are and how complacently we humans have seen in them only the shapes of our own ambitions, not 'the great wisdom' (412).

If the Clouds on the one hand are symbols of rarified speculation and airy sterility, on the other they open wide vistas upon the abundance of nature, with its joys of simplicity, health, and Dionysiac energy. It is they, with their atmostphere of nature's soundness, who restore Strepsiades to something of his rustic vitality and honesty. In a sense they 'untwist' him. Proclaiming at the end (1458–62) the stern morality which Strepsiades would have imbibed from Aeschylus in his youth, they force him to accept both his age and his rusticity. Under the shock of their reversal he now joins both of these realities into a single utterance: 'positively enticing an old rustic astray' (1457; trans. Sommerstein). They recall him too to his moral responsibilities (1462 ff.), though they cannot reconvert Pheidippides. Stunned back into lucidity and the lean rustic realism of his antecedents, Strepsiades now recognizes the quackery of the *phrontistērion* and the foolishness of depriving the world of a moral centre by dethroning Zeus for Whirl (1468–77; cf. 563 ff.). When he attacks the *phrontistērion*, the Clouds make no move to protect it, no outcry. Socrates' deities desert him.

In this final action of the play, the Clouds reveal the positive side of their nature. They release in Strepsiades the energy for his closing gesture, which is, at the same time, the most intelligent thing he has done. Where Socrates' educational methods have failed, the Clouds have succeeded.

The Clouds bring at the end something of that vitality which glows in their opening lyrics (275 ff.). In this way they are connected with *physis*, but not the *physis* of the Unjust Argument. In the *Birds*, which is also much concerned with the *nomos–physis* dichotomy and the effects of over-civilization, the Hoopoe's subjects, who embody the freedom of *physis*, can be called upon to sanction father-beating, yet are also models of pious care for parents (*Birds* 755 ff., 1345 ff.). The aspect of *physis* with which the Clouds are in touch is, like that of the *Birds*, not the negation of all human

---

[33] Whitman, *Aristophanes and the Comic Hero*, 128.

order, but the reservoir of energy, good health, good sense. Strepsiades' words near the end, *diōke, balle, paie* (1508), suggest the spirited urgings of the Adikos Logos to 'use nature', *chrō tēi physei, skirta, gela* (1078). But these free energies, though equally natural, have a more positive source and a more salubrious effect.[34]

The destruction of the *phrontistērion* emanates from this healthy aspect of *physis*, that instinctive good sense which preserves life and has its roots in our connections with nature's rhythms and the ultimate simplicity of our real needs. Aristophanic comedy affirms the goodness of such needs and banishes the befogging complexities which prevent us from recognizing them. Strepsiades' coupling of 'the accursed Chaerephon' with Socrates at this point (1465) completes the expulsion of the deathlike, sterile investigations of which 'half-dead' Chaerephon (503), 'who knows the tracks of fleas' (831), serves as a recurrent symbol.[35] Death and darkness are driven off, and it is part of the sophisticated irony in the design of the play that the figures whose nature comes closest to fog dispel it.[36] The vitalism of their function in nature prevails over the momentary darkness which their appearance in the sky heralds.

Thus the destruction of the *phrontistērion* is in this play the counterpart to the exuberant marriage feast or the orgiastic indulgence which ends other comedies. Strepsiades' kindled torch, a brilliant substitute for the bridal torch which ends other plays, finally clears away the darkness of the opening lines; and Socrates

[34] If Hermes is the speaker of these lines, as seems possible since R and V attribute them to him, the lines would have the sanction of Olympian authority. It is not, however, necessary to assign them to the Clouds, as Beer, Meineke, Zielinski, Starkie, and others do. See Rogers, *The 'Clouds' of Aristophanes*, ad loc. and Starkie, *Aristophanes, 'The Clouds'*, ad loc. Dover, *Aristophanes, 'Clouds'*, ad loc. keeps the attribution to Strepsiades.

[35] For Chaerephon and these trivial investigations see 144–52, 156–64, in addition to the passages cited in the text. Strepsiades' 'accursed Chaerephon and Socrates' in 1465 symmetrically balances Pheidippides' 'wretched Socrates and Chaerephon' at the beginning (104), where Socrates gets the epithet. The parallel reinforces the irony of the reversal in Strepsiades' position. Though it is certainly plausible, as Dover, *Aristophanes, 'Clouds'*, p. xcvii suggests, that Aristophanes 'intended to bring Chairephon into the revision, that 104 and 1465 belong to that early stage of revision, and that this intention was abandoned', I do not think, for the reasons given in my text, that it necessarily follows that 'neither in 104 nor in 1465 does the prominence given to Chairephon serve by itself any discernible humorous or dramatic purpose' (ibid., p. xcv).

[36] For the Clouds' association with fog and deception, see Reckford, 'Aristophanes' Ever-Flowing Clouds', 223, 231–2, who notes the cloud-deceptions of Pindar, P. 2, and *Iliad* 14. Also Dover, *Aristophanes, 'Clouds'*, p. lxviii.

and the inhabitants of the *phrontistērion* are, appropriately enough, choked by the smoke (1504; cf. 320, 330).[37]

It is, however, the sudden flash of tragic wisdom in the Clouds' last speech (1454 ff.), which brings the comedy and its main protagonist back to an heroic (or comically heroic) decisiveness and energy. The Clouds, in taking a lofty tone, seem to regain a fuller measure of their own essence. They come closer to the serene, removed dignity with which they first appeared to us (275 ff.). As they resume what we may call their 'higher' nature, they also restore Strepsiades to 'himself'. Indeed, they do more. They lift him above his trivial concerns and put him back into touch with the rustic energy of his background, the qualities of those 'holm-oak' and 'maple-wood' Marathon-fighters of his father's generation whom Aristophanes praises in the *Acharnians* (179–81) as opponents of all humbug and chicane. Sanity and good sense come upon the scene with a burst of vitality—as did the Clouds themselves earlier (275 ff.). Here we have actions, not sophistic words; the bustling, single-minded comic victor, not the theorizing sophist.

If the Clouds are to be associated with the positive side of *physis*, with the sources of the vibrant, life-filled energies in ourselves, it becomes clear why both Strepsiades and Socrates fall afoul of them. Both men would confine their expansive power, their contact with the grandeur of nature, to their own petty ends, *phlaura pragmata*. The late fifth century was keenly aware of the dangers of circumscribing the elemental forces of our world. Yet the Clouds, unlike Euripides' Aphrodite or Dionysus, are benign, as indeed *physis* in general is for Aristophanes and perhaps ultimately for most comedy, believing as it does in the saving power of our instincts and the sanity of our physical being. Nature can spring the safe fastenings of human institutions (*nomos*). But it can also point the way out of the entanglements of those institutions into the sun, out of phrontisteric mists into the light (cf. 2 ff., 285 ff., 508, etc.). If clouds suggest obnubilation, they are also, after all, a form of fresh air.

On the other hand, any interference with *physis* is likely to cause a greater reaction than was bargained for. Hence, if the Clouds bring an order of a sort, they also bring, in the closing lines, intimations of chaos which are not resolved. As embodiments of Dionysiac energy and the life-force celebrated by comedy, their concern is to wash

---

[37] For this association of smoke and pretentious intellectuality, cf. Theseus' scornful description of Hippolytus as *pollōn grammatōn timōn kapnous*, E., *Hipp.* 954.

away blockages in the stream of life, to overwhelm false seriousness, gloom, and depressive inertia—what Democritus calls *lypēn adespoton psychēs narkōsēs* (68B290 DK)—with 'the force that through the green fuse drives the flower'. But, in doing so, they may impel a more violent flood than is strictly necessary; and this process too holds a very ancient form of *dikē* (see *Iliad* 16. 384–93). Thus if the *phrontistērion* and Strepsiades himself are justly punished, Pheidippides is still left on the rampage. More important, the action with which the play ends is primarily destructive. This closing scene is a strong foil to the life-giving lyrics of 275 ff. Aristophanes is perhaps deliberately showing us two opposed, but complementary effects of the energies which comedy contains and celebrates, as Euripides does with Dionysus in the *Bacchae*.

The Clouds are rightly to be regarded as deities, but they have to retain also the mysteriousness of deities. It is this quality which Socrates, despite the ironic comparison of the *phrontistērion* to *mysteria* (143), would strip away. He approaches them with a superficial optimism characteristic of some of the Sophists and repugnant to many of their contemporaries, notably Sophocles and Euripides. He assumes that these free, changeful beings are friendly to his purposes. But the Clouds' very first words—concrete, traditional, poetic words, not the new abstractions—lead in the other direction. They exercise their cloudy prerogative by making a sudden (though not entirely unexpected) change. As *daimones* too they have a right to retribution; and the Aeschylean frame into which they cast their final speech is a concluding counter-statement both to Socratic–sophistic optimism and to Strepsiadean pettiness.

Aeschylus, present though unnamed in 1458–62, is for Aristophanes the poet *par excellence* of big words. In the *Frogs* he is the fashioner of 'utterances fixed fast with bolts' and the wielder of 'Lycabettuses and the magnitudes (*megethē*) of Parnassuses'.[38] Despite himself Strepsiades gets from the Clouds the 'big wisdom' (*megalē sophia*) and the 'big thoughts' (*megalai gnōmai*) that earlier he so cheekily and smugly rejected in favour of his own small desires (412, 432–5) and the little 'thoughtlets' (*gnōmidia*) of Socrates.[39]

---

[38] *Frogs* 823–5, 1056–7.

[39] *Clouds* 321. See Whitman, *Aristophanes and the Comic Hero*, 140: 'Perhaps more important, all the clouds' lofty rumblings do not bring about any grand change, but only small thoughts, constantly struck off in diminutives, "thoughticals", "speechlets", characteristic of the piddling concerns of rhetoric and philosophy, here packaged as one.'

10

The *Parodoi* of the Aristophanic Comedies

BERNHARD ZIMMERMANN

Thoughts on the Typology and on the Function of the Entrance of
the Chorus in the Comedies of Aristophanes

I

While there are plenty of books and articles that deal with the
chorus of tragedy and the function of the chorus's utterances,
especially of the lyrics,[1] and also detailed treatises upon the compo-
nent parts of tragedy,[2] the *merē tēs tragōidias*, we still have no
interpretation which treats thoroughly the chorus of comedy, the
role and function of the chorus in the dramatic action, the influence
which the co-operation of chorus and actors has on the structure of
the play and the function of the lyric in each comedy. An answer to
these questions can be found especially in the *parodoi*, which
introduce the chorus, and in the *amoibaia*, which integrate the
chorus into the action by lyric dialogue.[3] Since because of its
theatre experience the contemporary audience could expect a
chorus in each play we could make clear by an interpretation of
the *parodoi*, how the poet plays with the expectations of the audience, how he fulfils or disappoints them.

---

[1] See e.g. W. Kranz, *Stasimon: Untersuchungen zu Form und Gehalt der griechischen
Tragödie* (Berlin, 1933); W. Kraus, *Strophengestaltung in der griechischen Tragödie*, i:
Aischylos und Sophokles, SAWW, 231–4 (Vienna, 1957); H. A. Pohlsander, *Metrical
Studies in the Lyrics of Sophocles* (Leiden, 1964).

[2] See W. Jens (ed.), *Die Bauformen der griechischen Tragödie* (Munich, 1971).

[3] I define 'amoibaion' as a lyric dialogue between one or several actors and the
chorus; cf. my *Untersuchungen zur Form und dramatischen Technik der Aristophanischen
Komödien*, i: *Parodos und Amoibaion* (Königstein/Ts. 1984), 150–2.

Before starting with the subject I want to explain the term
'parodos': in chapter 12 ($1452^{b}22$–3) of the *Poetics*—if chapter 12 is
really genuine—Aristotle defines *parodos* among the *merē tēs tragōidias* as *hē prōtē lexis holē chorou*, 'as the chorus's first utterance
taken as a whole',[4] which has a certain length. In the *Nicomachean
Ethics* ($1123^{a}23$–4) he uses the term in a more general sense also for
comedy: here it means 'entrance of the chorus', but also implying
the sense 'entrance song' or 'entrance utterance'. This variation in
use of the term 'parodos' can also be found in the modern literature;
so to avoid terminological difficulties I'll use 'parodos' in the sense
'*meros tēs kōmōidias*, of a certain length'. But it causes difficulties if,
following Aristotle's definition, you try to divide the *parodoi* from the
preceding and following parts of the comedy so that it makes sense.
One reason for this is that entrance and *prōtē lexis* do not always
coincide;[5] another more important one is that the entrance of the
chorus is often linked with the preceding and following passages so
closely that a rigid separation of single parts would violate the
structure of the comedies. So it seems better not to pay as much
attention to the *merē* as to the whole structure, which is the result of
the *systasis pragmatōn*, that is, to different stages of the dramatic
action. Therefore I'll use the term 'parodos' only 'for convenience'
sake' as Pickard-Cambridge has already suggested.[6]

II

Looking through the eleven preserved comedies of Aristophanes you
can see that the part 'parodos' has several functions. First the
chorus is introduced into the play ('entrance of the chorus') making its first utterance. As already mentioned the entrance of the
chorus and the first utterance don't have to take place simultaneously. Then the first meeting of the chorus with the actors occurs.
The chorus can meet a friend, whom it supports, or it appears with
hostile intentions having no ally among the actors. It reacts to the
action of the prologue and utters its opinion about the plan of the
comic hero, whom it supports or fights against. So the course of

---

[4] A. M. Dale, *Collected Papers* (Cambridge, 1969), 35–6.

[5] e.g. *Av.*, *Th.*, and *Ec.*; in *Nu.* and *Ra.* you can hear the chorus before you see it.

[6] A. Pickard-Cambridge, *Dithyramb, Tragedy, Comedy* (Oxford, 1927), 304 n. 1; cf. O.
Taplin, *The Stagecraft of Aeschylus*, (Oxford, 1977), 470–6.

action in the *parodos* is determined by the chorus, which on entry
gives fresh impulses to the development of the action. So I'd propose
to divide the *parodos* from the following parts at the very point
where the chorus as a participant in the action is put in the
background and loses the initiative to the actors. This is particularly obvious in the comedies in which the chorus's entrance is
followed by a battle scene.[7] As soon as the chorus is willing to
listen to the arguments of the actor it loses its influence on the
dramatic action. The interest of the audience now concentrates on
the speech of the actor. Regarding the chorus's attitude to the actors
and to the plan of the comic hero, that is, in Klaus Koch's words, to
the 'Comic Subject' ('Komisches Thema')[8] we can differentiate three
types of *paradoi*:

Type 1. *Acharnians* 204–346, *Lysistrata* 254–386. In these two
comedies the chorus enters with *scaena vacua* to prevent one or
several of the actors from performing an action, which is not to
its liking. It hasn't got a friend or an ally among the actors, but only
one or several opponents. The hostile attitude of the chorus is
shown in the battle scene following its entrance. Since the chorus
does not meet its opponent at once it has got enough time to speak
about itself and its opponent.

Type 2. *Knights* 242–77, *Peace* 296–345, *Plutus* 253–321. The *parodoi*
of these three comedies belong to a second type. The chorus appears
to support an actor. For this type the actor's cry for help[9] is typical,
which links the prologue and the *parodos*. The transition from
prologue to *parodos* is smooth in the *Knights* and *Peace* as—in
contrast to the *Plutus*—the chorus's entrance doesn't take place
with an empty stage. In the *Plutus* we can find a variation of this
type: the chorus isn't called by an actor, but brought by the slave
Carion. On its entry these three choruses are immediately involved
in the action. They start a quarrel or a dialogue with an actor. So
the meeting of the chorus with the actors takes place during its
entry. That is, the entrance of the chorus and the battle scene

---

[7] *Ach., V., Av.*

[8] K. Koch, *Kritische Idee und komisches Thema: Untersuchungen zur Dramaturgie und
zum Ethos der Aristophanischen Komödien*[2] (Bremen, 1968).

[9] See A., *Dictyulkoi,* fr. 178, H. J. Mette, *Die Fragmente der Tragödien des Aischylos*
(Berlin, 1959), 19–22 S., *Ichneutae,* 33 ff.; Taplin, *The Stagecraft of Aeschylus,* 218–21;
Zimmermann, *Untersuchungen zur Form und dramatischen Technik der Aristophanischen
Komödien,* 12.

coincide. So the chorus hasn't got the opportunity to talk about itself when entering. It is forced to act at once.

Type 3. *Wasps* 230–525, *Thesmophoriazusae* 279–371, *Frogs* 316–459. In these three comedies the chorus assembles from habit. In the *Thesmophoriazusae* and *Frogs* to celebrate a festival, in the *Wasps* to follow its usual business. In all three plays the chorus knows less than the audience, which has already been informed in the prologue and knows the situation with which the chorus is confronted. When the chorus enters it is not linked with the 'Comic Subject' and the dramatic action as it has not got any idea of what is going on and only discovers it slowly. This is the way in which Aristophanes creates the 'genre-picture from old Athens'[10] in the *Wasps*, the parody of the opening of the Athenian *ekklēsia* in the *Thesmophoriazusae* and the procession of the initiates in the *Frogs*.

These three basic types can be combined and altered in various ways: the *parodos* of the *Clouds* (263–456) belongs to the second type. The chorus is called by an actor. According to their nature as goddesses the *Clouds* approach, singing solemn hymns, which can be heard before they enter the *eisodos*. The scene in catalectic anapaestic tetrameters (314–456) is substituted for the battle scene: Socrates and Strepsiades react to the arrival of the chorus and are concerned with it on an intellectual level.

Also the *parodos* of the *Birds* (209–450) belongs to the second type. After the song of the hoopoe in anapaestic dimeters—a *solo a cappella*, which links the prologue with the *parodos*—the chorus is called together by Tereus' aria (227–62) and appears without knowing what's going on. Having been informed, it doesn't agree to Tereus' plan, so that it comes to a hostile encounter in the battle scene (327ff.). After Tereus' successful intervention the 'information-*amoibaion*' (406–33) is the transition to the arrangements (434–47), which usually precede the epirrhematic *agōn*. Also in *Wasps* only after having been informed by Philocleon's monody (317–33) about Bdelycleon's intrigues does the chorus get involved in the action and in a battle scene. So the battle scene can be linked with all three types. Finally the *parodos* of the *Ecclesiazusae* could belong to type 3: the women assemble according to the arrangements they made before the opening of the play. Both the typology of the *parodoi* and the variations and combinations of these basic

[10] H. J. Newiger, *Metaphor und Allegorie: Studien zu Aristophanes* (Munich, 1957), 74.

structures show the variety of this part of the dramatic action. The
poet plays with the possibilities of the production of the chorus's
entrance. The audience expected the entry of the chorus and
Aristophanes exploits skilfully their expectations. He rouses and
disappoints them, accelerates and slows them down, seems to, or
actually does, duplicate them, and causes the action to take an
abrupt turn.[11] The audience pays attention to the way Aristophanes introduces the chorus into the play, how he makes it relate
to the comic hero and the action, how he characterizes it, and how
he organizes the entrance of the chorus and its involvement in the
dramatic action.

III

After having worked out a typology of the *parodoi* referring to the
content I'd like to show how this typology can be supported by
formal and structural interpretations on the one hand and metrical
analyses on the other hand. At first I want to illustrate by the
parodoi of type 1 how we can support the typology on the formal
and structural level. Then I want to show by the interpretation of
the *parodos* of the *Wasps* how the metrical composition accompanies
and reinforces the content and dramatic action.

Both in the *Acharnians* and the *Lysistrata* the chorus appears
spontaneously to defeat the intentions of the comic hero. The
different role of the two choruses finds its expression in the different
arrangement of the epirrhematic composition. In the *Acharnians* the
chorus vehemently rushes into the orchestra searching for
Amphitheos. The action takes place in the epirrhema (204–7). Not
discovering its opponent, the chorus turns to lyric metres. It complains about the burden of old age and the loss of the nimbleness of
youth (208–18). In the *antepirrhema* it calls itself back to the present
and continues looking for Amphitheos (219–22). In the *antode* (223–
33) it utters threats before starting once again to search for
Amphitheos (234–6). The recitative tetrameters are dedicated to

---

[11] See T. Gelzer, 'Some Aspects of Aristophanes' Dramatic Art in the *Birds*', BICS 23
(1976), 1–14; Zimmermann, *Untersuchungen zur Form und dramatischen Technik der
Aristophanischen Komödien*, 141–9.

the action; either the chorus acts itself or is asked to act. The lyric parts contain reflections and emotional utterances.

The entrance of the old men in the *Lysistrata* is significantly different from the composition of the *Acharnians*' appearance. After the 'katakeleusmos' (254–5) of the chorus-leader the chorus complains about the uncertainties of life in general and especially about the women's insubordination (256–65) before it pulls itself together and walks on during the *epirrhema* (266–70). In the *antode* it remembers the glorious days of its youth (271–80); in the *antepirrhema* (281–5) it again refers to the present, the occupation of the Acropolis. In the lyric parts the chorus reflects on a higher emotional level whereas in the *epirrhemata* it acts or—at least—starts acting. The epirrhematic composition of the two *parodoi* is a good opportunity to introduce the chorus with *scaena vacua* both as an agent and as a reflecting person. The chorus, since it does not meet its opponent at once, has got enough time to develop, especially in the lyric parts in which it expresses its emotions. So the content determines the form: in the Acharnians the sequence *epirrhema–ode–antepirrhema–antode* shows the chorus at first as an acting group whereas in the *Lysistrata* the old men enter slowly during the *katakeleusmos*; they are out of breath and start complaining and reflecting before they act. In both *parodoi* the odes pick up the metre of the *epirrhemata* in lyric form. So the characterizing effect of the entrance metre is found in the lyric parts, too: the cretics and paeonics are a lyric translation of the trochaics of the Acharnians' entry. In the *Lysistrata* the lyric iambics pick up the catalectic iambic tetrameters of the *katakeleusmos*.[12]

After the chorus's entrance it comes to a combat, which is delayed in both comedies. In the *Acharnians* the charcoal-burners observe Dikaiopolis celebrating the Rural Dionysia before they attack him. In the *Lysistrata* we expect that the old men after having reached the Acropolis will meet Lysistrata and the young women; instead of this they encounter the old women in the orchestra. So the chorus of old men does not meet its actual opponent, but an unexpected enemy. Thus Aristophanes creates a situation in which the quarrel takes place on two levels—between the half-choruses and between Lysistrata and the *proboulos*. The two

---

[12] See Zimmermann, *Untersuchungen zur Form und dramatischen Technik der Aristophanischen Komödien*, 34–56.

half-choruses take part in the action longer than the choruses of
other plays because they are not involved in a direct confrontation
with the comic hero and need not listen to his arguments in the
agōn. Only when they are reconciled do they recede into the background. The reconciliation in home politics is followed by the
reconciliation in foreign politics.[13]

If we compare the two plays we clearly see how Aristophanes
using one basic structure creates the scene of the chorus's entrance
without any schematism and how he formally adapts it to the
requirements of the dramatic action as is demonstrated especially
by the different use of the epirrhematic composition.

The interpretation of the *parodos* of the *Wasps* will show now how
Aristophanes fits the metrical composition to the dramatic action
and how he uses the metrical form for a characterization both of the
chorus and the actors. The interpretation also seeks to help to
explain the function of the different lyric metres in the course of
action.[14] Before the *parodos* of the *Wasps* Aristphanes plays with
the audience's expectation: Philocleon, who is in a desperate
condition as he can't get out of his house, calls his fellow
jurors, who constitute the chorus (197). The audience—because
of its theatre experience—now expects the arrival of the chorus.[15]
But the old jurors do not appear yet. Bdelycleon reacts to his
father's call for help and asks his slave to be very cautious: in
the early morning he'd expect the arrival of his father's friends.
Obviously they had got up too late today as they had usually
arrived a short time after midnight carrying torches and humming
old-fashioned songs à la Phrynichus to call Philocleon out of the
house. Soon after this announcement of the chorus the old fellows
appear telling each other to hurry. The chorus is accompanied by
some boys, whose support the old men need when walking by
twilight.

A *katakeleusmos* of the *coryphaeus* opens the chorus's entrance
(230–47). The metre is—as in the *Lysistrata*, *Plutus*, and *Ecclesiazusae*—the catelectic iambic tetrameter: a metre which serves to

[13] H.-J. Newiger, 'War and Peace in the Comedy of Aristophanes', in J. Henderson
(ed.), *Aristophanes: Essays in Interpretation*, Yale Classical Studies, 26 (New Haven,
Conn., 1980).
[14] See Zimmermann, *Untersuchungen zur Form und dramatischen Technik der Aristophanischen Komödien*, 93–111.   [15] See above (type 2).

characterize old men.[16] They walk slowly, shuffling. This is especially obvious in the opening line, which has the largest number of long syllables which the metre permits.[17] Lines 244 and 246 are significant exceptions: whereas usually—up to line 243—sense-units and verse-ends coincide, we get enjambment in 244 and in 246 a resolution of the second longum. As soon as the old jurors try to be quicker the structure of the verses changes, too.[18]

The diction of the old men fits in perfectly with their entry. The sentimental and nostalgic reminiscence of the glorious days in Byzantium is expressed in a naïve manner of speaking, in a paratactic sequence of events (237, 239 *kaita*). In the following dialogue (248–72) with one of the boys there is a variation of the entrance iambics. The delivery of the 'Euripideans' can't be different from the delivery of catalectic iambic tetrameters as the chorus-leader explicitly announces in lines 270–3 that he is now going to sing.[19]

The change of the metrical form must have been expressed by the way the old people walked. MacDowell[20] assumes a 'slight increase in speed'. The effect of the syncopation could have gone even further. In the *parodos* of the *Lysistrata* the syncopated iambic tetrameters express that the old men get out of breath. This can be fitted in with MacDowell's interpretation: while talking with the boys the old men's walking becomes livelier, and so they get out of breath. The effect of the syncopation must have been a short pause and a new beginning, which is underlined by middle diaeresis.

By including the boys, Aristophanes can dramatize the *parodos* as a dialogue without the actors. The conversation between the chorus-leader and his son serves to further characterize the jurors: the chorus consists of old men, who live in the past, who chatter about unimportant things, and who feel so shaky that they need the help of their sons. Their parsimony rooted in their poverty is near to avarice, but also shows that they are dependent on their daily income from the courts. The impudent answer of the son to his father's reproach reveals the helplessness of the old

---

[16] See F. Perusino, *Il tetrametro giambico catalettico nella commedia Greca* (Roma, 1968), 41.

[17] See D. M. MacDowell, *Aristophanes, 'Wasps'* (Oxford, 1971), 162.

[18] See ibid. 165.

[19] See Perusino, *Il tetrametro giambico catalettico nella commedia Greca*, 35–6; A. Pickard-Cambridge, *The Dramatic Festivals of Athens²*, rev. J. Gould and D. M. Lewis (London 1968), 156 ff.   [20] *Aristophanes, 'Wasps'*, 166.

men—a helplessness which seems to be contradictory to Bdelycleon's warning about the chorus.

Because of the content, and for metrical reasons, I do not follow
Srebrny's and Russo's[21] transposition of the lines 266–89 between
316 and 317.[22] So the dialogue is followed by the chorus's song (273–
89), by which they want to call Philocleon out of the house. The
mixture of ionics and dactyloepitrites[23] is an excellent metrical
characterization of the old men. Through the ionic opening their
old-fashioned special liking for Phrynichean tunes is expressed as
Bdelycleon has already announced (217–21). The dactyloepitrites in
the manner of Pindar[24] also characterize the old jurors as lovers of
old times and melodies. The musical accompaniment reinforces the
characterization, which was already expressed in the nostalgic
reminiscence of their entry. Another function of the metre consists
in the comic effect which is the result of the tension between
content and language on the one hand and the metrical form on
the other:[25] the thoughts about the reasons of Philocleon's absence
with their absurd conclusions are opposed to the form and thus
create a comic atmosphere.

The clausula of the song (289) is followed by the chorus-leader's
order to the boy in the same metrical shape (io io). The old man is so
exhilarated by his favourite tunes that the order to the boy becomes
lyric, too.

In the following *amoibaion* (291–316) between the chorus-leader
and the boy, the metre is continuously ionic, too. Prato's[26] note on
this *amoibaion*, 'Gli ionici sono parodici, come *Thesm.* 101 sgg. e *Ran.*
323 sgg.', needs some modification as the three quoted passages
show different functions of the ionic rhythm: there is no parodic
intention in the *parodos* of the *Frogs*. Ionics appear in connection
with Dionysus' worship. In the *Thesmophoriazusae* the ionic monody
characterizes the poet Agathon as female and weak. In the *Wasps*

---

[21] St Srebrny, 'Aristophanea', *Eos*, 50 (1959–60), 43–51; C. F. Russo, 'Die *Wespen* "im
Umbruch" und ein Modul von 18 × 2 Tetrametern' (1968), in H.-J. Newiger (ed.)
Aristophanes und die Alte Komödie (Darmstadt, 1975).
[22] See my argumentation in *Untersuchungen zur Form und dramatischen Technik der
Aristophanischen Komödien*, 95–7.
[23] See my analysis (ibid. 97–9), which is different from MacDowell's (Aristophanes,
'Wasps' 170–1) metrical explanation.
[24] E. Fraenkel, 'Lyrische Daktylen', in *Kleine Beiträge zur Klassischen Philologie*,
(Rome, 1964), 227–8.   [25] See MacDowell, *Aristophanes*, 'Wasps', 170.
[26] C. Prato, *I canti di Aristofane* (Rome, 1962), 99.

this metre has got a different effect: it serves the characterization of the old men as lovers of old times. In the *amoibaion* a parodic effect is created by the tension between content and form: the boy's request for a little present in lyric metres. In lines 306–8 there is a further comic element. 'The boy absurdly slips into a quotation from Pindar.'[27] This quotation (fr. 189 Sn.-M.) leaves the level of colloquial language which prevailed in the strophe. Now the dialogue turns to paratragedy. In a 'little *thrēnos*'[28] the boy complains about his fate whereby the reason for his lament exclamation (309, 315) and the desperate question (311) is contrasted comically with the lamenting exclamation (309, 315) and the desperate question (311). So Aristophanes doesn't parody a certain original, but a tragic situation, the melodramatic lament.

The paratragic end of the *amoibaion* is followed by Philocleon's answer—a parody on content and metre of Euripidean monodies. The aria parodies the way Euripidean heroes express their grief and pathos in threnodic monodies. The lyric polymetrical form[29] is in comic contrast to the fate of the singer. The pathos of the opening line with the typical Euripidean bacchaic dimeter[30] and the address *philoi*[31] is destroyed by the following trivial content and slips into bathos. 'You just have to imagine how *dia tēs opēs* and *elthōn epi tous kadiskous* might be sung'.[32] In this monody metre and language are used with parodic intentions. According to P. Rau's typology[33] Philocleon's aria belongs to the group of 'parodic imitation'—the imitation of the long *thrēnoi* found in Euripides' tragedies. The monody serves as a transition from the skilfully portrayed chorus's entry to the battle scene. Having been informed by Philocleon's song about the situation and seeing that their arrival in the early morning hasn't been successful, the old men turn to action now. Bdelycleon's impudent attempt to confine their colleague leads to the chorus's burst of indignation (334ff.). Philocleon recites tetrameters, the angry chorus sings in free lyric trochaics (334–5, 342a–345). The *epirrhema* in catalectic anapaestic tetrameters (346–57)

---

[27] MacDowell, *Aristophanes' 'Wasps'*, 175.

[28] P. Rau, *Paratragodia: Untersuchungen zu einer komischen Form des Aristophanes* (Munich, 1967), 192.

[29] See my analysis in *Untersuchungen zur Form und dramatischen Technik der Aristophanischen Komödien*, 103–4.

[30] See E., *Supp.* 990 = 1012, 1002 = 1025, *Ion* 1465, *Tr.* 321, 587–8, *Ph.* 1290, *Or.* 1437–9; Ar., *Th.* 1018–19, 1143–4, *Ra.* 1346.   [31] See Ar., *Th.* 1015; Rau, 71, 151.

[32] Rau, 151.   [33] *Op. cit.*, 15.

with a *pnigos* (358–364) contains considerations about the possibilities of escaping and a nostalgic reminiscence to former times. In
the *antode* (365–78) Philocleon has got the ingenious idea of gnaw-
ing the net which surrounds the house. The chorus is on guard to
help Philocleon in the case of emergency. The parallelism of the
whole syzygy is disturbed because of the content. Whereas part 1
with ode, *katakeleusmos, epirrhema,* and *pnigos* is complete part 2 has
only got *antode, antikatakeleusmos,* and *antepirrhema.* In line 395
Bdelycleon awakes and rushes to prevent his father's escape, which
explains the absence of the *antipnigos.* So the *antepirrhema* actually
ends in line 394.[34] The next lines prepare the following battle scene,
to which Philocleon's cry for help (400–2) is the transition. The
chorus reacts in a trochaic song (403–14) announcing that they
will show their *cholē* as *sphēkia.* The strange idea of the old men that
someone who wants to stop their *philodikia,* which *toin theoin
psēphismata* (378) guarantee, is an enemy of democracy and a future
tyrant is especially expressed in the lyric *pnigē* of the odes (410–14,
468–70).

The form of the epirrhematic syzygy is used in the battle scene to
divide two parallel scenes: the chorus-leader's *katakeleusmos* (403–4)
and the following 'battle-song' of the chorus (405–14) introduce a
real battle scene, which Bdelycleon and his slave win. After the
antode (463–70) with the chorus's angry outburst about Bdelycleon's tyrannical behaviour in lyric trochaics they finally agree
in the *antepirrhema* (471–525) to use words instead of violence.

The interpretation of the *parodos* of the *Wasps* has shown how the
metrical, that is the musical, composition accompanies the action
and how it is used to characterize the actor and the chorus. The old
men, who come near Philocleon's house while it is still dark, enter
with iambics (230–47). The syncopated iambic tetrameters ('Euripideans') illustrate that the old men have difficulties with walking
and get out of breath (248–72). The following song shows the jurors
as admirers of old-fashioned melodies *à la* Phrynichus (273–88b).
They sing their serenade to call their colleague using a mixture of
ionics and dactyloepitrites, which may have been significant for
Phrynichus. Once they have been set going they remain in the
ionic metre in the following *amoibaion,* too (291–316). Being

---

[34] See Gelzer, *Der epirrhematische Agon bei Aristophanes. Untersuchungen zur Struktur
der attischen Alten Komödie* (Munich, 1960), 20.

informed by Philocleon's paratragic monody about his son's intrigues their anger, their waspish character is expressed by the trochaics of the odes of the two syzygies—a metre which fits with an aggressive mood. The change of metre reflects the transition to another type of parodos: type 3 (chorus assembles habitually) changes into type 2 (chorus encounters with an opponent when entering). It is significant that the metre of the *epirrhemata* of the syzygies is different. The first syzygy (334–402) is composed in catalectic anapaestic tetrameters, the second (403–525) in catalectic trochaic tetrameters. So the trochaic metre is also in tetrameter passages a means to underline an aggressive mood whereas catalectic anapaestic tetrameters fit with a discussion as it takes place in the first syzygy.

IV

With these two examples I hope to have shown how masterfully Aristophanes composed his comedies and how skilfully he used metre, rhythm, and music to reinforce the dramatic action. So my article could be regarded as a rehabilitation of 'Aristophanes as a lyric poet', to quote Michael Silk's article of 1980.[35] Silk emphasizes the conventionality of Aristophanes' poetry compared with Pindar and the tragedians. But he overlooks one important point: the function of the lyric in the context of the comedies, which I tried to illustrate by my interpretation of the *parodos* of the *Wasps*.

I think that a thorough interpretation of the eleven plays can show that Aristophanes was in no way bound to rigid forms of composition, which he had to keep because of the tradition of Old Comedy, but that he could manage them freely and use them according to the requirements of the dramatic action—as we can expect from a great poet.

---

[35] M. Silk, 'Aristophanes as a Lyric Poet', in J. Henderson (ed.), *Aristophanes*.
This essay is a revised version of a paper given to the Greek seminar of the University of Cambridge.

II

Some Aspects of Aristophanes' Dramatic Art in the *Birds*

THOMAS GELZER

The Old Comedy of Aristophanes, as is well known, differs in many respects from other dramatic genres such as tragedy, satyric drama (despite its comic character), and the New Comedy of Menander. Several elements that in the other genres have been considered typical of the dramatic art-form are either virtually absent or are of only minor importance. The methods of other types of drama correspond much more closely to those to which we are accustomed in our own modern drama than do those of Aristophanic comedy; for despite the brilliance of Aristophanes' imagination no later writer ever used his work in all its various aspects as a model for his own writing. In any attempt to get to grips with Aristophanes' dramatic technique the first difficulty that has to be faced is simply that of finding the right questions to ask.

It was no coincidence that those elements which go to make up the typical structure of Old Comedy were only discovered and adequately described, gradually and very late, in the second half of the nineteenth century, and that these discoveries were at first by no means the result of attempts to answer questions of dramatic technique, but came about in the course of narrowly technical investigations into metrical construction and form.[1] Only very slowly were these results brought to bear on problems of Aristophanes' technique as a dramatist.[2] Until the twentieth century no

---

[1] Whereas the parabasis was already recognized as a form in antiquity, A. Rossbach and R. Westphal, in their *Griechische Metrik* (Leipzig, 1856), 88 f. 199, were the first to describe the *agōn* as an 'antisyntagmatische Form'.

[2] T. Zieliński, *Die Gliederung der altattischen Komödie* (Leipzig, 1885). He went, however, rather far in contrasting the 'epirrhematische Komposition' of comedy with the 'epeisodische Komposition' of tragedy. J. Poppelreuter, *De comoediae Atticae*

attempt was made to build up from these insights a coherent picture of the 'composition' of Attic Old Comedy, a picture in which these conventional forms, the way in which the action of the complete plays is structured, and the resources available to the dramatist would all find a place.[3]

Since then, of course, very many apt observations have been made, and if we look at the most recent general accounts of Aristophanes we see that the present-day picture of his dramatic work is a very different one.[4] Now and again, however, a certain reluctance can still be found in some quarters to admit that the basic elements out of which he built up the action of his plays were very different from those of other genres. Attempts are even made, it seems, to 'rescue' him for respectable drama by trying somehow to prove that his plays too keep to those rules according to which we are accustomed to judge works from other dramatic genres.[5] If, however, we consistently approach the plays of Aristophanes with the same questions that we ask, justifiably, when we discuss the other types of drama, then, as we know by now, the answers we shall get concerning his dramatic technique will be quite inadequate. But then, our job is not to justify it but, to start with at least, simply to understand it. In order to put Aristophanes' technique in the right perspective we must start from these special conventions of the genre. Of course, we can hardly expect that it will prove totally different from that of other types of drama; Aristophanic comedy too is drama, and therefore naturally employs methods that are of importance in any dramatic genre. But these techniques are none the less used to a very different extent, since they must achieve their intended effect against a background of different conventions and with different ends in view.

Some very acute critical observations have already been made in this direction, and what follows will naturally be based on them,

---

primordiis particulae duae, diss. (Berlin, 1893), 23 ff. then described the typical structure of the 'second part' of the plays.

  [3] P. Mazon, *Essai sur la composition des comédies d'Aristophane*, thesis (Paris, 1904).
  [4] See e.g. C. F. Russo, *Aristofane autore di teatro* (Firenze, 1962), and K. J. Dover, *Aristophanic Comedy* (London, 1972); for the *Birds* in particular: Russo, 231 ff.; Dover, 30 ff., 140 ff.
  [5] See e.g. H. Erbse, 'Sokrates im Schatten der aristophanischen Wolken', *Hermes*, 82 (1954), 385–420; P. Händel, *Formen und Darstellungsweisen in der aristophanischen Komödie* (Heidelberg, 1963); M. Landfester, *Die Ritter des Aristophanes* (Amsterdam, 1967).

although I have not the space here to acknowledge each one in detail;[6] but there remains a great deal to do. It is of course difficult to describe Aristophanes' dramatic art in terms appropriate to tragedy and New Comedy, types of drama which have much in common with Old Comedy and yet are so very different; I propose therefore to start not from abstract concepts but from a study of the way in which his dramatic technique works in practice; in the short time available I would like to look in detail at a few concrete examples of its use in the *Birds*.

Right from the beginning the Prologue gives us an introduction of a masterly kind to the fantastic atmosphere of the piece. The dramatic means which are employed in the later parts of the comedy, with a great profusion of people, things, and musical and metrical forms, are already present in essence here.

In front of a stage-set which as yet betrays nothing of what is concealed behind it, two old men are moving around in uncertain direction in the orchestra: tired, heavily laden, and lost. Only trees (1), a wood (92), undergrowth (202ff., 256), rocks (54) are obviously visible—a wilderness, but no house, no entrance, no trace of any inhabitants whatsoever, and no indication of where they might come from. All this is, on the contrary, what the two men are themselves looking for, and what they discover only after an ostentatiously produced detour. The audience is therefore at first totally uncertain about what they are being given to look at, and the emphasized lack of certainty about what they are given to see at the beginning, and about the stage décor and the appearance and movements of the actors, arouses a general curiosity about what must be going to transpire here. By these means Aristophanes establishes in a masterly way, right from the beginning, a sense of anticipation which carries the audience along. The audience knows, of course, that the uncertainty will not last, but that this will be a play in which actors and a chorus, under generally well-known conditions, and in forms which it knows of old, will present a comedy. The especially wide divergence between this quite particular expectation on the one hand, and the possibilities of foreseeing how it will be fulfilled this time on the other, creates a tension which stimulates the curiosity of the audience to a remarkable degree. The

---

[6] For a very useful select bibliography, see now H.-J. Newiger, *Aristophanes und die Alte Komödie* (Darmstadt, 1975), 487–510.

way in which the information, essential for understanding the comedy, is revealed step by step compels the audience to concentrate on virtually every word which is said, and creates a readiness to follow, almost without knowing it, Aristophanes' train of thought—and this readiness is then the basic means by which the audience is drawn into Aristophanes' comic inventions. Their dramatic penetrating force is intensified by the economy with which he plays with this expectation, now accelerating, now decelerating.

At first the audience's attention is directed towards the two birds, the crow and the jackdaw, whose directions the two men are following in their erratic wanderings. By this means the audience learns, it is true, why they are proceeding in such an apparently random zigzag course—but not, on the other hand, where they are going and to what purpose. Above all, however, the two confess that they have no idea where they are (9–10). Attention is therefore drawn additionally to the mysterious deserted wood; but its significance and identity are still withheld: the audience's curiosity is excited even more strongly. But then one of the characters addresses the spectators directly in two small monologues (13 ff., 27 ff.). Now the audience is entitled to expect that it will be put straight in the picture, in the usual way of prologues,[7] about the situation and the purpose of the whole enterprise. Well, it learns something at least: first the starting-point and destination of the journey on which the two are engaged. They have bought the two birds in Athens, in the bird market, as guides to take them to Tereus, who has been transformed from a man into a hoopoe—so the motive for their vague search is revealed. Then the reason for their journey is made clear: they have left their city in order to escape the excessive litigation. Thereby they are identified as true-born Athenians, and the luggage which they carry becomes meaningful. The purpose of the basket, the pot, and the branches of myrtle, as equipment for the sacrifice at a new foundation is not explicitly stated, but any spectator with his wits about him can deduce it from the circumstances. One learns too that Tereus is not the ultimate aim of their journey, but is only to be a source of information to tell them from his experience where they might find a *topos apragmōn* in

---

[7] See e.g. *Ach.* 1 ff.; *Eq.* 40 ff.; *Nu.* 1 ff., 41 ff., 60 ff.; *V.* 54 ff.; *Pax* 20 ff., 50 ff.; *Ec.* 1 ff.; *Pl.* 1 ff.

which ultimately to settle. What they have in mind to do there is not yet let out.

A new expectation is aroused, and a consequent curiosity, but at this moment the monologue is interrupted. The economical play with the withholding of information has begun. What happens is that the birds now make signs indicating that they have reached a spot which they want to show to their owners. Now the mystery about the forest scenery begins to clear. The audience's anticipation has been directed towards the habitation of the hoopoe Tereus. Aristophanes increases their curiosity by putting the first encounter between the two Athenians and the inhabitants in the form of a door-opening scene (53 ff.). As with the monologue addressed to the spectators, a scene of this form is thoroughly conventional in the prologue.[8] So, Aristophanes is again able to play with quite precise expectations of the audience. He does so immediately, by drawing attention to the fact that this is not a real door, but that they have to knock on a rock, and that they are calling out not an ordinary 'concierge', but a hoopoe, slave of a hoopoe. Thus the audience's expectation is concentrated in a quite particular direction: two birds are already present, the crow and the jackdaw, which are to serve as guides to their fellow bird the hoopoe; compared with these two very large birds a hoopoe is a relatively modest animal, and all the more so is the *pais* of a hoopoe. The two men conduct themselves accordingly: after some frivolous jokes about the manner in which they can knock and what form of summons to use, the one who knocks insists very impatiently that he should not be kept waiting unnecessarily by the door-keeper and have to knock again. The fact that they are kept waiting also serves to heighten the tension: what will come out of this so-called 'door'? It is a surprise: instead of a tiny little bird there rushes out a man-sized monster which opens an enormous beak. The mood changes totally on the instant, from wanton high spirits to mortal terror for their lives, which can be exploited for immediately effective situation comedy.

But Aristophanes does not only build and heighten the tension—he also makes the surprise more effective in a quite particular sense: by leading the audience's anticipation plausibly and positively to expect a harmless animal to appear—and then fulfilling it in a

---

[8] See e.g. *Nu.* 131 ff.; *Pax* 178 ff.; *Th.* 25 ff.; *Ra.* 35 ff.; other 'door-opening-scenes', after the prologue, e.g. *Ach.* 393 ff.; *Lys.* 424 ff.; *Ra.* 460 ff.; *Pl.* 1097 ff. etc.

different way: by the monster with this beak. He exploits the situation thus created: he makes the one who has caused their panic by his appearance cry out at the same moment, himself in terror (62), 'Good god—these are bird-hunters', and then introduce himself as a perfectly harmless little *trochilos* (plover) who has been changed, together with his master, into a bird. Right to the last this panic is exploited: the two Athenians are compelled to confess mutually what cowards they are (85 ff.), and that because in their terror they let their birds fly away. Even from this, from getting rid of these props which are no longer necessary, he makes use of the opportunity for jokes inherent in the situation.

All this is played *prestissimo* in about fifty lines. This information and expectation of the audience which he has thus created is employed further without delay, but this time with inversion: we have seen only the servant—what will his master be like? The two Athenians are just engaged in confessing their fear—and once again Aristophanes uses the door which is not a door for a surprise. They are interrupted by a voice from inside: still invisible a king is heard commanding in mock-tragic parody of Sophocles' *Tereus* (92), 'open wide the oak, that I may go forth'. The reaction of the two is bound to be a new terror: the expectation is now that something quite enormous must come. This time the surprise consists in that this king comes out, so to speak, in his underclothes. He has just been roused from his siesta, and in addition he happens to be moulting, and his feathers have gone. This time it is a suppressed laughter, for which the two have to find a fibbing excuse. The beak which at the first sight terrified them (61) is now the alleged cause of their hilarity. Without following up all the innocent jokes by which the two parties, in a mock-tragic dialogue, now introduce themselves to one another (and by doing so of course in the first place also to their audience), I shall just give a brief résumé of the techniques which Aristophanes uses at this stage of the action: first of all, surprise: the voice interrupts the dialogue; then, building up of tension: from inside something is heard which is not yet seen; third, creating an expectation which then is revealed as erroneous: instead of a frightful tragic tyrant there pops out a moulting bird without any of the royal insignia; the effect is of suppressed laughter instead of the anticipated terror. But above all we should note the manner in which the whole scene is designed: it is obviously a duplication of the pattern which has been used just before. Once again an as yet unidentified person comes out of the door, and we can see what Aristophanes makes of this repeated pattern: he plays careful variations. Look at the two scenes in parallel:

First time (49 ff.)		*Second time* (92 ff.)
Circumstantial knocking at the door; waiting; innocuous jokes about the so-called 'door' by those outside	I	A sudden movement from inside surprises those outside—dramatizing joke about the door made by one inside
Reaction of fear at the sight of the slave's beak	II	Reaction of laughter at the sight of the king's beak
There appears an unknown little bird which is taken for a monster, but is in fact a devoted slave	III	There comes out the expected hoopoe, but not as a royal appearance even though he is in fact the king of the birds
The two are reduced to fibbing with invented birds' names because of their dread, in order to save their dignity	IV	They are reduced to fibbing with an alleged reason for their laughter, in order to preserve the proprieties.

In addition, both scenes serve indirectly the purpose of introducing the players by giving information about their identity as well as through their conduct.

By this duplication Aristophanes is able, without adding anything new and by the mere parallelism of the process, to use expectations, aroused by the fact that apparently exactly the same is going to happen again, to delude and surprise his spectators, making them anticipate by analogy what is in fact *not* going to happen: in the repetition of the pattern the king appears *un*summoned and his appearance is the *opposite* of frightful; the two Athenians are *not* compelled to present themselves as—despite all appearances—dignified foreign birds; and yet the same items are used: the door, the birds' costume, the beak; and the same situation is the basis of the scene, namely the first introduction of the two parties. It is precisely through all this repetition that the audience's expectations are deluded and surprised.

How self-consciously employed an artifice this technique of repetition is can be seen right from the most minute elements, even when they are on a far smaller scale than complete repetition scenes of the sort which we have just examined. Even single jokes may be based in and receive their point from this kind of deceptive analogy. I shall take only three examples from the prologue which we have just dealt with. Right in the opening lines we have an instance which by the almost pedantic regularity of its structure can serve as a paradigm. Two introductory verses in the form of a question establish the level of expectation (3 ff.):

> Why are we wandering up and down, you rogue?
> This endless road will make an end of us,

and the corresponding first remark:

> To think that I, poor fool, at a crow's bidding,
> Should trudge about, an hundred miles and more!

and now the parallelism:

> To think that I, poor wretch, at a daw's bidding

(up to this point almost word for word analogous—and now comes the variation:)

> Should wear the very nails from off my feet!

The in-itself-innocent image for the hardship of the journey, 'wear the very nails from off my feet', is given added point because at one and the same time it is an expected continuation by structural analogy of the first remark, and gives this expectation a surprising turn by the ridiculous self-pity of the colloquial expression.

In a more spaciously developed but quite identically structured example we soon meet the following. The hoopoe asks them both (127 ff.):

> What sort of city would you like?

The first answer:

> A city where my first trouble would be such as this:
> A friend at daybreak coming to my door
> And calling out:
> 'Take your bath early, then come round to me
> You and your children to the wedding banquet . . .'

and so on. And the hoopoe's ironical remark:

> Upon my word you are quite in love with troubles.

Now the parallel pattern. The hoopoe asks the other:

> And you?

Then the answer:

> I love the same,

which turns out to be only a provisional answer, because then comes the unexpected continuation which is there only to provide this parallelism. The hoopoe asks again:

> But tell me what.

And he is now given the answer parallel to the first:

> A city where the father of some handsome lad
> Comes up and chides me with complaints like these:
> 'Fine things I hear of you Stilbonides,
> You met my son returning from the baths,
> And never kissed, or hugged or fondled him . . .'

etc. And again the hoopoe's second ironical remark:

> Poor poppet you are in love with ills indeed.

The whole superfluous development of the second answer is given structurally comic point, because through the analogical pattern of repetition the expectation of a second definition of what sort of happiness would make the New City desirable is reduced to the bathetic revelation of a harmlessly obscene sex fantasy. In this second reply many of the same themes appear as in the first: an invitation by the father, the bath, and even the wedding—in a sense.

And now the third example. In the smallest space and with the greatest economy this schema is used with a whole cascade of repetitions in the reply (113 ff.) that follows this question:

> What brings you here?

Answer:

> You were a man at first, as we are now

(this shows the pattern which is now to be repeated:)

> And had your creditors, as we have now,
> And loved to shirk your debts, as we do now;
> And then you changed your nature and became a bird.

Again two verses are entirely superfluous 'And had your creditors . . . And loved to shirk your debts . . .' and these statements are witty only because they are an unexpected parallel to 'You were a man at first' with the additionally repeated phrase *hōsper nō pote*.

It is in the stereotyped duplication, or even multiple repetition, of the same structure, and even with an identical addition, that the joke consists—the joke of a quite definite expectation and its subsequent frustration. The mechanical repetition of the phrase *hōsper nō pote* creates in the smallest space the well-known Lekythion effect. On a larger scale we meet it with repetition of a whole scene, and we shall meet even more luxurious developments of it where whole sequences of scenes are treated that way, in the second part of the comedy.

It is only now—after these last questions and answers—that Aristophanes takes up again the thread that he had dropped before. His audience needs and wants to be put in the picture about what the two are actually going to do here. Curiosity had already been aroused in the first monologues to the audience, which were then on purpose interrupted. At that point the economy consisted in postponing the satisfaction of this curiosity by interception and the distraction of other unexpected jokes which, nevertheless, served at the same time to reveal in part, and step by step, the basic information for the plot. This curiosity can now be reactivated: what are the two men really after? From the conversation with the hoopoe it appears that they are looking for a city which fulfils their wish for 'the good life', and incidentally they discover that the birds themselves might be likely to offer this good life (161).

Thus—the audience is induced to conclude—they are going to live under Tereus with the birds. Now at last the solution is found. But this too is a deception. Again there comes a surprise, and again an unexpected interruption. Peisetairos does not ask, as one might have expected, the hoopoe Tereus for advice how to do that, but he gives him advice, which leads once more to something new and entirely unexpected. Quite clearly the solution for which we have been waiting is coming at last. Now Aristophanes begins to play with the audience's expectations in deadly earnest. Nothing is given away prematurely. At first, as in a vision, in a sibylline manner a general announcement (162 ff.):

> Oh the grand scheme I see in the birds' reach,
> And power to grasp it, if you'd trust to me!

Now then:

> Trust you in what?

and to that quite a few futile answers such as:

> Don't fly about . . . like birds

. . . and so on.

> . . . but what we ought to do
> Tell us!—Found one State!

But:

> What sort of state are birds to found?

Really that is precisely what everybody wants to know now. But now Peisetairos gives himself airs. First he makes the poor hoopoe guess himself and search: on the floor, in the air—and find there heaven and clouds. Then he defines *polos* and *polis*, and the air as the area of transit of the gods, until he reaches finally the unexpected conclusion: it is the air we will have to colonize and to fortify, so we can compel the gods to surrender us the power. So, that is now the final plan. It is on, and the audience knows finally what kind of an action there is to be in this comedy, what the display of stage-set, props, and movements was aimed at, and the plan can immediately be put into practice.

One condition, however, is still named on which the whole progress of the action rests. It must be secured that the birds are willing to execute this scheme, and that they are going to execute it following the advice of Peisetairos. But all that is nothing but a question of purely technical organization, and, although every word now contains concrete directions according to which the following action really will proceed, that is not a matter of humour but—in dramatic terms—only of practical significance for the continuation of the play. Thus everything is precisely indicated, but here economy demands the opposite procedure from hitherto: here there is no delay, but actual acceleration. In less than ten lines (198–205) all practicalities are disposed of. The significance of this procedure is quite clear: the interest lies not so much in what the content of the action is going to be, but purely in how it will happen. The practical organization is there only to serve as a basis for the development of those dramatic games which are the cause of this action being Comedy. These games in scarcely any case serve to promote the action, but almost exclusively cause delay. And even this delay is used with great economy to rouse tension and curiosity, whose unexpected resolution then releases the relief of laughter.

The prologue over, the audience once more knows what must come next, namely the *parodos* of the chorus. Here, as elsewhere, the spectators have, and always have had, a general idea of what will follow, because Old Comedy has its structural conventions. Aristophanes does not, therefore, have to create anticipation, only exploit it. Let us look briefly at the way in which he plays with it this time. First of all, he contrives once more to distract the attention of the spectators and to keep them in suspense; before he really introduces the chorus there are plenty of surprises in store. The excitement of wondering how it will come on is intensified by his trick of not letting the audience see what initially claims its attention. Everything happens in the foliage, and in this game of inside–outside the device of having the two men waiting outside and making lively comments expressive of their expectations provokes and maintains the audience's curiosity, as it is meant to. Everything needed for the appearance of the chorus is carefully prepared before they actually enter.

The hoopoe disappears into the foliage and first sings a delightful song to wake his nightingale; her answering song is rendered by flute music. We may conclude from the words of the two Athenians that the invisible music rises to a climax: first comes this solo *a capella* (209–22), then flute music alone for the nightingale (223–4); now everything would be ready for the entrance of the chorus. But now another surprise: instead of the entry of the chorus, the Epops begins to sing again; now comes the thrilling bravura aria, a solo with flute accompaniment, in which the hoopoe summons all the birds from their nests to an assembly (227–62). All attention is directed to the music; the audience can see nothing. Now the suspense of waiting for the chorus has reached a climax—but nothing happens. 'See any bird?', asks Peisetairos, with reason; 'not I, nor sign of one', his companion answers, and 'the hoopoe whooped it up for nothing then, down in the rushes' is the flippant comment we get from them both. The audience now turn their eyes expectantly to the sky: 'and I've got my mouth and eyes open too, gazing up at the sky' (263–6). But in that direction there is nothing—Aristophanes keeps us in suspense a little longer. Yet another surprise: somewhere a bird calls *torotix torotix*.

Only the fact that the metre changes (268ff.) from iambics to tetrameters, the usual metre for this section, with accompaniment from the flute, shows the audience that the *parodos* is now beginning. And now come four birds dressed up in dazzling colours; but they do not come from the *parodos*, as one would expect, and not as a chorus, but singly. The hoopoe, who has meanwhile re-emerged from his thicket, gives detailed information about their names and costumes; he is now wearing his complete royal panoply, ready for the arrival of his bird subjects (268–93).

Ah, the chorus is dressed up like that this time, and the *choreutai* are going to come down individually this time from various elevated points. But no—here again Aristophanes has led us up the garden path. While the audience searches the heights of the *skēnē* expectantly for new exotic manifestations, the birds are suddenly gathered in the orchestra, having entered very quietly and stealthily from a *parodos* (294ff.). The fact that the birds have arrived in silence is a special surprise, after the spectators had been led by the great aria and the cries of 'torotix' to believe that it was all leading up to a fantastic burst of song from the chorus. And what has now come is not a new collection of exotic flying creatures, but twenty-four ordinary denizens of Attica's woods and fields, some of whose names the two old men already know (297–301): they are then all listed in a brilliant piece of versification (302–5). The four exotic creatures that came in before, one by one, don't even belong to the chorus.

Once again, as at the beginning, complicated and confused movements make it impossible to see where the birds are going and what they are going to do (307). They all turn their beaks towards the three actors (308–9), a threatening gesture which scares the two Athenians once more, as had the first encounter with the *trochilos*; but their fears are, thank goodness, groundless this time too. The birds haven't even noticed yet that the hoopoe is not alone, and he has first to apprise them of the fact (301–21); very comforting! But now yet again a surprise: these guests are not welcomed as the king's *proxeroi* after all, but they see the same reaction as with the *trochilos* (322–35): men are arch-enemies of the birds, they are bird-catchers. Now they have come too close, and suddenly things start to happen. The chorus, which until now has been in complete disorder, gets ready—but not to sing; they line up for an attack (336ff.).

Now every Athenian knows exactly what is going on; the ringing cries are parodies of commands that every trained soldier (i.e. every Athenian citizen) knows exactly how to carry out (343–53). A parody of a proper battle follows. The opposition—the two Athenians—reacts immediately, and jumps to defend itself. The props that the men have brought with them for their journey and for the foundation of a new city (bowl, spit, saucer) are suddenly used for a completely different purpose, as rampart and stockade (354–63). The command to attack rings out (364–5); the audience is now looking forward to a proper fight, but yet again they are disappointed. The hoopoe comes forward to separate the warring factions (366–85) and by using his skill as a mediator, equipped with all the tricks of the sophists and the orators, he gets them to agree to an armistice (438–47). The final orders to the hoplites are to hang up their weapons again next to the hearth (434–5) and to dismiss home, but stand by on alert (448–50); these orders arouse in every Athenian familiar feelings of relief, now that the worst is over again for the moment.

Thus Aristophanes exploits to the full every chance given to him by the first meeting of chorus and actors in the *parodos*. Every part of the action, even the shortest, brings a new surprise, and the emotions of the spectators continually see-saw from suspense to relief and back again. It should be emphasized, in passing, how in these and later scenes the opportunity repeatedly presents itself to make capital out of the expectations of the audience, who are familiar with the conventional forms and structure of comedy. The function of every anticipated section of the play is varied and altered somewhat in the *Birds*, so that Aristophanes can thus indulge in dramatic surprises. This is the case with the *parodos*, where the chorus enter in silence, and with the first epirrhematic *agōn* (327–99), here used for the battle described above; then come the main *agōn* (451–626), in which here for the first time the usual argument between two people is replaced by a manifesto speech made by Peisetairos alone, and then the parabasis (676–800), where in this play the poet does not speak in his own person but makes the birds base their claim to hegemony on their primeval origins.

One example will suffice to show how Aristophanes can exploit expectations too that do not arise from these fixed forms of Old Comedy themselves but are still the result of the audience's knowledge of what usually happens in such a play.

Once the birds, convinced by Peisetairos' speech, have agreed to carry out his plan (627–38) the audience knows that it is now time for the actors to leave the stage so that the chorus can go on to the parabasis. At this point Aristophanes repeats his game with the 'door', although this time it is not a matter of an exit but of an entrance. The spectators expect the actors to go off through it, but they are repeatedly surprised and kept waiting by one delaying tactic after another. The hoopoe invites the two Athenians with due courtesy to be guests in his nest (645 ff.). 'You are both most welcome.' 'We accept gladly.' 'Then please come in here.' And they agree to do so: '*iōmen*, let's go!' But first there is a slight difficulty about who should go first, which delays their exit for a moment: (to the hoopoe) 'Go first and lead the way for us', to which the hoopoe replies, '*ithi*, please, after you'—'oh, but wait a minute, please come back for a moment'. First they must think about the problem of getting wings for the two men, so that they will not have to live like the fox with the eagle. The problem is quickly solved (649–55) and now they think about leaving again (656 ff.) '*houtō men eisiōmen*; now we can go in then!' But once more something holds them up; the hoopoe is unexpectedly held up, for the chorus-leader would like the nightingale–flute-player to be sent out to entertain the birds; he expresses his wish now in tetrameters, which this time surely mean that the parabasis is really beginning (658–60; cf. 268 ff.). But the metre changes once more; the parabasis is not starting yet after all, and the nightingale really does come out; in a surprising interlude she has to take her mask off quickly to let Euelpides kiss this beautiful girl (661–74). Then they start to exchange courtesies again over precedence: (675) the hoopoe says '*iōmen*', Peisetairos answers '*hēgou dē su nōin* ('Lead on')', and the spectators expect yet another such delay—but they are wrong; the three actors really do go in and the parabasis can now commence. But a final surprise is still to come: the chorus does not simply launch into the parabasis in the tetrameter rhythm already used by their leader; instead he sings a short glyconic song, for a *kommation*, and not at all expected

(676–84); only then does he change to the long-awaited tetrameters of the parabasis (685 ff.).

Finally, I would like to take a look at the last part of the comedy, that following the parabasis. The audience knows once more just what to expect, namely, the 'revue', that series of scenes in which one new arrival after another is dealt with by the main actor, in this play therefore by Peisetairos. However, as Paul Mazon so rightly remarked,[9] 'du point de vue dramatique toute cette seconde partie de la comédie prête infiniment moins d'intérêt que la première'. The reasons for this are that all the scenes are by definition more or less similar and that the same sketch form can be used over and over again without limit. Aristophanes therefore uses every technique of variation he knows to try to avoid monotony. Not only are the personages whom he brings on, one after another, very different, but he also has new properties at his disposal each time; finally he sees here a chance to show his skill in parody of various musical, metrical, and linguistic patterns.

However, we have no time to discuss here in detail all the nineteen or twenty visitors, their greater or lesser degree of characterization, or the jokes about their activities, or their speech. Let us look only at the dramatic structure of this whole section. Aristophanes actually exploits the repetitions and the opportunities they offer for echoes and parallelisms to produce here some of his best effects.

The first point to notice is that here too nothing is left to chance; the whole sequence is carefully planned. In a short scene (801–50) he prepares the ground very carefully so that when everything is ready the fun can start. Once the parabasis is over the two Athenians come out again from their foliage and first only remark: so much for that, 'so far so good' (801). The new feather costumes are briefly introduced and laughed at, and now the preparations for the second part begin. The name Nephelokokkygia is bestowed on the new city, and now, as always in technical matters, the speed with which these details are dealt is positively emphasized; on this occasion only nine lines are needed (837–45) to get everything ready so that the plot can continue as planned. Euelpides is sent off with the following instructions: he is to help the birds with the fortification of the new city in the air; he must see to it that a system of

[9] *Essai sur la composition des comédies d'Aristophane*, 175.

watches is set up to guard it; one herald is to visit the gods, and another mankind, to inform them of the new order; the herald sent to mankind should then report back.

Secondly, he does not simply tack the sketches on to each other, but uses two fair-sized choral interludes (1058–117, 1313–34) to split the series up into three sections: the first (801–1057) deals with the foundation ceremony, for which a sacrifice is needed, the effects of the building of the new city having not yet become apparent; the second uses four messengers to give preliminary reports on the completion of the project (1118–1312); the third section then gives us a picture of the effects of this foundation on men and gods (1335–1719).

The first section, then, is concerned with the sacrifice that must be made as part of the foundation ceremony. The characters who appear are all parasites, eager to cash in on the sacrifice. Variety is provided by the different methods used by Peisetairos on each occasion to foil their schemes. The first, a priest, is simply sent away, because he summons so many mighty predatory bird-gods to the sacrifice that any one of them would just make off with the skinny victim in front of the others' noses (859–94). The second, however, a poet, most unexpectedly receives a present, though this is admittedly only his own servant's threadbare shirt (903–56). The next arrivals are not so lucky. First to come on is a soothsayer, who is rewarded with anti-oracles, beaten, and driven off (957–91). Then, surprisingly after these anonymous figures, we see the astronomer Meton. What sort of a present will he get? He is first courteously warned—and then thrown out (992–1020). Then comes an inspector who wants to be bribed—he is driven out without a warning (1021–34), and then a statute salesman, who gets his beating without delay (1035–47). But then we are surprised to see the inspector return and declare his intention of acting as a prosecutor in accordance with just such a statute; the pair of them are thrown out together (1048–57). Aristophanes gradually speeds things up so as not to let these sketches become monotonous; the first two are the longest, and after the first comes a short choral song; but then the sketches become shorter and follow rapidly and directly on one another until the climax of the double beating is reached. The poet has 48 lines, the soothsayer 34, Meton 28, the inspector 14, the statute salesman on his own 9, then the unexpected partnership is disposed of in 7 lines; as a final irony, the sacrifice is not offered on the stage, but inside (1055–7). Clearly, each of these sketches in isolation would hardly have been dramatically effective; only in the context of the whole series, by answering the same expectation each time with a different unexpected twist, can Aristophanes really exploit the technique of variation.

After the second parabasis another laconic remark is made in a single line: the sacrifice has proved satisfactory (1118). In the second series of sketches the four messengers arrive; they all make it clear that Euelpides has completed his various missions, and all have a report to make on the foundation of the city or on its consequences. This time variety is provided not by acceleration but by deceleration: first we hear a short, anodyne description of the building of the city (1119–67), then a somewhat more exciting report from a sentry: a winged god has got past the guards and flown in (1168–87). There follows a short interlude in which the chorus sings a martial song to heighten the excitement (1188–95). Then the deity appears in person, but, as it turns out, is no warrior, only another messenger, namely the messenger of the gods, Iris, bringing a command from Zeus. She is treated with utter contempt, molested, and finally driven off (1196–1262). This scene too brings a few surprises: first, these mortals are unexpectedly visited by a god; secondly, the visitor is no warrior-god, but a lady, a messenger; and finally, a new and unprecedented variation on the theme of beating and driving off is found for her: she escapes through the air, assisted by the crane. After the antistrophe, which already celebrates the victory over the gods (1262–8), the herald from earth returns with a report full of pathos, in which Peisetairos is already beatified as the ruler of the world (1271–1303). The speech corresponds in form and in content to that of the 'exangelos', who describes the glorious fulfilment of the plan that was decided on in the first part of a play and put into operation in the second. The expectations of the audience are therefore guided in one particular direction: for now they anticipate the transition to the exodos—but again Aristophanes is only teasing them. To everyone's surprise the last four lines (1304–7) introduce a new development: now crowds of human beings will come here and beg you for wings and talons. Peisetairos is not carried off in triumph by the chorus, as everyone expects: instead he and the chorus in alternation indulge in a little pantomime at the expense of a lazy slave, who has to bring on the props for the following scenes (1313–34).

And thus—a real surprise this—the third series of sketches follows; these make the *Birds* the longest ancient play still extant. They come on one after another, without a break: a parricide, the dithyrambic poet Kinesias, and a sycophant. The mockery of Kinesias, of course, like that of Meton, is all the funnier because of the company he is keeping here. The repetitions lead to a climax, but here in reverse: the parricide gets a pair of wings from the huge pile, together with a complete panoply, the poet gets nothing, and the sycophant a beating. The wings are then removed (again in a single line) and Peisetairos leaves the stage (1469); everything is ready for the exodos. But the chorus does nothing more than sing an ode, which admittedly starts off as though it were going to lead to the exodos (1470 ff.): 'Marvels yet unknown to science have I seen in bird's-eye view' but then turns out to be an ordinary piece of mockery directed at two men, Kleonymos and Orestes. There is one final surprise in store for us: after this ode we expect at least a few well-known personages to appear and be dealt with in the proper manner. But Aristophanes gives the 'revue' an entirely unexpected twist: he brings it to an end with a different class of being, the climax of this whole procession: heroes and gods. The Iris scene had apparently exploited every possibility in this direction; but Aristophanes makes the universal dominion of Peisetairos lead to a surprising state of affairs: not only mankind, but also the gods, want something from Peisetairos. Now, however, beating is out and diplomacy is demanded. Another situation is now exploited: cut off from the stream of sacrifices, the gods are starving. One of the gods almost gets something to eat. Prometheus first tells Peisetairos what he must do to bring his negotiations with the approaching delegation to a successful conclusion; in this advice a new and unexpected aspect of Peisetairos' world dominion is revealed: if he plays his cards right he can even demand the 'royal power' from Zeus (1494–1552). This time, in the last of these conversations, the point lies again in repetition of a motif, but now the roles are reversed. Peisetairos negotiates with the three gods who now appear, Poseidon, Herakles, and the Triballian, in the manner of an accomplished sophist. Like the inspector and the statute salesman, whom he had thrown out, he now produces some dubious interpretations of Attic law, which, together with a promise, of a meal of roast birds, are enough to persuade the starving glutton

Herakles to cast his vote in favour of the bird-city: his hopes of a meal are, however, dashed in the end (1565–1693).

And now everything is ready for the exodos; the meal will be a wedding-feast, Basileia the bride (1688 ff.). A real 'exangelos' now announces the birds' triumph over the gods (1706–19). Basileia really appears (1720–30), and after all these preparations the feathered figure of Peisetairos leaves the stage to the strains of the Hymenaios (1731–42) in one of the most spectacular triumphal processions in Aristophanic comedy (1743–65).

It is clear that Aristophanes' teasing of the expectations of his audience is an important aspect of his dramatic technique, a trick which he uses again and again. He achieves a comic effect by arousing curiosity, turning the expectations in a certain direction, and then disappointing them finally by an unexpected denouement. We can tell how carefully he uses the resources available to him by the fact that he is never prodigal with his comic inventions but exploits fully every opening they give him; equally significant, he always drops a theme as soon as it has served its purpose and is no longer useful for new jokes but would be more of a hindrance than a help.

It is rewarding to note what elements he uses to arouse the expectations of his audience. Firstly, of course, there are the simple things like scenery, props, and the peculiar behaviour of the characters. He uses them for his own ends; one way of doing this is the single or even multiple repetition of whole scenes, trains of thought, or just single sentences.[10] Repetition, of course, in certain circumstances has of its nature something funny about it, but Aristophanes hardly ever uses it in its purest form, but rather as a basis for that kind of variation in which expectations aroused by means of parallelisms are disappointed and a comic effect achieved.

And finally, he makes use of expectations which he does not have to foster, but which the audience has as a result of its knowledge of the structure, forms, and methods of expression of Old Comedy.

---

[10] This may also account for the fact that so often in the second parts of his comedies Aristophanes makes people appear on the scene, whether together or immediately following one another, in pairs of opposite characters; see e.g. *Ach.*: Megarian–sycophant (729–828), Boeotian–Nicarchus (860–958), unhappy farmer–happy bridegroom (1018–68), Lamachus–Dicaeopolis (572–625, 1069–94, 1174–1226); *Pl.* poor, just man–sycophant (823–958), old woman–youth (959–1069), deposed Hermes–appointed priest (1097–1190).

These expectations make up a latent resource which he can potenti-
ate when necessary by suitable hints. We have already seen how he
makes use of them right from the start, with the aimless movements
of the two men in the orchestra, with the monologues addressed to
the spectators and the door-opening scene; then how he plays
around with the form and the content of the *parodos*, *agōn*, and
parabasis, and finally with the conventional structure of the 'second
part' of the comedy, including the messenger speech of the
'exangelos'. All these possibilities are enriched by the fact that the
poet and the audience can already look back to decades of performances of plays belonging to the genre and art-form of Old Comedy.
For the poet to be able to sport with its conventional elements, not
only must the forms of the plays have become somewhat traditional,
but the public too must be completely familiar with them as a result
of years of watching and evaluating the work of its poets. Similar
developments can therefore be seen in the contemporary late phase
of tragedy too.[11] Precisely in the period of Aristophanes' writing
from which the *Birds* is the first extant play, this game with
traditional forms, which are then made to produce unexpected
effects, is particularly striking. In this light, it seems not at all
surprising that these fossilized forms, once this last chance, their
playful use for purposes different from the traditional ones, was
played out, very soon finally disappeared.

When the *Birds* was produced, however, this game still offered
excitingly new and unexplored possibilities. Aristophanes, by playing with variations on these forms and their functions, is really, with
a roguish wink, letting the audience participate fully in the process
of building up a comic situation. He makes every single spectator
feel something of the satisfaction of the connoisseur who knows how
it's done and who is therefore allowed by the artist to look over his
shoulder; thus he creates a certain intimacy between himself, the
poet, and the *sophoi* among the spectators,[12] those who understand
him and can judge his work with almost a sense of identification.

The very fact that these conventional elements of Old Comedy not
only exist in their own right, but are also used by the comedians
themselves as important factors in the creation of comic effects in
their plots, explains of course the existence and the maintenance of

---

[11] See e.g. W. Geoffrey Arnott, 'Euripides and the Unexpected', *G & R*, 20 (1973),
49–64.   [12] *Sophoi* and *dexioi theatai*; see e.g. *Nu.* 521 ff., *Ra.* 1119 ff.

these significant differences between Old Comedy on the one hand and tragedy and New Comedy on the other. These conventional elements of Old Comedy are an integral part of its nature, not something secondary that happened to find its way into the genre.

The few aspects of Aristophanes' dramatic technique that I have here tried to illustrate, using the *Birds* as an example, give us an idea of the conscious artistic skill with which he has built up his dramatic plots. If we want to search for some kind of unity in his plays, this is the road most likely to lead us to it. His technique, it seems, is inseparably bound up with the traditional structure of Old Comedy. The question how far the poets of Old Comedy themselves were conscious in detail of the rules of their *technē* or, to put it another way, to what extent they would themselves have been able to formulate these rules theoretically, divorced from actual practice, and to render account of them in the Platonic sense, is another matter which need not detain us here. It is, however, a question that may be asked in much the same way about Old Comedy as about all other types of pre-Hellenistic poetry.[13] This much has in any case become clear: if we take as our starting-point the interdependence of the specific structure of Old Comedy and its comic effects, we shall be able to make many more interesting discoveries that will help to illustrate Aristophanes' dramatic art.[14]

---

[13] Old Comedy with its possibility of breaking the dramatic illusion, however, enables Aristophanes to say more about his technique than poets in other genres. For what he says, see *RE*, supp. vol. 12 (1970), 1392–1570: 1538 ff., and for what he does not say, ibid. 1542 ff.; reissued separately under the title *Aristophanes der Komiker* (Stuttgart, 1971).

[14] It is a pleasure to express my gratitude to the heads of the Greek departments of the Universities of St Andrews, Leeds, Reading, Cambridge, and the Institute of Classical Studies in London, who invited me to read this paper, in a slightly reduced form, as their guest under the British Council's Academic Interchange with Europe Scheme in Oct. 1974. Special thanks are due to Drs A. W. and P. A. Bulloch and to Mr. J. Parry, who assisted me in translating it into English. For the metrical translations of Aristophanes I have made free use of B. B. Rogers's translation.

12

Comic Myth-Making and Aristophanes' Originality

CARROLL MOULTON

I

Aristophanes' comments on the other playwrights of Old Comedy show that he was keenly aware of his place within a tradition.[1] His status as poet was inextricable from his profession as dramatist.[2] The numerous exploitations of dramatic conventions in the comedies (such as Trygaeus' address to the crane operator at *Peace* 174–6) and the complex network of vaunting and lyrical images that Aristophanes applies to his own poetry (such as the choral *pnigos* in *Wasps* 1050–9) are thus aspects of the same, self-conscious perception of the poet *vis-à-vis* his precursors and contemporaries.[3]

Aristophanes' appreciation of his own originality typically combines elements of fantasy and elements of realism. It is generally couched in boasts of cleverness:

But in the future, wondrous friends, love and cherish the poets who look for and invent something new to say, and store up their thoughts: throw them in your chests with the apples. If you do that, your clothes will smell all year—of cleverness (*dexiotētos*)! (*Wasps* 1051–9)

---

[1] See e.g. the remarks on Magnes, Cratinus, and Crates at *Knights* 506–44. Part of the fun, of course, is that the 'tradition' of Athenian stage comedy is relatively brief, dating back only to 486 BC.

[2] It is well to remind ourselves that neither the Greeks nor the Romans were aware of the possibility of writing drama in prose, and the modern separation of 'dramaturgy' and 'poetics' would have been meaningless to them.

[3] For an illuminating reassessment of the relationship between Eupolis and Aristophanes, see Ian C. Storey, 'Notus est omnibus Eupolis?', in A. H. Sommerstein, Stephen Halliwell, Jeffrey Henderson, and Bernhard Zimmermann (eds.), *Tragedy, Comedy and the Polis* (Bari, 1993).

Since Aristophanes, in this parabasis, has just made the chorus upbraid the audience for ignoring the virtues of his own play of the previous year (*Clouds*), it is clear which of 'the poets' this passage has in mind. His plays, the dramatist claims, are veritable feasts, whose aroma is the scent of cleverness. They thrive on novelty (*kainon*, 1053); *Clouds* surpassed the efforts of Aristophanes' rivals (in the author's own estimate, if not in actual fact) because it was fertile with 'the most novel ideas' (*kainotatais . . . dianoiais*, 1044).

Cleverness and novelty. They are conjoined as well in the parabasis of *Clouds* (545–8):

I'm not a poet who puts on airs, and I don't try to deceive you by bringing on the same acts two or three times; but I'm always inventing clever new routines (*kainas ideas*) for you, each one different and all of them ingenious (*dexias*).

The assertion of novelty and cleverness is, at first sight, disingenuous. Shortly before this passage in *Clouds*, Aristophanes has disarmingly declared that his comedies avoid all of the following: obscene joking with the phallus, mockery of bald-heads, the *kordax* (a vulgar dance), witless old men with stale jokes, and wild commotions with torches and clamour (*Clouds* 537–44). But the fact is that we can document most, if not all, of these elements in Aristophanic comedy, and several of them are especially evident in the revised version of *Clouds*.[4]

Comic rivalry and infighting, which are alluded to in the chorus's accusation (*Clouds* 553 ff.) that Eupolis plagiarized Aristophanes' famous eel simile in the *Knights* (864 ff.), make the whole passage suspect—not in terms of its authenticity, but in the sense of its rhetorical quality as a smoke-screen. The poet pretends not to employ the very techniques that in fact he favours. He boasts of his great originality and cleverness, and for good measure he attacks his rivals, who are charged with being far less original and clever. Ironically, the frequency of such tactics and their typical concentration within the parabases suggest that the boasts

---

[4] Line 543 is in fact a good description of the end of the play, where Strepsiades uses a torch to set the *phrontistērion* on fire; one of the students actually cries *iou iou* (cf. 543 with 1493).

of novelty and cleverness were well-known formulas of Old Comedy.[5] The paradoxical fun for the audience, we may speculate, was in the expectation of these formulas from the comic choruses, and in the uncertainty about which poet would invent the most outrageous tongue-in-cheek routines. To be successful, jokes must build on both the familiar and the unfamiliar, and Aristophanes' appreciation of this dynamic is crystallized in the exchange between Dionysus and Xanthias in the opening lines of Frogs, where—even as the god of the theatre and his porter satirize the 'old jokes'—they elicit the spectators' laughter (Frogs 1–18).

Aristophanes also belied his boast of novelty by often reusing material that proved successful.[6] The evidence for this practice ranges from the simple level of personal attack to more complex repetitions or variations of metaphor, theme, and parody. For example, it is striking that many of the minor scoundrels of contemporary Athens are referred to not just once but twice or more within individual plays. To take only one comedy, the Birds: we find Exekestides and his citizenship at 11, 764, and 1527; Chaerephon as a bat at 1296 and 1564; Orestes, the hooligan, at 712 and 1490; Opountius, the one-eyed informer, at 153 and 1294; Teleas at 168 and 1025; and the cowardly Cleonymus at 290 and 1475. Some of these doublets may possibly involve a principle of audience preparation: the poet familiarizes the spectators with the target in his first jab, only to unleash an even wittier assault later, to greater laughter.[7]

When we look beyond the confines of a single play, we notice the same technique, such as the repeated jabs at the fat and cowardly Cleonymus over a period of more than a decade, or the mockery of the effeminate Cleisthenes.[8] On a more imaginative level, Aristo-

---

[5] On dexiotēs, see K. J. Dover, Aristophanes, 'Frogs' (Oxford, 1993), 10–14. See also Thomas K. Hubbard, The Mask of Comedy: Aristophanes and the Intertextual Parabasis (Ithaca, 1991), esp. 85–7 and 103 ff., and cf. the interesting remarks of A. W. Gomme, 'Aristophanes and Politics', CR 52 (1938), 108–9.

[6] One could, I suspect, systematically document this practice in most of the successful playwrights who lived after Aristophanes, including Menander, Plautus, Shakespeare, and Molière. My remarks on Aristophanes' reuse of material are necessarily circumscribed by the fact that about 75 per cent of the playwright's output is lost. If more plays were extant, the picture might change in detail, but I think its basic contours would remain the same.

[7] See the brief comments of S. Halliwell, 'Comedy and Publicity in the Society of the Polis', in Sommerstein et al. (eds.), Tragedy, Comedy and the Polis, 330.

[8] For Cleonymus see Ach. 88, Clouds 353, Wasps 20, Birds 290, 1475; for Cleisthenes see Ach. 118, Knights 1374, Clouds 355, Birds 831, Lys. 621, Th. 574 ff., Frogs 426.

phanes recycles some key metaphors: compare the personification of Polemos as a drunken symposiast (*Ach.* 979 ff.) with the presentation of Polemos as a nefarious host in a dramatic episode written four years later (*Peace* 236 ff.).[9] The self-reflectiveness of Aristophanic comedy is striking when we notice, in turn, that the scene early in *Peace* is a comic parody of the revel at the end of plays like *Acharnians*, *Birds*, and *Peace* itself—where the hero, engaged in preparing a banquet, is regularly interrupted by offensive impostors (*alazones*). At the beginning of *Peace*, Polemos' preparation for a grisly meal, in which he will devour the Greek cities, functions as a thematic and structural inversion of Trygaeus' triumphant banquet at the end.[10]

Peace also provides numerous examples of the imaginative reuse of motifs from earlier plays. Both Trygaeus and Dikaiopolis extensively parody the situation of Euripidean tragic figures (Telephus and Bellerophon, respectively, at *Ach.* 280 ff. and *Peace* 58 ff.).[11] In both *Peace* and *Acharnians* there are elaborate, humorous, and quite fantastic accounts of the origins of the Peloponnesian War (*Ach.* 515 ff.; *Peace* 605 ff.). Just as we learn in the prologue to *Wasps* that Philocleon suffers from a new illness (71), so the master in *Peace* is said by his slaves to be under the spell of a strange mania (54 ff.).[12] In the prologues to both these plays, slaves jest with the interpretation of riddles (*Wasps* 20, *Peace* 47). Part of the parabasis of *Peace* is directly quoted from *Wasps* (compare *Peace* 752 ff. with *Wasps* 1030 ff.). Finally, in both plays Aristiphanes includes particularly emphatic abuse of the crablike Karkinos and his sons (*Wasps* 1501 ff.; *Peace* 781, 864).

All this does not prove, of course, that *Peace* is a derivative play. Similar evidence could be adduced for all the fifth-century comedies. The same motifs, images, and jokes, once they have entered a comedian's repertory, are likely to be used again if they 'play' well. This rationale applies even to larger-scale repetitions and

---

[9] The fundamental discussions are by H.-J. Newiger; see his *Metapher und Allegorie* (Munich, 1957) and Ch. 8 above.

[10] On the imagery for the feast of Polemos, see C. Moulton, *Aristophanic Poetry* (Göttingen, 1981), 85–92. Intertextuality within and among the Aristophanic comedies is a major theme of Hubbard, *The Mask of Comedy*.

[11] Helene P. Foley presents interesting and persuasive arguments for the specific appropriateness of the parody of *Telephus* in *Ach.* See Ch. 7 above.

[12] An especially nice touch in the later play is the twofold reference to this disease (within as many lines) as *kainon*.

adaptations, such as the parodies of the Euripidean *Telephus* in
Acharnians and *Thesmophoriazusae*. Aristophanes' penchant for presenting the same play in two versions (*Clouds, Peace, Thesmophoriazusae,* and *Plutus*) may also be linked with the urge to reuse
material, even if it was not initially popular (as with *Clouds*).

But even as we acknowledge the playwright's return to old
material (and are thus forced to take his claim of novelty with a
few grains of salt), Aristophanes' imaginative achievement remains
intact. Very seldom are motifs and characters exactly duplicated.
And the novelty of Old Comedy, in a deeper sense, is connected with
the fact that Aristophanes and his contemporaries undertook a task
from which the tragedians were largely exempt: the job of dramatic
myth-making. The Middle Comedy poet Antiphanes is almost plain-
tive in his reminder that, whereas tragedians may retell the well-
known stories of legend, comic dramatists must invent 'new names,
new business, and new plots' (fr. 191).[13] And so Peisetairos, the hero
of *Birds*, is duly admired by the chorus as an old fellow who is 'of
novel judgement' and an 'accomplisher of novel deeds' (*kainos
gnōmēn kainōn t'ergōn engcheirētēs* 256–7). The birds themselves
become the 'new' gods (*kainoisin theois*, 848, 862). And, in a passage
that might come from *Clouds*, the distracted poet Cinesias tells
Peisetairos that he wants to acquire wings so that he may hang
suspended in the air, plucking snow-clad preludes for his dithy-
rambs. In this way, he can assure that his poems will be novel
(*kainas*, 1384). Let us now turn to a more detailed analysis of
Aristphanic novelty, drawing our examples first from *Birds* and
then from *Lysistrata*.

II

The parabasis of *Birds* (676–800) affords an excellent illustration, not
only of the comic myth-making process, but of Aristophanic style as
well. In some respects this poem is unusual: at 125 verses, it is the

[13] See the recent perceptive discussion of this fragment by Eric Handley in P. E.
Easterling and B. M. W. Knox (eds.), *The Cambridge History of Classical Literature*, i:
Greek Drama (Cambridge, 1989), 159–61. Handley stresses Antiphanes' 'conception
. . . of organically constructed comedy about fictional people' and links the fragment's
contents with Aristotle and Menander, whereas my focus below is on the notion of
kainon as a touchstone for Aristophanic comedy.

longest parabasis in the extant plays; the artistic claims of the poet
are not advanced; and the chorus maintains its dramatic persona
throughout. Furthermore, a mute character, the nightingale (who
has entered at 665 before the parabasis commences), seems to
remain on stage during the choral address to the audience, accompanying the poem on the flute (682–4).

The introduction invokes the nightingale and her sweet song
(676–81). The bird is then entreated to 'begin the anapaests', the
usual metre for the parabasis proper (684).[14] In the latter, the birds
address earthbound mortals, 'shadowy, dreamlike ghosts, creatures
of a day' (685–6), purporting to instruct them on the origins of the
universe and the majesty of birds, the original divinities. In a parody
of Hesiod's *Theogony* (and probably of the Orphic hymns as well) the
birds proclaim the beginnings of the cosmos in Chaos and darkness.
Black-winged Night laid a wind-egg, from which hatched Eros,
gleaming with golden wings (695–7).[15] Eros in turn mingled with
Chaos and begat all subsequent generations of birds.

In case we have failed to notice that this is the stuff of myth, the
birds continue with a pastiche of Homeric diction, Hesiodic structure, and a dash of the Presocratics here and there (notably
Empedocles). Eros is said to have brought together all things in
mingling (700–1), and only then did the race of immortal gods
begin. In a recapitulation of Peisetairos' earlier arguments in the
agōn of the play, the birds boast of their associations with beauty,
youth, love, the seasons, the blessings of nature, and even divine
oracles (703–22; compare 465 ff.). The parabasis proper concludes
with a pun on the very word *ornis* (which may mean both 'bird' and
'omen'). The birds proclaim themselves a collective 'Apollo' for
mankind (722); Apollo, of course, was associated with prophecy
and divination.

The third section of the great parabasis is the *pnigos*, or 'choking
lyric'—so called because some ancient scholars believed it to have

---

[14] For metrical analysis and commentary, see Bernhard Zimmermann, *Untersuchungen zur Form und dramatischen Technik der aristophanischen Komödien*, ii: *De anderen
lyrischen Partien* (Königstein, 1985), 214 ff. On some artful touches of the unexpected
just before the beginning of the parabasis, see Ch. 11, above.

[15] William Arrowsmith has insightful, provocative comments on the connection of
wings with *eros* in his essay 'Aristophanes' *Birds*: The Fantasy Politics of Eros', *Arion*,
NS 1/1 (1973), 119–67. I am less inclined than Arrowsmith, however, to interpret the
play as an indictment of Athenian *polypragmosynē*.

been said all in one breath.[16] As with the mention of the anapaests at 684, the chorus specifically identifies this section of the parabasis (726). The birds promise a cornucopia of goods to men, if only mortals will tender them their proper worship and substitute them for Zeus and the Olympian gods as the true divinities (723–36). With the conclusion of this section, we reach the end of what may be called the first movement of the parabasis.

The four-part syzygy that follows constitutes the second movement, in which the birds provide specific examples of the benefits they can confer upon mankind. The syzygy consists of *ode* (O), *epirrhēma* (E), *antode* (AO), and *antepirrhēma* (AE). Lyrics alternate with trochaic tetrameter. O (739–51) draws attention to the overall parabatic structure by presenting a second invocation of the nightingale, the 'woodland Muse', whose sacred melodies suggest the honey-sweet tragic choruses of Phrynichus.[17] AO (769–84) corresponds with O both with respect to metrical structure and theme; here the swans, sacred birds of Apollo (see Plato, *Phaedo* 84e), gather by a river praising the god with their songs and the noise of their wings.

E and AE are pungently satirical in tone, but certain motifs—especially the notion of flying and the pun on *nomos* (meaning 'melody' at 745 and 'law' or 'established custom' at 755 and 758)—connect these passages to O and AO.[18] The birds hold out tantalizing prospects to men if they will join them in the new city. Like the cocks, they may beat their fathers if they feel like it; branded slaves may escape to liberty, like speckled francolins. In fine, all that is prohibited by the laws and customs of society (755) is not only legal but admirable in birdland.

AE (785–800) expands this notion by linking wings to the smashing of a number of taboos. With the help of wings, a man may

[16] For the *pnigos*, see now Hubbard, *The Mask of Comedy*, 20; for his comments on the parabasis of *Birds*, see 163–71.

[17] Hubbard (ibid. 169) rightly regards as unproved the suggestion of Kakridis ('Phrynicheisches in den *Vögeln* des Aristophanes', *WS*, NS 4 (1970), 38–51) that the lyric portions of the syzygy are a patchwork of references to a bird *hyporchēma* by Phrynichus.

[18] The punning network is more extensive than these references alone might imply: cf. *synnome* and *xynnome* at 209 and 678, *synnomōn* at 1756, and the exchange between Peisetairos and the father-beater at 1345–6. The pun receives a new dimension at 1287 with the use of the differently accented *nomon*; B. B. Rogers ingeniously referred to 'laws' and 'lawns' in his translation of this line.

escape from boring tragedies at the theatre, or fly away to answer
nature's call, or even expedite a secret adulterous affair. Finally, one
of the central dreams of comedy, to exchange obscurity for power, is
illustrated by the chorus with another ridiculous pun involving
'Captain Horse-Cock' Dieitrephes, a minor military official whose
promotions in the service were, presumably, inversely proportional
to his competence. The chorus fancifully adduces the fortune he has
made in manufacturing wicker 'wings' (or handles) for wine-flasks
(798–800).

The parabasis of *Birds* is a *kainos logos*—a novelty—in the fullest
sense.[19] Aristophanes' parody ranges over the whole of Greek
literature and philosophy since Homer and Hesiod. This is intertextuality with Joycean scope, if not on a Joycean scale. The poet uses
numerous echoes of prior speculation about the beginnings of the
universe to invest his fantastic myth of the cosmic wind-egg with a
certain credibility. If the best romance is grounded in reality, so too
are the most evocative fantasies—since the fantastic operates
through a precise reversal of reality, and hence the very process of
fantasy contains a code for the world that produces it.[20]

Within the parabasis itself, this polarity is crystallized in the birds'
summation of life in birdland (755–6):

All the things that are shameful here and forbidden by the law are beautiful
(and legal) among us, the birds.

The contemporary debates of such Sophists as Protagoras, Antiphon, and Prodicus (the last is mentioned by the chorus at 692)
on the relationship of *nomos* and *physis* may lurk in the background
here, but it would be a mistake to extract an Aristophanic 'position'
on them. It is simply more fantastic, and funnier, to imagine law and
nature, fathers and sons, birds and gods, turned topsy-turvy.[21]

[19] Cf. the extensive discussion by Heinz Hofmann in *Mythos und Komödie: Untersuchungen zu den 'Vögeln' des Aristophanes* (Hildesheim, 1976). Hofmann sees the
overarching structure of the play as an exemplar of comic myth-making, involving
an ornithomachy and a story of divine succession. Although his emphasis is quite
different from mine in this chapter, I am in essential agreement with his approach.
See pp. 177–96 for his comments on the parabasis of *Birds*.
[20] See Eric S. Rabkin, *The Fantastic in Literature* (Princeton, 1976).
[21] In contrast to such critics as Arrowsmith ('Aristophanes' *Birds*'), I think that on
balance it is myth, rather than satire, that drives this particular comedy. But the
fusion of the fantastic and the satirical in Aristophanes is often seamless: see my
comments on the genre of the abuse lyric in *Aristophanic Poetry*, 45 ff.

As the division of the parabasis into two major movements suggests, Aristophanes' comic myth-making operates on two levels. First is the fanciful evocation of a past golden age (the birds' hegemony); second is the construction of a future utopia (men's growing wings to become birds). As if to underline this structure, the first movement of the parabasis (676–722) looks backward—not only to previous Greek literature, but also to the earlier arguments of Peisetairos within this play. The second movement (723–800) looks forward, especially in AE, where the vignette of the Muses, the Graces, and Apollo suggests a divine royal wedding and anticipates Peisetairos' climactic union with Basileia and his apotheosis (1718 ff.).

The myth of golden age and utopia also elegantly suggests that the arc of history from a fantastic past to an idealized future is really circular. The parabasis contains a clear example of ring composition (the tawny nightingale at 676 and the tawny Dieitrephes at 800, the first and last verses of the poem), and the nightingale's presence, in both music and language, furnishes a unifying theme. The rhetorical structure of AE is also evidence of carefully planned composition: note the repeated expression *katepteto* ('flew back again') at verse end (789, 792, 796), as well as the symmetry of *hypopteros* ('winged') at 786 and 797. Since two of the examples of the utility of wings are specifically set at the theatre (786–92), there is perhaps an oblique hint in the birds' suggestion of escape from tragic tedium that it is comedy (and, above all, Aristophanic comedy) that serves to fulfil the most grandiose human dreams.[22]

Immediately after AE, when the flute music of the nightingale ceases, Peisetairos enters with precisely the accoutrements the chorus has praised ('there is nothing better or more pleasurable than growing wings' 785). Perhaps glancing at Euelpides, but more probably adopting the stance of a spectator of the parabasis itself, Peisetairos metatheatrically comments, 'So much for that part of the play. By God, I've never seen anywhere a funnier affair than this!' (801–2).

As an addendum to this discussion of the parabasis, we may

[22] It may not be superfluous to point out—given the lingering notion that Aristophanes' plays are rambling, artless creations—that the proportion of the first movement (676–722) to the parabasis as a whole (37.6 per cent) is virtually identical to that of the first part of the play (1–675, before the parabasis) to the play as a whole (38.2 per cent).

observe that besides the sheer novelty of the avian cosmogony, the merging of past and future, and the fantasy of men growing wings, the comic myth-making in *Birds* also derives energy from its reinterpretations of existing myth. Such is the impulse behind the passages dealing with Procne, the nightingale (her name in some versions of the myth is Philomela). The traditional myth of Tereus, Philomela, and Procne was a ghastly story of lust and revenge.[23] Aristophanes, however, has radically altered the myth to suit the festive connotations of Peisetairos' quest in *Birds*. In three passages of the play, invocations to the nightingale provide a highly lyrical impulse: see the hoopoe's song at 209–22, and compare the very similar lines 676–84 and 737–51 in the parabasis. Is it too much to claim that these passages together comprise a leitmotif? The sweetness of the nightingale's song is an auditory emblem of the land of heart's desire in the play. The flute that imitates her voice provokes elaborate praise from Euelpides (223–4), and her actual appearance just before the beginning of the parabasis instantly kindles the lust of both oldsters (667 ff.).

Comic myth-making metamorphoses the nightingale into a joyous, rather than tragic, symbol of Eros. Even though she is said in the hoopoe's song to chant laments (*thrēneis*, 211) and the boy Itys is mourned 'with many tears' (*polydakryn*, 212), Procne's song—and by extension she herself—is called 'pure' (*kathara*, 215). Her songs enjoy the antiphonal response of Apollo (217–22). Her hymns are associated with the sounds of spring (683) and the sweet verses of Phrynichus (748–50). In short, the nightingale, far from evoking the destructive powers of Eros, is reinvented and transformed.[24] She is now the central figure of a new myth: the comic fantasy of utopia.

---

[23] The best-known accounts are in Apollodorus 3 and Ovid, *Metamorphoses* 6. King Tereus raped Philomela, sister of his wife, Procne, and then cut out her tongue to prevent her from exposing the outrage. But Philomela, mute and imprisoned, managed to inform Procne of the crime by weaving the story on a tapestry and sending it to her sister. Procne enacted a hideous revenge on Tereus. She slaughtered their child Itys and served him up to Tereus at a banquet. When she told him of the atrocity, Tereus attacked her in a rage. But the gods put an end to the savage misery of all three characters by intervening to transform them into birds: Procne became the nightingale, Philomela the swallow, and Tereus the hoopoe.

[24] Cf. Eu. *Hel.* 1107–13, a passage that may have been influenced by *Birds*.

III

The finale of *Lysistrata* also illustrates the power of Aristophanic myth-making. In this case the 'novelty' proceeds both from a deliberate revision of myth and from a bold transformation of history. With the entrance at 1241 of the principals, who come from a great symposium honouring the truce between Athenians and Spartans (and between men and women), the stage is set for the concluding lyrics. However we order the lines, the Spartan semi-chorus has the majority (they sing 1247–72 and 1297–1320 in the Budé text).[25] The two semichoruses in this *exodos* obviously balance the earlier choruses of old men and old women, graphically under-lining the play's central equation between political and domestic strife.

The Spartans begin by recalling the battles of Artemisium and Thermopylae at the beginning of the fifth century. The Athenians are praised as 'godlike' for their heroism at Artemisium; as for Leonidas and his followers at Thermopylae, they are accorded an elaborate Homeric simile (1254–8; compare *Iliad* 20. 168ff.). In this passage the Persian Wars are recalled as an idealized example of the co-operation between Athens and Sparta. Present strife begins to be gradually transformed by evocations of glorious, antique heroism; we may contrast Lysistrata's ambiguous topical allusion to the role of the Persians in the Peloponnesian War (1133). The language for Leonidas also recalls the Iliadic narrative of Greek unity in a war in the more remote past; even the Trojan conflict will be romantically transformed in the Spartans' second lyric at 1297ff.

The Athenian semichorus intervenes to invoke a long series of divinities. Special emphasis is laid on the Graces (1279), who head the list, and on Hesychia (Serenity) and Aphrodite (1289–90), who conclude it. Dionysus and his maenads are mentioned (1284–5): this reference is complemented by the Spartans in their concluding song (1312–13). Cries of victory are raised (1291ff.), but it is the victory of Hesychia, not of Ares, that the chorus celebrates.

The final lyric invokes the Spartan Muse to celebrate Apollos at Amyklai (1298) and the cult of Athena Chalkioikos (Athena of the Brazen House) (1300, 1320). The Spartans create a charming vign-ette of young maidens by the river Eurotas; the maidens' chorus is

[25] See the ed. and comm. by Jeffrey Henderson (Oxford, 1987).

like that of Dionysus' Bacchae. But the surprise is that the leader of
this chorus is none other than Helen, daughter of Leda, who is now
hagna choragos euprepēs, the 'pure and fair leader of the dance'
(1315). Helen has been referred to once before in this play in quite
a different context. When Lysistrata explains her plan of the sex
strike to the women, the Spartan Lampito recalls that Helen's
seductive charms sufficed to make Menelaus forget his rage after
the Trojan War and forgo vengeance upon her (155–6). The tradition that Menelaus 'dropped his sword' when he was reunited with
Helen was extensively explored by Euripides in tragedy of this
period. In the *Trojan Women* (415 BC), for example, Menelaus is set
up as the judge of his own wife's guilt but is clearly shown to
weaken. Although the actual reconciliation of the couple is not
presented, the chorus prays apprehensively that the pair not be
allowed to return to Greece together on the same ship, thus allowing love to thwart justice (*Troades* 941–1114).[26]

But in the context of comic myth-making the 'dropping of the
sword', or the triumph of love (*erōs*) over strife (*eris*), is eminently
desirable. This explains the mention of Helen by Lampito and the
chorus's reference to her in the concluding lyric. Instead of the
catalyst of war, she is pure and lovely, an emblem of war's exorcism. She is the leader of an imaginary chorus, sacred to Dionysus,
that imaginatively parallels the on-stage chorus at the end of the
play. As such, her beauty is beneficial, like that of the personified
Reconciliation (Diallage), and she complements the mention in the
previous song of Hesychia and Aphrodite.[27]

[26] For discussion of Euripides' 'new Helen' of 412 BC (cf. Aristophanes' reference to
kainēn Helenēn at *Th.* 850), see C. Moulton, *Aristophanic Poetry*, 135–9. The similarities
of Euripidean and Aristophanic style are implicit in the celebrated phrase of Cratinus
(fr. 307), which refers to *euripidaristophanizein* ('to write like a Euripidaristophanizer')
in a context that seems to highlight the novel qualities of both dramatists' plays. But
we have more than this fragment as evidence. Both playwrights created novel works;
both indulged in metrical innovations; and the practice of including a parabasis is
attested in tragedy only for Euripides (see Pollux 4. 111, where the grammarian
mentions the lost play *Danae* and 'many [other] dramas' as exceptions to the norm
whereby parabases were restricted to comedy). In addition, we may compare *Birds*
209–19 with *Helen* 1107–13 and *Thesmophoriazusae* 253–65 with *Bacchae* 830–6 and
925–44. For a brief discussion of comic elements in the *Orestes*, see Edith Hall, 'Political
and Cosmic Turbulence in Euripides' *Orestes*', in Sommerstein *et al.* (eds.), *Tragedy,
Comedy and the Polis*, 277.

[27] Henderson, edn. of *Lysistrata*, takes a somewhat different view on Helen; he
comments *ad loc.* that 'the epithet here shows that we are to think not of the
unfaithful wife of heroic myth but of the maiden goddess of Spartan cult'. Yet the

The epithets *hagna* and *euprepēs* are arguably *kaina onomata* in Antiphanes' sense of 'new names', and the poetry of Aristophanes converts even Helen's ambiguous charms to beneficence. In effect, the comic poet constructs a new myth about the Trojan War: the conflict is poetically refashioned and limned in the glow of heroic, pan-Hellenic unity. Just as Helen is exculpated, so the cult of Athena of the Brazen House, ostensibly an *aition* leading up to the Peloponnesian War, is similarly transformed. Thucydides reports that the Athenians claimed that, through the death of Pausanias, the Spartans had brought a curse upon themselves, since Pausanias had sought refuge in Athena's sanctuary.[28] Athens demanded reparation, in response to the Spartan demand for restitution after the curse of Kylon. The final lyric of Aristophanes' *Lysistrata*, however, skilfully transforms these acrimonious preliminaries to war into a graceful, unifying salutation. Athena of the Brazen House links the patron of the Acropolis (prominently identified with the play's entire action) with Spartan cult. The curses associated with the pre-war embassies are implicitly expiated with the invocation of the goddess.

The finale of *Lysistrata*, then, shows comic myth-making as an exorcism of strife. Aristophanes recasts metonyms of the Trojan War, the Persian War, and the Peloponnesian War into a new historical panorama. Like the nightingale in *Birds*, Helen is re-envisioned as pure. Thermopylae and Artemisium serve as examples of pan-Hellenic harmony. Athena Chalkioikos transmutes curses into blessings. The whole scene is an impressive re-enactment of the past for the benefit of the future.[29] Through metaphor, rhetoric, and selective historical reference, Aristophanes creates a poetic myth of peace for an audience still painfully at war in real life—surely something *kainon*, a novelty in the most profound sense of Antiphanes' term.

play was written for performance at Athens, and the prior mention of Helen at *Lys.* 155 is decidedly ambivalent: see Henderson's note on a probable allusion there to Eu. *Andr.* 629 ff.

[28] Th. 1. 128 ff.

[29] Cf. the relationship in the comic mythopoiesis of *Birds* of the golden age and utopia, discussed above.

13
The People of Aristophanes

MICHAEL SILK

No one has yet succeeded in constructing a complete and coherent theory of character.

(Mieke Bal, *Narratology*)

I personally would like to bring a tortoise onto the stage, turn it into a racehorse, then into a hat, a song, a dragon and a fountain of water.

(Ionesco, *Notes and Counter-Notes*)

I

Aristophanes is not, in the ordinary sense, a difficult writer, and many of the incidental difficulties which he does pose—say, those involving intricate verbal jokes—are well understood by his interpreters. The diverse creatures who people his plays, however, pose special problems of interpretation. Consider the following representative instances from *Thesmophoriazusae*, which serve to suggest some pertinent questions. The instances are transparently uncomplicated—and therefore convenient to begin with.

Thesmophoriazusae is a striking mixture of (*inter alia*) broad comedy and devotional lyrics. Some of the broad comedy and all of the devotional lyrics are carried by one set of people, the women at the Thesmophoria—some of them in the chorus, some ostensibly among 'the characters'.[1] The women combine two main roles. They

---

[1] Except for the possibility that the 'Lady Herald' may be the chorus-leader (cf. K. J. Dover, *Aristophanic Comedy* (London, 1972), 166–7), it is customary to assume that the two groups are wholly separate. However, it is not obvious what distinguishes for example, 531–2 (traditionally ascribed to the chorus) from 533 ff. (ascribed to the anonymous 'First Woman'). The groups certainly share the same alignment and indeed the same virtual anonymity: two of the women (we learn incidentally) have

are humorous figures, aggressive assailants of Euripides, and they
are devotional figures, pious hymn-singers who celebrate the gods in
five separate choral songs. The question arising here is simply this:
what sort of relationship is there between the two roles, and what
sort of entities are the women who play them?

The two central characters of *Thesmophoriazusae* are clever Euripides and his dumb and docile relative Mnesilochus.[2] Early in the
play Euripides concocts a plan to get a man disguised as a woman to
infiltrate the women's festival. Euripides cannot go himself. His
fellow dramatist Agathon has the wit and the performing-skills
required, and Euripides asks him to do the job. When Agathon
refuses, Mnesilochus offers his services instead—although (on the
evidence of his bumbling performance to date) he patently lacks any
qualification for such a delicate mission:

EURIPIDES. Poor, poor Euripides! done for!
MNESILOCHUS. My dear cousin, don't give up.
EURIPIDES. What can I do?
MNESILOCHUS. Tell him to go to hell: how about using me?
EURIPIDES. Well, in that case . . .

$$(209-13)^3$$

The comic possibilities of Mnesilochus' failure duly form the basis
for most of the subsequent action. Euripides, one notes, never
actually suggested that Mnesilochus should take the part.
That—one might say—is because it won't work, and Euripides
would be too clever to suggest it. Why, then, does the clever
Euripides accept such an implausible offer at all? And why does
the dumb and docile Mnesilochus suddenly thrust himself into the
part in the first place?—a part which, while all goes well, he
proceeds to perform with gusto and some considerable inventiveness. It is not an answer to say, 'The plot requires it.' This moment

typical names (Mik(k)a, 760; Kritylla, 898), but then so do *choral* individuals elsewhere
(e.g. Drakes, *Lys.* 254; Nikodike, *Lys.* 321; etc.). Need it be assumed that the groups are
wholly separate in fact?

[2] The name Mnesilochus, as is well known, is not used in the text, but derives from
schol. R. This notwithstanding, it is both convenient and harmless (cf. the use of the
name Homer), whereas the alternatives (the favourite English alternative is 'Kinsman') tend to be frigid and distracting.

[3] Quotations from Aristophanes follow the text of A. H. Sommerstein but for *Th.* (as
here) the text of F. W. Hall and W. M. Geldart (eds.), *Aristophanes comoediae*', OCT
(Oxford, 1906).

is itself part of the plot; and anyway that kind of answer only converts the first set of questions into a second set: Why is it acceptable, on the level of what we call character, for the plot to 'require' it? In these various examples we seem to observe inconsistencies of behaviour in varying degrees on the part of the women, Euripides, and Mnesilochus. Why, and how, are such inconsistencies acceptable?

Consider again the women in *Thesmophoriazusae*. Their duality produces (or is produced by) not only inconsistencies of behaviour in the ordinary sense, but also inconsistencies of linguistic behaviour. There is a moment in the play when, after Mnesilochus in disguise has spoken up for Euripides (466–519), the women react furiously. One of them threatens, obscenely, to shave his (supposedly her) pussy (*choiros*, 538), a threat to which Mnesilochus responds with understandable alarm ('Please, ladies, not my *pussy*!', 540). Up to this point the women have been fairly restrained in their language, not only in the songs with all their religiosities ('come thou, mighty maiden . . . come thou, dread lord of the sea', 317ff.), but in the dialogue too. The sudden use of the word *choiros* represents, for them, a stylistic switch: the level suddenly drops. If asked to 'explain' this switch, we might point to the speaker's anger, as if the change were explicable in terms of a real individual's real emotional reaction. Such a rationalizing explanation is certainly available in this case. But stylistic switches abound in Aristophanes, and most of them are not explicable in such terms. One case in point, among many others, is a comparable vulgarism early on in the play, this time on the lips of Euripides. Mnesilochus, who is again the recipient of the obscenity, purports not to be able to remember who Agathon is. Euripides puts him wise:

MNESILOCHUS. The one with the untidy beard?
EURIPIDES. Haven't you ever seen him?
MNESILOCHUS. No—not consciously, anyway.
EURIPIDES. Well, you must at least have fucked him—not consciously, of course.

(33–5)

Up to this point Euripides, like the women later, has spoken in a restrained idiom. His remarks to Mnesilochus have been equable in tone, and there is nothing now to suggest that his mood has changed. Nor is there anything in his characterization to come which would suggest that obscenity is a fundamental trait of his, as it is, by contrast, of Mnesilochus. This vulgarism, certainly, is hardly open to rationalization.[4]

In Aristophanes the stylistic level of a speaker's (or a singer's) words switches frequently and, often, drastically. In interpreting his plays we tend to rationalize such switches, or (failing that) to explain them away as 'comic effect'—thus resorting to a tautology which in a sense points to the true explanation of the phenomenon and yet, in itself, explains nothing. The fact is that both our rationalizings and our ascriptions of 'comic effect' presuppose what is not the case: that, irrespective of any contrary indications, the speakers, and the singers, of Aristophanic comedy must ultimately conform to realistic norms.

For a stylistic idiom to be compatible with realism, it must involve a range of expression which is *consistently* related to a vernacular language, a language of experience, a language of life. Either the idiom is felt to amount to a 'selection of the language really spoken by men', as Wordsworth called it;[5] or alternatively it involves a broadly consistent stylization, like (for instance) the stylization of Greek tragic language, which does not constitute anything like a language of life, but is, nevertheless, fixed and conventionalized at a set, comprehensible distance from some hypothetical and more naturalistic idiom, which *would* pass

---

[4] On Aristophanes' stylistic switches, see my discussion in 'Pathos in Aristophanes', *BICS* 34 (1987), 78–111. Regarding the tone of *binein*, H. D. Jocelyn, *LCM* 5 (1980), 65–7, has argued interestingly that (unlike, for example, English 'fuck') the word is not obscene, partly on the grounds of its distribution within Attic comedy (esp. its use by females), partly on the grounds of its supposed occurrence in a Solonian law (Hsch. s.v. *binein* = Sol., *Test. Vet.* 448 Martina). He suggests that the word, instead, had an 'intimate' tone. Against this: (1) the overwhelming occurrence of the word is in low literature (largely comic—cf. the representative citations in *LSJ*—but note also Arch. 152. 2 West, Hippon. 84. 16 West): if this (given the sense of the word) does not suggest obscenity, it is not clear what would. (2) 'Intimacy' is not actually incompatible with obscenity: it is a known feature of current English (certainly British English) usage that the obscene 'fuck' is used by some couples (including female members of couples) in intimate contexts, and one recalls D. H. Lawrence's thoughts in this general area (see e.g. 'A propos of *Lady Chatterley's Lover*' in D. H. Lawrence, *Phoenix II*, ed. W. Roberts and H. T. Moore (London, 1968), 514). (3) The presence of an 'intimacy' in a law, however, seems appreciably less likely (even) than that of an obscenity. (4) But in any case the actual source of the 'Solonian' citation is as uncertain as its detail (on which Jocelyn himelf remarks (67): 'this entry [in Hsch.] is obscure and has been much emended'). All in all, Jocelyn's challenge to the established view can only be called insubstantial.

[5] Preface to *Lyrical Ballads*, ed. R. L. Brett and A. R. Jones, rev. edn. (London, 1965), 244 (1802 variant).

for a language of life *à la* Wordsworth. In the latter case, specifically colloquial vocabulary, phraseology, syntax, and so on, will
tend to be excluded, not capriciously or opportunistically in one
play or in one part of one play, but *throughout* the play or plays.
And the same principle of consistency applies to the more conspicuous, if still limited, presence of archaisms, conventional
tropes, and the other familiar features of an elevated language.[6]
This principle of consistency is complicated, but not subverted, by
a gradation of stylization into different levels—like the levels
represented by song and speech in Greek tragedy, or narrative
and direct speech in many novels, or the direct speech of one
character and the direct speech of another character in much
narrative fiction and much drama too. In Aristophanes the inconsistency within a given speaker's range of idiom points the opposite way. The style in which his people are made to express
themselves is incompatible with any kind of realism; and more
fundamentally, as this consideration of style serves to suggest, the
people of Aristophanes *per se* are not strictly containable within
any realist understanding of human character at all. Their linguistic and their non-linguistic behaviour[7] may cohere, but in neither
case on a realist premiss. And as such, these beings are distinguishable from their counterparts in the central tradition of
Western fiction, in drama or outside it.

This whole non-Aristophanic tradition we may call the *realist
tradition*. It is the tradition within which 'l'effet du réel'[8] is not so
much characteristic as ultimately decisive. In agreeing to call it

---

[6] Cf. Arist. *Po.* 22; M. S. Silk, '*LSJ* and the problem of Poetic Archaisms: From
Meanings to Iconyms', *CQ*, NS 33 (1983), 303.

[7] *Pace* the curious pretence (current among some literary theoreticians) that
linguistic behaviour ('text') is everything. 'Outside of language there is neither self
nor desire,' says one theorist (J. Frow, 'Spectacle Binding: On Character', *Poetics
Today,* 7/2 (1986), 238). In drama (which includes silent films and ballet), as in life
(which extends to deaf and dumb illiterates etc.), this is self-evidently untrue. Cf. (in
the classical context) the welcome discussion by D. Wiles, 'Reading Greek Performance', *G & R* 34 (1987), 136–51.

[8] The phrase was coined by Roland Barthes in an essay itself entitled 'L'Effet du
réel', *Communications*, 11 (1968), 84 ff. For Barthes the stress is on 'effet', not on 'réel',
because of the structuralist anxiety to see literature as removed from reference to real
life. However, the fact that all fictional characters (like everything in literature) are
constructed apart from real life (which is what we mean by 'fictional') does not affect
their referential capacity to evoke that outside reality. Cf. G. D. Martin, *Language,
Truth and Poetry* (Edinburgh, 1975), 68–106.

'realist', one is using 'realism' not (like many literary historians[9]) as
a period term, but to designate 'a perennial mode of representing
the world' in its 'consequential logic and circumstantiality', a mode
which has no 'single style' and whose actual style, or styles, in any
given age vary according to cultural norms, and whose 'dominance
at any one time is a . . . cultural option'.[10] So defined, the realist
tradition is the tradition canonized by Aristotle's theory and Menander's practice, and the tradition which reaches its fullest expression
in the nineteenth-century novel. And so defined, the tradition
includes instances of the two contrasting types of fiction, the
narrative and the dramatic: narrative fiction, with (typically) its
'omniscient' narrator who can tell us about a character, as well
as seeming to show us that character in action; and dramatic
fiction, which presupposes the individual human presence of the
actor—whose performance, furthermore, introduces a variable
which (except in a marginal case like oral-epic recitation) has no
equivalent in the narrative sphere. The differences between narrative and drama are large and important, but, for present purposes,
inconsequential.

Within the realist tradition we encounter a wide variety of ways
of representing fictional people. Sometimes we feel called on to
comprehend these people as 'characters', sometimes (to use Chris-
topher Gill's distinction) to empathize with them as 'personalities'.[11]
Some presentations seem to expand or diffuse single traits, some
seem to produce 'rounded' characters. The presentation may
impinge as two-dimensional or as three-dimensional; as more or
as less inward-looking; as a matter of status at least as much as of
temperament; as a matter of types or as a matter of individuals. And
interpreters may have good reason to draw attention to the differences between the presentations of (say) the Greek tragedians and
Eugene O'Neill, or Shakespeare and his predecessors, or Euripides
and *his* predecessors, or (most commonly) the modern European

[9] Most commonly of 19th-cent., as opposed to earlier, fiction, but also of 'modern'
as opposed to 'ancient' fiction (so, for instance, among classicists, G. M. Sifakis,
Parabasis and Animal Choruses (London, 1971), 7–14, esp. 9). See further the refs. in
nn. 10 and 12 below.
[10] J. P. Stern, *On Realism* (London, 1973), 32, 28, 52, 79, 158. On the history of the
term 'realism', see R. Wellek, 'The Concept of Realism in Literary Scholarship',
Neophilologus, 45 (1961), 1–20.   [11] See n. 21 below.

novel and *its* predecessors.[12] But all such presentations have one thing in common. The people presented have what we may see as a constant relationship with 'reality'—with the world outside as we perceive it or might be presumed to perceive it—because they stand at a constant distance from that real world.[13] They impinge as sentient beings, each with a tendency to be (in Aristotle's language) 'appropriate', 'lifelike', and 'consistent'.[14] At its most clearcut this tradition produces figures in which we detect a wealth of recognizable detail, with each detail corresponding to some possibility of life, and each detail connectible with or continuous with some other—even *each* other—detail, and the product of the details a recognizable yet also unique creation. It is within this tradition, and only within this tradition, that characters can be seen to do what we call 'develop'.[15] Such development (it might be argued) implies a progression from one perceived state to another via shifts of emphasis between the identifiable details—perhaps like phonetic changes taking place via a continuum of allophones.[16] Within this tradition development is possible, though most certainly not invariable or even always usual: it is most characteristic of the nineteenth-century novel, though we seem to see it first attested in eighth-century BC epic, in the shape of Homer's Achilles.[17]

Aristophanes (I suggest) does not strictly belong to this tradition. There are, it is true, some Aristophanic characters that lend themselves reasonably well to a realist interpretation. Take Strepsiades in *Clouds*. He is a recognizable type, in opposition to his equally typical son Pheidippides. The son is a corruptible, extravagant young urban sophisticate:

PHEIDIPPIDES. How nice to be *au fait* with everything clever and chic, and have the chance to look down on traditional values. In the days when all

---

[12] As (variously) J. P. Gould, 'Dramatic Character and "Human Intelligibility" in Greek Tragedy, *PCPS*, NS 24 (1978), 43–67; K. Newman, *Shakespeare's Rhetoric of Comic Character* (New York, 1985); J. Jones, *On Aristotle and Greek Tragedy* (London, 1962), 239–79; I. Watt, *The Rise of the Novel* (London, 1957), 9–34.

[13] Cf. Stern, *On Realism*, 55.

[14] Arist. *Po.* 15; see D. W. Lucas (ed.), *Aristotle: 'Poetics'* (Oxford, 1968), and most recently, S. Halliwell, *Aristotle's 'Poetics'* [London, 1986), 159–65.

[15] It is not uncommon to find the capacity 'to develop and change' virtually equated with 'character' *per se* (as by Newman, *Shakespeare's Rhetoric of Comic Character*, 1).

[16] On which see e.g. M. L. Samuels, *Linguistic Evolution* (Cambridge, 1972), 126.

[17] See M. S. Silk, *Homer, 'The Iliad'* (Cambridge, 1987), 83–96.

I could think about was racing, I couldn't put two words together
without making a gaffe. But now . . . [Socrates] has got me out of that,
and I spend my time on subtle ideas, arguments, preoccupations, I think I
can show that it's morally right to whack your father.   (1399–1405)

The father is a thrifty, crude old peasant, crafty but not brainy, and
deeply conservative:

STREPSIADES. So how can you be entitled to get your money back, if you
    don't know about meteorology?   (1283–4)

STREPSIADES. How mad I was, then, when I actually threw the gods out—all
    because of Socrates!   (1476–7)

It is not difficult to list the leading characteristics of the two figures
(in this instance they are inseparably matters of status and temperament), or to see how, with Strepsiades in particular, actions and
words are aligned to each other: how they are evocative, that is, of
various character-traits *as a continuum*. The old man's coarse
language, for instance, is suggestive of an earthy background *and*
of a certain intellectual mediocrity *and* of a fundamental antipathy
to the Socratic enlightenment. All three characteristics, accordingly,
are shown to belong together:

SOCRATES. O most holy Clouds, you have hearkened to my call in visible
    form. [*To St.*] Did you hear their voice in the awesome thunder's roar?

STREPSIADES. Yes, and I'm in awe, all right, O most honoured ones, and I'm
    so nervous and shaken up I feel like farting back at the thunder. Maybe
    it's right and maybe it's wrong, but the fact is I need a shit this minute.

                                                              (291–5)

Furthermore, Strepsiades even begins to develop. He learns from
experience. He sees his past in a new perspective, and is therefore
able to identify what went before as his mistake ('how mad I was',
1476), like (say) Cnemon in *Dyscolus* (713) or Creon in *Antigone*
(1272). These are real, if minimal, instances of development. They
are distinct, for instance, from the differential revelation of character we encounter in (say) *Bacchae* with Pentheus, who begins as
strident autocrat and ends as susceptible psychopath, but (we infer)
was actually ('really') both all the time. The development of a
Strepsiades, a Cnemon, or a Creon, of course, is slight compared
with the development of (say) an Isabel Archer:

Madame Merle was already so present to her vision that her appearance in the flesh was like suddenly, and rather awfully, seeing a painted picture move. Isabel had been thinking all day of her falsity, her audacity, her ability, her probable suffering . . . She pretended not even to smile, and though Isabel saw that she was more than ever playing a part, it seemed to her that on the whole the wonderful woman had never been so natural.   (Henry James, *The Portrait of a Lady*, ch. 52)

Such a complex response as Isabel's here, with its intricate mixture of positive and negative feelings, presupposes a fully explored personal history, which presupposes, in turn, a development over a substantial period of fictional time, even (as with James's novel) a period of years. Full development, one might say, requires at least the time-span of a Shakespearean tragedy (or an *Iliad*)—the span sufficient, for instance, to show us a 'progress' like Macbeth's from a guilty recklessness ('come what come may', I. iii; 'If it were done when 'tis done, then 'twere well | It were done quickly', I. vii) to the several stages of moral dissolution that follow ('I am afraid to think what I have done', II. i; 'What man dare, I dare', III. iv; 'I have almost forgot the taste of fears', v. v.). A Greek tragedy (or New Comedy) tends, instead, to centre on an expanded moment of crisis and the magnification of an individual's response to it. Such patterns, nevertheless, are obviously conducive to the presentation of character development, however embryonic; and it is symptomatic that they should be as generally uncharacteristic of Aristophanic comedy as they are characteristic of Greek tragedy.

Most (perhaps all) of Aristophanes' characters belong in *some* degree to the realist tradition, and some of them (like Strepsiades) might be construed—without too much forcing of the evidence—as belonging wholly to it. However, most (perhaps all) of them partake also of a different mode of representation, which, for lack of a better term, I propose to call *imagist*. Words used in images—that is, words used tropically, and especially words used metaphorically—disrupt the terminological continuity of their context.[18] Like words used literally, they evoke some reality.[19] Unlike words used literally, they evoke their reality through discontinuity. Verbal sequences that involve imagery rarely consist entirely of disruptive terminology

[18] See M. S. Silk, *Interaction in Poetic Imagery* (Cambridge, 1974), 6–14.
[19] Cf. Martin, *Language, Truth and Poetry*.

(an exception is the ancient allegory). Commonly, the image is part
disrupt*ive* terminology (the 'vehicle'), part disrupt*ed* terminology
(the 'tenor').[20] Aristophanes' characters, similarly, have their realist elements, or moments, or sequences, disrupted by imagist
elements, or moments, or sequences. And though realist elements,
or moments, or sequences, remain, the presence of the disruptive
serves to differentiate the representation as a whole from realism
proper. In the discontinuities of imagist presentation, accordingly, it
is reasonable to see a factor of decisive importance.[21]

To avoid any misunderstanding at this stage in the argument, it
should be noted that some of Aristophanes' characters, especially
some that we may think of as his 'non-fictional' characters, invite
comparison with images on quite different grounds. Take Socrates
in *Clouds*. This figure may or may not have traits comparable with
those of the historical Socrates. What he certainly has is exaggerated traits—recondite scientific interests, pretensions to authority,
spokesmanship of new deities, an indifferent attitude towards the

[20] Cf. Silk, *Interaction in Poetic Imagery*, 8–14.
[21] This analogy between character and image is (as far as I know) my own. Various
critics and theorists have suggested that there is a tendency towards discontinuous
characterization in *comedy in general*: e.g. N. Frye, *Anatomy of Criticism* (Princeton,
1957), 170; and notably L. Pirandello, *L'umorismo* (1908), who suggests that serious
writing 'composes' a character 'and will want to represent him as consistent in every
action', whereas 'the humorist . . . will *decompose* the character . . . and . . . enjoys
representing him in his incongruities' (trans. A. Illiano and D. P. Testas *On Humor*,
University of North Carolina Studies in Comparative Literature, 58 (Chapel Hill, NC,
1974), 143). Discontinuity in Aristophanic characterization has been discussed, but
without what I take to be the necessary emphasis, e.g. by Dover, *Aristophanic Comedy*,
59–65. Remarkably, theories of character as a whole tend to ignore the fact that there
is such a thing as discontinuous presentation at all. This is the case with such diverse
and wide-ranging discussions as C. C. Walcutt, *Man's Changing Mask: Modes and
Methods of Characterization in Fiction* (Minneapolis, 1966); P. Hamon, 'Pour un statut
sémiologique du personnage', in Roland Barthes, Wolfgang Kayser, Wayne C. Booth,
and Philippe Hamon, *Poétique du récit* (Paris, 1977); S. Freeman, 'Character in a
Coherent Fiction', *Philosophy and Literature*, 7 (1983), 196–212; Frow, 'Spectacle
Binding'; S. Chatman, 'Characters and Narrators'; U. Margolin, 'The Doer and the
Deed: Action as a Basis for Characterization in Narrative'; C. Gill, 'The Question of
Character and Personality in Greek Tragedy' (all four essays in *Poetics Today*, 7/2
(1986), 189–273). Structuralist–semiotic attempts to 'dissolve' character into 'text' are
no exception (see e.g. J. Weinsheimer, 'Theory of Character: *Emma*', *Poetics Today*, 1
(1980), 195; cf. Hamon, 'Pour un statut sémiologique du personnage'; Margolin, 'The
Doer and the Deed'; Frow, 'Spectacle Binding'): *all* character is simply subjected to a
common reinterpretative principle. Margolin, however, briefly considers the phenomenon of texts (e.g. the *nouveau roman*) which frustrate expectations of 'a unified stable
constellation' of '[character] traits or trait-clusters' ('The Doer', 207).

two arguments, Right and Wrong—which collectively amount to a
cartoon of the new intellectualism. But what sort of cartoon is it?
Not the emblematic, metonymic kind (as Uncle Sam is a metonym
for the USA or John Bull for England). Rather the metaphorical
kind—like the lumbering cart-horse which the cartoonist Low
regularly used to represent the Trades Union Congress in Britain
between the wars, or the infant of tender years he once used to
represent the human race in the new atomic age ('Baby play with
nice ball?'). So in *Clouds* the new Enlightenment is personified as a
mad scientist, called (for convenience) Socrates. So (more transparently) in *Knights* the relation between the people and their leading
politicians is represented metaphorically as the relation between an
old man (labelled Demos, as he might be in a modern cartoon) and
his slaves, old and new.

Whatever else he is, Euripides in *Thesmophoriazusae* is partly an
image of this kind. For intance, despite his original disinclination to
disguise himself, Euripides in fact goes through three disguises, the
last of which is the disguise of the old madam. Why *that* disguise?
Because Euripidean tragedy (in Aristophanes' eyes) is a new and
morally subversive kind of drama, fascinating but disturbing: lower
in tone than the heroic tragedy of an earlier age (its heroes in rags
were notorious), more seductive in its persuasive techniques.[22] This
is all summed up in the representation of Euripides himself as an old
hag bringing on a girl to seduce the forces of law and order (here the
Scythian policeman) and thereby distracting and (literally) disarm-
ing them. More generally, the Euripides of this play is an image in
the same sense: he is a personification of the 'real' Euripides' own
plays. Among the other salient characteristics of those plays (as
seen by Aristophanes) are melodramatic emotional moments, flashy
ideas, modishly difficult thoughts, and a penchant for the unexpected. Accordingly, throughout this play the character Euripides is
melodramatic ('today will tell if Euripides is to live on or die', 76–7),
full of flashy ideas ('brilliant and up to your best standard' (Mnesilochus), 93), given to modishly difficult thoughts ('you can't *hear*

---

[22] See e.g. *Ra*. 939–44, 954 (lowering the tone); 842, 1063 (rags); 771–6 (persuasion).
The mode of transference seems to recall the technique of the (later) ancient
biographers of Greek authors: 'the smallest hints of personality in conventional
statements [in their works] could be developed into character traits [in their
authors]' (M. R. Lefkowitz, *The Lives of the Greek Poets* (London, 1981), p. ix).

what you'll soon be here to *see*', 5–6), and, 'by introducing something new and clever' (1130), constantly doing the unexpected.[23] In
these respects Euripides is evidently, in my terms, a figure belonging
to the *realist* tradition. Irrespective of his relation to the historical
Euripides or to the historical Euripides' plays, his characterization
endows him with the set and stable features of a realist character—
albeit a realist character comically stylized by its construction
around a few limited traits.

The representation of Euripides as 'unexpected', in the image of
the unexpected twists and turns of his plays, brings us back to the
imagist presentation in the sense that primarily concerns us.
Images, characteristically, work by discontinuing the context they
presuppose. Imagist characters, accordingly, act discontinuously,
and unexpected behaviour, verbal or visual, is therefore their
imagist prerogative. In the particular instance of Euripides in
Thesmophoriazusae a version of discontinuity is *also*, ingeniously,
converted into a realist character-trait. It is almost as if one were
to act on Aristotle's instruction that an inconsistent character
should be portrayed as *consistently* inconsistent.[24] However, as the
examples already considered suggest, the point (in these Aristotelian terms) is that imagist characters are *inconsistently* inconsistent.

The mobile, continuous characters of the realist tradition do, or
can, develop: they do, or can, do so by gradual movement between
their particular traits. The imagist characters of Aristophanes are
fundamentally different. If and when they change, they change
abruptly and, perhaps, entirely—like the women at the Thesmophoria, dropping their respectability and picking it up again; like the
clever Euripides, abruptly accepting Mnesilochus' offer to help
(which *might* be explicable in terms of Euripides' own traits of
character); or like the stooge Mnesilochus, suddenly assuming the
role of hero by making that offer (which is not apparently explicable
in such terms). In short, the realist tradition, at its extreme, permits
character development, whereas the Aristophanic mode of representation involves, at *its* extreme, a binary principle: instead of
development, it permits inversion or reversal. Imagist representa-

---

[23] For these as characteristics of Euripidean drama, see e.g. *Ra.* 1330–63 (melodramatic moments and constant surprises: the Euripidean predisposition towards the
unexpected is summed up in the word *strephein*, 957); and 892–9 (modish thoughts
and flashy ideas); cf. W. B. Stanford (ed.), *Aristophanes: 'The Frogs'*[2] (London, 1971) on
both passages.   [24] Arist. *Po.* 15.

tion, it will be gathered, accepts a merely sequential view of time. In the realist tradition, by contrast, time is perceived as a (literally) *con*sequential matter, as an Aristotelian process of events that follow the laws of 'probability or necessity'.[25]

It is usual to discuss 'character' in Aristophanes in terms of alternatives which belong to the realist tradition rather than the imagist. Are his characters (for instance) 'types or individuals'? Such a question is eminently discussible in respect of Menander, and it is discussible in respect of Aristophanes the more his characterization approximates to the Menandrian–realist. It is therefore a more appropriate, and a more meaningful, question to ask of Strepsiades in *Clouds* than it is of (say) Philocleon in *Wasps*. That old man begins his play as a sort of caricature of Athenian legalism—and ends it as a sort of personification of the self-expressive life-force, abusing, drinking, and dancing. When we first see him, he is totally lacking in self-confidence, pining in captivity (317). Later on, he exudes total self-confidence ('much the most outrageous of them all', 1303). He is, no doubt, both an individual and a type at different times, perhaps even at the same time, but that formula is not illuminating: the important thing is his capacity to reverse. In this connection it is revealing to note that various interpreters of Aristophanes, from Süss to McLeish, have sought to identify his characters with a neo-Aristotelian set of character-types derived from the *Ethics* and elsewhere: notably the *eirōn* (the dry wit, who understates himself), the *alazōn* (the charlatan, who overstates himself), the *bōmolochos* (the buffoon).[26] What these attempts show is that the 'types' cannot be consistently equated with Aristophanes' *characters*, but may be equated with their *functions*. Beyond a certain point, in other words, the analysis is bound to resemble a Proppian analysis of narrative functions,[27] in which a

[25] Ibid. 7. To dissociate Aristophanes and development is not to ascribe a non-developmental tendency to comedy as a whole, as S. K. Langer did in *Feeling and Form* (New York, 1953), 335–6. Different again are the 'semantic reversals' which are reasonably taken to be a sign of inner 'psychic process' (i.e. of one form of realist characterization) by Newman, *Shakespeare's Rhetoric of Comic Character*, 11.

[26] Arist., *EN* 2. 7, 4. 7–8; *EE* 3. 7; ʿH. 3. 18: see W. Süss, *De personarum antiquae comoediae usu et origine* (Bonn, 1905); id., 'Zur Komposition der altattischen Komödie', *RlM*, 63 (1908), 12–38; K. McLeish, *The Theatre of Aristophanes* (London, 1980), 53–6, 74–5. The three types occur as a set in the *Tract. Coisl.*: see R. Janko, *Aristotle on Comedy* (London, 1984), 39, 216–18, 242.

[27] See V. Propp, *Morphology of the Folktale* (Bloomington, Ind., 1958).

given function may be seen to be transferred from one character to another. So whereas Mnesilochus, for instance, begins *Thesmophoriazusae* as the buffoon, in the later stages of the play the buffoon's function is transferred from Mnesilochus to the Scythian, while Mnesilochus himself acts as a sort of 'dry wit' in his speech at the women's assembly, when he catalogues the vices of the sex from (purportedly) a woman's point of view. The transferability of such 'functions', however, is largely, if not entirely, a corollary of imagist discontinuity. The application of these types to the discussion of Aristophanes, therefore, leaves a plausible realist interpretation of his characters as unattainable as ever.

It is a necessary, though not a sufficient, condition of imagist representation that it should involve figures whose appearance is decisive for their being. It follows that if such figures are disguised, they change. In life we suppose that this is not true. In this kind of art, however, it has the appearance of truth—hence the wonderful repeated joke in the second half of *Thesmophoriazae*, that by appearing to be Menelaus, Euripides can rescue Mnesilochus, if Mnesilochus appears to be Helen; and by appearing to be Perseus, Euripides can rescue Mnesilochus, if Mnesilochus appears to be Andromeda. Mnesilochus himself makes the principle explicit:

Thank heaven! There's still hope. My man won't let me down. He just shot past as Perseus. It was a sign that I must be Andromeda.   (1009–12)

The topic is prefigured, programmatically, by Agathon, earlier on in the play. The writer must 'identify with', and therefore disguise himself as, his own parts:

I wear the clothes that fit in with my projects. A playwright, you see, must tailor his own life-style to the dramatic task in hand. If it's a play about women, his own physical being has to have something of their style.   (148–52)

Role-playing, disguise, and identification, of course, can and often do figure within the realist sphere. In the imagist tradition, however, they have a distinctive significance.

II

Realism of some kind seems to dominate fictional writing in the
Western world from Aristophanes' own day to the beginning of the
present century. More precisely: outside Aristophanes the best
examples of imagist representation seem either to belong to the
twentieth-century avant-garde or to be naïve—perhaps in the
ordinary sense of that word, or else in Schiller's sense, whereby
(say) Homer is naïve, and the word tends to imply *early*.[28] We do
indeed find hints of imagist representation in Homer, especially in
the *Iliad*, where (with the notable exception of Achilles) characters
have fixed qualities which they either live up to or fail to live up to,
and where the prospect of any such failure is felt as a threat to—
because a reversal of?—personal integrity. So Hector, besought by
Andromache to hold back from the fighting where he will risk his
life and her future, grants the validity of her fears but points to the
constraints of public opinion *and his own nature*:

Woman, all this is on my mind as well as yours. But I am too much in awe
of the Trojan men and the long-robed Trojan women to skulk away from
battle like a coward. Nor is that what my own heart bids me do, for I have
learned always to be valiant and fight among the leading men of Troy and
win great glory for my father and myself. (6. 441–6)

'Yes,' says Hector in effect, 'you are right: I *will* be killed. But what
else can I—*being me*—do? *Ich kann nicht anders.*' His obstinacy,
however, is prompted not by any sort of Lutheran conscience, but
by a consciousness that cannot conceive of—and is not conceived in
terms of—a flexible response.[29]

Perhaps the simplest, and certainly the most naïve, type of
imagist representation is found in the fairy-tale. The ugly frog
who changes into a handsome prince is a typical instance. The
character is represented as an unchanging being—except that it
can go into binary reverse and become its own opposite. Compare
the transformation of Demos from ugly old man to handsome

---

[28] Friedrich Schiller, *Über naive und sentimentalische Dichtung* (1795–6). Examples
from 'carnival' literature might be adduced to support the correlation between
imagist and naïve. There are, however, some surprising counter-examples of sophisticated imagism: the Duke in Shakespeare's *Measure for Measure* is one.
[29] The reference is to Luther's speech at the Diet of Worms, 18 Apr. 1521.

younger man at the end of *Knights*.[30] Compare, too, similar transformations in surviving forms of traditional popular culture like the
pantomime.

In our own century many writers, especially dramatists, have
opened up the possibilities of imagist representation in a more
self-conscious, experimental way, by reacting against the whole
realist tradition as no Greek of Aristophanes' day either needed to
or could. Against familiar stabilities and traditional expectations of
development the new age puts a series of challenging questions.
Sometimes the challenge is mounted on behalf of what many would
think of as a marginal artistic tendency—stream of consciousness,
surrealism, the absurd. For Strindberg, it is associated with a neo-
realist perception that modern people, 'living in a transitional era
more hectic and hysterical' than earlier ages, are, and should be
represented as, 'more vulnerable . . . torn and divided'.[31] For Pirandello, questions give way to new answers: 'My drama lies entirely
in this one thing . . . in my being conscious that each one of us
believes himself to be a single person. But it's not true . . . each one
of us is many persons.'[32] Accompanying and often underlying these
new positions is the rejection of the 'substantial unity of the soul' by
influential thinkers like Nietzsche and Freud.[33] Marxist theory too
produces its alternative to the realist tradition, above all in the work
of Brecht. In *Der gute Mensch von Sezuan*, for instance, 'the "good
woman" Shen Te assumes a mask of harsh oppressiveness and turns
into the businessman Shui Ta, so that each of her twin personalities
recalls the possibility of the other'.[34] As early as *Die Dreigroschenoper*
(1928) Brecht is seen to be exploring norms of imagist representa-

---

[30] Despite the arguments of L. Edmunds, *Cleon, Knights, and Aristophanes' Politics*
(Lanham, Md., 1987), 43–4, it may be assumed that when Demos is pronounced
'handsome' (*kalon ex aischrou*, 1321) the ordinary associations of this phraseology
would point to some sort of rejuvenation. It is true that, for example, at X. *Smp.* 4. 17
we learn that old men can be called handsome (*kaloi*) too, but only by way of a refined
qualification to the everyday perception that 'good looks soon pass their prime'—i.e.
that 'beauty' and 'youth' do belong together, as of course they do in a host of familiar
contexts from Homer (e.g. *Od.* 6. 108) to Aristophanes himself (e.g. *Lys.* 647).

[31] From Strindberg's preface to *Miss Julie* (1888), trans E. M. Sprinchorn, in B. F.
Dukore (ed.), *Dramatic Theory and Criticism* (New York, 1974), 567.

[32] The father's words in *Six Characters in Search of an Author* (1921), trans. F. May
(London, 1954), 25.

[33] The phrase 'substantial unity of the soul' is used (as a target) by T. S. Eliot in
'Tradition and the Individual Talent' (*The Sacred Wood* (London, 1920), 56).

[34] R. D. Gray, *Brecht* (London, 1961), 66.

tion. At the final peripeteia of the drama, for instance, we find the arch-criminal, Macheath, suddenly snatched from the gallows by royal decree and raised to a peerage, exchanging his crude curses on the police and farewells to fellow criminals and lavatory attendants for the lofty operatic observation that the greater the need, the more imminent the rescue—this frog having become a prince after all.[35]

In classical Greek drama as we have it, imagist characterization is much more characteristic of comedy than of tragedy; but the 'progress' of comedy (in the fourth century), as of tragedy (in the fifth), is clearly towards the realist mode. If one is prepared to extrapolate backwards from that tendency, it might be conjectured that early drama, tragedy as well as comedy, contained various imagist elements. One likely context would be the chorus—the stylized speaking or (especially) singing group, which both forms of drama eventually found to be incompatible with their aspirations towards realism, and sought to eliminate. The Aristophanic chorus, certainly, is—still?—markedly imagist. In no extant Aristophanic comedy, in fact, 'does the chorus have a consistent and unalterable dramatic character'.[36] The women in *Thesmophoriazusae*—in or out of the chorus—actually constitute a modest specimen of group variability. The chorus in *Wasps* begin as creaky old men, turn into fierce wasps, and end as earnest commentators on the action.[37] The chorus in *Peace*, as the play's most recent editor observes, actually has 'four or five distinguishable identities' in the space of 500 lines.[38] But in tragedy too the identity of the chorus is often—in realist terms—elusive: the 'Theban elders' in *Antigone* are a classic case in point.[39] More fundamentally, though, it may be that imagist characterization is originally implicit in the very rhythms of Greek drama—in the alternative reversals from happy man to sad man (common in tragedy) and sad man to happy man (usual in comedy). That Aristotle should have interpreted such

---

[35] 'Die Mordgesellen, Abtrittsweiber, | Ich bitte sie, mir zu verzeihen. | Nicht so die Polizistenhunde'; 'Ja, ich fühle es, wenn die Not am grössten, ist die Hilfe am nächsten'; Bertolt Brecht, *Versuche* 1–12 (Berlin, 1959), 217–18.

[36] Sifakis, *Parabasis and Animal Choruses*, 32.

[37] *V.* 230ff., 1450ff.: cf. Silk, 'Pathos in Aristophanes', 87–90, 110–11.

[38] Aristophanes, *Peace*, ed. A. H. Sommerstein (Warminster, 1985), p. xviii.

[39] See M. S. Silk and J. P. Stern, *Nietzsche on Tragedy* (Cambridge, 1981), 267–8.

patterns as essentially and primarily sequences of *action* testifies to
his overwhelming concern with classic tragedy and his own penchant for realism.[40] And that latter prejudice, no doubt, *is* broadly
justified by classic tragedy as we know it, where the imagist presence is a marginal one. Outside the chorus, in fact, it is chiefly
visible in the dramatic experiments of Euripides. His *Medea*, for
instance, reveals *both* the progressive realist who explores the
woman's inner agonies about killing her children *and* the avant-
garde anti-realist who offers us her transfiguration from oppressed
victim to divine agent of vengeance at the end.

III

The obvious positive feature of imagist presentation of character is
discontinuity; and if one seeks confirmation of the plausibility of an
imagist reading of Aristophanes—a reading that sees discontinuities
of characterization as essential, not incidental—one will find it
above all in the evident kinship between such discontinuities and
others elsewhere in the text or texture of Aristophanic drama.[41] I
have already instanced Aristophanes' stylistic shifts and reversals as
symptomatic of the mode of character presentation that they
contribute to. With the word 'imagist' in mind, we can hardly
overlook the fact that no mechanism is more characteristic of
Aristophanic writing in general than metaphor, the discontinuous
stylistic feature *par excellence*[42]—just as nothing is more characteristic of his verbal humour than the surprise joke (*para prosdokian*).[43]
An equivalent discontinuous tendency is apparent in the organization of his dramatic fictions. This is what we commonly discuss
under the heading of 'breaches of illusion'; and no one can dispute
the propensity of Aristophanes' characters to be the carriers of these
'breaches' *without undermining their own peculiar mode of existence.*

---

[40] See Arist. *Po.* 6; and (on the endings of tragedies and comedies) cf. M. S. Silk,
'The Autonomy of Comedy', *Comparative Criticism*, 10 (1988), 27–9.

[41] Cf. Silk, 'Pathos in Aristophanes', esp. 103–8.

[42] See esp. J. Taillardat, *Les Images d'Aristophane* (Paris, 1965).

[43] 'The instances of comic surprise in Aristophanes are legion' (W. J. M. Starkie, *The
'Acharnians' of Aristophanes* (London, 1909), p. lxvii). It may be noted that the ancient
theorists who established the principle of humour *para prosdokian* themselves tended
to interpret it very narrowly, as e.g. did Demetrius (*Eloc.* 152), who classified it as
merely one among many humorous mechanisms (ibid. 137–62).

'Master, shall I tell you one of the usual jokes that always get the audience laughing': whatever else is true of such an opening to a play, it is certainly true that it alerts us to a kind of character presentation which is not going to be that of a Menander (let alone a Henry James).[44] One notes, however, the frequency of such moments in twentieth-century avant-garde drama, including that of Brecht.[45]

Going deeper into Aristophanes, one could also relate his character presentation to the discontinuities of his plot construction, notably those associated with the loose connection of episodes in the latter parts of many of his plays. Here too Brecht offers a valuable point of reference—the Brecht of theory even more than the Brecht of practice. As he repeatedly urges us to see in his theoretical writings on the theatre, seemingly unrelated aspects of drama in fact hang together—above all, aspects of his own innovatory 'epic theatre' as against aspects of the traditional dramatic, or 'Aristotelian', theatre. In particular he allows us to sense a connection between Aristotelian theatre's 'evolutionary' treatment of character and its 'linear development' of plot, as against the concern of his own epic theatre with 'jumps' and 'curves'. Traditional theatre means *growth*; his own means *montage*, where, in place of a 'natural' whole, the individual events are tied together in such a way that 'the knots show'.[46]

One might, with profit, lay still more stress on a different affinity. The tendency of Aristophanes' imagist characters to reverse themselves surely belongs to a vast pattern of reversals, inversions, and oppositions in Aristophanic comedy as a whole. *Thesmophoriazusae*

---

[44] *Ra.* 1–2: cf. Sifakis, *Parabasis and Animal Choruses*, 7–14.

[45] A representative example from *Die Dreigroschenoper*: the address to the audience in the theatre by Macheath's rival, Peachum, explaining the thinking behind the royal pardon for Macheath ('wir haben uns einen anderen Schluss ausgedacht': Brecht, *Versuche* 1–12, 218).

[46] Bertolt Brecht, *Schriften zum Theater* (Frankfurt, 1963–4), ii. 117, vii. 67. The relevance of Brecht's theory to Aristophanes' practice is briefly, but properly, stated by Sifakis, *Parabasis*, 21, 113 n. 46; cf. W. Görler, 'Über die Illusion in der antiken Komödie', *A & A* 18 (1973), 44–57; K. von Fritz, *Antike und moderne Tragödie* (Berlin, 1962), pp. x–xxviii; H. Flashar, 'Aristoteles und Brecht', *Poetica*, 6 (1974), 17–37; D. Bain, *Actors and Audience* (Oxford, 1977), 3–5. Before Brecht, Pirandello had anticipated the connection between discontinuous character and discontinuous dramatic form: the 'decomposed' and 'incongruous' characters of 'the humorist' (see n. 21 above) are related to 'all that is disorganised, unravelled and whimsical, all the digressions which can be seen in the works of humor' (*On Humor*, 144–5).

again offers an apt instance with (among much else) its women
playing at being men (*ekklēsia* and all); one man (Mnesilochus)
playing at being a woman *ad hoc*; another man (Cleisthenes) who
habitually takes that role; a member of the dominant sex (Mnesilochus) taken captive by the weaker sex (women), but himself
reversing roles when he kidnaps their 'baby'. Within the action of
the play we have a whole series of reversal tableaux, like the weak
man Cleisthenes being put down by the strong women ('stand
aside—I'll do the interrogating', 626); or the vocal representative
of the dominant sex (Euripides) being forced to ask for terms from
the supposedly weaker women; and another member of that weaker
sex (the dancing-girl) overcoming another member of the stronger
sex (the Scythian), who (as a laughable foreigner) is an inversion of
establishment domination in his own right. Within such a series of
reversals and inversions, details like the women's sudden coarse-
ness, or Mnesilochus' sudden assumption of the strong man's role
and Euripides' eager response to it, fall into place, unnoticed. Everywhere we meet (as Bakhtin says of the medieval carnival) 'the
relativity of prevailing truths and authorities . . . the peculiar logic
of the "inside out"'.[47]

Furthermore, all such reversals and inversions belong to a still
larger system of fundamental oppositions, notably those expressed
in agonistic terms, around which so many of the plays are constructed: men and women (as *Thesmophoriazusae*), men and gods (as
Birds), peace and war (as *Acharnians*), new and old (as *Clouds*),
young and old (as *Wasps*). The oppositions, of course, may be
subject to inversion themselves. In *Wasps*, for instance, the normal
pattern whereby the young resist the orthodoxies of their elders (cf.
the end of *Clouds*) is reversed, so that the son Bdelycleon labours in
vain to reduce his father to order, the imagist corollary of which is
that the old man *becomes* 'young' in his own right.[48] And pervading
all the plays is the opposition between higher and lower, serious and
non-serious, a particular version of which we find alluded to in a
contrasting pair like Euripides and Mnesilochus, and another ver-

[47] M. M. Bakhtin, *Rabelais and his World*, trans. H. Iswolsky (Cambridge, Mass.,
1968), 11. On inversions in *Thesmophoriazusae*, cf. F. Zeitlin, 'Travesties of Gender
and Genre in Aristophanes' *Thesmophoriazusae*', in H. P. Foley (ed.), *Reflections of
Women in Antiquity* (New York, 1981).
[48] *neos gar eimi* ('I'm only young, you see') (1355). On the implications of this
'becoming', see Silk, 'Pathos in Aristophanes', 109–11.

sion in the stylistic switches discussed earlier. This, arguably, is the opposition from which, above all, Aristophanic comedy gets it bearings.[49]

IV

This discussion of imagist representation can hardly be regarded as comprehensive, either in a theoretical sense or in respect of Aristophanes. I hope to have answered one question: the inconstancies of behaviour which the people of Aristophanes exhibit are acceptable because they presuppose Aristophanic 'norms' of discontinuity both on the level of character and elsewhere. And I hope, in answering it, to have shed some light on the possibilities (and actualities) of character presentation in general. At the same time, various other questions have been left unconsidered. Their existence should at the very least be acknowledged, if only as a gesture towards the ideal of a comprehensive treatment.

In the first place, my discussion of Aristophanes has been essentially behaviourist. I have concentrated on the words and actions of his people and have generally evaded their minds and thoughts. As imagist beings, can they actually be said to have minds and thoughts? In realist representation, characters are assumed to have minds and thoughts which work like those of real people in real life. Real people have experiences, whether we know about them or not; they have habits that imply responses to those experiences; and in general they have memories of their experiences. Fictional people, necessarily, have experiences only when we know that they do, and responses and memories only when these are made public in some way. Within this limitation, however, the characters of realist fiction impinge on us as sentient beings: so far as we see and know them, they act from their minds (experiences, responses, memories), and their behaviour is referable to their minds. Are we to make any such reference with imagist characters, and if so, when and why? Picture Mnesilochus taking his decision to help Euripides, and it is hard to deny imagist characters any mental capacity at all. Think of Xanthias' anti-illusionary

---

[49] Cf. Silk, 'The Autonomy of Comedy', 16; O. Taplin, 'Fifth-Century Tragedy and Comedy: A *Synkrisis*', *JHS* 106 (1986), 163–74.

question to Dionysus at the start of *Frogs*, and it is hard to see what
sort of experiences, responses, or memories such a being needs to be,
or can be, credited with.

Secondly, it is easier to say (as I have said) that Aristophanes'
presentation of character is both imagist and realist than to assess
the relative strength of each element in any given dramatic
sequence. The general principle (I would say) is clear enough.
And this is that Aristophanic comedy presupposes a non-realist
sense or logic of human *being* and *behaving*. As such it admits
realism, in so far as realism suits its own logic.[50] However, the
particular problem, as it concerns particular sequences, remains
unsolved. For instance (thinking back to the previous unanswered
question), we might ask: Do we credit the character Xanthias with a
mind ('of his own') when he talks to Dionysus 'in character', but not
when he makes anti-illusionary remarks like the one at the start?
Do we in fact—can we conceivably—switch mentalist assumptions
on and off like a tap in this way? Is the truth that even when we
credit Xanthias with a mind, we always do so on some non-realist
terms, which remain to be specified?

Finally, a comprehensive discussion must certainly come to terms
with the evaluative implications of the modern experiments in
imagist representation, whose diversity and sophistication suggest
that while we may argue for the superiority of realism, we cannot
simply assume it. As John Gould reminds us in his discussion of
tragic character, realist character in fiction—from Greek tragedy to
Eugene O'Neill—is a construct, not a hidden pre-existing reality.[51]
This is hardly to devalue realist characterization, since our sense of
a human character in life, arguably, must always be as much of a
construct as a response to a hidden reality itself.[52] And certainly it
does not justify us in describing realist characters as 'systems of
rule-governed equivalencies' (like Philippe Hamon) or, more simply,

---

[50] Cf. Silk, 'The Autonomy of Comedy', 23–7.

[51] See n. 12 above. Gould (I hasten to add) is at pains to *contrast* Greek tragedy and
O'Neill, and he does not give them any common 'realist' label, as I do.

[52] See e.g. E. Goffman, *The Presentation of Self in Everyday Life* (Garden City, NY,
1959); J. Lacan, *Écrits* (Paris, 1966), 93 ff.; cf. P. E. Easterling, 'Constructing Character
in Greek Tragedy', in C. B. R. Pelling (ed.), *Characterization and Individuality in Greek
Literature* (Oxford, 1990), 83–99. A similar conclusion about (realist) characterization
is reached by Newman, *Shakespeare's Rhetoric of Comic Character*, 127–8.

as 'predications' (like Todorov).[53] But it does encourage us to see that the constructional quality of imagist representations does not in itself invalidate their claim to serious attention.

[53] Hamon, 'Pour un statut sémiologique du personnage', 144; Todorov, *Grammaire du Décaméron* (The Hague, 1969), 27–30.

14

Aristophanes and the Demon Poverty

A. H. SOMMERSTEIN

Aristophanes' last two surviving plays, *Assemblywomen* and *Wealth*, have long been regarded as something of an enigma. The changes in structure—the diminution in the role of the chorus, the disappearance of the parabasis, etc.—as well as the shift of interest away from the immediacies of current politics towards broader social themes, can reasonably be interpreted as an early stage of the process that ultimately transformed Old Comedy into New, even if it is unlikely ever to be finally agreed whether Aristophanes was leading or following this trend. The decline in freshness, in verbal agility, in sparkle of wit, in theatrical inventiveness, which is perceptible in the earlier play and very marked in the later, may be put down to advancing years and diminishing inspiration. Such an explanation squares with the evidence of a marked decline in Aristophanes' productivity towards the end of his life. Whereas in the first seven years of his career (427–421) he seems to have produced, or had produced for him, not less than ten plays,[1] and in the years 420–405 approximately another eighteen, the twenty years or so that followed *Frogs* yielded a further eleven at the very most[2] unless some titles have been completely lost; and since it is not likely that after

[1] Certain are *Daitalēs, Babylonians, Acharnians, Knights*, the original version of *Clouds, Proagon, Wasps*, and *Peace*. Almost certain are *Holkades* (cf. Hypothesis 3. 33–7, M. Platnauer (ed.), *Aristophanes: 'Peace'* (Oxford, 1964) to *Peace* and fr. 407, 411) and *Georgoi* (cf. fr. 100, 107, 109).

[2] Certain are *Assemblywomen, Wealth*, the late *Kokalos* and *Aiolosikon II*, and also *Storks* (cf. fr. 431, 439); probable are *Telemessians* (cf. fr. 538) and also the first version of *Aiolosikon* in view of the 'Middle Comedy' nature of the plot (Platon., *Prolegomena de comoedia* 1. 22–31, W. J. W. Koster, *Scholia in Aristophanem I. 1a: Prolegomena de comoedia* (Groningen, 1975)), which cannot have differed much from that of the later version. In addition a number of plays are not readily datable on the information we have, or at most can only be assigned a *terminus post quem*; of these *Danaids, Lemniai, Phoinissai*, and *Polyidos* may be later than *Frogs*, though the only evidence is the absence of known references to persons and events of earlier date.

the outstanding success of *Frogs*, and the public recognition that followed it,[3] Aristophanes would have experienced any difficulty in securing a chorus, the explanation can only be that he was writing less. But the truly puzzling feature of the two late plays we possess is the apparent sea-change in the author's social orientation. In his fifth-century plays, from *Acharnians* to *Frogs*, as has been shown (in my view conclusively) by de Ste Croix,[4] Aristophanes reveals himself as one who instinctively speaks the language and thinks the thoughts of the well-to-do, even if at the same time he can laugh with the common man at ostentatious and useless wealth in the shape of Pyrilampes' peacocks,[5] Leogoras' pheasants,[6] or the sultan-like garments of an Athenian imperial official[7]—as one who was happy for the Demos to be sovereign so long as it was willing to be guided by the advice of its 'betters', the *kaloi te kagathoi* of, for example, *Knights* 738 or *Frogs* 727–9, and to leave them in the quiet enjoyment of their property. At first sight in *Assemblywomen* and *Wealth* this seems to have changed almost diametrically. In both plays a central concern is the sufferings of the poor, many of whom, we are constantly reminded,[8] are not in a position to feed or clothe themselves adequately; and in both a fantasy project is set on foot to end these sufferings, a project which is bound to harm the living standards and life-style of the rich in ways that would have drawn screams of horror from the Aristophanes of twenty or thirty years before. In *Assemblywomen* Praxagora abolishes all private property: land is to be held in common, town houses merged into a single residential complex,[9] and personal chattels surrendered to the state, which will maintain all citizens through public dining-halls. In *Wealth* the miraculous healing of the god of wealth results in all and only those who are of good character becoming rich, whereas

---

[3] Attested by one of the *Vitae* (*Prolegomena* 228. 40–3 Koster) and by Hypothesis I to *Frogs* citing Dichaearchus. I have discussed the honours awarded to Aristophanes in my ed. of *Acharnians* (Warminster, 1980), 24–5 n. 10; I would now date them fairly confidently to late 405 or early 404, since the advice of *Frogs* 718–37 would be unlikely to appeal much to Athenians who had experienced the rule of the Thirty.

[4] G. E. M. de Ste Croix, *The Origins of the Peloponnesian War* (London, 1972), 355–76.

[5] *Ach.* 63.   [6] *Clouds* 109.   [7] *Birds* 1021.

[8] *Ass.* 353, 380–2, 408–26, 566; *Wealth* 219, 253, 263, 283, 504, 535–46, 562, 594–7, 763, 842–7, 952–4.

[9] *Ass.* 673–4. The abolition of individual housing reappears in Plato (*R.* 3. 416d, 5. 458c); for its appearance in later collectivist utopias and at least one actual collectivist society (pre-conquest Peru) see I. R. Shafarevich, *The Socialist Phenomenon* (New York, 1980), 198–9.

previously one could become rich only through crime;[10] thus all those who were formerly rich are made poor, at least until they reform themselves morally. De Ste Croix[11] has rightly called attention to Aristophanes' acceptance, in his earlier work, of the usual Greek upper-class equation of 'the rich' with 'the good'; but in these two plays we find Aristophanes explicitly equating the rich with the bad.[12]

It is natural that critics should be reluctant to credit the notion that Aristophanes underwent, in middle life, so apparently complete and radical a transformation in his socio-political attitudes—though we should remember that if there was a change, it may well not have been as sudden as, on our limited evidence, it inevitably seems. For those who wish to avoid supposing a transformation, there seem to be three possible approaches. One is to seek evidence of a radical 'left-wing' viewpoint in the fifth-century plays; this has been attempted, without general success, by Helmut Schareika.[13] Another is to see the two late plays as simply comic fantasies, influenced both by the Utopian tradition within Old Comedy[14] and by discussion in philosophical circles of new models of society, but not intended to have any serious effect on the thinking of members of the audience on contemporary social issues; on this view[15] *Wealth*, which as comedy is weak, must be accounted a failure.

Most prominent, however, in recent discussion have been a variety of approaches which, while differing in detail, agree that Aristophanes takes in these plays a negative attitude towards the kind of radical social changes that the plays depict. Since on the surface the two revolutions are triumphantly successful, this must mean that Aristophanes has presented them and their results in an

[10] *Wealth* 30–1, 35–8, 45–50, 352–90, 502–3, 569, 754–6, 774–81.
[11] *The Origins of the Peloponnesian War* 358–9.
[12] In addition to the passages from *Wealth* cited in n. 10, see *Ass.* 426 (implying that the wealthy Nausikydes has never done any good for the community), 603 (a man with much money must have acquired it by perjury), 608 (the rich are the biggest thieves). De Ste Croix, *The Origins of the Peloponnesian War*, 360, misses these passages, and explains those in *Wealth* by 'the nature of the plot', which begs the question why Ar. chose to make a plot of this nature (and twice!).
[13] *Der Realismus der aristophanischen Komödie* (Frankfurt, 1978).
[14] On this tradition and its reflection in Aristophanes (esp. in *Wealth*), see F. Heberlein, *Pluthygieia: Zur Gegenwelt bei Aristophanes* (Frankfurt, 1980).
[15] For which see (among others) R. G. Ussher, *Aristophanes* (*G & R* New Surveys in the Classics, 9 (Oxford, 1979), 18–19 and A. H. Sommerstein, *Aristophanes: The 'Acharnians', The 'Clouds', 'Lysistrata'* (Harmondsworth, 1973), 14.

ironical manner, intending at least the discerning spectator to realize that the new social order would be unworkable and/or would bring no real benefits; or alternatively (as has recently been suggested, in relation to *Wealth*, by Konstan and Dillon)[16] that he has adroitly confused different conceptions of the causes and cure of poverty in order 'to dissolve the issue of exploitations and inequality into a vague nostalgia for a golden age'.

Ever since Wilamowitz[17] the ironic interpretation of *Assembly-women* and *Wealth* has been that of most German scholarship, and even Heberlein[18] in his recent discussion of *Wealth* maintains this interpretation despite his rejection of the greater part of the evidence on which it had usually been based. Outside this tradition, too, recent studies by Saïd,[19] Foley,[20] and Konstan and Dillon seek by different routes to understand the two plays as hostile to radical social change.

In both plays, certainly, there is material which could well be used to support one or another variety of this general thesis. We may consider, for instance, the second half of *Assemblywomen*, which consists of three scenes exemplifying the consequences of the new social order. In the first of these (730–876) we meet a character who notwithstanding Praxagora's new law is determined to keep his property and not surrender it to the state: I shall refer to this man as the Dissident.[21] The Dissident is not only himself refusing to comply with the law; he is confident that many others will refuse

[16] D. Konstan and M. Dillon, 'The Ideology of Aristophanes' *Wealth*', *AJP* 102 (1981), 371–94.

[17] See the essay on *Assemblywomen* appended to his *Lysistrata* (Berlin, 1927), e.g. (p. 220) 'Aus Andeutungen entnehmen wir, dass der Dichter die Sinnlosigkeit der Pläne Praxagoras uns zu verstehen geben will'—though Wilamowitz may not have been entirely content with this interpretation, for he added 'Nicht viele Zuschauer werden ihn verstanden haben.' His successors have not been deterred from following him by this perceptive remark: see esp. W. Süss, 'Scheinbare und wirkliche Inkongruenzen in den Dramen des Aristophanes', *RhM* 97 (1954), 289–313, and H. Flahar, 'Zur Eigenart des aristophanischen Spätwerkes', *Poetica*, 1 (1967), 154–75; rep. in H.-J. Newiger (ed.), *Aristophanes und die alte Komödie* (Darmstadt, 1975), 405–34; and as Ch. 16 in this volume.

[18] F. Heberlein, 'Zur Ironie im *Plutus* des Aristophanes', *WJA* 7 (1981), 27–49.

[19] S. Saïd, 'L'*Assemblée des femmes: les femmes, l'économie et la politique*', in J. Bonnamour and H. Delavault (ed.), *Aristophane: les femmes et la cité* (Fontenay-aux-Roses, 1979).

[20] H. P. Foley, 'The "Female Intruder" Reconsidered: Women in Aristophanes' *Lysistrata* and *Ecclesiazusae*', *CP* 77 (1982), 1–21.

[21] He is never named in the text. His *nota personae* in the MSS is generally *pheidōlos*; the scholia (Σ^R 853, 869) refer to him as *ho mē katatheis*.

as well (769–77, 787–829), and confident also that despite his disobedience he will be able to wangle his way into the communal dinner. Moreover, if we take a later passage[22] literally, he succeeds in this. The next scene (877–1111) shows an unfortunate young man, whom I shall call Epigenes,[23] being fought over by three old and hideous women, all of whom, under another new law, claim a prior right to receive sexual satisfaction from him; he comes close to being torn to pieces (1083–90) for no fault at all, and his disappointed girlfriend is made to argue (1038–42) that the new sexual communism will result in large-scale incest. And in the final scene it seems twice to be hinted (1147–8, 1175–8) that the magnificent communal feast has no real existence. It might be felt that there was enough evidence to lead us to Saïd's conclusion that the attempt to establish universal equality and communality is presented as failing because of the persistence of selfishness, which no law can abolish.[24]

In *Wealth* there have been some rather captious doubts of the purity of motive of the hero Chremylus. It is pointed out[25] that he asks Wealth to make him rich, whether justly or unjustly (233), and says to the god that he loves his only son 'more than anything else—except you' (251). That so much has been made of these remarks merely shows how very little there really is to be said against Chremylus. If the first remark were taken literally, it would be inconsistent with the whole plot of the play. The Wealth-god has no wish to enrich anyone unjustly; he has only done so in the past because he was blind, and could not see who was honest and who was not; and in future, when he has been cured, in accordance with Chremylus' own wish (386–8) he will favour only the virtuous. We must therefore understand 'whether justly or unjustly' as a polar expression used loosely, as is the Greek habit with such expressions,[26] to mean (as the scholia say) 'by any means'. As to Chremylus' admission that he loves Wealth more than anything else, this is not a sign of avarice, only of frankness;[27] for in Chremylus' view *every* human being has an insatiable desire to be wealthy (188–97),

---

[22] 1132–3, where Blepyrus is told 'Out of more than thirty thousand citizens, you alone have not dined.'

[23] We are told in 934 and in 951 that the young man who enters at 934 is the same person whom the old woman was talking about in 931 and 933 and whom she then named as Epigenes.   [24] Saïd, 'L'Assemblée des femmes', 55.

[25] Flashar, 'Zur Eigenart des aristophanischen Spätwerkes', 159–60 (in the rep.: 412–13).   [26] Amply illustrated by Wilamowitz on E. *Heracles* 1106.

[27] As Chremylus himself explains (252).

and he does not pretend that he himself is an exception. Where he does differ from most is in wanting others to be wealthy as well as himself (345, 386–8): as we shall find, generosity and its opposite, miserliness, are quite important themes in this play.

Some other features of *Wealth*, especially in its latter half, have also been seen as lending themselves to an ironic interpretation; these will be examined later. But by far the most important evidence suggesting that at least not all the right is on Chremylus' side comes from his *agōn* with the goddess of Poverty (487–618).

Chremylus and Blepsidemus are about to take Wealth to be healed in the temple of Asclepius when they are interrupted (415) by a hideous and terrifying old female who identifies herself as Poverty, 'who has been living with you these many years' (437). The two men declare their intention of driving her out of Greece (463); she undertakes, on the contrary, to prove that if they do so they will be doing great harm to themselves and humanity, and a formal debate is duly held, its special status being signalled by a change of metre to anapaestic tetrameters and a typical two-line *katakeleusmos* by the chorus-leader.

Chremylus is first to speak, and that in itself may be regarded as significant; for in almost every other Aristophanic debate in *Lang-versen*[28] the first speaker is the ultimate loser. He argues that justice demands that wealth should be the reward only of virtue, adding (for the first time in the play) that if this is done everybody will become virtuous (497) since virtue will be in their material inter-est.[29] His words for 'virtuous' and 'wicked' are mostly vague and general—*chrēstos* and *agathos* on one side, *ponēros* on the other—but he also describes the wicked or one class of the wicked, as godless (491, 496) and says that in the better world of the future all men will be god-fearing (497). This may well seem hard to square with the actual outcome of Wealth's healing: what happens then is that all men turn to Wealth alone in worship while the other gods

---

[28] I use this expression, rather than *agōn*, in order to exclude those scenes (*Birds* 451–638; *Ass.* 571–709) which possess all or most of the formal characteristics of an *agōn* but are exercises in persuasion by a single speaker rather than debates between two speakers. Among genuine debates the only exception to the generalization in the text is *Knights* 303–460, where the first *epirrhēma* (335 ff.) opens in noisy confusion with both antagonists demanding to be allowed to speak first.

[29] This contrasts sharply with the existing state of society, which offers the virtuous so little hope of success that Chremylus himself, anxious for his son's well-being, had almost resolved to bring the boy up to be a criminal (35–8).

and their priests starve for lack of offerings (1099–1190). Nor does Chremylus' prediction of universal reverence and piety sit well with his earlier assurance to Wealth that once the latter regains his sight 'the sovereignty of Zeus and his thunderbolts [won't be] worth three obols' (124–6). One may feel that if anyone in the play deserves to be called godless it is Chremylus himself.[30] In reply to Chremylus' initial presentation and defence of his proposal, Poverty argues (507–16) that if everyone is wealthy, and hence able to live in comfort without working, no goods or services will be produced. Chremylus, like Praxagora (*Ass.* 651), counters that the work will be done by slaves, but he is unable to explain satisfactorily how slaves will be procured, and is confronted with the prospect of being 'compelled to plough and dig and do the rest of the hard work yourself' and lead 'a far more wretched life than now' (525–6)—to which the only answer he can find is a curse (*es kephalēn soi*). It seems to have been shown, paradoxically, that universal wealth must lead to universal misery.

Chremylus' vivid description of the horrors of poverty, in a passage to which we shall have to return (535–47), is a splendid piece of soap-box invective but has hardly any relevance to Poverty's argument: at most it establishes that the existing situation is bad, not that it would be improved by the healing of Wealth. Moreover, or so Poverty claims, it rests on a failure to distinguish between beggary, which she admits is an evil, and being poor, which she regards as a good (548–50). The latter she defines as 'living austerely, concentrating on one's work, not having any surplus but not having an insufficiency either' (553–4), in short, living at subsistence level; and she says it produces 'wiry, wasplike men, deadly to their enemies' (561)—men, no doubt, like the Wasps of an earlier play who defeated the Persians by land and sea (*Wasps* 1060–1101)—whereas the products of wealth are 'gouty, pot-bellied, thick-calved, obscenely fat men' (559–60) who are inclined to be hubristic (564) and, if they are in politics, to plot against the people (569–70). And here (571) Chremylus admits that Poverty is telling the truth.

Two further arguments by Chremylus—that poverty must be an evil because men shun and flee from it (575) and that wealth must be better than poverty because Zeus is wealthy and Zeus surely

---

[30] Cf. Süss, 'Scheinbare und wirkliche Inkongruenzen in der Dramen des Aristophanes', 311–12.

knows what is best (579–80)—are rebutted in turn by Poverty, and with that rational argument virtually ends. It may well be felt that Poverty has made the most solid points; at any rate she has put forward at least two arguments to which Chremylus has failed to find a satisfactory answer:

1. that if all men are made rich, and so are able to live in idleness, free men will abandon productive work and slaves will become unobtainable, with the result that the new life will be much more miserable than the old (507–34);
2. that a state with a mainly poor (but not *very* poor) population will be better able to defend itself than one whose people have been enervated by wealth (558–61).

These arguments are far from invulnerable. They are inconsistent with one another (for how can people be enervated by a wealth that will reduce, not increase, their standard of living?), and the first is not even consistent with itself (since possession of money will not deter people from working if there are no goods on which they can spend the money). Nor is it hard to find rational rejoinders to them (e.g. that slaves could be bred or obtained by warfare; that a rich state could defend itself by building a powerful fleet and hiring mercenary soldiers and sailors). But the fact is that Chremylus offers no such rejoinder. Throughout the debate, once his initial statement of his case has been challenged, his main weapons of argument are emotionalism, cursing, and sarcasm. Again, how does the *agōn* end? At the close of a normal Aristophanic *agōn*, either the loser admits defeat[31] or the chorus or other arbiter declare a winner[32] or declare themselves convinced by the single speaker.[33] Here it is Chremylus who breaks off the debate, and the words in which he does so suggest on the face of it that he is intellectually convinced that Poverty is in the right, and that only emotion and prejudice make him deaf to her arguments (598–600):

Get to hell out of here, and don't utter another sound—because you won't persuade us even if you convince us.

Poverty, after brief resistance, departs with the words, 'I tell you, the time will yet come when you'll send for me to come back here' (608–9),

---

[31] *Clouds* 1102.
[32] *Knights* 943–59 (Demos takes his ring from Paphlagon and gives it to the Sausage-Seller); *Wasps* 725–6; *Frogs* 1467–71.   [33] *Birds* 627–8; *Ass.* 710.

to which Chremylus replies, 'When we do, you'll come back; but for now, *get out!*' (610), which, again, might be thought to suggest that he recognizes despite himself that the banishing of Poverty cannot be permanent, but prefers even a brief experience of wealth to none. It has been argued, too, as by Heberlein,[34] that when Chremylus does become wealthy his wealth takes decidedly inconvenient forms, with kitchen utensils being turned to gold, silver, ivory, and other such materials (812–15), which in some cases results in their being quite unsuitable for their proper purposes. Even if we are not prepared to put as much weight as Heberlein does on a single casual reference, in a quite different context (287), to the legend of Midas, we may still wonder if Chremylus has not fallen into the same trap as the Phrygian king.[35]

To this point I have been putting the case, as fairly as I can, for the ironic interpretation of *Assemblywomen* and *Wealth*. But can it be upheld? Are the plans of Praxagora and Chremylus in fact presented as failures? And which side, if either, are we really to take to be victorious in the *agōn* of *Wealth*?

The second halves of both plays consist of a series of self-contained scenes, and we may begin by considering these in turn. The first relevant scene in *Assemblywomen* is that between Chremes[36] and the Dissident. The naïvety of the former is no doubt sometimes laughable, but the opportunism of the latter is contemptible, especially when he abruptly changes his attitude as soon as he hears of the splendid free dinner (834–52) and says he will use violence and robbery, if necessary, to get a share of the food (860–6)—a procedure which he describes as 'helping the community' (861): in his opinion the duty of a good citizen is to take all the benefits the state offers while contributing as little as possible in return (cf. 777–9). His attitude, if at all widespread, would be the ruin of any society, and he is given no positive qualities whatever. He does, indeed, at the end (872–6) give us to understand that he has had an idea (he does not tell us what it is) that will enable him to get in and have dinner;

---

[34] Heberlein, 'Zur Ironie im *Plutus* der Aristophanes', 45–6.

[35] The story of Midas' 'golden touch' was known to Aristotle (*Pol.* 1257^b 14–17), and it may safely be assumed that it was known to Aristophanes and his audience: see L. E. Roller, 'The Legend of Midas', *Classical Antiquity*, 2 (1983), 310.

[36] For convenience I designate thus, with Rogers and Ussher, the character who in this scene is preparing his property for surrender to the state, but I doubt very much whether he is in fact intended to be the same person as the Chremes of 372–477; see my paper in 'Act Division in Old Comedy', *BICS* 31 (1984), 139–52.

but before he makes this prediction we have already had opportunities to form an opinion on his powers of prophecy. He did not believe that the public would surrender their possessions (772); later we hear that they are already doing so, in Chremes' neighbourhood at any rate (805–6). He expects that the women will 'piss' on him (832), i.e. treat him (and men generally) with disdain; in fact they are at once heard issuing a general invitation to dinner. After these wrong predictions the natural expectation, when he goes off in the hope of cheating or forcing his way into the dining-hall, is that he will be wrong again; and if he does prove to be wrong, no spectator will regret it. The statement in 1133 that Blepyrus is the only citizen who has not yet dined is hardly to be taken as evidence that the Dissident has succeeded in getting in; even if it were legitimate to take 1133 as an implied reference to a one-scene character about whom we have had no occasion to think for over 250 lines, *monos*, 'alone', would be an unsafe word on which to base such deductions, considering how often it is used in an exaggerated way to splotlight an individual with little or no thought of literal accuracy.[37]

The lot of the young man Epigenes, who becomes the victim of three lecherous crones, is much more likely than the Dissident's to gain our sympathy, particularly as he at any rate has done nothing to deserve it.[38] This scene has been very variously evaluated in recent scholarship. Konstan and Dillon[39] view it positively, 'not as a critique of the women's communist experiment but as its most glorious expression, the randy, boisterous, grotesque triumph of comic energy'; for Saïd[40] on the other hand it is pervaded with the miasma of death, and serves as a refutation of Praxagora's

---

[37] In Aristophanes, cf esp. *Clouds* 365 (contradicted by 264–5, 423–4, etc.); *Peace* 130 (the same fable that says the beetle flew to heaven also says the eagle flew there first!), 739; *Frogs* 1453 (the second half of the line contradicts the first); *Wealth* 948. The characterization in *Ass.* 730–876 has been well discussed by G. Maurach, 'Interpretationem zur attischen Komödie', *Acta Classica*, 11 (1968), 3–7, although his term 'Dummkopf' is distinctly unfair to Chremes, who has quite enough sense to know when the Dissident is trying to take advantage of him (867–71).

[38] We cannot hold it against him that he wishes to seduce an unmarried citizen girl. Under the old dispensation this would have made him a *moichos*, the equivalent of an adulterer, but Praxagora has established full sexual freedom for citizen women (except for certain rules prescribed in the interests of equality) and has indeed effectively prevented men from resorting instead to slaves and prostitutes (718–24). Epigenes therefore is acting as Praxagora expected and intended that men should act.

[39] Konstan and Dillon, 'The Ideology of Aristophanes' *Wealth*', 382.

[40] Saïd, *'L'Assemblée des femmes'*, 58–60.

promise of a world free from hate and jealousy, theft and abduction, discord and misery. We may perhaps derive some assistance in our interpretations by considering more generally the attitude of Old Comedy to youth and age. If we do, we will find that Old Comedy, in marked contrast to New, throughout displays a systematic bias in favour of older and against younger men. The rejuvenation of the old is a favourite theme, and in other plays as well as this one sexual success with attractive young women is the almost exclusive pre-rogative of the older male.[41] The Aristophanic comic hero, if male, is regularly old;[42] indeed young male characters of any kind are rather rare, and when they do appear they are quite often shown under-going some kind of discomfiture. Bdelycleon in *Wasps* may succeed in weaning his father away from the life of a juror, but thereafter he proves totally unable to control the old man, who even succeeds in knocking him down (1384–6), and by the final scene (1474–1537) Bdelycleon seems to have given up the struggle. In *Birds* the father-beater (1337–71) and the young *sykophantēs* (1410–68) both fail to gain what they expected to gain from their visits to Cloud-cuckoo-ville. In *Lysistrata* the only young male character, Cinesias, is thoroughly bamboozled by his wife. Aristophanes' young men are typically self-confident, cocksure of their ability to get their way, and arrogant in their superiority to other forms of humanity; and it appears to be one of the functions of comedy to take them down a peg. Sometimes they are worsted by older men, sometimes by women; that a young man of the most objectionable type, Pheidip-pides, walks out of *Clouds* insolently triumphant[43] is one of many

[41] Dikaiopolis (*Ach.* 1198–1221); Demos (*Knights* 1389–95); Philocleon (*Wasps* 1341 ff.); Trygaeus (*Peace*); Peisetairos (*Birds* 1634–end); Blepyrus (*Ass.* 1138). No young free male enjoys such a success in any surviving Aristophanic comedy; there is only the Scythian slave in *Th.* 1172–1225, and even he is being duped by the elderly Euripides and has to pay heavily for his few minutes with young Elaphion—he loses his quiver and his prisoner, and can probably expect severe punishment for neglecting his duty.

[42] Dikaiopolis; Strepsiades (*Clouds*); Trygaeus; Peisetairos; Euripides' kinsman ('Mnesilochus') (*Th.*); Chremylus. Dionysus in *Frogs*, as a god, is of indeterminate age, but he is fat (*Frogs* 200) and physically unfit (128 and the rowing scene). In *Wasps* the young Bdelycleon is formally the hero, since it is he who conceives and imple-ments the 'Great Idea' (on this concept see my edn. of *Ach.* 11–13), but Philocleon is more comic, more ingenious and more lovable, and he triumphs in the end (see text above). Only the Sausage-Seller in *Knights* is unequivocally a hero and unequivocally young.

[43] Martha Nussbaum, 'Aristophanes and Socrates on learning Practical Wisdom', *YCS* 26 (1980), 78, suggests that Pheidippides goes into the *phrontistērion* at 1475 and is

uncomic features of that play. The general pattern is clear, and our
scene of *Assemblywomen* conforms to it. Indeed, from the comic
point of view it may actually be a merit of Praxagora's scheme
that it enables conceited young men to be treated as Epigenes is
treated here, while benefiting older men by giving them preferential
treatment as regards opportunities for sexual activity[44] and providing communal dinners which they are shown as particularly enjoy-
ing.[45] It is true, as Saïd has noted, that the Epigenes scene is
unusually dark in tone and heavily overladen with the imagery of
death;[46] that this contrasts sharply with the brightness of his and
the girl's love-songs earlier in the scene (952–75); and that she
suffers as well as he, though not so much. Yet perhaps the morbid
imagery only brings to our attention how absurdly Epigenes is
exaggerating his plight. He is not, after all, going to be killed, nor
under the terms of the new law[47] can there really be any question of
one of the old women detaining him (1099); and we may add that
unlike Blepyros (619–20) he will have quite enough energy left to
cope satisfactorily with his young lady when the two older ladies
have finished with him, for he must surely be supposed no less
capable than Peisetairos (*Birds* 1256) or Demos (*Knights* 1391,
where see my note) or the chorus of *Acharnians* (994) of copulating
three times in quick succession.

As to the claim made by the girl (1041–2) that 'if you establish this
law, you will fill the whole land with Oedipuses', if this is really an
attempt to raise an incest scare it is wildly misguided. There is no
reason why Praxagora's new social order should lead to any
increase in the incidence of Oedipal incest: for although children
will not know their fathers (635–50), there is no mention of any

thus caught up in the subsequent conflagration; but it is hard to believe that
Strepsiades would thus endanger the life of his only son, whom at 1464–6 he
regarded as dearest and a fellow victim of Socrates' and Chaerephon's villainy.
More likely Pheidippides goes impudently into his father's house, or nonchalantly
off by one of the side-passages, a godless father-beater who has got off scot-free.

[44] *Ass.* 626–34, 702–9.   [45] *Ass.* 848–50.
[46] *Ass.* 994–6, 1030–6, 1073, 1101 (see Ussher's note), 1105–11.
[47] The law provides only that a man wishing to have intercourse with a young
woman must first, on demand, give the same satisfaction to an older woman (*Ass.*
617–18, 693–701, 939–40, 986, 990, 1013–20, 1049–51); there is no indication that the
older woman has the right to detain him indefinitely. Epigenes at 947 does not say 'If
only I could have the pretty one!', for he knows that eventually he *will* have her; he
says 'If only I could have the pretty one *and her alone* (*monēn*)!'

proposal, such as was made by Plato[48] and by some later socialist
theorists,[49] for breaking the connection between a child and its
natural mother. In any case, incest is irrelevant to the context of
the girl's remark. She is not saying that the old woman is Epigenes'
mother, only that she is old enough to be his mother (1040); and it
seems likely that Aristophanes is here taking the same humorous
attitude to the Oedipus story as is taken in *Frogs* 1193–4; the most
terrible thing that happened to Oedipus was that he married a
woman much older than himself—the fact that this woman was
his mother was a trifle in comparison. If Aristophanes had wanted
to suggest that sexual communism would lead to widespread incest,
he could have directed our attention to the fact that under Praxagora's scheme it would be impossible to prevent accidental incest
between fathers and daughters unaware of their blood relationship;[50] but he has not dropped the least hint of this.

The allegation[51] that the communal feast at the end is unreal
partakes more than a little of unreality itself. Where, if not at the
feast, has the maidservant managed to get so gloriously drunk
(1112–24) on such high-quality wine? The joke that the entire
audience can look forward to an excellent dinner 'if they go off
home' (1148) is the same joke at their expense that we find made
at much greater length in two choral songs in *Lysistrata*,[52] where a
whole series of magnificent free-gift offers are dangled before the
audience and then unexpectedly snatched away. The audience of

[48] *R.* 5. 460c–d.
[49] Cf. Dom L. M. Deschamps, *Le Vrai Système* (Geneva, 1963), 170–1: '*Les Enfants
n'appartiendraient qu'à la société* ... Les femmes, qui auraient du lait sans être
enceintes, donneraient leur sein aux enfants indistinctement, et sans se soucier de
savoir s'ils sont ou s'ils ne sont pas à elles.' This was written about 1770; for more
recent examples of the same idea in theory and practice see Shafarevich, *The Socialist
Phenomenon*, 246, 270–1.
[50] Plato avoided the problem by imposing so strict a control over sex and procreation that each man could easily identify (by their dates of birth) the relatively small
subgroup of the younger generation which would contain his own biological offspring
if he had any (cf. Pl., *R.* 5. 461b–e). In Praxagora's society, on the other hand, sex and
procreation are completely unrestricted (*Ass.* 614–15) except for the two laws giving
priority to the old or ugly (nn. 44, 47).
[51] For which, see e.g. Süss, 'Scheinbare und wirkliche Inkongruenzen in der
Dramen des Aristophanes', 291–7.
[52] *Lys.* 1043–71, 1189–1215; cf. E. Fraenkel, in *Greek Poetry and Life: Essays Presented
to Gilbert Murray* (Oxford, 1936), 273–4. The idea of a pseudo-invitation to the
audience to share the characters' dinner reappears in Plautus, *Rudens* 1418–22
('you can all come to my party—in sixteen years' time), *Pseudolus* 1331–4, *Stichus* 775.

Assemblywomen had never expected to partake themselves of a feast which, like Blepyrus and Praxagora and the maid, belonged to the dramatic fiction; and the same character who extends the bogus invitation to them shows at once that *he* regards the feast as real enough, for his very next line is 'Now I'm going to hurry off to the dinner' (1149).

At the very end of the play, indeed, after describing the main dish of the feast in a lip-smacking word of seventy-nine syllables,[53] the chorus say to Blepyrus (1175–8):

Now you've heard this, get yourself a bowl, quick and fast, and then dash off there—taking some porridge to dine on.

And it may be asked: why should Blepyrus take a bowl of porridge with him, unless because he will find, on arrival at the dining-hall, that the fabulous meal is a mirage? Against this we may note that the chorus, like Blepyrus before them, promptly show by their own words ('we shall be dining', 1181) that they do *not* believe it a mirage.[54] The reason why Blepyrus is urged to take the precaution of bringing along some food of his own is more probably that there is a risk of his discovering that he has arrived too late and the food has all been consumed. Attendance at dinner has replaced attendance at the Assembly as the main duty of the Athenian male; and as formerly only punctual arrivals could be sure of receiving their pay for attending the Assembly (282–4, 290–3, 380–93), so now only punctual arrivals can be sure of getting their meal—and Blepyrus is the very last arrival (1133). Most of the others had finished about 200 lines earlier,[55] and now Blepyrus can only be assured that there is some Chian wine 'left over' (1139). There is no reason to believe that the feast in *Assemblywomen* is any more unreal than those which occur at or near the end of most other Aristophanic plays.

To come to more general considerations about *Assemblywomen*, both Saïd[56] and Foley[57] have argued that whether or not Praxagora's scheme is shown to be workable in its own terms, it is

[53] A small suggestion for the improvement of this word: for the obviously corrupt *-parao-* (1171) read *-paralo-* 'lightly salted' (cf. *Ach.* 1158 with my note): salt is in place here as a seasoning, between silphium and honey.

[54] This is ignored by Süss, 'Scheinbare und wirkliche Inkongruenzen in den Dramen des Aristophanes', 297.

[55] Epigenes, when he enters at 938, is evidently coming *from* the meal; his situation is similar to that foreshadowed in 691–701.   [56] Saïd, *L'Assemblée des femmes*, 55.

[57] Foley, 'The "Female Intruder" Reconsidered', 16–18.

presented as resting on a value system which the audience are intended to find unacceptable. When, however, we ask what this supposedly unacceptable value system is, it turns out to be identical with that which commonly prevails in Old Comedy. For Saïd, the new order is presented as a bad one inasmuch as it assumes that the sole legitimate interests of human beings consist in 'the satisfaction of their alimentary and sexual needs'. I leave on one side the brilliant demonstration by Igor Shafarevich[58] that precisely this assumption has been made over many centuries by the majority of theorists of utopian or revolutionary socialism, and content myself with observing that in Aristophanic comedy generally, it is precisely food, drink and sex that are the typical rewards of the successful male hero. What Praxagora has done is to make these universally available—to enable every male Athenian (especially the older men) to live the life of a Dikaiopolis or a Trygaeus. If we like we can say, with Foley, that the men are 'reduced to living a drone-like life of pleasure in a world run by others'; but we could say just the same about the mythical inhabitants of the Isles of the Blest. The normal man in Old Comedy may, in Dover's words,[59] be the man who works and fights, but he would be a very abnormal man if he did more of either than he had to.

In *Wealth*—to pass now to that play—there are effectively five scenes which follow the entry of Wealth, healed of his blindness, into the house of Chremylus, and illustrate different aspects of the new order of things which his healing has inaugurated. In the first brief scene (802–22) Cario describes the new-found wealth of the house itself. We have seen that some of the blessings listed have been thought to be of little more benefit than Midas' golden bread and cheese, but the leading place in the recital is taken by things that are very obviously beneficial and of which Chremylus had often been short in the past[60]—corn, wine, oil, figs, perfume (806–11). The only item in the list that can really be accused of being a mixed blessing or worse is the ivory *ipnos*, if, as is probable, this means

[58] Shafarevich, *The Socialist Phenomenon, passim*; he summarizes his findings on pp. 258–69 (cf. also pp. 3–6, where he shows that Praxagora's programme as a whole is almost identical with 'the classic statement of the Marxist program contained in the *Communist Manifesto*').

[59] K. J. Dover, *Aristophanes, 'Clouds'* (Oxford, 1968), p. liii.

[60] Like the members of the chorus, he had often had to supplement his diet by gathering wild plants (253).

'oven'; for an ivory oven would quickly destroy itself by burning. We need not, however, suppose that the audience are meant to deduce that this (still less Wealth's other gifts) is not worth having. As Sobolevsky has pointed out,[61] poor men's fantasies about being rich are not restricted by considerations of practicality or convenience. The Russian peasants whose saying Sobolevsky cites—'If I were rich I'd lie summer and winter on a hot hot stove wearing a fur coat, and I'd eat fat cabbage soup with honey-cakes'—were not saying that being rich can be hazardous to your health; they were saying that rich people, unlike themselves, were never cold or hungry. In this connection it is worth noting how often in this play we are reminded that poverty and hunger are close companions.[62]

In the second scene (823–958) we see the restoration to prosperity of an honest man who had become poor not through extravagance nor even through bad luck, but because he did what everyone should do[63] and helped his friends when they needed help (830); and we also see the deserved impoverishment of an informer (sykophantēs). The honest man has come to Chremylus' house in order to dedicate to Wealth the cloak and shoes which for thirteen years were the only ones he had (842–8), and inevitably it has been suggested by some[64] that we are meant to regard his piety as hypocritical because his offering is of very small value. Small indeed it may be, but surely he offers it because it is all he has to offer. Everything else he possesses has just been given him by the Wealth-god, and he evidently feels, very humanly, that he wants to thank the god by giving him something of his own: one does not show one's gratitude to a benefactor by handing back one of his gifts almost immediately after receiving it. And if there is no irony in this part of the scene, there is certainly none in the rest of it, nor any sign that we are intended to see any redeeming features in the informer.

The scene that follows (959–1096) seems to show the new system

[61] S. J. Sobolevsky, Eirene, 1 (1960), 98–9. Earlier in the same article Sobolevsky makes out a convincing case for 'oven' as the meaning of ipnos here.
[62] Wealth 219, 504, 536, 539, 543–4, 562, 594–7, 628, 762–3, 1005.
[63] K. J. Dover, Greek Popular Morality in the Time of Plato and Aristotle (London, 1974), 177–8 cites ample evidence for the proposition that 'a good man was expected to invite his friends to share his good fortune'.
[64] e.g. Maurach, 'Interpretationem zur attischen Komödie', 10.

working much less satisfactorily: we see a young man, far less attractively presented than Epigenes in the earlier play, repudiating with scorn and insult an elderly mistress who had plied him with lavish gifts to retain his affections. It is true that the woman describes him as *chrēstos* (977), but she is there speaking of the past (975, 978), and in any case is referring not to his moral qualities but to his (obviously mercenary) attentiveness to her needs (977–8). Only two things are we told that can be thought to count in his favour. Yet these two things are crucial. They are that the young man was poor (976) and that he had the burden of supporting his mother and at least two unmarried sisters (984–5). The woman, on the other hand, was rich—the kind of person who can travel in a carriage to Eleusis for the Mysteries (1014–15); and both by the standards of Chremylus (223–6, 345) and by those of the honest man of the previous scene (830) she ought to have shared her wealth ungrudgingly and without making any demands in return. Certainly the youth was sponging on her, but as he shows by his behaviour when once independent of her, he hated every minute of it: we must presume that like so many others in these two plays, he had no other means of making an adequate living. With no marketable asset except his good looks, he has been forced into a life that he finds repugnant, and his reaction when able to escape is natural. If it makes him forget a moral obligation he has incurred,[65] Chremylus makes him accept that obligation—perhaps (though this is not made explicit) under threat of losing his new-found wealth if he does not. The old woman's complaint that Wealth has not fulfilled his promise 'always to help the victims of wrong' (1026) is ill founded, as perhaps even she will admit in the end when she gets the young man back after all (1201) and incidentally retains her own riches (at any rate she never complains of having lost them).

The fourth scene (1097–1170) brings Hermes down from heaven to fulminate threats of destruction against Chremylus and his household. It appears (1113–16) that since Wealth has regained his sight, no one any longer sacrifices to the (other) gods. It has been complained[66] that he wished 'the wicked and the godless' to become poor, and to his expectation that in his new world every-

[65] The obligation to treat well a person who has treated him well (1029) and not to discard her merely because she is of no further use to him (cf. 1084–5).

[66] e.g. H.-J. Newiger, *Metapher und Allegorie: Studien zu Aristophanes* (Munich, 1957), 157, 174.

body would be 'virtuous and rich and reverent towards the gods' (497). What, though, does reverence towards the gods (*to ta theia sebein*) mean? It means reverence towards those gods who hold power at any given time. Zeus is lord of the universe now, and so men should revere Zeus; but in the Golden Age (Hesiod, *Works* 109–111; Cratinus, fr. 165K = 176 Kassel–Austin), and when Kronos was lord of the universe, it was men's duty to revere Kronos. If on the other hand Zeus should be deposed by (say) Peisetairos and the birds, it would become men's duty to revere Peisetairos and the birds. What is dangerous and wrong, because it risks incurring the anger of Zeus, is to deny his power and the duty owed him *while he still holds that power* and demands that duty: this was the religious offence of Socrates in *Clouds*. We should know by now that Greeks believed it was their duty to obey the gods, not because the gods were good or deserved obedience, but because they were powerful and could punish disobedience. And in *Wealth*, as Chremylus told the incredulous Wealth-god early on (124–6), the power of Zeus to punish disobedience, or to enforce his will in any way, evaporates as soon as Wealth recovers his sight. Wealth himself is now the greatest of divine powers, and all human worship is naturally turned to him (823–48, 958, 1088–9, 1191–3). Treason against the gods, like treason against one's sovereign or country, is only punishable if it fails. As Hermes himself points out, by means of an allusion to the seizure of Phyle by Thrasybulus in 403 (1146), what Chremylus and his friends have done is to *lead a successful revolution* against the selfish divine oligarchy that ruled the universe and to install Wealth as a benevolent, democratically minded despot.

The final scene, involving the priest of Zeus Soter, continues this theme, and we learn that Zeus Soter himself has deserted to his enemy's camp.[67] His behaviour is the final proof of Chremylus'

---

[67] That this, as recently argued by Konstan and Dillon, 'The Ideology of Aristophanes' *Wealth*', 383 (cf. earlier Rogers *ad loc.* and R. F. Willetts, *Blind Wealth and Aristophanes*, Inaugural Lecture, (Birmingham, 1970), 4–5), is the correct interpretation of *Wealth* 1189–90 I have no doubt at all. The interpretation offered by the scholia, followed e.g. by van Leeuwen, *ad loc.* and Newiger, *Metapher und Allegorie*, 171, is that the Wealth-god is being spoken of as the new Zeus Soter; but this does not fit what is said:

CHREMYLUS. Zeus Soter is with us here; he has come of his own accord.
PRIEST. That's all right, then.

The Wealth-god did not come to Chremylus' house *automatos*: he was brought there by Chremylus, and was decidedly reluctant to enter (230–44). Nor would the priest

earlier statement (146) that 'everything is subordinate to wealth'. Zeus, like everyone else, would rather be rich than poor; and if the only way to be rich is to become a subject instead of a ruler, then he will become a subject! Thus in the end after all there is no question of men being disobedient to the gods. Men and gods are all on the same side: they are all worshippers of Wealth, they all have the blessing of Wealth, and they can all unite in escorting Wealth to his new home (or rather his old home) in the opisthodomos of the Parthenon (1191-3).

So far then as these 'exemplificatory' scenes are concerned, there is no reason to doubt that the audience are intended to take a positive attitude both to the revolution of Praxagora and to that of Chremylus. It is true that certain important questions, which any thoughtful modern student of economics or political science would raise, are in these plays neither raised nor answered. Thus in *Assemblywomen*, as Saïd and Foley have both recently emphasized,[68] the *polis* is reorganized essentially on the model of an *oikos*, as is natural seeing that the reorganization is done by women (expert managers of *oikoi* who have hitherto had no part whatever in the management of the *polis*), and the result is that, by and large, only those aspects of life are catered for which normally come within the framework of the *oikos*—food (*Ass.* 673-92), clothing (653-4), sex (613-34) and procreation (implied in 635ff.). Agricultural work is to be done by slaves (651), but the hundred and one other kinds of work necessary to the life of a civilized community are not mentioned at all.

This omission can perhaps be set aside as a simplification, passing over details of little comic value; if Praxagora had been pressed on the matter we may suppose that she would have replied, like Chremylus[69] and Phaleas of Chalcedon,[70] that the crafts too would be in the hands of slaves. It would be a more serious inadequacy if it were true, as Foley claims,[71] that Praxagora's scheme ignores such

have replied with an expression of satisfaction (*pant' agatha*) to the news that the very name of his own patron god had been usurped by another: rather he is saying in effect 'I am glad to know that Zeus Soter has become a worshipper of Wealth, because it means that I, his currently starving (1174) priest, can safely do likewise.'

[68] Saïd, 'L'*Assemblée des femmes*', 52; Foley, 'The "Female Intruder" Reconsidered', 14-21.
[69] *Wealth* 517-18.
[70] Arist., *Pol.*1267^{b}15. We do not know whether Phaleas proposed, as Praxagora does, that agricultural labour also should not be personally performed by citizens.
[71] Foley, 'The "Female Intruder" Reconsidered', 18.

crucial aspects of civic life as legislation, judgement, and war. But in fact these are not ignored. The entire second half of the play is based on, and displays the consequences of, two legislative enactments made by the women, that for the communization of property and that for equal rights in respect of sex. No doubt the feminine tradition of leaving well alone (215 ff.) will ensure that these laws once made are not altered, but this is to be seen as a welcome change from the baffling succession of enactments, repeals, and re-enactments to which, according to the characters, male Athens has become addicted.[72] As regards judgement, there is indeed no provision for private civil litigation, because there is no private property to be the subject of dispute (655–61); but there can still be crimes against the community which require punishment, and machinery will exist to provide it (663–6). That the punishment proposed is of a domestic character—deprivation of food, seemingly a common disciplinary measure for slaves[73]—does not in itself mean that it is inappropriate for a *polis*: it is the nearest equivalent in a moneyless, propertyless society of that most common of Athenian penalties, the fine.[74]

As to war, while it is certainly unlikely that Praxagora's state would wage aggressive war (for its citizens are presumed to have everything they need for a contented life), defensive war is by no means ignored: indeed special measures are proposed to honour the brave and put the cowardly to shame (678–80), and the title chosen for Praxagora is not, say, 'ruler(ess)' but 'general' (246, 491, 727, 835). What Praxagora's new Athens does apparently renounce is participation in international power politics; and just as well, considering what an incoherent mess the men have made of it (193–203).

In *Wealth* one must presume that international power politics will itself be abolished. If 'everything is subordinate to wealth' (*Wealth* 146), then all wars must have economic causes, and once everybody is rich there will no longer be anything to fight about. The most

---

[72] *Ass.* 193–203, 797–8, 812–29.   [73] Cf. *Wasps* 435.

[74] It duly reappears two millennia later, in 1652, in the 'platform' of the English Digger leader Gerrard Winstanley (see G. Winstanley, *The Law of Freedom and Other Writings* (Harmondsworth, 1973)). In the society he envisages, the final punishment for a wide variety of offences (from assault on a public officer and abduction of another man's wife to failure to work, persistent waste of food, and offering or accepting wages) is temporary or permanent enslavement under a taskmaster, and if enslaved persons 'prove desperate, wanton or idle . . . the taskmaster is to *feed them with short diet*, and to whip them' (p. 335; cf. pp. 379–89).

obvious flaw in the utopia of *Wealth* is rather that the whole thing is based on a miracle: in real life there is no way of ensuring that all and only the virtuous are wealthy. Or is there, perhaps? What if one assumes, as the characters in the play do,[75] that all large fortunes have been acquired dishonestly? If that is really so, then in a democratic state it is only necessary for prosecutors and jurors to do their duty and convict the rich of whatever crimes they have committed, and distribute the proceeds of confiscation among the poor, thereby abolishing before very long both inequality and poverty. If this has not in practice been done, it is because most prosecutors are selfish (like the one who is a character in the play) and most jurors less than conscientious, sitting not to do justice but to draw pay, and cheating the allotment system to increase their earnings.[76]

However, that line of thought is not deeply explored in *Wealth*: the play is content to assume a miracle. In this it resembles many another Aristophanic comedy in which a fantasy solution is found for a very real problem. In *Wealth* the audience are asked to suspend disbelief and assume it to be *possible* to have wealth distributed in accordance with desert, and the question for debate in the *agōn* is whether such redistribution would or would not be *desirable*.

We have already seen (pp. 257ff.) how one might interpret the *agōn* in an ironic sense, regarding Poverty as the real winner of the argument. But does the author intend his audience to take it so? This question may be divided into two:

1. Are the two strong arguments that Poverty advances (507–34, 558–61) intended to be accepted as valid?
2. Does the general tone of the debate suggest that Poverty is right when she complains that Chremylus and Blepsidemus are displaying mental blindness (581) in refusing to listen to her?

Heberlein holds that Poverty's argument from the uselessness of wealth when there is nothing it can buy (507–34) is to be accepted as valid;[77] this he sees as being proved by the fact that Chremylus

---

[75] See the passages cited in n. 10.

[76] *Wealth* 972 (alluding to jurors who sat to try cases on days when they had not been selected by lot to do so), 1166–7 (alleging that 'all the jurymen' contrive to get themselves registered in more than one of the ten standing panels of jurors so as to increase their chances in the daily allotment).

[77] Heberlein, 'Zur Ironie im *Plutus* des Aristophanes', 44–5.

answers it, not with counter-argument, but with a curse (526). Certainly there are some weaknesses in the position taken up by Chremylus hereabouts. In reply to Poverty's claim that if people can live in wealthy idleness they will not want to work and nothing will be produced, Chremylus says that the slaves will do all the work (517–18); and when he is challenged to explain where the slaves will come from, Aristophanes carefully avoids letting him give the easy reply 'from among the barbarians'; his slaves are going to be Greeks, kidnapped and sold by bandits in Thessaly (520–1). Thus he lands himself in a contradiction, for the new order which was going to abolish crime (497) will itself have to be kept going by crime. Nor does he, as he might have done, pre-empt the whole question by pointing out that the bounty of the Wealth-god will in future make work unnecessary—an idea well in the tradition of Old Comic utopianism exemplified by Crates' *Beasts* or Pherecrates' *Miners*.[78] In short, the author makes Poverty's argument seem a good deal stronger than it actually is, and logically at 526 Chremylus seems beaten.

But is he? Poverty's argument has culminated in the claim that after the redistribution of wealth, Chremylus will find himself 'leading a far more wretched life than you do now' (526). And to this an answer *is* given. It is given, with tremendous power, in 535–47. It is that for very many people, a more wretched life than their present one is inconceivable. The grinding misery of it all is described in words that can scarcely be paralleled in Greek literature:[79]

What good thing can you provide, except bath-house blisters[80] and crowds of half-starved kids and old women? Not to mention the innumerable lice and gnats and fleas that torment us, buzzing around our heads, making us wake up and saying 'You'll starve; up you get!' And then, having a bit of rag instead of a cloak; for a bed, a rush mattress full of bugs that won't let one sleep; for a carpet, a rotting mat; for a pillow, a good big stone at one's head; to eat, not bread but mallow shoots, not barley cake but dry radish leaves;

---

[78] Crates, fr. 14–15K = 16–17 Kassel–Austin, Pherecr., fr. 108; cf. Pherecr., fr. 130, Telecl., fr. 1, Metag., fr. 6, Nicophon, fr. 13K = 20 Edm.

[79] The passage might have served well as an epigraph for de Ste Croix's *Class Struggle in the Ancient Greek World*, which in fact never quotes it nor (so far as I can discover) refers to it.

[80] Alluding to the practice of poor people frequenting the public baths in winter to warm themselves at the stoves (cf. 952–4).

instead of a bench, the top of a broken jar; instead of a kneading-tray, a rib of a casket, and broken at that. Doesn't that [Chremylos sarcastically concludes] show what *great* benefits you bestow on all mankind?

No warmth, no proper clothing or bedding or furniture, no food worthy of the name: *that* is what real poverty is—and such a person has nothing to lose. Nor is this condition much more extreme than what we have seen and will see in other parts of the play. Chremylus himself, indeed, is not abjectly poor; but we have already been told that there are 'many . . . honest men who had no corn' (218–19) and that his friends will probably be found 'toiling themselves in the fields' (224)—they at any rate will not be frightened by Poverty's prediction of a future in which they will have to do their own work! Twice we hear that these men eat wild thyme roots (253, 283), which chimes with the mention of mallow shoots and dry radish leaves in 544; and their life is described as 'cold and comfortless' (263). Later, we meet an honest man who has worn the same cloak and shoes for thirteen years (842–7), and we can no doubt see for ourselves how full of holes they both are; in winter this man had haunted the public baths for the sake of warmth (952–4; cf. 535). In fact almost all the miseries described in 535–47 appear elsewhere in the play, and in no case is there any suggestion that they are imaginary. Indeed if anything Chremylus is underplaying one important concomitant of poverty, namely disease and early death, no doubt because this is a subject that comedy habitually avoids[81] (though even this taboo is broken by the Aristophanes of our period, who mentions pleurisy as a scourge of the poor in winter in *Ass.* 417).

In other words, though Poverty's argument might have some force in a case like that of Chremylus himself, it has none at all as applied to those who, as he and the audience know, are truly, desperately, radically poor.[82] However little revolution is likely to benefit such people, their actual situation is so hopeless that it is natural and inevitable that they will want revolution nevertheless. Poverty does not see this, because she is thinking only (one might say) in terms of economic theory, and thinking, moreover, from the

---

[81] It has often been noted that comedy makes no known reference to the great plague of 430–426.

[82] I borrow this last expression from V. Ehrenberg, *The People of Aristophanes*[2] (Oxford, 1951), 172.

standpoint of the well-to-do. Note how in 528–30 she argues that universal wealth will dry up the supply of *luxury* goods (coverlets, perfumes, coloured clothes), which are of little interest at present to Chremylus and less to the chorus.

Chremylus' splendid tirade at last forces Poverty to recognize the misery of the very poor, but she dismisses it (548) into a separate category of beggary rather than being poor, using a verbal distinction that has rightly been characterized as sophistic.[83] Her definition of the good kind of being poor (533–4) is something fairly close to the sort of life Chremylus himself has been leading: 'living austerely, concentrating on one's work, not having any surplus but not having insufficiency either'. The distinction does not appeal to Chremylus.

Demeter! what a happy life you've set down for him—scrimping and toiling, and at the end not leaving enough behind to pay for his funeral!

In any case, every poor person in the audience would know that being poor can easily slide into beggary in times of adversity, for instance as a result of poor crops, illness, or war. If it is agreed that beggary is bad (and apparently Poverty now concedes this), then being poor must be bad too: walking on a tightrope over a crocodile-infested river is but little better than being thrown into it.

The argument that poverty makes better soldiers than wealth (558–561) is one that would have been fairly generally accepted,[84] but it presupposes one thing: that the soldiers are adequately fed. That is why Chremylus' one-line reply is devastating:

I suppose it's in order to make them waspish warriors that you starve them.

Nor does he have any difficulty with Poverty's next argument, for it suits his case as well as it does hers. It is that rich men are typically hubristic, dishonest, and anti-democratic (564–70). Chremylus entirely agrees: only, while he believes that these men are rich because they are dishonest (30–1, 35–8, 502–3), Poverty's argument only has force if she assumes that they are dishonest because they are rich—and she herself gives the lie to any such assumption by letting it slip out that the men in question (assumed to be politi-

---

[83] W. Schmid, *Geschichte der griechischen Literatur*, iv (Munich, 1946), 380, speaks of 'prodikeische Synonymik'. On sophistic features of Poverty's arguments in general, see Heberlein, 'Zur Ironie im *Plutus* des Aristophanes', 40–2.

[84] Cf. Pl., *R.* 4. 422a–c, 8. 556b–e; for other references, see Dover, *Greek Popular Morality in the Time of Plato and Aristotle*, 111–12.

cians) become rich 'on public money' (569) *after* having made a start
in public life as poor, honest democrats (567–8). Like the men who
are driven by poverty to be thieves and burglars (565), they become
dishonest while and because they are poor, and their dishonesty
(embezzlement) makes them rich.

Thus it can be seen that three successive arguments raised by
Poverty have all been rather weak; and since even her strong
economic argument first had its effect blunted by the unsatisfactory conclusion on possible shortages of luxury goods (528 ff.) and
was then followed by Chremylus' great tirade, the balance of the
debate is now definitely against her. And now Chremylus produces
his own best argument. Poverty has been trying to prove that it is
better (better for the individual concerned) to be poor than to be
rich; but the universal consent of mankind holds otherwise (575).
Poverty replies that mankind are merely foolish (576–8) and the
gods know better; but that reply commits her to the most sophistic
and implausible of all her arguments, for she has to maintain that
Zeus is not rich (581–6). We and Chremylus know she is wrong: we
have already been told, and by a god, that if Zeus withholds wealth
from deserving mortals (whether Olympic victors or ordinary honest folk) he does so neither from poverty nor from benevolence but
from malice (87–92). The last word (594–7) is left to Chremylus, and
it combines several themes: that poverty is the main cause of crime,
that poverty equals hunger, and that it would be better even for the
gods if men were less poor:

You can find out from Hecate whether it's better to be wealthy or hungry.
She'll tell you that the 'haves' and the rich send her a dinner every month,
but the poorer mortals snatch it away before it's even set down.

There are men, in other words, who are desperate enough to
commit sacrilege for the sake of something to eat.

Thus from 527 onwards the whole trend of the *agōn* has been
against Poverty. Her arguments have become increasingly strained
and sophistic. She has extolled the blessings (themselves rather
dubious) of moderate poverty and ignored the widespread existence, and the even more widespread fear, of extreme poverty,
which Chremylus has vividly brought before the audience. At the
end of all this it scarcely matters that seventy lines earlier she
succeeded in establishing the theoretical point that a system of
universal wealth would be self-stultifying—and in any case, even

if she was right about that, it would leave most people no worse off
than they were to begin with. The order of presentation is strongly
in Chremylus' favour. So, let us not forget, is the horrific *appearance*
of Poverty (cf. 422–4). This is not the only place in the play where
the loser in an argument is allowed to make an effective point to
which no reasoned reply is given. In 907–19 the informer argues
that he and his like are essential to the control of crime. He is then
much abused, but no one suggests how he can be replaced—unless
indeed Aristophanes trusted his audience to remember that under
the new dispensation there would be no longer any crime to control.
In earlier plays too the losing side in an *agōn* is sometimes allowed to
state its case reasonably effectively, most notably Euripides in *Frogs*;
it remains the losing side. The final silencing of Poverty by Chremylus and Blepsidemus (598–612) no more proves her in the right than
the silencing of Pheidippides in *Clouds* 1447–51 proves that he was in
the right to offer to beat up his mother just before.

The ironic interpretation, then, of *Assemblywomen* and *Wealth*
cannot stand; nor can the subtler recent approaches which, while
varying in the details of their analysis, all agree that Aristophanes
takes a negative attitude to the sort of radical alterations of society
depicted in the plays. We seem driven after all at least to entertain
the possibility that a straightforward reading of the two plays is
correct. Let us sketch out what the main lines of such a reading
might be.

Assemblywomen and *Wealth* alike are simultaneously moral and
social comedies. From the moral point of view, *Assemblywomen* puts
the finger on selfishness as a major cause of Athens's current
political and economic difficulties. In determining state policy,
citizens take account only of personal or sectional interests (*Ass.*
197–8, 206–8); they obey laws and decrees only when it suits them
(762–8, 853–4) and would not even attend the assembly unless paid
to do so (183–8, 289–310, 380–2, 390–2); they never ask what they
can do for their country, but only what their country can do for
them (cf. 778–9.)[85] Hence the idea of turning over the city to the
women, who by the nature of their social role live mainly for others,
and who do not commit any of the common crimes to which
selfishness leads (435–54). But not only should the moral evil of

---

[85] The editors all assign these words to the Dissident as a statement of his
philosophy, but they are better taken as an indignant rhetorical question by Chremes.

selfishness be abolished: abolished too, if possible, should be the social evil of poverty[86]—the poverty that forces two typical Athenians to miss a meeting of the assembly because each has lost his only cloak (352–3, 535–48); that makes men dependent on state pay for their food (380–2); that makes January the month for going down with pleurisy (416–17); that leaves many without beds and bedding in winter (418–21) and makes it understandable when there is talk of compulsory requisitioning of corn for the benefit of the poor (422–6); that coexists with substantial wealth for other individuals (591–3); that is the main cause of crime (605, 667–9). This is achieved by Praxagora's scheme for the communization of society. It is true that in her new order no provision is made for luxuries (except in the sphere of food); but no one complains of their absence. It is true, too, that Praxagora's sexual communism may be felt to go a little far; but it is much more to the point that she is headed in the right direction. For what is being suggested is that the community will not prosper until its members think, or are made to think, of the community's interests first and not their own; nor can it be healthy while there is absolute, desperate poverty in its midst. It may well be that the citizen will be prepared to think a little less of his selfish interests without those interests having to be abolished by law. It may well be that the rich will see that the alleviation of poverty is in their interest as well as in that of the poor, and that moderate measures effecting some degree of redistribution will make extreme measures unnecessary. But something, somehow, has to be done about both evils. *Acharnians* did not advocate the declaration of what might now be called a 'war-free zone'[87] in defiance of assembly decisions; but it did advocate the making of peace.[88] *Clouds* did not advocate the violent destruction of philosophers' houses; but it did express hostility to philosophers. *Assembly-*

[86] On poverty and selfishness as the main evils against which Praxagora is struggling, see Saïd, '*L'Assemblée des femmes*', 49–51.

[87] It has become difficult to continue describing Dikaiopolis' private peace treaty as 'an impossible fantasy. . . that by its very nature could never actually happen' (de Ste Croix, *The Origins of the Peloponnesian War*, 365), when scores of British local authorities have espoused the yet more fantastic notion that the best way to secure immunity from nuclear attack is to undertake that you will do nothing to help deter such an attack or minimize its effects, and to do this (unlike Dikaiopolis) without gaining any reciprocal undertaking from the other side.

[88] Those who find this statement naïve should consult de Ste Croix, ibid. 363–7, 369–70 and D. M. MacDowell, 'The Nature of Aristophanes' *Acharnians*' *G & R* 30 (1983), 143–62.

women does not, at least not necessarily, advocate the abolition of private property; but it does advocate an attack on the evils of selfishness and poverty, and moreover implies that the two are interrelated.

In *Wealth* poverty is again in the centre of the author's field of vision, but the moral theme is perhaps more diffuse. Much is made of the virtue of generosity, which in the world as it is brings no benefits: the Honest Man found that the friends whom he had helped in the past cold-shouldered him when he was in need, and everyone is amazed when Chremylus invites his friends to share in his newly won good fortune (*Wealth* 340–2). Even the Old Woman is rewarded in the end for her liberality to her young man (1201). Much is made too of the contrary vice of meanness, of the person who has good fortune himself and grudges it to others—the miser. The archetypal miser in this play is Zeus, who blinded Wealth because he resented the prosperity of the virtuous (87–92), and who is not prepared to give even an Olympic victor a prize of real value (583–92). Wealth himself draws us a vivid little picture of the human miser (237–41):

If I happen to enter a miser's house, he at once buries me down under ground; and if then some honest friend of his comes asking to borrow a small sum of money, he says he's never seen me in his life.

Closely linked with miserliness is ingratitude—the ingratitude of Zeus, who 'is honoured only by the virtuous and just' (93–4) but does nothing for them in return (quite the contrary); of the gods generally, who have given men no recompense for their worship and sacrifice (1116–17, 1124–5); of the Honest Man's friends, who never repaid the help he had given them; of the young gigolo, who, whatever excuses can in fairness be made for him, is ready to break his mistress's heart as soon as he is no longer dependent on her. But the acme both of generosity and of gratitude is Wealth himself, who is only too willing, once he recovers his sight, to dispense his blessings freely to all who deserve them, and most of all to Chremylus, who was responsible for his cure. He is also the link between the moral and the social themes. The social theme is simple. As things are, wealth is almost exclusively in the hands of criminals, and this must be put right; once it is, the inhuman burden of poverty will be eased. In the play, the unjust distribution of wealth is rectified by a miracle; in real life it can be done by making malefactors of great wealth pay the proper penalty for their crimes. We have come a long way from *Knights* and *Wasps*. In those plays it was the villains, Cleon and his associates, who posed as the champions of the poor and were represented as persecuting the rich, and Aristophanes with the help of characters such as ‵Bdelycleon exposed what he saw as their humbug. Now a generation later it is the heroes, Praxagora and Chremylus, who are the champions of the poor; and Praxagora is allowed no effective opponent, Chremylus only the hideous, sophistic figure of Poverty and the detestable Informer. Clearly, something has changed; and the simplest hypothesis is that the change has been in the author.

Inevitably one is led to speculate (though we do not have the information to do more than speculate) on the causes of this change; and we are able to point to three or four factors that may have been at work. It is possible, indeed likely, that Aristophanes himself may have been among those who were considerably impoverished as a result of the defeat of 404. *Acharnians* 652–4 is often taken as evidence that Aristophanes lived or owned property on Aegina. If so, he will have lost his estate and become, not positively poor, but at any rate a good deal poorer than he had been. Thereafter, like everyone else, he had experienced the rule of the Thirty. These were some of the very men in whom a year or two earlier, in *Frogs* 718–37, he had recommended the Athenians to put their trust, and it would not be surprising if their tyrannical behaviour, and their shameful betrayal of all Athenian interests, created a particularly strong revulsion in the mind of one who had hitherto been inclined to regard their sort as *chrēstoi* and *kaloi kagathoi*.[89] Then, as Athens settled down under the restored democracy, and a comic dramatist could resume his normal activities, Aristophanes will soon have become aware that his spectators were on the whole worse off economically than they had formerly been, and that many of them (as some contemporary speeches show)[90] were very ready to listen to abuse of the rich; and even if he had no strong feelings of

[89] Giuseppe Mastromarco (in correspondence) has compared the possible effect on Aristophanes of the defeat of 404 and the rule of the Thirty with the way in which in Italy after the fall of Mussolini 'molti che erano stati convinti fascisti si trovarono a combattere il fascismo in nome di una ideologia contraria'.

[90] See esp. Lys. 22; also Lys. 7. 27; 14. 41–2; 16. 18; 18. 16–19; 19. 45–52; 27. 10–11; Isoc. 20. 11.ff.

his own, he may have felt it wise to accommodate himself somewhat to the feelings of his audience.

I suspect, however, that a factor as potent as any of these may have been Aristophanes' deep emotional involvement with the Attic peasantry. Seemingly a child of the city himself,[91] well versed in the latest artistic and intellectual fashions, he yet saw the country people as the healthiest element in Athenian society, as play after play makes plain;[92] and these country people had been injured far more than the townsmen by the war and its aftermath, their houses and fruit trees destroyed not once but twice, while those who had been settled abroad were suddenly uprooted and bundled back to Attica without thought of their chances of making a living. The backbone of the Athenian people was being crushed, and something had to be done about it. And Aristophanes—for whom, by the nature of his profession, nothing could ever be too fantastic to contemplate—became ready to dream radical dreams of what might be done.[93] Having for nearly a quarter of a century spoken unmistakably in the language of the well-heeled, he began to write like a spokesman of the barefoot, because the class he most admired had lost their shoes.[94]

[91] He was a member of the city deme of Kydathenaion (Platon. *Prolegomena de comoedia* 28. 2. 29a. 3, 32b. 2 Koster; cf. *IG* ii² 1740. 24 = *Agora* 15 12. 26), so presumably his family had lived in the city since before 508.

[92] Esp. *Acharnians*, *Peace*, and *Wealth*; cf. also *Knights* 805–8, *Birds* 109–11, *Ass.* 300–10. In *Wealth* it is worth noting that Chremylus appears to loathe the urban *cheirotechnai* almost as much as he does Poverty (617–18).

[93] It does not fall within the scope of this essay to inquire to what extent and in what form ideas similar to those expressed in *Wealth* and especially *Assemblywomen* had already been put before the public by others. In addition to the discussion by R. G. Ussher (*Aristophanes 'Ecclesiazusae'* (Oxford, 1973), 15–20), the essentials of this question have been briefly and well presented by G. B. Kerferd, *The Sophistic Movement* (Cambridge, 1981), 160–2, and I would agree with him that 'while we are unable to make particular attributions it can be taken as virtually certain that revolutionary theories about the rights and the position of women [and, I would add, about the structure of society generally] were in the air throughout Aristophanes' lifetime'. On the question of a specific written source for the proposal for community of women and children, with its remarkable parallels to Pl., *R.* 5, it should be noted that Aristotle's statement (*Pol.* 1266ᵃ 34–5) that no one but Plato had recommended these innovations refers, as the context shows, exclusively to writers of *politeiai*, i.e. *systematic* blueprints for improved forms of human society: he is not saying that similar ideas were not discussed before Plato in writings of other kinds.

[94] Versions of this paper were read at the Annual General Meeting of the Classical Association at Nottingham (14 Apr. 1983) and at a seminar at the Working Men's College, London (14 May 1983). Comic fragments are cited from Kock (K) unless otherwise stated.

15

The Assemblywomen: Women, Economy, and Politics

SUZANNE SAÏD

An assembly in which women, disguised as men, decide to entrust
the running of the state and the entire administration of all public
affairs to women; a 'generalissima' who founds a communism
even more radical than the communism of the *Republic* (all goods
are shared by all citizens and all women are available to all men,
whereas Plato limits the possession of goods, women, and children to the guardians alone); this is the picture of a topsy-turvy
world offered by Aristophanes to his Athenian audience in 393,[1]
in a comedy that with one blow does away with masculine
power, property, and marriage, the three pillars of the Greek
city. Is this, therefore, an apolitical work, an escapist play, a
gratuitous fantasy aimed at 'making people laugh by artificial
means, ungrounded in reality', as H. Van Daele proposes in his
introduction?[2]

It is easy to say, and it is not difficult to back up the argument. We
must, however, take the *Assemblywomen* seriously, if for no other
reason than because it puts gynaecocracy and communism on
stage, and thus brings together ethnography and philosophy. In
the ethnographic stories, from Herodotus to Strabo, these two
themes are used primarily as ways of talking about what is unciv-

---

[1] In the absence of didaskalia, we must rely on the allusions to the historical
situation present in the text itself, and the explanatory comments of scholia, in
order to date the *Assemblywomen*. All things being equal, it is agreed that the comedy
appeared during the archonship of Demostratus (393/2). R. G. Ussher *Aristophanes'
'Ecclesiazusae'* (Oxford, 1973), pp. xx–xxv discusses the question at length and
considers it could have been presented from the spring of 393 on.

[2] *Aristophane*, v: Budé edn. (Paris, 1930), 5–12.

ilized, and of keeping at arm's length things foreign to the socio-
political system of the Greeks.[3] In Plato's *Republic* they are used to
give a critical analysis of the existing order[4] and to contrast the
corrupt Athens of the fourth century with a utopian state. A utopia
in both senses of the word: 'a nowhere country' (ou-topia), since
this 'model (*paradeigma*) of the state as it should be' (472e) does not
yet exist and one can doubt that it ever will exist (Socrates himself
speaks of a 'pious wish', 450d); but also the 'country of happiness'
(eu-topia), since there the guardians will lead 'a happier life than
the blissful life of the victors of Olympia' (465d).

It is worth taking a look at the *Assemblywomen* and examining
the meaning of both gynaecocracy and communism in the comic
utopia, because nothing is gained by dissociating the two and
treating Praxagora's communist project as an after-thought introduced by Aristophanes 'to enliven the play'.[5] We would be even
farther from the point if we looked outside the play for 'political,
literary, personal, and moral reasons' to explain the choice of
themes and justify the extraordinary changes in 'the form, the
substance, and the spirit of this comedy' compared with previous
works of Aristophanes.[6] Let us rather pursue the three themes of
women's power and the common sharing of goods and of women, in
the order in which they appear in the play, and thereby bring to
light a series of parallels and connections. These themes develop
along the same lines: both use utopia as satire at the beginning ('it's
going badly' and no one has anything else to suggest) and again at
the end (an official statement of failure). At the same time they are
inevitably connected to each other: the common sharing of belongings is the necessary consequence of power exercised by women as
women, and the sharing of women is introduced only in order to
make the sharing of belongings possible.

[3] See S. Pembroke, 'Women in Charge: The Function of Alternative in Early Greek
Tradition and the Ancient Idea of Matriarchy', *Journal of the Warburg and Courtauld
Institute*, 30 (1967), 1–35, and M. Rosellini and S. Saïd, 'Usages de femmes et autres
nomoi chez les "sauvages" d'Hérodote', *Annali della Scuola Normale Superiore di Pisa*, 8/
3, 949–1005.
[4] On the link between criticism and utopia, see N. Frye, 'Varieties of Literary
Utopias', repr. in *The Stubborn Structure: Essays on Criticism and Society* (London,
1970), 111, and M. Finley, 'Utopianism Ancient and Modern', in *The Critical Spirit*,
coll. H. Marcuse (Boston, 1967), 3–5.
[5] As do Van Daele, *Aristophane*, and Ussher, *Aristophanes 'Ecclesiazusae'*, p. xv.
[6] See Van Daele, *Aristophane*, 6–7.

I. FROM THE 'POWER OF THE PEOPLE' (DEMO-CRACY) TO THE 'POWER OF WOMEN' (GYNAECO-CRACY)

Disruption: From the Failure of Democracy to Gynaecocracy

From the outset, when Praxagora, the heroine of the *Assembly-women*, decides to 'take in hand the affairs of state to give them a healthier impetus' (107–8), there exists, as always in Aristophanes, dissatisfaction with the way things are. This dissatisfaction takes a particularly strong form in a comedy in which the heroine asserts that 'everything's going badly', or, if one accepts Palmer's correction, that 'everything is absolutely rotten' (175).[7]

After the statement come the reasons why. Praxagora places the responsibility on the 'miscreants' (*ponēroi*) to whom the people always turn. It seems that things get worse with time because the 'honest chap' (*chrēstos*) quickly becomes a 'miscreant' and is always followed by someone even more of a miscreant than he (177–9).

This picture of an Athens in the grip of an incurable decadence owing to the corruption of its leaders is not new. As K. J. Dover recently pointed out,[8] attacking the current politicos, doubtless encouraged by a community nothing loath to see its leaders publicly belittled, is one of the themes dear to the heart of ancient comedy. In the *Assemblywomen*, however, these attacks on individuals, perhaps the inverse of a profound belief in the value of democratic institutions,[9] become blurred[10] and are replaced by a questioning of the community itself. But if we are to believe the oligarch who wrote the *Constitution of the Athenians*, such criti-

---

[7] The MS's text (*kai pherō ta tēs poleōs hapanta bares pragmata*) is kept by Ussher, *Aristophanes' 'Ecclesiazusae'*, and J. Huber, *Zur Erklärung und Deutung von Aristophanes' 'Ekklesiazusen'*, diss. (Heidelberg, 1974). The correction is adopted by Van Daele, *Aristophanes*.

[8] *Aristophanic Comedy* (Berkeley, 1972) 34–5. For the subjects of these attacks, see A. Meder, *Der athenische Demos zur Zeit des Peloponnesischen Krieges im Lichte zeitgenossischer Quellen*, diss. (Munich, 1938), 124–51, and J. Taillardat, *Les Images d'Aristophane: Études de langue et de style*,² (Paris, 1965), 408–23.

[9] C. H. Whitman, *Aristophanes and the Comic Hero²* (Cambridge, Mass., 1971) 200–1. I. Muller, 'Der Wandel der Stoffwahl und der komischen Mittel in den Komödien des Aristophanes durch die Krise des attischen Polis', in E. C. Welskopf (ed.), *Hellenische Poleis: Krise, Wandlung, Wirkung* (Berlin 1974), iii.

[10] There are only two allusions to Agyrrhius (102–4, 184–5). For their significance, see the comments of Ussher, *Aristophanes' 'Ecclesiazusae'*, and Huber *Zur Erklärung und Deutung von Aristophanes' 'Ekklesiazusen'*.

cisms were officially forbidden.[11] This is a far cry from the
Acharnians (425), in which Aristophanes made it clear that the
attacks were on individuals only, 'not the state, remember that I
said not the state' (515–16).[12] We are nearer the *Birds* (414), in
which Euelpides declares that he does not dislike Athens, at the
same time rejecting a state in which democratic equality is
nothing more than an opportunity for anyone to be ruined by
lawsuits or by fines (36–8); and nearer still to *Lysistrata* (411), in
which attacks on individuals are almost non-existent,[13] where
women lay the blame on a 'tempestuous populace' (170)[14] and
draw up a document of failure of 'the politics of the male' (the
male citizens continually make bad decisions on the most important questions (511), and everything goes from bad to worse
(517)). One should also cite the *Thesmophoriazusae* (411), in
which the women address just reproaches to men in general
(830–1); and the *Frogs* (405), in which the chorus calls the
citizens idiots (733) and invites them to 'change completely'
(*metaballein*) their actions and their way of choosing leaders
(734–5). The idea is pursued in *Plutus* (388), which shows an
Athens whence all justice has fled to the point that even the
blind know that a person can make a solid profit by doing
nothing good in times like these (48–50).

It is precisely because corruption has touched the whole of the
populace, all men act like 'rogues, thieves and sycophants' (436–8),
everyone has chosen to act unjustly by betraying the secret of the
council's deliberations (*boulē*) and by refusing to return the funds
that were entrusted to them before witnesses (446–50), that the
remedy can only be a fundamental change in the state. In the
Birds, the characters went looking for another 'place' (*topos*, 44),
in other words another 'state' (*polis*, 48), because for the Greeks,
man, the 'political animal', can only live within the bounds of a
polis. Given the impossibility of finding an acceptable one on earth,
they decide to establish one in the country of the birds. In the
Assemblywomen, they do not go off into the clouds, but prefer to

[11] Ps.-Xen., *Ath. Pol.*, 2. 18: 'We don't let comic poets make fun (*kōmōidein*) of the
people or malign them'.
[12] See also *Knights* (1356), in which the Sausage-Seller says that Demos is not
'responsible' (*aitios*) for past mistakes.
[13] There are only two jokes at the expense of Eucrates (103) and Peisandros (490).
[14] On the meaning of this line, see Taillardat, *Les Images d'Aristophane*, 386–7.

change the state while staying in place. The Athenians and the pupulace are replaced by women whose status in Athens is that of foreigners,[15] and they therefore constitute a separate group.[16]

This power acquired by the women constitutes a true revolution that only a total failure of the 'men's club',[17] called democracy, can justify. We have seen it before in *Lysistrata*[18] and we hear it again in the *Assemblywomen* in the two speeches in which Praxagora successfully pleads for a women's government.

In the first speech, a sort of general rehearsal, Praxagora begins by denouncing the people (that is, the men): 'It is you, the people (*dēmos*) who are responsible for all this' (205). At another moment she posits the arrival of women to power as the only way to be saved: 'It is into the hands of the women, you hear, that we must entrust the state' (210–11).

In the second speech she gives before the Assembly, reported by Chremes, the proposal to 'put the state into the hands of the women' (430) is justified by a criticism of the men, which follows a eulogy of the women (435–6).

Continuity: Gynaecocracy, Final Stage of the Corruption of Democracy

So the break from democracy to gynaecocracy is total, at least in appearance. But in reality the decision to hand over the power to the women is the logical result of certain tendencies, very deep but also very disastrous for Athenian democracy, and the utopia is here simply a displacement of the satire. This radical and absurd innovation is in line with the traditions of a people known for their penchant for innovations and crazy ideas.[19] And the form that

[15] In the *Thesmophoriazusae* they have a pimp who is none other than Cleisthenes, the effeminate youth (576).
[16] In the *Thesmophoriazusae* women and 'the Athenian state' are carefully distinguished (304–5) and 'the community (*dēmos*) of the Athenians' and 'the community of the women' are contrasted (306–7, 335–6). Concerning the asymmetry between the two sexes expressed by these phrases ('women' are not contrasted with 'men', but with 'Athenians'), see N. Loraux, 'Sur la race des femmes et quelques-unes de ses tribus', *Arethusa*, 11/1–2 (1978), 53.
[17] The expression is H. I. Marrou's in *Histoire de l'éducation dans l'Antiquité* (Paris, 1948) 63.
[18] See Rosellini and Saïd, 'Usages de femmes et autres *nomoi* chez les "sauvages" d'Hérodote'.
[19] See *Ach.* 556; *Knights* 1055; *Clouds* 587–8, 898, 919; *Peace* 689; *Lys.* 511, 517–20, 522, 1228; *Frogs* 734, 1503.

this innovation takes, power given to women, is dictated by the evolution of a state in which the real men have been put aside in favour of effeminate men whose unmanly gossip has taken the place of political discussion.

Thucydides is not the only one to have expressed through the mouth of the people of Corinth the Athenian's taste for innovation (1. 70. 2). As Praxagora recalls, 'if the city of the Athenians congratulated itself on a certain practice, it would still not consider itself saved unless it contrived to do something unprecedented' (218–20). Government by women remains 'the only thing never to have been done' (456–7). This extraordinary measure not only shows to what lengths the taste for novelty can go; it also serves to expose the absurdity of a policy that constantly innovates. It is replaced by a return to tradition when power is taken over by those who do everything 'as before'. This is the height of absurdity since it is this very refusal to innovate that determines the people to innovate by giving power to the women.[20]

But can we really speak of innovation? It is doutbful, when one considers what the administrative personnel of democracy and the people itself had become. In all Aristophanes' attacks on the men of politics, their effeminate character returns like a refrain.[21] The *Assemblywomen* is not far behind in this tradition: it attacks Agyrrhius, who is never anything but a woman dressed up in a borrowed beard (102–3). It extends this criticism to the whole populace and to a theatre audience that one might be tempted to address as 'ladies' (165–8). In fact this is what explains the success of Praxagora's stratagem. Why should not women, disguised as men and wearing false beards, be thought of as men and play a role in politics, when so many effeminate men have done just that?[22]

For the same reasons, Praxagora can also imagine substituting a 'woman's voice' for the political voice. Normally the two are incompatible. The women, who anxiously wonder why a gang 'with women's hearts' (*thēluphrōn*) can 'speak to the people' (*dēmēgorein*) in lines 110–11, recognize this, and Praxagora, who is waiting for them to stop chattering so that she can invite the orators to 'speak in public' (*agoreuein*, 130), implicitly admits it. But as a good

---

[20] See *Ass.* 221–32.

[21] See e.g. the attacks on Cleon, *Ach.* 664, *Knights* 379–81, 877–8, *Peace* 48, 758.

[22] See *Ass.* 101–4.

sophist she also knows how to turn the argument against into the
argument for, showing that skill in rhetoric, far from being incompatible with femininity, is actually associated with it (111–14). In the
Knights the Sausage-Seller describes the effeminate men as the
source of all orators (421–5).[23] In the *Clouds* Unjust Reasoning
recalls that catamites now make up the pool from which are
recruited all those who give political speeches, whether in the
lawcourts, the theatre, or the Assembly (1088–94). In the courts,
Aristophanes compares the triumph of rhetoric to 'gossip';[24] in the
theatre, there are only 'women's plays' and 'airs with a female
smell';[25] things destined to please a public made up mainly of
catamites.[26] Under these circumstances, the women, whose talent
for 'gossip' is unequalled,[27] have every opportunity to cut an
honourable figure in an Assembly where gossip has become the
rule.

Revolution, or rather the logical end of an evolution—women's
power—in the *Assemblywomen* seems therefore to be a solution (and
even the only solution) to the problems of Athens. But it is a comic
solution, or a simpleton's remedy. Out of the frying-pan into the fire:
the public is perishing because of womanish men, so it seeks to be
saved by women. In a mad world there's no hope for logic; all that
can be done is to counter the absurdity of reality with a greater
absurdity[28] and hope that 'the wildest and most senseless decisions'
will lead to success and turn to the 'advantage of those who made
them'.[29] This paradoxical cure was successful in the *Knights*: Cleon
is thrown out and an even more 'disgusting' (*bdelyros*, 134) individual is placed in power; and Demos, youthful again, is as he was in
the good times at Marathon when he banqueted with Aristides and
Miltiades.[30] In the *Assemblywomen* Praxagora promises the state
perfect happiness and at the end of the play a servant also proclaims the supreme happiness of the people.[31] But before examining
whether the reality in the comedy corresponds to the image attrib-

[23] See also 879–80.   [24] *Clouds* 931.   [25] *Th.* 130–1, 151.
[26] *Clouds* 1096–1101.
[27] In the *Thesmophoriazusae* Aristophanes calls them 'the gossipers' (393) and they
recognize themselves as such when they ask in the *Assemblywomen*: 'Which of us, my
dear, doesn't know how to gossip?' (120).
[28] See Whitman, *Aristophanes and the Comic Hero*, 56.
[29] *Clouds* 587–9; *Ass.* 473–5.   [30] *Knights* 1325.
[31] *Ass.* 558, 573, 1112, 1129, 1134.

uted to it, we must linger over the picture of women in power as presented by Aristophanes.

2. POWER IN THE FEMININE MODE

The Faces of Gynaecocracy

In a Greek universe where it is accepted fact, according to Aristotle in his *Politics*, that 'men are by nature more apt to command than women' (1. 12. 1. 1259^b1–2) and 'the relationship of the male to the female is by nature that of the superior to the inferior and the governed' (1. 5. 7. 1254^a 13–14), female power is by definition abnormal. This has already been said by P. Vidal-Naquet in an article that likens women's power to that of slaves, and analyses the forms of gynaecocracy in tradition, myth, and utopia.[32] However, one can point out, in line with him, that this abnormality can take clearly opposing forms and result in a masculinizing of women if the women become adapted to the nature of power; or, the opposite, a feminization of power if the women adapt the power to their own nature and make the domestic more important then the political.

The society of the Amazons, as described by Diodorus[33] and Strabo,[34] is an excellent example of the first type of gynaecocracy.

Among the Amazons, power is defined by certain masculine characteristics, and the exercise of power continues to require military and political abilities, normally for the Greeks the exclusive property of males. Women can therefore only exercise power if they are transformed into men at the price of actual mutilation: the right breast of girls was cut off in order to make them more fitted for war by suppressing an organ that might get in the way of drawing the bow.[35] By paying this price, women were then capable of such masculine activities as hunting, war, and politics. Strabo has the boldest among them practise hunting and war;[36] in Diodorus they exercise complete political power. Their state is a 'gynaecocracy'[37] of

---

[32] 'Esclavage et gynécocratie dans la tradition, le myth et l'utopie' in *Recherches sur les structures sociales dans l'Antiquité classique* (Paris, 1970), *passim*.
[33] Diod. 2. 45–6 (the Amazons of Thermodon) and 3. 52–5 (the Amazons of Libya).
[34] Str. 11. 5. 1–2.   [35] See Diod. 2. 45. 3, 3. 53. 3.   [36] See 11. 5. 1.
[37] Diod. 2. 45. 1, 3. 53. 1.

which the chief is a woman[38] and 'the women fill all magistracies
and all public offices' (III. 53. I), and they also make war.

Inversely, the men, if they are not completely excluded from this
society (which is the case in Strabo's, Plutarch's, and Philostratus'
descriptions),[39] take the place of the women. They act 'like Greek
wives' and are assigned feminine tasks such as working with wool
and looking after children. On the other hand, they are rigorously
excluded from politics and war: 'They take no part in expeditions, do
not occupy magistracies, and cannot give advice in the Assembly'.[40]
This transformation is possible only at the price of a mutilation
parallel to that undergone by the women. The Amazons of the
north sever the nerves of the arms and legs of boys, since there
resides the warrior's power.[41]

All in all, the contrast between the sexes remains intact, even if
the roles are redistributed. The gynaecocracy of the Amazons is a
topsy-turvy world which only reproduces, turned upside-down, the
fundamental structures of Greek society.

Nor does the Amazonian society question the split between the
inside and the outside, and the rigid opposition between the domestic and the political that it reflects. For the Greek man, 'domestic
space, an enclosed space with a roof (protected) has . . . a feminine
connotation. Space ouside under the sky, a masculine connotation.
The woman is in her kingdom at home, she should not leave it. The
man, however, represents the centrifugal element of the *oikos*: it is
his business to leave the comfortable enclosure of the home to face
the fatigues, dangers, and unforeseen events of the exterior'.[42]
Among the Amazons it is the women who go off on expeditions;
the men do not accompany them, they stay at home and spend the
rest of their lives there.[43]

The Assemblywomen: *A Comedy of Amazons?*

One might think that the *Assemblywomen* offers the same picture of
an upside-down world where men and women exchange roles,

[38] Diod. 2. 45. 1, 4; 46. 1–3.
[39] Str. 11. 5. 1; Plu. *Pomp.* 35. 6, Philostr. *Her.* 215–16, ed. C. L. Kayser (Teubner,
1871).   [40] Diod. 3. 53. 2.   [41] Diod. 2. 45. 3.
[42] J. P. Vernant, 'Hestia-Hermès: Sur l'expression religieuse de l'espace et du
mouvement chez les Grecs', in *Mythe et pensée chez les grecs* (Paris, 1965), i. 131.
[43] See Diod. 3. 53. 2.

where the women go out dressed as men and the men are indoors dressed as women.

When the play begins, we indeed see the women leaving their usual place. At the call of their companions they leave their houses and discuss more or less at length the difficulties, or the ease, of the enterprise.[44] As their disappointed husbands point out, the women 'are not at home' they have 'gone out' (325), indeed 'sneaked out' (337). Leaving in this way, according to Blepyrus,[45] is clearly a revolutionary infraction. One could allow that a woman might leave her house to go into another domestic space and join other women in their houses, for example to have breakfast with a neighbour (348–50) or to help another woman give birth (526–35). But this time the women leave the domestic space to invade the political space. Indeed they are about to 'sit in the Assembly' (*ekklēsiazein*, 161).

To enter into this masculine space normally forbidden to them, the women have decided 'at the Skira' (18) to 'become men' (121). It is probably not by chance that they chose this occasion. The Skira, like the Thesmophoria, is a festival at which women gather together.[46] Also, the name evokes a ritual of transsexual disguise since an essential element of the festival of the Oschophoria consists of a procession to the temple of Athene Skiras led by two boys dressed up as girls.[47] If one can believe Praxagora, who at the end of the enterprise congratulates them on their 'virility' (519), the transformation is successful.

The women have made themselves hairy. They have thrown away their razors in order to be hirsute all over (65–6); their underarms are 'bushier than a jungle' (60–1), and they have given themselves false beards (68–72). Abundant black hair was a mark of virility for the Greeks. In the *Thesmophoriazusae* the image of a tragic poet as a true man includes 'a full beard' (32).[48] In *Lysistrata* the aggressively virile old men of the chorus also have 'a thick growth' (800) and the

---

[44] See *Ass.* 30–2, 35–7, 48, 50–5.   [45] *Ass.* 325–6, 338.
[46] For this feast, see H. W. Parke, *Festivals of the Athenians* (London, 1977), 156–61.
[47] For this ritual, see Parke, *Festivals of the Athenians*, 77–80. P. Vidal-Naquet ('Le Chasseur noir et l'origine de l'éphébie attique', *Annales ESC* 23 (1968), 956–8, and 'Esclavage et Gynécocratie sur les structures sociales dans l'antiquité classique', 79) shows the link between this ritual and the themes of the comedy.
[48] See also *Th.* 160, 190.

valiant warriors in Myronides' time had 'thighs black with hair' (802–3). Women, however, are supposed to have smooth skin. In Aristophanes' comedies there is always talk of women who shave or pluck themselves,[49] and gay men like Agathon are recognized because they leave their razors at home and have no beards.[50] This being so, the first thing to do to change a man into a woman, as we see in the *Thesmophoriazusae*,[51] is to shave him and pluck him; vice versa, to change a woman into a man, she must be provided with hair.

The women had also uncovered themselves in the sun in order to acquire a tan (62–4), since bronzed skin is also a mark of virility. In the *Thesmophoriazusae*, the manly poet is 'sunburnt' (31). Women, however, shut up in the house, characteristically have a pale complexion, as we see on vases and in the theatrical masks. This paleness is therefore synonymous with beauty.[52] Among men, it is a sure mark of effeminacy.[53]

And finally, the women have borrowed male clothing. In a comedy where all the roles were played by men, the costume, along with the mask and the phallus, indicated the different sexes much more effectively than when feminine roles are played by women. In the theatre, a man wore a 'cloak' and 'Laconian shoes'.[54] In order to 'play a man', the women of the *Assemblywomen* simply have to appropriate the distinctive signs of manhood: the 'cloak', men's shoes ('Laconians' or *embades*) and the 'staff '.

The men, on the other hand, have to 'play at being women'. The two husbands who appear at the beginning of the play after the women have left the stage are confined to the indoors and cannot go to the Assembly as they would like to (351). Since the women have borrowed their clothes, they have to dress in women's garb, 'the little round cloak' (317–18), 'the little yellow dress' (331–2), or 'the little tunic' (374), and put on women's 'Persian' shoes (319) or 'platform shoes', thus being forced to adopt the costume that characterizes the gay man Agathon in the *Thesmophoriazusae*

---

[49] *Lys.* 89, 151, 825–8; *Th.* 538–43; *Frogs* 516; *Ass.* 13.

[50] *Th.* 191, 217–19. This is also true of Cleisthenes, who is a perfect example of the effeminate; *Ach.* 119; *Knights* 1373–4; *Frogs* 423–4. See also *Clouds* 1083.

[51] *Th.* 215–45, 589–90, 1042.   [52] Cf. *Birds* 667; *Ass.* 699.

[53] It is the same for Agathon in the *Thesmophoriazusae* (191) and for the little man who was unable to run in the Lampadodromia in the *Frogs* (1092). See J. Henderson, *The Maculate Muse: Obscene Language in Attic Comedy* (London, 1975), 211.

[54] *Th.* 142.

(136–9) and is enough to transform Euripides' relation into a woman (250–63).

The Assemblywomen, *or the Impossible Exchange of Roles*

Can we then speak of a true reversal of the feminine and masculine in an upside-down world? I do not think so, because the disguise in the *Assemblywomen* is clearly just that. In this comedy we see men disguised as women, and women who try 'not to look like women at all' (67) and act like men (*mimeisthai* appears twice in lines 277 and 545), mimicking the character of the old rustic and copying their husbands' gestures. But the humour of the first part of the play (up to the moment when in line 499 Praxagora orders the women to change their clothes and become once again what they have never ceased to be) comes precisely from the incomplete and unsuccessful disguise that at no moment deceives.

The Limits of Disguise

The scene showing the men dressed as women (311–75), and ending with the entrance of Chremes returning from the Assembly, is based on a quite different brand of humour from that in the scene with Agathon in the *Thesmophoriazusae*. There, the laughter was for a man so effeminate that his true sex eventually becomes a problem.[55] Here, the laughter is about two obviously virile men weighed down by garments that look quite incongruous on them, as we are told in the neighbour's remarks (329–32) and those of Blepyrus (374). Far from accomplishing a transformation of the men into women, the feminine garments only serve to accentuate the virility of those who wear them.

Equally unsuccessful is the attempt of the women to look like men. Had it succeeded, this cross-dressing could have been used to emphasize the very conventional character of the differences between the masculine and the feminine, and to discuss the reasons for the cultural asymmetry between the sexes. In the *Assemblywomen*, however, it serves to show the characteristics of a female nature that reveals itself in spite of the efforts made to disguise it.

Although the women stay out in the sun, they do not acquire a

[55] See *Th.* 134, 145.

tan like the men. Their bronze is a borrowed bronze, through which
their original paleness shows, in defiance of all realism. They are
compared to 'grilled squid' (126–7). They are never taken for men.
At the best, they can be grouped with 'cobblers' (385–6), artisans
who lead an enclosed life as do women and have, like them, pale
complexions (387). All the efforts of Praxagora only serve to have
her taken for a gay man. The portrait Chremes gives of her as 'a
young man with a handsome, pale face' (427) reminds those who
have read the *Thesmophoriazusae* of the description of Agathon, also
'pale' and 'handsome' (191–2).

The other outward signs of virility sported by the women are
equally as artificial and incongruous.

The beards are false pieces 'sewn' (24–5) by the women, and we
are not allowed to forget it: the women enter carrying them in their
hands, on stage they brandish them (68–72) before sticking them on
their chins,[56] and they take them off in front of the audience (503).
Thus the beards only serve to underline the femininity of those who
wear them, and their incongruity is supposed to cause laughter, as
the adjective 'ridiculous' (*katagelastos*) suggests (125, 127).

The men's cloaks are borrowed plumes, and have been 'filched'.[57]
The text reiterates this point several times: one woman tells of the
trouble she had to get the cloak away from her husband (40); a man
complains that his wife has gone off with his cloak (341); Praxagora
wants to take hers off and put it back (510–13) and, surprised by her
husband, tries to justify borrowing it as well as she can (526–9).
These cloaks, just like the beards, are put on and off on-stage, thus
removing their credibility in advance.

What goes for the cloaks goes also for the shoes, which the
women put on (269) and take off again on-stage (507–8). In lines
46–7 the attention of the audience is drawn to the clumsiness of the
women in their borrowed shoes, and Praxagora underlines the
distance between copy and original by inviting the women to tie
the shoes in the way they have seen their husbands do it (269–71)
and use them to imitate a man's walk (544–6).

The staffs,[58] which are supposed to give the women manly
attitudes when talking and walking[59] (they enter with them (47),
walk about leaning on them (276–7) like the old countryman in the

---

[56] *Ass.* 99–100, 121–2, 273, 494.   [57] *Ass.* 26, 75, 275.
[58] *Ass.* 74, 76–8.   [59] *Ass.* 149–50, 546–7.

Acharnians (682) or the heliasts in the *Wasps*),[60] are still their
husbands' staffs.

The Errors of Discourse

Betrayed by their disguise, the women are also given away by their
discourse. For the Greeks, femininity is revealed in language. To play
a woman in a comedy is not just to 'look like a woman', but also to
'speak like a woman' (*gunaikizein*) in a convincing manner, in other
words to 'chatter' (*lalein*), as Euripides reminds us in the *Thesmophoriazusae* (266–8). To play a man, however, would be to submit to
the rules of political speech instead of chattering. The whole first
part of the play demonstrates the women's handicap in this area:
they make one blunder after another.

Before the Assembly sits there is a purification ceremony. The
animal sacrificed is not, however, the customary pig, but a weasel
(128), the animal most familiar to women and the most feminine
since it is greedy and thieving as they are.[61]

The women who prepare to speak know that they have to crown
themselves first,[62] but they mistake the meaning of the wreath,
which they associate with banquets and drinking, and they ask
for a drink as soon as they have put it on, instead of beginning to
speak (131–4).

They show themselves to be women by the very words they
pronounce: they swear by the two goddesses (155), as do women
and only women,[63] and address the members of the Assembly as
'ladies' (166).

The transformation of women into men in the *Assemblywomen*
never gives the illusion of reality. It is also very temporary. It lasts
only as long as the Assembly sits, and then we see the women put
off all their masculine trappings and become women-women again,
in contrast to the Amazons and the women 'with manly hearts'
who 'can speak like wise men', such as Clytemnestra in the
Agamemnon.[64]

---

[60] Cf. *Wasps* 33, 1396.

[61] Cf. *Wasps* 363; *Peace* 1151; *Th.* 558–9. This is why the woman is compared to a
weasel (*Ass.* 925) or made to be the same thing (*Ach.* 255).   [62] Cf. *Birds* 463.

[63] Cf. *Wasps* 1396; *Lys.* 51, 112, 148, 732; *Th.* 383, 566, 718, 875, 897, 916; *Ass.* 532; *Pl.*
1006.   [64] A., *A.* 11, 351.

The Triumph of Femininity

Defined as women, acting as such in order to gain power, the women in the *Assemblywomen* finally entrust to themselves the administration of the affairs of state for reasons connected with their femininity, as is revealed in Praxagora's justification speech, starting with a 'Here's why' (211).

Women and Stewardship

'We trust them', she says, 'with the guardianship (*epitropos*) and stewardship (*tamia*) of our homes' (211–12). The first justification thus refers to the traditional domain of women, the home, and in Greek society the functions mentioned were normally carried out by women, as we see in Xenophon's *Economics*.[65] Not that this means she can hold the purse-strings of the state and manage the public treasury,[66] because, as the commissioner says in *Lysistrata*, 'It's not the same thing' (496).

But what is very clear is that the assumption of power by those who are defined as housekeepers only makes sense in a state in which the problems of housekeeping have become of primary importance. And surely this was the case in Athens after the defeat of 404 and the end of the empire.

Before 404, while the empire still existed, the main problem was to draw enough revenue from abroad to meet the expenses of the

[65] See 7. 3, 4, 7, 16. In Aristophanes' comedies, the woman's function as housewife is taken for granted (*Lys.* 493–6) and she feels the loss of it is an intolerable blow (*Th.* 418–21).

[66] The movement from private to public is made easier here by the presence of *epitropos* along with *tamia*. *Tamia* is generally used for the woman who manages the household (or the man, cf. *Wasps* 613, 964; *Knights* 948, 959) but can also refer metaphorically to the one who looks after the sea (Poseidon is the 'manager of the trident', *Clouds* 566) or to the person who manages the state (sovereignty is Zeus' general 'manager' and in particular oversees the arsenals and the *triōbolon*, *Birds* 1538, 1542). But *epitropos* is more ambivalent and designates the confidential agent in both the political and private spheres: in *Peace* it is used as a substitute for *prostatēs*, the leader of the people (684–8), and in the *Knights* the verb *epitropeuin*, 'to administer', twice has *dēmos*, 'the state', as its complement (212, 426); but the verb is also used in the *Knights* to substitute for *tamieuein* (948–9), and the noun is associated with *tamia* in a fragment (fr. 294K). H. J. Newiger (*Metapher und Allegorie: Studien zu Aristophanes* (Munich, 1957)) shows the role these two terms play in the construction of the action in *Knights* (46–9).

democracy and to use the tribute money (*phoros*) for salaries
(*misthos*).[67] Aristotle was not the only one to have made, in the
Constitution of Athens, a connection between empire and democracy,
saying that 'the tributes, the taxes, and the allies provided for
twenty thousand men' (the traditional number of citizens) and
gave the people 'the means to support themselves' (24. 3). On the
eve of the expedition to Sicily, Thucydides said that for the majority
of the soldiers the war represented immediate income and the future
power to guarantee 'indefinite salaries' to the citizens (6. 24. 3.) And
in Aristophanes' comedies before the defeat, either in the *Knights*,
the *Wasps*, or the *Birds*, we find the same picture of Athens drawing
its resources from outside itself and living on the profits of the
empire. In the *Knights* the triremes 'instructed to raise tribute'
(*argurologos*, 1071) are also 'the ones who bring the citizens their
salaries' (*misthophoros*, 555), and the Greek empire consequently has
a heliast living in Arcadia with a salary of five obols (797–9). The
veterans in the *Wasps* consider the *triōbolon* a just price for their
trouble in rowing ships, serving in the infantry, or laying siege to
cities (684–5); they even find a perfect balance between the tribute
and their salaries, and in lines 1115–21 they complain that the
people who stayed in Athens 'devour the tribute which is the fruit
of their labours' and the men who have taken up neither oar nor
lance 'swallow up the salary they receive'. In the *Birds* it is not
surprising therefore to find Sovereignty managing both the arsenals
and the *triōbolon* (1537–41).

Without the empire, there is no question of the city having
sufficient income from abroad; it can only subsist by staying
inside, using its resources to run Xenophon's programme in the

[67] In the *Constitution of Athens* (24. 1) Aristotle establishes a direct relationship
between the hegemony of Athens and the upkeep of its citizens in the advice he has
Aristides give: 'Aristides advised the Athenians to seize the authority and to come
down from the countryside into the city; they would all find a living . . .'. The link
between democracy and empire is also touched on in the *Constitution of Athens* by
Pseudo-Xenophon (1. 2), who establishes a cause-and-effect connection between the
role of the people and of poor people in the navy, therefore in the empire, and the
power they have in the state, as in Xenophon's treatise *On the Revenues*, in which the
partisans of the empire say they are 'forced to abandon justice with regard to other
states because of the poverty of the people' (1. 1). Concerning the inevitable link
between imperialism and democracy in the Athens of the 5th cent., read the analyses
of M. I. Finley in *Démocratie antique et démocratie moderne* (Paris, 1976), 99–106.

Economics. [68] Production thus steps ahead of acquisition. To express this opposition in metaphorical terms, with the state represented by a house (*oikos*), as Aristophanes does in the *Knights*,[69] one could say that, given the Aristotelian distinction between chrematistism and economics,[70] in imperial Athens the former (i.e. the art of acquiring riches) is more important than the latter (i.e. the art of managing acquired riches). So it is impossible to imagine a state run by women, who by definition have no experience in acquiring. On the other hand, in a state that no longer has imperial revenues, economics and the art of money management are all-important. Hence the authority that women can acquire—women, who by definition are housekeepers.

Women's power in the *Assemblywomen* is therefore not justified by a transformation of the women into men, but by a transformation of the political situation. This is what contrasts the regime imagined by Aristophanes with the gynaecocracy of the Amazons and the *Republic* of Plato. Among the Amazons, the rigid separation of within and without and the activities of the two sexes continue to exist, but there is a transposition between the women and the men in comparison with the Greek model. Plato, on the other hand, calls into question the rift between male and female and their different activities as a function of sex. While recognizing a difference in the natures of man and woman (5. 453b), Plato's position is that there is no occupation specific to women or to men in the government of the state (as also in the running of the household) (5. 455d). Their natural aptitudes having been equally divided between them, the woman, according to her nature, can participate in all the traditionally male activities (5. 455d–e). That is why Plato installs 'female guardians' along with the male guardians. Aristophanes, however, holds that the nature of the female is specific to her and continues to think of politics as a masculine endeavour. It is therefore the nature of power itself which changes from the moment it arrives in the hands of the women. More precisely, women becoming powerful is a way of saying that the power has changed, that politics as such exist no more, and that economics has invaded everything, in the same

---

[68] Xenophon's problem is to 'find out if the Athenians could subsist on the resources of their own country' (1. 1.)

[69] For the development of this metaphor, see Newiger, *Metapher und Allegorie*, 11–49.

[70] *Pol.* 1. 8. 1–2. 1256^a 1–14.

way as the acquisition of power by a sausage merchant in the *Knights* indicates that politics has been downgraded to cooking.

3. COMMUNAL PROPERTY AND THE LOGIC OF DEMOCRACY

The women's regime, aiming at happiness for everyone,[71] begins by decreeing the most radical communism possible: 'Everyone', says Praxagora, 'must have everything in common' (590). First of all, possessions: 'I shall make the land', she says, 'common to all; money too, and all personal belongings' (597–8). Food is also affected. The women will make an entirely unique kind of existence, the same for everyone (594); the citizens will live on common funds (599) and their lives will be lived communally (673).

This startling entry of communism into the women's programme is surprising. But it is a measure that obeys the same logic as does the decision to give over the government to the women and is a result of analysing the ills from which Athens was suffering.

The End of Inequality

As presented by Praxagora, communism is a way of ending poverty. There will be no more destitute citizens (*gymnos*) and indigents (*penēs*) (566). From her point of view, this is not an end in itself, but a necessary condition for restoring morale. Indigence must disappear so that relations among citizens can again be dictated by justice (*dikē*) and respect for each other (*aidōs*), both of which are the foundation of social life and the basis of the city's existence. Praxagora states this quite clearly in lines 561–7; these verses contain an impressive catalogue of the political and social dangers of poverty. Where poor people are found, there hate is also found (they 'envy' (*phthonein*) their neighbours), theft (they 'relieve' (*lōpodutein*) passers-by of their valuables), abuse (*loidoreisthai*), and a perverse use of legal practices both by the poor acting as sycophants and by the rich seizing their debtors. In a few lines she paints a complete picture of the city's crisis. As proof, one can turn to book 8 of Plato's *Republic*, where we find the same appreciation of the dangers to society from a class of indigents. Social dangers first: in a

[71] *Ass.* 557–8, 573–5.

state in which there are beggers (*ptōchoi*), there will also be, though well hidden, 'thieves, pickpockets, the sacrilegious and miscreants of all sorts' (522d). Then political dangers: ill-feeling between poor and rich divides the city and turns a single, united state into two enemy camps.[72]

Goods in common contribute to re-establishing normal conditions among the citizenry. In the *Assemblywomen* poverty and riches are both defined by possession of land: to be rich is 'to have a lot of land to cultivate' (592); to be poor is 'to have not even enough ground to be buried in' (592), that is, to have no land at all. This is an amazing definition in a mercantile city such as Athens, where real estate was certainly not the only, nor even the privileged, source of wealth;[73] a definition, too, full of instruction. We know how important property was to the Greeks for its material proof of participation in the state and its close relation with citizenship, and the following facts go to prove this: in Athens non-citizens usually had no right to buy land (except for special permission, foreigners were forbidden to acquire real estate in Attica),[74] and the citizenship of those who had no land was questioned. We know from a speech by Lysias that, soon after the restoration of democracy, Phormisius proposed that *politeia* (the full rights of citizenship) should be reserved for landowners only.[75] The theoreticians can also be cited in this respect. In his *Politics* Aristotle clearly states that 'citizens must possess a piece of the land' (2. 1. 2. 1260[b]). And in the *Republic* Plato is indignant that people can still be citizens after having given up their estates (*klēros*) (8. 552a). As a result, to abolish private property and replace it with collective possession of the land is to re-create the citizenship–landowning relationship.

But to own a *klēros* is not in itself sufficient for citizenship; the leisure to be politically active is needed, and therefore it is necessary to have slaves. In the Athens of the fourth century, some citizens had become so poor that they had no slaves,[76] while the rich had several (593). By setting up a regime in which the land would be

[72] Pl., R. 4. 422e, 8. 555d.

[73] *Ass.* 601–2: 'And he among us who has no land but has money and gold coins? Such a fortune is invisible!'

[74] For *enktēsis*, see V. Ehrenberg, *L'État grec* (Paris, 1976), 75, and for its development in the 4th cent., see E. Will, C. Mosse and P. Goukowsky, *Le Monde grec et l'Orient: Le IVe siècle et l'époque héllénistique* (Paris, 1975), 121–2.

[75] Cf. Will *et al.*, *Le Monde grec et l'Orient*, 106.

[76] On the absence of a single slave as a sign of indigence, see Lys., *For the Invalid* 6.

cultivated exclusively by slaves (650), Praxagora gives everyone the opportunity of taking part in political life.

The End of Egoism

Praxagora's communism is not just an egalitarian regime that would end the social imbalance and normalize the political life; it is also a community regime that would be a remedy for the individualism which threatens the civil spirit and the very existence of the city.

In Aristophanes' comedies, particularly after 411, we find a picture of an Athens in which the egotistical impulses of political figures and even of some citizens were in conflict.[77] In the *Assemblywomen* this situation is exaggerated and affects all the citizens, who have eyes only for their own interests. People are in favour of the compensation that rewards attendance at the Assembly, and Agyrrhius is praised when they receive it; they are against it only when they arrive too late to get it (183–8). Everyone votes for or against the war according to the advantages or disadvantages it offers them. 'Should we launch a navy? The poor say yes, but the wealthy and the farmers are against it' (197–8), because the poor become sailors, so the war represents wages for them, whereas it is costly for the rich, since they have to maintain the warships and contribute a large amount to the war chest, and costly too for the farmers who have to abandon their fields to the ravages of the enemy in the event of an invasion. We are far from the ideal Athens of Thucydides' funeral oration, in which wealth or poverty are never put before the interests of the state (2. 42. 4).

In addition, the institution of compensation reveals a creeping perversion in the relationship of citizen to state. Praxagora accuses the citizens by saying: 'You waste the state's money in the compensation you get and each of you is concerned only about your personal profit, while the state, like Aisimos, can muddle along' (205–9). In the ideal democracy, private and public interest are one and the same, and it was even held that it was better to be

---

[77] See *Th.* 360, 383–4; *Frogs* 359–65, 1427–30. For the increase in individualism and its denunciation after 411, see J. de Romilly, 'Les Phéniciens d'Euripide et l'actualité dans la tragédie grecque', *Revue de Philologie* 91 (1965), 28–46, *passim*, and E. Levy, *Athènes devant la défaite de 404* (Paris, 1976), 223–8.

poor in a prosperous state than rich in a floundering state.[78] There
was a balanced exchange between citizens and state: the soldiers
gave their lives to the public to receive privately eternal praise and a
distinguished burial;[79] the responsibility of the magistrates' position
was rewarded by the honour accorded them;[80] *eranos* is described
here, the share that each one brings to a communal meal,[81] and it
was the individual who took the initiative of generously offering his
life to the state. The *Assemblywomen* gives a different picture of a one-
sided relationship between a subsidized citizen who only receives and
a welfare state that is expected to give. The tribunals and the
assemblies, 'the expression of the politics of the community',[82]
have become an opportunity to receive the *triōbolon*. Men go to the
tribunal and agree to judge only in order to support their families
(460–1). When they play public prosecutor, they do it not to defend
the interests of the state but to receive a living wage (561–3). The
assemblies only function because of money. Aristophanes will say it
clearly in *Plutus* (171); now he shows it in the *Assemblywomen*. If they
hurry to get there, it is not good citizenship that drives them, but the
threat of not getting the *triōbolon* if they arrive late (289–92). If the
attendance at the Assembly has become more numerous, it is due
not to a surge of patriotism but to an increase in compensation from
one to three obols (299–304). Such decadence is made more conspicuous when nostalgia evokes the good old days, which here correspond to Myronides' era, when no one would have been impudent
enough to receive pay for managing the affairs of state (304–6).

Communism: Scandalous Innovation or Logical Result of Democracy?

Even if it is the logical result of the list of ills the city suffers from,
Praxagora's communism is still incredibly bold and appeals to the
Athenian love of innovation (583–5). Democracy in Athens recognized private property. The judges in their oaths and the ruler in his
inaugural declaration solemnly swore to respect beliefs and guarantee the ownership of real estate.[83] Praxagora's imaginary regime

[78] Cf. S., *Ant.* 188–90; Th., 2. 60. 2–3; X., *Mem.* 3. 7. 9.   [79] See Th. 2. 43. 2.

[80] See Isoc., *Panathenaicus* 145.

[81] See Th. 2. 43. 1. See L. Gernet, 'Droit et prédoit en Grèce ancienne', in
Anthropologie de la Grèce antique, (Paris, 1976), 194–5.

[82] Ehrenberg, *L'État grec*, 103.

[83] See D., *Against Timocrates* 149, and Arist., *Ath. Pol.* 56. 2.

seems to go even further in communism than any regime known to the Greeks. When Aristotle carefully distinguishes in his *Politics* between the communal as regards property (*ktēsis*) and the communal as regards goods (*chrēsis*), he gives examples of one or the other among the barbarians, but names no group that practiced both forms of communism at the same time (2. 5. 1–4. 1262^{b}37–1263^{a}21).

The rupture is total, but more apparent than real. According to L. Strauss,[84] 'there is one link between the novel order and the order preceding it: egalitarianism'. Praxagora's communism does indeed develop certain egalitarian tendencies present in Athenian democracy.

We find this in the text of the *Assemblywomen*. At the meeting in which power is transferred to the women, Praxagora is preceded by a speaker who expresses himself 'quite democratically' (411). What he proposes is simply a preliminary sketch of communism. From now on, the well-lined citizens will give the needy what they lack: 'If the fullers give everyone who needs it a wool cloak as soon as the nights become long, no one will catch pleurisy. Let everyone who has neither bed nor covers go and sleep at the tanners after the bath' (415–20). Blepyrus outdoes these suggestions by proposing a free distribution of food: 'He might have added . . . if the flour merchants do not give the indigent (*aporoi*) three quarts of barley meal for dinner, they'll be very sorry' (422–4).

All this follows in the footsteps of the rites that made the wealthy responsible for a certain number of public services and occasioned a transfer of money from the rich to the poor.[85] In addition, these proposals in favour of the poor expand the measures taken by Athens to help certain categories of citizens such as invalids.[86]

---

[84] *Socrates and Aristophanes* (New York, 1966), 272.

[85] Cf. S. Lauffer, 'Die Liturgien in der Krisenperiode Athens: Das Problem von Finanzsystem und Demokratie' in Welskopf (ed.), *Hellenische Poleis*, i. The author of the *Constitution of Athens* (1. 13) bitterly noted the injustice of a measure destined to 'enrich the poor at the expense of the rich'.

[86] See Lys., *For the Invalid*, *passim*. Demosthenes, in the *Fourth Philippic* (37–42) also agrees that it is just that the rich should see that the poor 'lack nothing', because all citizens must be regarded as fathers of the state and duties imposed by the law concerning parents should be observed (in particular, care for their welfare).

Communism and the Primacy of the Domestic

A revolutionary measure that is in fact the logical result of certain traits of democracy. The same logic, taken to its extreme, is used for sharing goods as it was for transferring power to the women. These two themes are not just developed in parallel, they are closely linked. K. J. Dover, one of the rare critics to have thought about the relationship between a government of women and a regime that abolishes individual property, is content with recalling that Athenian women were excluded by law from owning property and were never involved in transactions, except as intermediaries in the transference of goods (marriage portion or inheritance) from one man to another.[87] It is possible to go even further and show that giving power to the women, who only know how to manage households, inevitably makes of the state one single household and abolishes private property. This indeed is what Praxagora says in lines 673–4: 'I intend to make the city (*astu*) a single household (*oikēsis*) by breaking down all the walls and joining it all up so that we can all go to each others' houses' (673–4).

By thus putting everything 'in the centre' (602) Praxagora does away with the distinction between private and public, not, as one might think, to abolish the private sphere, but to allow the domestic to invade everything. And the lack of connection in Aristophanes' text between a political definition of communal goods and its domestic realization is revealing.

Praxagora speaks of making 'wealth' (*chrēmata*, 712) communal, in other words land and money. And Chremes consequently announces that he will make an inventory of his 'property' (*ousia*) and put it at the disposal of the state. But we only hear about 'furniture' (*skeuē*, 728), and a complete household invades the *agora*. The very centre of public life is thus filled with objects that belong to the private sphere. The audience is treated to a kitchenful of utensils: a flour sifter (730), a casserole (734), a water pitcher (738), a mill (739–42), a bowl with honeycombs (742), a tripod (744), a bottle (744), not to speak of all the little pots and pans (745). The *agora* is transformed into a dining-room, just as Praxagora had warned.

The replacement of the political (or rather the politcal–religious)

---

[87] *Aristophanic Comedy,* 200.

by the domestic is also emphasized by a theatrical contrivance. In order to bring his kitchen utensils on stage, Chremes organizes a procession (*pompē*, 757) and performs a parody of the great Panathenaea.[88] The sifter plays the part of the *kanēphoros* (*kanēphorein*) since it is, like the latter, covered in white powder (730–4). The casserole, 'black all over' takes the place of the 'litter-carrier' (*diphrophoros*), a woman of low rank, whose swarthy complexion doubtless contrasted with the aristocratic pallor of the *kanēphoros*. The water pitcher takes the place of the foreigners' wives who had to carry the pitchers (*hydriaphoros*) in the procession (738). The mill is the cithara player (*kiktharōidos*) (739–41). The bowls containing honeycombs represent the foreigners who carried them (742–3). This is not just 'an original and amusing way to stage an inventory'.[89] It has a meaning and clearly states that the city of Athens, which turned out in force for the Panathenaic processions, is now only a kitchen since the women have come to power.

4. THE DEMOCRATIZATION OF SEX: THE WOMEN'S COMMUNITY

Women's politics that are a negation of politics, a welfare state that emphasizes self-interest and turns towards brutishness. This failed utopia in the *Assemblywomen* would not be complete without adding sex, and sex introduces the worst tyranny.

We shall begin by looking at Praxagora's programme for the women.

Women in Common and Goods in Common

This is apparently a second, and secondary, measure to eliminate the last obstacle towards realizing communal property.

In an Athens where justice has given way to expedience (it is common practice to perjure oneself for money, 602), where the law is only respected when it coincides with self-interest, it is obvious that the citizens will turn in their property to the community chest only if they gain nothing by not doing so (610). Now that they have become bellies and their self-interest and the satisfaction of their

[88] On this procession, see Parke, *Festivals of the Athenians*, 41–50.
[89] Van Daele, *Aristophane*, 48 n. 2.

alimentary and sexual needs are one, a system must be thought up
in which these needs can be satisfied at no cost. Praxagora has
assured the citizens that food and clothing are free; they must now
be assured that sex is free, otherwise they would save their money to
purchase the favours of a pretty girl (611–13). So she declares: 'You
can screw for nothing. I am making women common property, any
man who wants can screw them and make them pregnant' (613–15).

This arrangement, which makes woman as common property the
necessary condition for communal belongings, obeys the logic of a
system in which both are closely related. In Greek society marriage
was a means of handing on property through legitimate children,
and only makes sense in relation to the *oikos*, its functioning and
continuity.[90] As Theomnestus says in *Against Neaera*: 'We have
women to procreate legitimate children and to be faithful guardians of our household'. If there is no private property because
everything has been given to the community, if there is no *oikos*
because the whole state has been turned into a big house, there is
no longer any reason to get married.

Women in Common and Democratic Regulations

In the *Assemblywomen* the abolition of marriage does not mean, as it
does for the savages of Herodotus, a return to a state of nature and
general promiscuity (*mixis epikoinos*) with random coupling, in spite
of the 'whoever wants to' of line 615. It is, rather, a democratic
regulation of sex, previously not regulated at all, except in so far as
it concerned marriage and the legitimacy of children.[91]

Praxagora draws the extreme consequences from the ideal of
equality before the law (isonomia)[92] and of equal rights.[93] In

[90] See Dover, *Aristophanic Comedy*, 200, and J. P. Vernant, 'Le Mariage', in *Mythe et
société en Grèce ancienne* (Paris, 1974).   [91] Cf. D., *Against Aristocrates*, 53.
[92] Concerning this word, 'which suggests rather than defines a regime in which
those who participate in the public life do so as equals and which would not be
expressed by the modern idea of equality before the law' (P. Leveque and P. Vidal-
Naquet, 'Clisthène l'Athénien', *Annales littéraires de l'université de Besançon*, 65 (1973),
31), and on its importance in the formulation of the democratic ideal (Herodotus uses
it along the same lines as *dēmos*, *dēmokrateesthai*, and *dēmokratia* to mean the regime
in which the people (*dēmos* or *plēthos*) have the power), see also 'Clisthène l'Athénien'
(25–32), V. Ehrenberg, 'Isonomia', *RE*, supp. 7, cols. 294–300, and 'Origins of Democracy', *Historia*, 1 (1950), 525–37, G. Vlastos, 'Isonomia', *AJPh* 74 (1953), 337–66, and J.
A. O. Larsen, 'Clisthenes and the Development of Democracy', in *Mélanges Sabine*,
(Ithaca, NY, 1948).
[93] *Isomoiria* is not, like *isonomia*, a purely political concept. It implies an economic

Athenian democracy this ideal existed only in the political sphere: all citizens had an equal part in power. For Praxagora it extends to everything: all citizens have an equal amount of property, of food, and of sexual satisfaction. The same quantitative apportionment is applied to sex as to power in the democracy. As Blepyrus crudely puts it, she has seen to it that 'not a hole remains empty' (623–4).

The problem, therefore, is to figure out how to apply democratic equality to an area in which the most pronounced natural inequality exists. The play shows this inequality in a particularly forceful fashion.

Not all women are equally as desirable and desired. There are those who are 'fresh',[94] others who are 'ugly and plain'.[95] Similarly, among the men, there are 'the handsome and the ugly',[96] 'men who look good' [97] and 'plain ones'.[98] How, then, to prevent all the men from seeking out the freshest girl and trying to make out with her (615–16) and, vice versa, to stop 'the women from running away from the ugly men and going to the handsome ones' (625)?

To balance out this inequality, Praxagora sets up a female lottery that puts a pretty woman beside an ugly one. The former can only be laid after the latter has been satisfied (617–18). Similarly, the ugliest men will stand guard over the handsomest and women will only be allowed to sleep with the latter after they have accorded their favours to the plainest and smallest (626–9).

This way of giving equal shares of sex recalls Herodotus' account[99] of the way in which the Babylonians brought equality to marriage. Defining marriage, as did the Greeks, as the acquisition of a woman and a marriage portion, they compensated the one by the other: a man paid to marry the prettiest (and all the dearer if she were very pretty), or received compensation for marrying the ugliest (and all the more the uglier she might be).

But the inequality where objects of desire are concerned is doubled among men by an inequality where subjects are concerned. As old Blepyrus says: 'If we old chaps lay the ugly ones,

---

reality and a sharing of land (see Leveque and Vidal-Naquet, 'Clisthène l'Athénien', and Ehrenberg, *L'État grec*, 96).

[94] *Ass.* 616, 696. The adjective *hōraios* in Aristophanes always qualifies those who are desirable, youths (*Birds* 138) and young women (*Ach.* 1148; *Frogs* 291, 514), as well as young gods (*Frogs* 394).   [95] *Ass.* 617.

[96] *Ass.* 625, 626, 702, 705.   [97] *Ass.* 702.   [98] *Ass.* 705.

[99] Hdt. 1. 196.

we won't have it in us for the next charge. We'll be routed!' (619–20). Nature will let democratic law function smoothly. The old men who have less drive are also less desirable, and the old and ugly women will voluntarily give up.[100]

The result is an apparently faultlessly fair system: 'Lysicrates' nose will have the same pretensions (*isa phronein*) as the Apollos' (630). But this is a ferocious caricature of democratic equality.[101] Praxagora emphasizes its 'democratic' character (631), but it upends the natural order by giving priority to old people of both sexes, who will be the only ones able to have intercourse with beautiful youngsters.

Aristophanes' text invites us, behind his derision of a system that proposes to eliminate physical differences, to see a political system that does not take into account social disparities. When Praxagora wants to show that the last shall be first, she contrasts not two physical beings, rather two social conditions. On the one hand, 'respectable people with seal rings' (632), on the other, 'a man who wears working shoes' (633) and who says to the former, 'you have the honour of letting me pass' (633). Back in line 617, she had contrasted the uglies not to pretty women but to 'respectable women'.[102] This double shift unites the *Assembleywomen* with several other texts which denounce the injustice of the arithmetical equality instituted by democracy.[103] Isocrates, Plato, and Aristotle agree in condemning a system that 'gives the same thing to propertied people (*chrēstoi*) as to those with nothing (*ponēroi*)' and 'lends a sort of equality to the equal and the unequal', and contrasts it with a geometric equality that respects proportion and gives each 'his due' (*prepon*).[104] More precisely, Aristophanes' insistence on the reversal of the normal order of priorities, with the image of the respectable man who is second in line (*deuteriazein*),[105] recalls the attacks in the *Constitution of Athens*[106] against a regime that gives

---

[100] *Ass.* 621–2.   [101] See Strauss, *Socrates and Aristophanes*, 270–2.

[102] By *semnos* Aristophanes means belonging to the social strata of the 'worthy' (*chrēstoi*) and the 'rich' (*plousioi*); see *Clouds* 48; *Wasps* 627–8; *Lys.* 1109; *Pl.* 940.

[103] See J. de Romilly, *Problèmes de la démocratie grecque* (Paris, 1975): 'Le Principe des deux égalités', 49–52.

[104] See Isoc., *Areopagiticus* 21–2, *Nicocles* 14; Pl., *Grg.* 508a, R. 8. 558c, *Laws* 6. 757b-c; Arist. *EN* 5. 1131^{a}19ff., *EE* 7. 9. 1241^b, 1242^b, *Pol.* 2. 7. 10. 1266^b 38–1267^{a}2, 3. 9. 1. 1180^a 11–24, 13. 1. 1283^a 23–9, 5. 1. 12–15. 1301^b 29–1302^{a}8.   [105] *Ass.* 631–4.

[106] Ps.-Xen., *Ath. Pol.* 1. 1, 2, 4.

people with nothing (*ponēroi*) a more enviable fate than people of property (*chrēestoi*) and attributes more to them.

Making sex part of democracy is translated not only in egalitarian regulations, but also in the exclusions of non-citizens. 'I intend', says Praxagora, 'that prostitutes shall give up their jobs, all of them' (718–19) and 'the slave-girls, because of their finery, should not steal a pleasure due by rights to the free-born' (721–2). In a world where there is no more marriage, it is logical that the rules which 'under the old regime' applied only to marriage should be extended to sexual life in general. We know that in Athens a law proposed by Pericles in 451/450 and reaffirmed after the return of democracy forbade Athenians to marry (to contract a union for the purpose of legitimate children) with women who were not legitimate daughters of Athenian citizens. But such a measure results necessarily from the application to sexual life of the rules of democratic sharing. Democracy is defined as a closed club that guarantees its members, the citizens, exclusive power and the profits attached thereto (*misthos*). From the moment that sex is managed democratically, the women want to keep the youths for themselves (720) and consider unions between slave women and free-born men as 'thefts' (722). Shared women and shared goods therefore create diametrically opposed situations as regards slaves: the former presupposes the exclusion of slaves, the latter depends on the activity of the slaves which allows the citizens to do nothing (651–3).

Praxagora's communal system, a reflection of the collective egoism of the citizens, is only adopted because it serves the personal interests of some among them. Blepyrus and Chremes, the only two citizens on stage, support the new system for the most self-interested reasons. Being old and ugly they have everything to gain, 'because, according to the decree, the ugly, half-dead men can fuck first' (705–6) and nothing to lose because the ugly women 'won't fight for them' (621–2). We can understand why they reply to Praxagora's question: 'Well, tell me you two, does that suit you?' 'Absolutely!' (710).

The Injustice of Egalitarianism and the Tyranny of the Law

As soon as Blepyrus hears that the women have taken over power, he is immediately worried that they will use it to force men to sleep with them (467–8) and right away denounces the scandal there would be if he himself were forced (471). It is this scandal that is staged in lines 877–1111 in a long scene of rarely appreciated caustic comedy pushed to the limit of the objectionable. Critics like G. Murray consider it 'wrongly handled, too long, unpleasant'.[107] Or, like Ussher, people try to avoid the problems that its interpretation uncovers by dismissing it as sheer buffoonery (as if the meaning could only be seen at the expense of the comic and particularly in its absence), or by dealing only with the question of scenery or the position of the various characters.[108] However, this scene, which shows three old women trying to grab a young man in spite of the efforts of his girlfriend, who is soon reduced to silence, is an explicit illustration of how the new regime works.[109] The three old women constantly refer to the 'law' (nomos) and to the 'decree' (psēphisma) and even recite its text at length.[110]

It is of course only a partial illustration and differs from the programme. Praxagora began by announcing the sharing of women as objects to the profit of men as subjects (614–15). Then she used two parallel examples of how the new system would work; on one hand, women (with no indication that they are old and ugly) rivalling each other to offer the men 'fresh' young girls (696), 'very white and pretty' (699), and only briefly indicating that they should sleep with them themselves before taking on the others (700–1); on the other hand, men (with an emphasis on their ugliness) who poke fun at the handsome youths and claim priority because of that ugliness (702a–709). So we hear how the system profits the men, but we actually see only how the old women benefit. This awkwardness is probably explained by the theme of the play. In a comedy about women's power they are naturally the subjects, and the way the new regime functions is seen from their point of view. But surely this is also the best way of portraying the absurd and oppressive, not to say mortal, character of the new laws by showing a double inversion of the natural order with the triumph of the old women over a young man.

We are led to expect an egalitarian regime in which all citizens, regardless of age, appearance, or social origin, have the right to the

[107] Aristophanes: A Study (Oxford, 1933), 196.
[108] Aristophanes' 'Ecclesiazusae', pp. xxx–xxxii.
[109] As recognized by Strauss, Socrates and Aristophanes, 275–80, and Huber, Zur Erklärung und Deutung von Aristophanes' 'Ekklesiazusae', 198–202
[110] See Ass. 944–5, 987–8, 1013–20, 1022, 1049–51, 1056, 1077–8.

same amount of pleasure, in which the seedy have the same
pretensions (*isa phronein*, 630) as the Apollos. We see on stage an
old woman who has pretensions far superior (*meizon phronein*, 937)
to those of an attractive young girl. Natural inequalities have been
replaced by others to create a topsy-turvy world in which youth and
beauty have become reasons for not obtaining sexual satisfaction
and in which ugliness is the basis for success. The action of the
scene, which is a sort of parody of the judgement of Paris (instead of
the youth awarding the prize to the most beautiful of the three
women who present themselves, he himself becomes the prize of the
ugliest woman), underlines the absurdity of the new order. To begin
with, an old woman whose beauty is borrowed (her skin is painted
with white lead and her cheeks reddened with alkanet)[111] tries to
take the place of a pretty young girl by citing the new law. The girl
manages to get rid of her with the threat of incest, but she is no
match for a second old woman, who is 'a sight worse than the first'
(1053) and whose only red is due to her bleeding sores (1057). The
latter sees her victory menaced by a third old woman, who is 'a
helluva sight worse than the other' (1070) since under her make-up
her shape is not even human; she is 'a fright covered in white lead'
(1072). She makes the young man follow her, nevertheless, in the
name of the law that sanctions, behind an egalitarian façade, the
precedence of the ugliest (1077-8).

The old women's scene also allows us to denounce a law that
regulates the natural exercise of sex by systematically opposing
nature. Normally, an old woman would have no other friend than
'Old' Geres (932) and no other lover than death.[112] Inversely, the
mutual attraction of the two young people is a fact of nature
underlined in the first part of the scene. We are shown a youth
who 'has no need of an old woman' (934-5) and wants only to be
alone with his girl and make love to her without having to screw
the old one first.[113] We are shown a young girl who is trying to get
rid of the old woman and does so temporarily.[114] So we have a duo of
lovers,[115] then some stage business echoed by a play on words
showing how the two desires accord with each other. The call of
the one replies to the call of the other (952a-b, 960-1), and both take

[111] *Ass.* 878. 929.   [112] *Ass.* 994-6.   [113] *Ass.* 938-40, 947-8.
[114] *Ass.* 949-50.
[115] On this duo, see C. M. Bowra, 'A Love-Duet (*Eccl.* 952-975)', *AJP* 79 (1958), 376-91.

up a refrain which is a prayer to Eros (958–9b, 967–8b). The young
man wants entrance by knocking on a door she is only too happy to
open to him. The stage business is all the more expressive since the
Greek words 'to knock' (*krouein*) and 'door' (*thura*) have an obscene
meaning and suggest the sexual act and the female genitals.[116] But
the free play of desire is prevented by the old woman reading the
law, which does not take into account the natural order and the
case 'in which a young man desires a young woman' (1015–16), but
opposes it and forbids the young man 'to make the girl' before
'knocking at the old woman's door' (1016–17). The law even makes
violence legitimate: if the young man refuses, 'the old women have
the right to drag him off by his "tool" ' (1019–20). Violence is now at
the heart of the law that should aim to proscribe it.

The women's laws are like their politics. Making sex democratic
only serves to worsen the woes it was supposed to alleviate and
results in insufferable tyranny and general lawlessness.

The law for the Greeks was 'the complement of liberty and its
guarantee'.[117] In the *Assemblywomen* it inaugurates a regime 'insup-
portable to a free man' (932) and introduces violence (*bia*) and
coercion (*anankē*)[118] in the area of desire where they have no
place. It creates a world where you *must*[119] go with an old woman
you loathe and lie with her, 'willy-nilly'.[120]

Praxagora's promises are gradually reduced to nothing. She gave
Blepyrus and Chremes a glimpse of a world in which there would be
neither hatred nor jealousy (*phthonein*, 565) between neighbours.
Instead we are shown a young and an old woman, whose house
doors are apparently next to each other, fighting over the same man
and feeling 'jealous hatred' (*phthonein*, 900, 1043) for each other.
There should no longer be thieves and pickpockets, since there is
nothing more to steal.[121] Even slaves should not 'steal' pleasure from

[116] Cf. Taillardat, *Les Images d'Aristophane*, 77, 103, and Henderson, *The Maculate Muse*, 137, 171. The whole scene depends on the double meaning of these terms. When the young man asks the girl to 'open the door', (962–3, 971) he is clearly playing on the two senses. The old woman who asks 'What are you knocking (*koptein*) for?' (976) and remarks: 'You were even pounding at the door' (977) is describing the stage business. But when she invites him to 'knock first at her door' (990) she is obviously also playing on the double meaning, as does the youth in line 989. Finally, in lines 1017, 1018, and 1021, *prokrouein* and *prokroustēs* have only obscene meanings.
[117] Cf. J. de Romilly, *La Loi dans la pensée grecque* (Paris, 1971), 19.
[118] *Ass.* 467, 471, 1021, 1029.   [119] *Ass.* 939, 1008, 1013, 1077, 1090, 1098.
[120] *Ass.* 981, 1097.   [121] *Ass.* 565, 667–9.

free women.[122] But we witness the successful efforts of old women to 'steal' their lovers from young women (921). No one should have to see the sad spectacle of debtors being dragged off by creditors and their belongings seized (567).[123] But the spectacle here is even worse, since the young man is 'dragged off violently'[124] by the two old women and by the law they represent and is forced to pay with his person. Instead of harmony reigning in the banquets where the life of the city is supposed to take place, it is a free-for-all, with the young man torn asunder (*diaspan*, 1076) and 'skinned alive' (*apoknaiein*, 1087); it is also the triumph of bestiality, with the two old women whom the young man likens to wild beasts (1104). Government by women, according to Praxagora, would inaugurate an era of perfect happiness for the city (558). Instead, it turns a source of pleasure into a source of misery by making the young man weep as he makes love (942), condemned to 'screw a senile old woman all day and all night' and after that to have to 'begin again with another even more frightful' (1098–1101). No wonder he exits crying 'woe'. As L. Strauss[125] has said, Praxagora's system 'has not eliminated happiness and unhappiness; it has only redistributed good and evil'.

---

[122] *Ass.* 721–2.

[123] On comparing the expression *(e)nekhurazomenon pherein* (567) with *Clouds* (241), where Strepsiades complains that his belongings are being seized saying: *pheromai, ta khrēmat(a) enekhurazomai*, I make *enekhurazomenon* masculine, as does Ussher, *Aristophanes' 'Ecclesiazusae'*.

[124] *Ass.* 1001: *agein*, and 1020, 1037, 1050, 1055, 1056, 1066, 1094: *heikein*.

[125] *Socrates and Aristophanes*, 278–9.

16

The Originality of Aristophanes' Last Plays

HELLMUT FLASHAR

I

The last two of Aristophanes' extant comedies, the *Ecclesiazusae* (probably staged in 392 BC) and the *Plutus* (388 BC), diverge in several respects from his other plays. First of all, the differences are formal. There is no parabasis, the chorus plays a diminished role, the metres tend to be simpler (iambic trimeters predominate), and the plays rely less on the characteristic conventions of Old Comedy, such as the *agōn*. But these changes in form merely reflect an intrinsic transformation of comedy itself. Athens' defeat in the Peloponnesian War and the subsequent disruption of democracy had deprived comedy of its traditional source of inspiration. It turned to more general social themes, ceasing henceforth to dramatize current political situations, to involve the audience in the play, to make the ridicule of leading politicians its main focus, and to offer political advice, instruction, or solutions. The public's taste has also changed, for it no longer enjoyed either crude jokes or fine but suggestive lyrics. Aristophanes, at first reluctant to adapt to this shift, eventually became resigned to it.

Critics such as Wilamowitz and Gilbert Murray have generally viewed this transformation of comedy as a symptom of decline, although the latter admitted that Aristophanes, with remarkable originality, had marked out the path to be followed by ancient and even contemporary comedy. In this sense, one may indeed regard his late plays as a transition to Middle Comedy, with which his work overlaps, and to the New Comedy of Menander. These plays anticipate several things we find in Menander, such as the progressive diminution of the chorus's role, the development of stock characters (e.g. Cario in the *Plutus*), the use of stereotypical names, and the outfitting of the stage with two private houses, as in the *Ecclesiazusae*. To be sure, we cannot accurately gauge Menander's indebtedness by concentrating on the extant comedies—for Aristophanes does not reflect the full range and variety of Old Comedy—not to mention other influences, such as Euripides and the Peripatetics.

On the other hand, these late comedies stand clearly within the tradition of the rest of the Aristophanic corpus. Not only do they preserve in their plots the overall structure exhibited by the remaining plays, but they also tie in with individual themes Aristophanes had already treated earlier. Both the *Ecclesiazusae* and the *Plutus* are political comedies, although they rely for their background not so much on a specific political situation but rather on the general conditions of the times. The *Ecclesiazusae* is obviously linked with the other women's comedies, for its main character Praxagora corresponds to Lysistrata, while the transvestism motif of the *Thesmophoriazusae* recurs in inverted form in the *Ecclesiazusae*. And the *Plutus*, after all, picks up motifs from Aristophanes' earliest comedies: the farmers' economic plight, as well as the issue of education viewed within the framework of father–son tensions.

But if there is clear continuity in these two comedies with the rest of the Aristophanic corpus, and if they in turn stand at a point where comedy begins to explore new forms and subjects, then we should re-examine the nature and character of these late plays. By refusing to incorporate contemporary affairs, comedy obviously lost the kind of humour which thrives on politics. What took its place? Here scholars present curiously contradictory views. While they maintain that by abandoning some outdated conventions Aristophanes allowed comedy to become more coherent and substantive, they fault precisely these two plays for a lack of cohesion in the individual scenes and for all sorts of other inconsistencies, which they claim arose because in both cases Aristophanes had hastily combined two different concepts. In the *Ecclesiazusae* he linked the idea of gynaecocracy with the critique of the communal sharing of possessions, a notion that allegedly had occurred to him shortly before the play's production, thus leaving no time for revising the whole drama. In the *Plutus* the idea that all men should become rich, opposed by Penia, is superimposed on the plan of Chremylus to enrich only the righteous, which may explain why many have viewed the entire Penia scene as interpolated.

Some scholars have correctly suggested that in these late plays irony is a comic device that Aristophanes employs against whatever ideas or theories he has snatched up. But it can in fact be argued that in so far as irony involves the plot, characters, situations, and actions of these plays, it represents the very essence of the comic, which in each case determines and shapes the development of the play as a whole. Whereas the second part of a comedy usually tends to illustrate ideas inherent in the main plot, here the poet uses ironic exaggeration to push the plot into the realm of the absurd, thus emphasizing the gap between plan and reality or feasibility. Instead of resolving this ironic tension, Aristophanes maintains it by reaching at the very climax of absurdity for a completely conventional ending. The recognition of such sustained irony in these plays shows that the objections raised against them are largely unfounded, for the supposed peculiarities and inconsistencies are rooted in a conscious and intentional ironic ambiguity. We can observe this in some detail in the last of Aristophanes' extant plays, the *Plutus*.

II

The prologue of the *Plutus* (1–253) conflates two Aristophanic prologue types: slave prologues, where the dialogue between two slaves explains the situation (*Knights*, *Wasps*, *Peace*), and journey prologues (*Birds*, *Thesmophoriazusae*, *Frogs*). Here, of course, we have (as in the *Frogs*) only *one* slave (Cario) and his master, Chremylus. Prompted by the oracle, they are on the last stage of a journey from Delphi to Athens following the blind Plutus. The prologue itself has already outlined the whole plot. Plutus is going to be healed and on regaining his sight will come to stay with the righteous, meaning primarily Chremylus. Hence the play falls into two parts, describing first the period before the healing of Plutus (1–770), and then the effect of his healing on humans (771–1209).

The prologue presents the situation by focusing on the main characters, Chremylus and Plutus. Chremylus and the chorus of peasants remind us of the early Aristophanic plays, where honest and upright farmers, such as Dikaiopolis in the *Acharnians*, have all the poet's sympathy, We are repeatedly told that Chremylus (28, 99, 1056) and the other farmers (219) are righteous, but on closer examination their claim to righteousness becomes exceedingly questionable. All the humour of the opening scene rests on the recognition that behind the façade of justice there lurks plain greed. This is not explicitly stated, but it is always implied. Typical is Chremylus' wish that Plutus fill his house with money 'justly and not' (233). He wants to get rich, not remain righteous. His question to the oracle, i.e. whether his son should become dishonest, unjust, and a good-for-nothing in order to succeed (32–8), had revealed a similar attitude. Indeed, Chremylus' desire for wealth overshadows his concern for his son, for as much as he may love him, his love for Plutus is greater (250–1). In a sense he is like Strepsiades in the *Clouds*, who sends his only son to learn the 'unjust logic' so that with its help he may rid himself of debts and creditors. But in this case the irony which attends the presentation of Chremylus determines the whole structure of the play.

Initially, the play's theme appears to be the unjust distribution of property, by which people remain poor while scoundrels grow rich. It would seem that the wish to eliminate such injustice by healing Plutus could only be the wish of a righteous man. However, by suggesting that Chremylus does not really want a just distribution of wealth but only one that benefits him, Aristophanes presents this plan and its realization from a highly ironic perspective. Because the whole plot revolves around the allegedly righteous disposition of Chremylus, the resulting tension between claim and reality puts him into a series of comical situations.

This is already apparent from the way the prologue presents the character of Plutus. In his conversation with Chremylus, the main issue from the beginning is whether Plutus should abide only with the righteous or should frequent others as well. Zeus had blinded him because he had threatened to consort only with the former (87–92), so that before his blinding he must have bestowed his particular boon—wealth—with no regard for justice. Now, however, if he regains his sight he plans to fulfil his threat and associate only with the righteous (95–6). Only at this point does Chremylus offer himself to Plutus as the most righteous man of all (106, 245), and in so doing initiates the healing process. Plutus agrees to it reluctantly after Chremylus explains to him Plutus' universal power (128–97), to which even Zeus is subject and of which Plutus himself had been curiously unaware (129, 136, 139, 143, 169, 186).

Yet the notion of rewarding the righteous coexists with another

view that Plutus himself accepts, namely that all humans are
essentially bad (111). They are righteous only when poor, but they
become scoundrels when they are rich (107–9). By equating
poverty with justice and wealth with injustice, Plutus has in fact
returned to the point from which Chremylus, drawing on common
experience, had started. Strictly speaking, these two ideas are
mutually exclusive, and the tension between the moral imperative
that the righteous ought to do well and the empirical finding that
wealth corrupts is never adequately resolved. From this very dis-
sonance, however, the irony of the whole play evolves, while the
constant interplay between these opposing viewpoints generates
much of the humour of the prologue: for example, when the blind
Plutus says that he has not seen a righteous man for a long time
(98), or when Chremylus combines the two outlooks in one contradictory line, 'It is probably true [i.e. that all the rich are essentially
bad], but surely not all are bad' (110).

The plot can develop in two ways; either Plutus will regain his
sight and assure a proper distribution of wealth by making only the
righteous rich, or whoever becomes rich will cease to be righteous,
in which case Plutus had better remain blind, which in fact is Zeus'
will. On the surface, the play seems to embrace the first alternative,
but the poet distances himself from it through various ironic hints
that derive from the second—which later, especially in the figure of
Penia, emerges as a sort of counterpoint to the first.

The following scenes explore these alternatives in greater depth.
First comes a traditional passage (322–414) after the *parodos*, in
which Blepsidemus, a minor character, significantly develops these
ideas. In this scene, which shows a reaction to the plan outlined in
the prologue, Blepsidemus essentially represents people looking to
their own advantage. Aristophanes' ironic depiction of the relationship of Blepsidemus, Chremylus, and the farmers is typical of the
play as a whole. Blepsidemus, for instance, wonders that Chremylus,
on the verge of becoming rich, issues an invitation to his friends—
quite contrary to native practice (342). The sharp contrast between
the (apparently) friendly and righteous Chremylus and Blepsidemus,
who cannot imagine anyone attaining wealth by honest means,
dominates the entire scene. That Chremylus' righteousness is a
sham becomes obvious when, soon after the healing of Plutus, he
finds his friends a bother (782–5); he thus appears to resemble
Blepsidemus far more than we had originally thought. Hence

when Blepsidemus marvels that Chremylus should have changed so much (365), we will not miss the irony: in reality, he has not changed at all.

Also ironic is Chremylus' remark that Blepsidemus, being one of his 'friends' (345), could share in his wealth. According to the provisions of the plan, however, Chremylus and his 'friends' are supposed to be the righteous, among whom Plutus, once healed, will abide in order to undertake a just distribution of wealth. When this prerequisite is applied to Blepsidemus, he immediately thinks of bribery (377–9), or even theft and burglary, as entirely proper, provided that the crimes remain undiscovered (566). It is therefore not the case that Blepsidemus fails to hear the conditions for obtaining wealth, but rather that neither the farmers' qualifications nor those of Blepsidemus himself are even remotely examined. Although this prerequisite is mentioned once again in very general terms (386–7), no one else is ever asked to produce concrete proof of righteousness.

At the same time, the irony is quite clear when an obvious trick of Blepsidemus is called 'friendly' (*philos*, 380), or when an astonished Blepsidemus asks if Chremylus is not going to send Plutus to his friends (398), even though shortly before he had characterized such an act as totally unconventional (340–1). The profound irony which permeates this entire scene calls into question not only the righteousness of Chremylus and his friends, but also the plan based on such a presumption.

The appearance of Penia determines and structures the scenes that follow. In the quarrel preceding the *agōn* itself (415–86), the plan of Chremylus is substantially expanded. Already in the scene with Blepsidemus the criterion for righteousness, the one qualification for obtaining wealth, was in essence defined only in terms of being counted a 'friend' of Chremylus. This definition is pushed a step further when the (supposedly) righteous are said to be all those who, like Chremylus and his friends, are poor. Thus Penia's argument begins with the assumption that she is going to be completely banished 'from the whole land' (430), a motif that Chremylus picks up in 463, saying that he wants to drive her out of Hellas. This plan is actuated by the desire to benefit all humans (461), which causes Chremylus gradually to abandon his original view that 'the righteous should be rewarded' and to embrace the idea that 'all men should get rich'.

For Chremylus, the 'righteous' are precisely all those who are not rich now, and, to the extent that all of them are to become rich, Penia must indeed fear for her existence. It is part of the unique nature of the play that this rather dubious equation between being 'not rich' and being 'righteous' turns out to be an apparently consistent (though ironic) extension of the initial situation expounded in the prologue.

All these elements are further developed in the subsequent *agōn* (487–618), which occupies the centre of the comedy. Thomas Gelzer has observed that the *agōn* in the *Plutus* is rather 'lopsided', lacking several components (such as an *antephirrhēma*) usually found in a 'complete' Aristophanic *agōn*. Concluding from this 'distintegration of forms' that the scene with Penia had not been adequately incorporated into the overall content and structure of the play, Gelzer felt that the *agōn* was used to deal with a sensitive contemporary issue that had little to do with the comedy. The *agōn* and whatever remained of the old forms were 'fossils' that were no longer properly understood. Thus Gelzer denied Aristophanes any conscious intent to transform comedy. Since his conclusions are relevant for assessing the role of Aristophanes' late works in the transition to Middle and New Comedy, it is important to determine their validity.

The lopsided structure of the *agōn* is neither accidental nor pointless. For here it is not a question of balancing opposing points of view, such as those of Plutus and Penia, but of presenting the plan of Chremylus—which, as the poet's ironic hints suggest, is not necessarily identical with that of Plutus. The plan is briefly recapitulated at the beginning and further refined (489–506) to become the starting-point for the much more detailed argument of Penia (507–91). Gelzer has correctly observed that Penia addresses not just the objections of Chremylus, but also the arguments of the prologue concerning the power of Plutus (128–98). Far from being cut off from the rest, the Penia scene is instead a coherent and interdependent part of the whole play.

The beginning of the *agōn* first outlines Chremylus' plan, stressing its particular benefits (493). As in the prologue, there is talk of the common experience that nowadays the rich, having obtained their wealth unjustly, are soundrels, whereas all decent people are poor (500–4). The plan's purpose is to invert the present situation, and we now learn the details. On being healed, Plutus will first turn to the righteous and avoid the wicked, but then he will make all men righteous and consequently rich (494–8). Obviously the expectation of wealth is meant to turn the unjust toward righteousness, which means that according to this plan those who are currently rich (and wicked) will lose their wealth only until they mend their ways. The goal is universal distribution of wealth, and it is therefore understandable that Penia should oppose this idea. It we cannot surmise from the way the comedy has developed so far that this plan is entirely utopian and presented with the utmost irony, such an inference is made explicit in the latter part. Here the question about man's relationship to the gods is a particularly important issue. The wicked, whom Plutus is initially supposed to avoid, are repeatedly described as 'godless' (491, 496), whereas all those who eventually have become righteous are called 'god-fearing' (497). Soon, however, it will become apparent that the actual implementation of this plan completely contradicts this passage.

As Penia presents counter-arguments to Chremylus' plan, the poet abandons the ironic development of ideas and takes the other side. Without necessarily identifying with Penia's point of view, Aristophanes suggests how far removed from reality the utopian design really is. Penia's argument develops in three stages. First she reveals the absurdity of the plan (507–62). Next she questions the moral qualifications of Chremylus, i.e. his righteousness (563–678). Finally she talks about the relationship with the gods, whom Chremylus had just mentioned (579–600). The interrupting comments of Chremylus and Blepsidemus revert to an ironic tone.

Penia shows the plan's absurdity by revealing its uselessness, which contrasts with the strong emphasis Chremylus had placed on its utility. The plan appears useless because its realization means the end of all work. Once all are blessed with wealth, no one will continue to work or be able to obtain the products of labour. If the mainspring of all crafts and efforts now appears to be not Plutus (as argued in the prologue, 160–9) but Penia instead, this is not essentially a contradiction but rather a different aspect of the same phenomenon. Advances in craftsmanship are prompted by necessity; they are meant to diminish poverty and contribute to well-being. Therefore, according to Penia's argument, universal wealth causes work, and with it the struggle against poverty, to come to a halt. This train of thought becomes fully intelligible once we see that Penia is not at all what Chremylus had thought her to be—namely beggary, hunger, and deprivation—but rather the restraint that prompts frugality and moderation, which is as far removed from superabundance as it is from scarcity. We may grant that sophistic theories lie behind this idea, and Aristophanes has employed the *agōn* elsewhere to discuss questions of general interest. This does not, however, affect the consistent development of ideas within the play, for Aristophanes intentionally allows Chremylus and Penia to talk past each other, so as to present the plan of Chremylus as one-sided and unrealistic.

The second point in Penia's argument pertains to the connection between poverty (in the sense of a balance between want and excess, as defined above) and righteousness. If Penia now elaborates by saying that after obtaining wealth men will become unjust (569), she merely repeats what Plutus had already advanced in the prologue as a reason why he might be better off blind (107–9). And even if Chremylus now agrees with her view (571), it is further evidence that this stricture applies to Chremylus and his friends, and that his plan rests on a set of fragile assumptions. In this respect, Penia approaches the position of Zeus, who wished after all to achieve the same end by blinding Plutus. At any rate, the (probably traditional) blinding of Plutus must be understood this way, for in what follows the poet himself links the figure of Penia with that context. Consequently, at the end of Penia's explanation a religious note is struck again, as she seeks to prove that Zeus himself, like her, is not rich but poor. Chremylus' invective against Zeus (587–9) shows all too clearly how untrustworthy his assurances are that decent people (among whom he counts himself) continue to be god-fearing even after they become rich (497). Already in the prologue, Chremylus had tried to prove that Plutus was more powerful than Zeus (128–9), and at the end of the comedy we find out that his claim to piety rests solely on his devotion to Plutus as the highest god—indeed, as the 'Saviour Zeus' (1189).

The *agōn* concludes with another ironic verse as Chremylus says to Penia: 'You will not convince me even if you do convince me' (600). The penchant for oxymorons of this sort to underscore utopian and unrealistic elements is characteristic of this play (cf. 119, 571). At the end of the *agōn*, the poet hints that Penia has actually won the debate, for she can be driven off only by brute force. Yet the second part of the comedy operates on the assumption that Chremylus is the winner. That this is true in only a superficial sense is clear from the *agōn* itself, which in the Penia scenes has moved to a new level of meaning that becomes the reference-point for all subsequent surface action.

Passing over the report of the slave Cario about the cure of Plutus in the sanctuary of Asclepius (627–770), we now turn to the episodic scenes which, as always in Aristophanes, elaborate and exemplify the resolution of the main plot—except that here, by way of irony, they also manage to set it aside.

Immediately upon regaining his sight, Plutus affirms his initial resolve to devote himself henceforth to the righteous (774–81). Thereupon, he showers wealth on the house of Chremylus, who now finds the friends he had just summoned to be a nuisance (782–3). Five separate scenes illustrate his new situation. The first three focus on the initial stage of the plan; the reward of the (supposedly) righteous and the punishment of the wicked by means of granting or removing wealth. The arrival at the second stage, where the wicked are transformed into the righteous (and rich) and where all live in the lap of luxury according to the expectations of Chremylus, is assumed in the last two scenes. To understand these scenes, we must heed the ironic manner in which they are presented, which alone enables us to account for their apparent difficulties and inconsistencies.

First we must realize that the new situation has come about through a simple reshuffling of existing conditions. The naïve equation of poverty with righteousness and wealth with injustice is merely inverted, so that all who are currently poor become rich, without ever a hint that the presumed righteousness is put to the test.

In the first of these scenes (823–49) a 'righteous man' appears, that is to say a pauper who has now become rich. As a token of gratitude, he wishes to dedicate his old mantle to Plutus. It is apparent that even here Aristophanes is only interested in showing the consequences of Chremylus' plan, not its feasibility or the particulars of its realization. We are told neither how this righteous man has suddenly become rich, nor anything else about him, except that he had been naïvely good-natured towards his friends. Such suppression of details is constructive in that it causes us to reflect, and hence it is no doubt intentional, so that we should not charge the poet with obscurity or inconsistency.

The second scene (850–958) presents us in turn with someone

who has become impoverised through Plutus. According to the
assumptions of Chremylus' plan, it would have been someone
previously rich and unjust, and indeed it is a sycophant (873) to
whom Plutus now denies his gifts. Considering himself to be righteous and a defender of the laws, he feels he has been unjustly
treated by the god, who he wishes would become blind again. He
misunderstands the plan as a promise 'to make all rich at once'
(864–5). This reintroduces the two contrasting ideas: the righteous
will become rich versus all will become rich. These ideas recur
throughout the play, although here they are scarcely in accord
with Chremylus' two-stage plan as outlined during the *agōn*, for
the sycophant is not at all ready to give up his occupation and show
himself worthy of Plutus. This, too, reveals not an inconsistency, but
rather a conscious intent, for in this manner the poet's irony points
up the distance between the plan and reality, thereby exposing it as
purely utopian. Another motif connects this scene with the previous
one, for as the sycophant's mantle is stripped from him, he is forced
henceforth to wear the righteous man's old and shabby mantle—
the cloak that he was about to dedicate to Plutus. Through this
particular detail, Aristophanes gives symbolic expression to the
sudden, drastic, even schematic inversion of man's relationship to
property as it now emerges in the play.

In the following scenes (956–1096), things are more complicated.
A fat old woman laments the loss of her young lover, whose favours
she had bought in the past. Now that he has become rich, he spurns
her and mocks her faded charms. In a playfully ironic manner,
Aristophanes calls into question here the resolution of the main
plot, thereby revealing its absurdity. The point pertains less to the
old woman than to the youth. Whereas the two preceding scenes
had presented us with what appeared to be a truly righteous and a
truly wicked man, now all proportions have become skewed. The
youth had only become rich because he had previously been poor.
The equation of poverty with righteousness clearly does not apply in
his case, since formerly when he had been poor he had merely used
the old woman as a source of income. In addition, he also knew how
to make her believe that he was motivated by love rather than
profit. Even though he had been anything but righteous and
decent, Plutus still enriches him on the grounds that he had
previously been poor, for Chremylus' plan assumes that all the
poor are righteous. The appearance of the youth himself leaves no

doubt about his sordid character, but Chremylus, who makes a feeble attempt to reconcile him with the old woman, does not even for a moment consider whether this young man has perhaps been unjustly enriched. The question of justice simply does not concern him any more.

The last two scenes again raise the issue about a proper relationship with the gods. In the first of these scenes (1097–1170), Hermes himself appears; in the second (1171–96), a priest of Zeus. Both lament that ever since Plutus has regained his sight no one wants to sacrifice any more. In the end, both enter the service of Plutus— the priest of Zeus at once and gladly, Hermes after first proclaiming the vengeance of Zeus (1107–9) and strongly condemning the healing of Plutus (1112). So much for the fear of god which, according to Chremylus, the newly affluent righteous would have. The gods do not matter, for no one heeds Hermes' message that Zeus will destroy everyone when the god's temple serves as an outhouse (1183–4). The 'piety' of the rich henceforth takes the form of recognizing as god only Plutus, whom Chremylus now calls Zeus Soter (1189), just as in the prologue he had placed Plutus' power above that of Zeus. By the last scene all have become rich (1178), probably because in the *agōn* Chremylus had intimated that, once rich, everyone would be pious and god-fearing (497). Plan and fulfilment are now set side by side.

The dethronement of Zeus and the rest of the gods is a favourite comic theme. In the *Clouds* the clouds are declared gods and the very existence of Zeus is questioned. In the *Birds* it is the birds who declare themselves gods and demand sacrifices formerly received by Zeus. But in the *Clouds* the Thinkery of Socrates, from which the clouds originate, is burned down, whereas in the *Birds*, a play that is quite fantastic as it is, there is an amicable arrangement with the Olympians. Whoever expects something similar in the *Plutus*, however, is surprised by a strikingly conventional ending (1197–1209). Chremylus leads the sacrificial procession and intends to dedicate the pots filled with sacrificial food to 'the god' (1198), that is to Plutus. The bearer of these pots will be the old woman who earlier had so bitterly lamented losing her lover, who even now derides her with a bad pun. Chremylus, on the other hand, plays the benefactor as if he had the same powers as Plutus, and he promises the old woman that her young man will visit her that evening. How Chremylus manages this we are not told. As the play ends, the

poet not only leaves the future of this union in suspense, but leaves
the reader quessing if and how the bold plan of redistributing wealth
will actually be fulfilled.

III

In the *Plutus* Aristophanes doubtless picks up contemporary political ideas about poverty and wealth, justice and injustice. But while
he stresses abuses and deplorable situations, discusses ideas and
plans, he offers no direct solutions, and all attempts to reduce the
comedy's meaning to a simple formula fail. It is not really a comedy
of character, for even though it does contain some stock figures,
such as the slave Cario, Aristophanes is not interested in making
Chremylus an entirely consistent character. Chremylus and his
friends, dissatisfied with their lot, have only one goal—to become
rich. They have no interest in questions of divine or human justice.
The less they reflect on the consequences of their wishes, however,
the more eager Aristophanes is to explore this topic. Yet whereas in
the *Clouds* Strepsiades and Pheidippides approach Socrates in utter
ignorance, become 'initiated' only with much difficulty, and still
remain quite unteachable, in the *Plutus* Chremylus becomes the
vehicle for ideas which the poet pursues not only through Plutus
and Penia, but also through Chremylus himself. As a result, his
character appears to be curiously fragmented. He seems to be a man
of honour and integrity, but what issues from his mouth conflicts
with that impression. Whenever the poet causes Chremylus to fall
short of the standards set by his own plan, he repeatedly places its
realization in doubt, implying thereby that the problems cannot be
resolved as they are in the play.

Only Penia is allowed to say so openly, and that is why she is an
essential character. Her absence would have radically altered the
whole play's structure. But Aristophanes shapes the plot in such a
way that although Penia's arguments win the *agōn*, she appears to
be in the wrong. The humour generated by the many small and
large absurdities and intentional 'inconsistencies' shows that the
final development of the plot in no way reflects the actual relationships and processes of the play but is rather to be understood
ironically. Such irony in the development of ideas is, however,
peculiar only to the late plays of Aristophanes. We may contrast

this technique with the poet's very different intent in the *Clouds*, where Strepsiades is beaten and his plans are completely thwarted when he tries to use his newly acquired skill to obtain money.

Among the extant plays of Aristophanes, such a subtle and thoroughly ironic treatment of a topic is otherwise found only in the *Ecclesiazusae*. Here, too, in the scenes that exemplify the proposed plan for sharing wives and property, the poet has created an ironic distance between the plan and himself, without actually allowing that tension to lead to a clear resolution. Whether or not the art of employing irony in treating comic themes is further developed and refined between the *Ecclesiazusae* and the *Plutus* is difficult to say. It is in any case a technique characteristic of these two plays, which gives them their distinctive nature and allows us to recognize all the objections that have been raised as unwarranted.

In Aristophanes' earlier comedies, we find ironic shifts in the specific utterances of individual characters, particularly in the heat of debate. The poet also depicts individual scenes ironically, for one can also apply the notion of irony to phenomena such as the breaking of the dramatic illusion or the lack of consistency and unity in a play. However, an ironic treatment that determines the structure and development of ideas within a whole drama is unparalleled in all of Old Comedy before the *Ecclesiazusae* and the *Plutus*.

Such treatment failed to influence post-Aristophanic comedy, however. New Comedy knows only a limited and, in comparison to Aristophanes, a more restrained form of irony, applied only to specific details and in such a manner that at the end the ironic tension is always clearly resolved. That a comedy should end with this kind of ironic ambiguity does not, as far as we know, happen in Menander. And Roman comedy differs from Greek precisely in that it tries to eliminate the ironic tension between idea and reality— either by intensifying the raucous humour (Plautus) or by opting for an unmistakable realism (Terence). Thus the last two extant plays of Aristophanes signal the transition to the New Comedy of Menander in a few formal details, but not in their essential attributes as comedies.

These late plays, with their characteristically ironic treatment of plot, characters, and the development of ideas, could not have played such a mediating role for the following reasons. The ironic treatment of art-forms, or the sustained differentiation of two levels linked to one another through irony, always characterizes a late stage of development, and for that very reason it excludes immediate imitation. Just as Aristophanes is less influential than New Comedy and Roman Comedy for the development of Western comedy, so are the late plays of Aristophanes doubly excluded from being models for imitation. Only when German Romanticism has helped to dispel a theoretical perspective that ultimately goes back to ancient literary criticism could one begin to see in Aristophanes the rough outline of Menandrian comedy. And now, in a literary age that has elevated irony virtually to a formative principle, the comedy of Aristophanes has also been linked with the notion of irony, albeit in the wider senses of fantastic inventions, of breaking the dramatic illusion, and of involving the audience in the play.

Aristophanes' influence can also be traced in Romantic poetry, most clearly in Ludwig Tieck's comedy *Puss in Boots*, which essentially employs irony as a structural principle. But here we do not find irony sustained throughout the play, nor have the Romantics recognized its importance in their theoretical observations about Aristophanes. And yet it is precisely the Romantic perception of Aristophanes that can help us understand how the irony of the many details in due course leads to the ironic cast of the whole plot, and how this phenomenon, as it appears in his last two comedies, therefore represents neither an inorganic break within the plays nor a decline of the poet's creative powers.

ACKNOWLEDGEMENTS

1. Erich Segal, 'The *Physis* of Comedy' From *Havard Studies in Classical Philology*, 77 (1973), 129–36. Reprinted with minor revisions by permission of Harvard University Press. Those referring to this essay for scholarly purposes are requested to consult the original version.
2. Oliver Taplin, 'Fifth-Century Tragedy and Comedy'. From *Journal of Hellenic Studies*, 106 (1986), 163–74. Reprinted with minor revisions by permission of the author and the Society for the Promotion of Hellenic Studies. Those referring to this essay for scholarly purposes are requested to consult the original version.
3. A. W. Gomme, 'Aristophanes and Politics'. From *Classical Review*, 52 (1938), 97–109. Reprinted in an abridged form by permission of Oxford University Press. Those referring to this essay for scholarly purposes are requested to consult the original version.
4. G. E. M. de Ste. Croix, 'The Political Outlook of Aristophanes'. From *The Origins of the Peloponnesian War* (Ithaca, N.Y., 1972), app. 29. Reprinted by permission of the author and publisher. The author has kindly allowed this material to be abridged and certain footnotes to be revised or omitted. Those referring to this essay for scholarly purposes are requested to consult the original version.
5. Jeffrey Henderson, 'The *Dēmos* and the Comic Competition'. From John J. Winkler and Froma I. Zeitlin (eds.) *Nothing to Do with Dionysos?* (Princeton, 1990). Reprinted by permission of the author and Princeton University Press. The author has kindly allowed this material to be abridged and certain footnotes to be revised or omitted. Those referring to this essay for scholarly purposes are requested to consult the original version.
6. Stephen Halliwell, 'Aristophanes' Apprenticeship'. From *Classical Quarterly*, 30 (1980), 33–45. Reprinted with revisions and corrections kindly supplied by the author for this volume, and by permission of Oxford University Press. Those referring to this essay for scholarly purposes are requested to consult the original version.
7. Helene P. Foley, 'Tragedy and Politics in Aristophanes' *Acharnians*'. From *Journal of Hellenic Studies*, 108 (1988), 33–47. Reprinted with minor revisions by permission of the author and the Society for the Promotion of Hellenic Studies. English translations have been kindly supplied

by the author for publication of the essay in this collection. Those referring to this essay for scholarly purposes are requested to consult the original version.

8. Hans-Joachim Newiger, 'War and Peace in the Comedy of Aristophanes'. Translated by Catherine Radford for *Yale Classical Studies*, 26 (1980), 219–37. First published as 'Krieg und Frieden in der Komödie des Aristophanes', in *Dorema: Hans Diller zum 70. Geburtstag* (Athens, 1975). Reprinted with minor revisions by permission of the author and publisher.

9. Charles Segal, 'Aristophanes' Cloud-Chorus' From *Arethusa*, 2 (1967), 143–61. Reprinted with minor revisions by permission of the author and publisher. Those referring to this essay for scholarly purposes are requested to consult the original version.

10. Bernhard Zimmermann, 'The *Parodoi* of the Aristophanic Comedies'. From *Studi Italiani di Filologia Classica*, 3/2 (1984), 13–24. Reprinted with minor revisions by permission of the author and publisher. Those referring to this essay for scholarly purposes are requested to consult the original version.

11. Thomas Gelzer, 'Some Aspects of Aristophanes' Dramatic Art in the *Birds*'. From *Bulletin of the Institute of Classical Studies*, 23 (1976), 1–14. Reprinted with minor revisions by permission of the author and the Institute of Classical Studies. Those referring to this essay for scholarly purposes are requested to consult the original version.

12. Carroll Moulton, 'Comic Myth-Making and Aristophanes' Originality'. From 'Aristophanes', in T. J. Luce (ed.), *Ancient Writers: Greece and Rome*, (New York, 1982). Reprinted with revisions by permission of the author and publisher.

13. Michael Silk, 'The People of Aristophanes' From C. B. R. Pelling (ed.), *Characterization and Individuality in Greek Literature*, (Oxford, 1990). Reprinted with minor revisions by permission of the author and publisher. Those referring to this essay for scholarly purposes are requested to consult the original version.

14. A. H. Sommerstein, 'Aristophanes and the Demon Poverty'. From *Classical Quarterly*, 34 (1984), 314–333. Reprinted with minor revisions by permission of the author and publisher. English translations have been kindly supplied by the author for publication of the essay in this collection. Those referring to this essay for scholarly purposes are requested to consult the original version.

15. Suzanne Saïd, '*The Assemblywomen*: Women, Economy, and Politics'. First published as '*L'Assemblée des femmes*: Les femmes, l'économie et la politique', *Aristophane, les femmes et la cité*, Les Cahiers de Fontenay (Fontenay-aux-Roses École Normale Supérieure), 17 (1979), 33–69. Translated by Janice Orion in an abridged form for this collection, by

permission of the author and publisher. Those referring to this essay for scholarly purposes are requested to consult the original version.

16. Hellmut Flashar, 'The Originality of Aristophanes' Last Plays'. First published as 'Zur Eigenart des aristophanischen Spätwerks', *Poetica*, 1 (1967), 154–75. Translated by Walter Moskalew for this collection. By kind permission of the author, the footnotes of the original version have been omitted. Those referring to this essay for scholarly purposes are requested to consult the original version.

GLOSSARY

adikia: injustice

agathos: good, noble

agōn: an argument between two characters, in which each vehemently attempts to convince the other; one of the fundamental structural units of Old Comedy

agora: assembly-place of the people

aidōs: shame

aischrologia: obscenity; abuse

alazōn: imposter, charlatan

amoibaion: dialogue in lyric metre between one or several actors and the chorus

anapaests: one of the typical metres of comic verse, based on the anapaestic measure ($\cup\cup$ —); the 'anapaests' may also refer to the second major structural unit of a comedy's parabasis, or the parabasis proper

angelos: messenger

antepirrhēma: speech by the chorus-leader, metrically identical to the *epirrhēma* (see below) that precedes it

antode: lyric choral song, metrically identical to the ode (see below) that precedes it

apatē: deception

apragmōn: inactive in politics, easy-going

archē: empire; magistracy, office

archōn: Athenian public official

aulos: the flute used for musical accompaniment of drama

beltistoi: noblest

bōmolochos: buffoon

boulē: council

chorēgos: producer of plays

chrēstos: honest, worthy

coryphaeus: leader of the chorus

daimōn: a superhuman spirit or force

dēmos: the people

deus ex machina: 'god from the machine', i.e. a divinity who suddenly appears at the end of a play (ordinarily a tragedy), and is suspende from the crane or *mēchanē* to solve an otherwise insoluble situation. By extension, a literary metaphor for an unmotivated ending.

dexios: clever, ingenious

dexiotēs: cleverness, ingenuity; skill at writing plays

diabolē: slander, abuse

dicast: juror

didaskalia: production notice or record

didaskalos: teacher (of the people): hence, a playwright

Dionysia: springtime Athenian festival in honour of the god Dionysus; the principal occasion for performance of tragedies and comedies

dramatis personae: characters of a drama

eirōn: wittily ironic man

ekklēsia: voting assembly of the Athenian citizenry

ekkyklēma: a stage platform which rolls out to reveal an interior scene

epieikeis: the upper or educated classes

epirrhēma: speech by the chorus-leader, usually in trochiac tetrameter

epirrhematic syzygy: group of four subunits within the parabasis of Old Comedy, comprising *ode, epirrhēma, antode,* and *antepirrhēma*. The syzygy can be used, in whole or in part, as a 'second parabasis' in a play

exodos: the final scene of a play, often ending with a song of the chorus as they march off

gerōn: oldster

hēsychia: peace

hippeus: knight

hubris: excessive pride; outrage; physical assault

kalos kagathos: gentleman; noble; aristocrat

katakeleusmos: exhortation

katharsis: purgation, purification

kolax: flatterer

kommation: brief song in lyric meter that marks the beginning of the parabasis in a comedy

kommos: lyric dialogue between a principal character and the chorus

kōmōidia: comedy

kōmōidodidaskalos: comic poet

ōmōidopoios: comic playwright

ʼbos: game resembling dice

mid-winter Athenian festival, sacred to Dionysus, at which plays
ʼrformed, especially comedies
ʼc subsidy or function, ordinarily borne by a wealthy citizen of

, deus ex machina
operator in the Greek theatre

mythos: story, or plot of a play

Nikē: the goddess Victory

nomos: law, custom, social usage

ode: lyric song of the chorus in a play

oikos: household

orchēstra: circular 'dance-floor' in the Greek theatre

parabasis: a structural unit of Old Comedy, the part of the play in which the dramatist employed the chorus or chorus-leader to address the audience directly. The term may refer to this entire part of the play (which in complete form comprises seven sections) or more narrowly to the parabasis proper, which is most often composed in anapaests (see above)

parodos: the chorus's entrance song (or first choral ode)

parrhēsia: verbal licence

peripeteia: the Aristotelian 'reversal' in tragic plots

phrontistērion: Socrates' 'thinkery' in the *Clouds*

physis: nature; essential quality

pnigos: short 'choking' lyric, a subunit of the parabasis, so called because it was said all in one breath

poiētēs: poet, playwright

-*pōlai*: suffix meaning 'sellers'

polis: city-state

politeia: state; constitution

ponēros: crafty; wicked; low-born

proboulos: Athenian city councillor

prologue: all that portion of a play before the *parodos*

prosōpon: mask; character in a drama

rhēsis: formal set-speech

rhētōr: orator

skēnē: the stage-building in the theatre

sōphrosynē: moderation; self-control

sykophantēs: informer (a stock character in ancient comedy)

synkrisis: comparison with juxtaposition

technē: craft; art

thrēnos: lament

tragōidopoios: tragic playwright

triōbolon: three-obal coin (a juror's daily pay)

trygōidia: parodic word for *comedy* (punning on *tragōidia*)